Karolyn, 1 year old

Every Time a Bell Rings

The Wonderful Life of Karolyn Grimes

By Clay Eals

Clay Eals

Karolyn, 6, as Zuzu in IT'S A WONDERFUL LIFE

Karolyn at 16

PASTIME PRESS

Cover photograph by Larry F. Levenson / Illustrations by Sandy Johnson

Karolyn today

Every Time a Bell Rings
The Wonderful Life of Karolyn Grimes

By Clay Eals

Published by:

PASTIME PRESS

4310-¹/₂ S.W. Raymond St.
Seattle, WA 98136-1444

First Printing 1996

Printed in the United States of America

Cataloguing-in-Publication Data

Eals, Clay.
    Every time a bell rings: the wonderful life of Karolyn Grimes / Clay Eals.
    248 p. ; 28 cm.
    Includes bibliography (p. 238) and index.
    ISBN 0-9654984-2-5
    1. Grimes, Karolyn. 2. Motion picture actors and actresses-United States-Biography. I. Title.
    PN2287.G69 1996
    791.43–dc20   96-92801
                                            CIP

What's inside

The quotations that accompany the opening of each chapter come from the script of It's a Wonderful Life.

Greeting

By James Stewart

You know, I've made a lot of movies in my career, but I think my favorite is still Frank Capra's *It's a Wonderful Life.*

Its enduring message of hope and charity and faith renewed is still so important, especially in these times when money is tight and the holding of family together can be difficult.

Karolyn Grimes visits with James Stewart in 1990.

But as George Bailey learned, and as the movie so poignantly reminds us, what really count in life are the things that you can't put a price tag on – family and friends and the belief in the possibility of miracles.

So for this holiday season I wish you love and happiness and all of the joys and wonders of *A Wonderful Life.*

[Mr. Stewart recorded this Christmas greeting in the fall of 1993 for the nationwide promotional tour of the "Bailey kids" from **It's a Wonderful Life***, sponsored by Target Stores.]*

Dedication

The spirit of the gracious help that made this book possible will, I trust, find its way into all of you who pick it up and call it your own.

It is to you that this biography is dedicated.

Clay Eals

About the author

As a journalist for 15 years, a journalism teacher for two years, a curriculum writer for three years and a publications editor for three years, Clay Eals has written more than 4,500 articles for two daily and two weekly newspapers and more than a dozen periodicals. Eals, who has supervised reporters, writers and college students for nine of those years, edited and directed production of a 288-page, large-format history book of the West Seattle/White Center area of Seattle, Washington (*West Side Story*, 1987, publisher: *West Seattle Herald/White Center News*). He is publications editor for the Fred Hutchinson Cancer Research Center in Seattle.

One of Eals' voracious, long-held interests is movies. He has written film reviews for newspaper entertainment sections, and he helped lead a successful three-year drive to save West Seattle's 54-year-old Admiral Theater from the wrecking ball.

A graduate of the University of Oregon School of Journalism, Eals grew up on Mercer Island, a Seattle suburb. He lives in West Seattle with his wife, also an experienced journalist, and 20-year-old daughter, a student at the University of Washington.

*I*s it Karolyn, or is it Zuzu?

Well . . . yes. Karolyn has made Zuzu a part of herself, but only a part, and a very healthy part at that. She is fully aware that those who step forward to meet her are coming to meet Zuzu. And it is in her comfort with being Zuzu that her fans get a profound sense of just who Karolyn is. Perhaps an example can shed more light.

One evening, Karolyn was signing autographs and Zuzu-related Christmas decorations. One of the people who approached her was a man whom most would consider unattractive. Karolyn listened as he poured out his heart to her about his relationship with *It's a Wonderful Life*. He had virtually memorized the movie. It was obvious that he had made it a large part of who he was.

He had come to meet Zuzu. He knew it, and Karolyn knew it. She accepted this wholeheartedly. And she did not measure his eccentricity as he was spilling over in his enthusiasm to relate his story. Rather, as she allowed him to meet Zuzu, she was the willing vessel into which he poured his effervescence, and, in the process, she subtly allowed him to meet Karolyn.

As he went away, he had added a new dimension to his relationship with the movie. He had substantiated his fantasy with the real, live warmth of a real, live person. It was a special moment, and Karolyn was beaming just as broadly as he when the encounter was over.

Karolyn is smart enough to know that her celebrity is an important part of who she is, but she is not consumed by it. The warmth in her eyes as she meets all of her fans is not the antics of an accomplished actress. Rather, it is the full-fledged giving of herself and the knowledge that she will receive the same warmth in return.

But what else is in her eyes? What else rests subtly next to the warmth? Whatever it is, it complements, does not detract from, the warmth. It makes the soul of this celebrity much more accessible to the fan stepping forward to meet her for the first time. I must say that I was baffled by this for the longest time. But as I began to learn more about Karolyn, I finally discovered the answer.

The other thing in her heart is the sadness that resides in one who has seen personal misfortune, and yet has chosen to live life rather than succumb to the torture of depression.

When she was just a youngster, she became an orphan. Losing one's parents is a blow difficult enough for any child. But add to this the fact that she was torn away from her already substantial work in Hollywood. Leaving this world of fantasy, she was plunged headlong onto what must have seemed like another planet – the rural Midwest. But by her own admission, it was there that she met real people and learned real values.

More recently, she lost a son of 18, and a husband of 25 years. But in the years since these deaths, Karolyn has continued to live her life as fully as she can.

Do these personal misfortunes explain the gentle sadness that we see in her eyes? I don't know. I can only guess that there must be some part of her that must wonder where her career would have taken her had she spent the last 30 to 40 years in Hollywood, and perhaps on Broadway.

But even if she wonders about a road not taken, she will not wallow in the

By Bill Campsey

Bill Campsey operates an embroidery shop in Leavenworth, Kansas. A theater enthusiast who is retired from the military, he met Karolyn Grimes in 1995 and produces her Zuzu T-shirts and sweatshirts. Campsey contributed this piece to Karolyn's fan-club newsletter, THE ZUZU NEWS, in the summer of 1996.

tragedy of unfulfilled opportunity. Rather, she will play with the cards she is dealt. And she will play hard.

Regardless of the full extent of the roots of her sadness, what is important is the richness it adds to her character. We want celebrities to be warm toward us, or at least to display to us a warmth. We never expect them to share so much of themselves as Karolyn does.

As you read Karolyn's story in the following pages, and if you are fortunate to meet her in person, take a moment to comprehend what you are experiencing. In her self-assured voice, her gentle, firm handshake, her radiant smile, and, most of all, in the depths of her eyes, you get all of Karolyn, all at once.

About the beneficiary

The Fred Hutchinson Cancer Research Center in Seattle, Washington, is internationally renowned for its groundbreaking research into the causes, treatment and prevention of cancer. The mission of the center is to eliminate cancer as a cause of human suffering and death.

It was founded by Dr. William Hutchinson in honor of his brother, Fred, a Seattle baseball hero and winning major-league pitcher and manager who died of lung cancer in 1964.

Led by Dr. E. Donnall Thomas, the Hutchinson Center pioneered the life-saving technique of bone marrow transplantation, earning Dr. Thomas the 1990 Nobel Prize in Medicine. The nation's first and largest cancer prevention research program also is housed at the Hutchinson Center.

One-third of all Americans born today will have cancer during their lifetime. One-fifth of all Americans will die from it. One million new cancer cases are reported each year. As Karolyn Grimes says, "Everybody is touched by cancer somewhere along the line."

From the post-publication sale of each copy of *Every Time a Bell Rings: The Wonderful Life of Karolyn Grimes*, $5 will go to the Hutchinson Center. For more information on the Hutchinson Center, please call (206) 667-6070 or 1-800-279-1618.

Zuzu was born with the angels.

   The little-girl character – whose wide-eyed, earnest utterance of "Every time a bell rings, an angel gets his wings" stands among the most beloved lines in film history – got her start in heaven.

Nearly forgotten movie scripts written by noted playwright Clifford Odets more than 50 years ago reveal her origin. During the closing months of World War II, around Christmastime 1944, Odets penned three scripts for Paramount Pictures under the working title of "The Greatest Gift." Each was a feature-length embellishment of a 24-page short story of the same name created by Philip Van Doren Stern as a holiday greeting card for friends. Paramount had purchased rights to the story for $10,000, intending for its box-office heartthrob, Cary Grant, to play the lead. The studio assigned the script to a trio of writers: Marc Connelly, who turned out a draft on October 12, 1944; Dalton Trumbo, who completed his version on December 19; and Odets, who composed three variations of his own and turned them in the following February 12, 23 and 27.

   Portions of all three men's work found their way into what eventually was shot and released as *It's a Wonderful Life*. But the first of Odets' scripts is special. It was here that the Zuzu role was born.

   This preliminary script is preserved in two film researchers' troves: the Margaret Herrick Library of the American Academy of Motion Picture Arts and Sciences in Beverly Hills, Calif., and the Wesleyan University Cinema Archives in Middletown, Connecticut. Page by yellowed page, the script is a fascinating glimpse into the soul of the child's character, particularly in light of the finished movie.

'Every time a bell rings, an angel gets his wings.'

(Origin of Zuzu, December 1944; present-day Zuzu, December 1994)

   On screen, in the version of *It's a Wonderful Life* that everybody knows, Zuzu appears only in the film's darker final third. Like a set of bookends, she straddles the "unborn sequence" in which her father George, through the inspiration of a guardian angel named Clarence, experiences a vivid vision of what life would have held in store for Bedford Falls and its inhabitants if George had not

A forlorn Zuzu wanders through heaven to open IT'S A WONDERFUL LIFE in Clifford Odets' first script.

Illustration created for this book by Sandy Johnson

entered the world. The Zuzu role is vital to her father's wholesale emotional turnaround.

   In Odets' first script, however, Zuzu takes center stage the moment the story begins. Had this version been filmed, the sprite's innocence – along with a health crisis that threatens her life and helps foreshadow her father's death wish – would have opened the film.

Imagine an enormous, clear, blue atmosphere filled with floating, swirling white clouds – nothing but sky as far as the eye can see. Then conjure up the agreeable image of a peaceful small town. It's a beautifully sunny summer day. Trees pleasantly line a residential street. Large, old houses rest comfortably on either side. Clouds sprinkle their wispy shadows as they pass.

But there is no life on this street, save for a tiny girl wandering ever closer. Her face begs concern. Her eyes bespeak wariness, timidity, even fear. The girl is lost. This is how Odets' script begins.

The girl approaches a conservatory – a stately, multi-floor stone building, with expansive bay windows at every turn. Hearing a sound from inside, she stops. Actually, it's a muffled cacophony of sounds, all musical. There are voices, the arpeggios of harps and tentative practice notes from a piano. Hope creeps over the girl's face, and she climbs the front steps.

Inside, paint peels from the walls. The floors are broad and wooden. In the distance, a man with a long-handled brush slowly sweeps his way down a long, wooden staircase as the strains of a roomful of harpists seep into the entryway from behind a nearby door. The girl approaches the man and asks him, "Is my mother here?" Gently but ominously, the man tells her that she must be in the wrong building.

There is no life on this street, save for a tiny girl wandering ever closer.

Her face begs concern. Her eyes bespeak wariness, timidity, even fear. The girl is lost.

As the man returns to his deliberate brushwork, the child silently trains her eyes upon him. He looks down again, then, in a whisper, asks her age. She quickly tells him 4 years and 2 months, to which the man shakes his head and observes, "That's very young to be here."

The child leans against the banister, then sits on the bottom steps. The man finishes brushing the last step and continues toward the front door, knocking his brush against the wainscoting with a clatter. He looks up, nods to an old-fashioned water-cooler and offers the girl a drink. With sorrow in her eyes, she declines.

Abruptly, a teacher's voice, in a German accent, suddenly echoes from the same room where the harps are playing. The door flies open. The teacher bursts out, admonishing the sweeping man for his "clicking-clacking," then huffs back into the room. There, he scolds his orchestra of 15 weary men and women of all ages at the same time as he urges them to make one more attempt to play a complicated composition.

One student in the back, a broken man of 60, poises himself to play. The teacher thrusts his baton for a downbeat, the class starts in, but the result is laborious, hardly unified. Strained expressions cross the teacher's face, but he continues for a few moments, then jettisons his baton, and one by one, the students stop playing. The teacher waits until only the 60-year-old man, oblivious, is plucking his harpstrings. A student next to him makes a hissing noise, indicating the teacher. Disoriented, the man stops. The teacher walks over and, with a smirk, asks him how long he has taken lessons there. "A . . . a long time," the man stammers. "Useless!" the teacher shouts. Confused, the older man eyes his hands. A doleful frown marks his face. Then he slips along the edge of the room, to the door, leaving the class and padding to the water cooler.

Outside the room, the sweeper is gone. The girl, still seated on the stairs, her face bowed to her hands, has been crying. She raises her eyes and, unseen by the older man, stares at him. The man swallows his drink, turns back for the door, then discovers her. Slowly, carefully, he asks what she's doing there. New tears stream down her cheeks as she sobs her plea:

> *"I don't know where to find my mother. I'm lost. No one speaks to me. . . . I want to go home."*

When the man tells her that she can't go home, a hint of defiance crosses her gaze as her lower lip pushes out. Tears then flood her face, and her voice approaches a wail as she speaks the words that seal her character's place in the proceedings:

> *"My name is Zuzu Bailey, and I want to go home. . . . 334 Sycamore Street I live, Bedford Falls. Please take me home."*

Stunned as this information sinks in, the man slowly repeats it aloud. He asks the girl if her father's name is George. She nods. The man picks her up, smoothes her hair and tries to comfort her. His voice drops to a whisper. He speaks directly, reverently, in a hush, addressing her by name and assuring her that he will take her home. Relieved, the girl snuggles into his arms, and he carries her out of the building.

With Zuzu asleep in his arms, the man instantly appears in the office of an angel whose official status is clear from the dozens of maps and framed pictures of Lincoln, Tolstoy, Pasteur and Beethoven on the walls. The pair of wings on this official's back also stand out, as they fit snugly into a chair equipped with cutouts just the size of the wings. The official establishes that the man's number is 1163, series B. More important, though, this angel informs the man that Zuzu does not belong in this ethereal place. "She's in-

A trusting, relieved Zuzu unknowingly snuggles into the arms of her grandfather Peter Bailey, an angel in search of his wings in Clifford Odets' first IT'S A WONDERFUL LIFE script.

Illustration created for this book by Sandy Johnson

between – very sick – but she's not dead," the official says, ascribing this error to the increasing clutter of his work. Then, noting offhandedly that "you don't have your wings," the official offers the man a chance to return Zuzu to Earth, where she is to have "a long, useful life." The man exults, but tears well in his eyes. He tells the official that Zuzu is his granddaughter. He, therefore, as any *It's a Wonderful Life* fan can surmise, is Peter Bailey, George's father.

Another town, on Earth, comes into view. This time, though, the weather is dastardly, wind howling through bent trees, lightning slicing the sky and fierce rain soaking the surroundings. The torrent dizzies the paths of passing birds and beats incessantly against the Bailey family home.

Through an upstairs window, a doctor in a tuxedo, called away from a social event, is seen in Zuzu's bedroom. As she lies motionless in an oxygen tent surrounding her bed, the doctor holds her arm, giving her an injection, with the

Back at home in bed, Zuzu is comforted by the presence of her parents and, in a picture frame, her grandfather Peter Bailey.

Illustration created for this book by Sandy Johnson

help of a worried nurse. Zuzu breathes haltingly. The doctor finds his stethoscope and gently places it on her chest. He listens. Then, with Zuzu's parents George and Mary and George's mother riveted to his every gesture, the doctor breathes a long sigh of relief. "I think there's a chance. . . . Damn good chance!" he concludes.

All attention focuses on the bed, but behind, on the dresser, a framed picture of Peter Bailey looks out, with the hint of a smile.

Up in the clouds, Peter Bailey suddenly appears next to the official angel, playing billiards in a heavenly poolroom. He admits to the official that when he accompanied Zuzu back to Earth, he looked in on his troubled son. The official turns, a glint in his eye, and leads him to a projection room where a movie is rolling. His son's early life is under way on the screen. With Zuzu's near-death still hanging in the celestial mist, the official squarely addresses Peter Bailey and sets the tone for the rest of the story.

"This is a solemn moment for you. I want you to review a few highlights of your son's life before you meet him as his guardian angel."

"What has to be done?" Peter Bailey asks.

"A niceness of judgment – on your part, not mine – is needed," the official replies. "George," he says, "is very close to suicide."

• • •

The crisp, harmonic chimes of 'Angels We Have Heard on High' echoed through the foyer, pealed by a dozen members of a youthful handbell choir from a local Methodist church.

Fast-forward 50 years, to Saturday, December 3, 1994.

As an escalator lifted Karolyn Grimes to the second-floor grand ballroom of the Seattle Sheraton Hotel and Towers, a familiar sound began to reach her ears. Faint at first, then stronger as Karolyn ascended, the crisp, harmonic chimes of "Angels We Have Heard on High" echoed through the foyer, pealed by a dozen members of a youthful handbell choir from a local Methodist church.

Here, as everywhere she's traveled in recent years, angels were picking up quite a few wings.

The teen-age bell-ringers made a fitting welcome for Karolyn, the crowning touch and special guest of the 1994 Holiday Gala fund-raiser for the Fred Hutchinson Cancer Research Center in Seattle, Washington – 1,850 miles from her home in suburban Kansas City.

A full year earlier, volunteers for the center had selected *It's a Wonderful Life* as their theme for the festive holiday event, and seemingly no angle escaped their notice. Owing to James Stewart's ill health, the publicist for the film's star had to turn down the Gala's request for an introduction letter, but other heart-tugging reminders of the holiday tale proliferated. Photographs from the 1946 movie illustrated the inch-thick auction program and swayed high in the air on giant cardboard ornaments above the ballroom floor. Evoking downtown Bedford Falls, "Bailey Building & Loan" and "Gower's Drugs" storefronts on a painted backdrop decorated the stage. Sprinklings of fresh-plucked rose petals flecked tables, on which rested more than 100 table centerpieces – glass-and-ceramic snowglobes encasing figurines of the Bailey family gathered around a tiny Christmas tree.

Yet, as if Clarence, the movie's angel, were again trying to earn his wings by guiding the Gala plans, further fortune had fallen upon the event. As Karolyn puts it, "There are no coincidences."

Unknown to the volunteers, Karolyn already had agreed nearly a year before the 1994 Gala to fly to Seattle that very day to take part in an angel celebration at the Rosalie Whyel Museum of Doll Art in Bellevue, a suburb five miles east. There, she would sign and sell dolls she commissioned in the likeness of Zuzu, the Baileys' youngest daughter, whom Karolyn played as a 6-year-old. Karolyn knew nothing of the cancer center Gala. But just a scant three weeks before her scheduled appearance in Bellevue, Diana Honda of the museum saw a newspaper notice about the *It's a Wonderful Life* theme slated for the Gala to be held the same night. Inspiration took hold, and Diana called the cancer center to see if Karolyn would fit in with the Gala's theme. The event's leaders responded with resounding excitement.

As if Clarence, the movie's angel, were again trying to earn his wings by guiding the Gala plans, further fortune had fallen upon the event.

Little did they know just how snug the fit would be. In May of that year, Mike Wilkerson, Karolyn's husband of 25 years, had died after a long struggle with lung cancer. Her personal experience paralleled the Gala's cause, and Karolyn readily agreed to appear at the Gala and auction a Zuzu doll.

So, as Karolyn stepped off the escalator her first evening in Seattle, Gala attendees lavished greetings upon her. They came one by one at first, then in groups of three, five and more. As word spread through the foyer, the guests crowded around to meet or catch a glimpse of the woman who was once Zuzu. While their suits and gowns retained their sophisticated snazz and sizzle, their faces and eyes turned round and bright as those of a child.

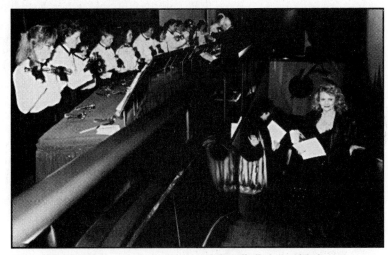

Greeted by the Tintinnabulators, the youth handbell choir of Lake Washington United Methodist Church from nearby Kirkland, Karolyn Grimes rides the Seattle Sheraton Hotel escalator to arrive at the 1994 Hutch Holiday Gala.

"Oh, I've watched your movie 20 times!" cried a woman in her 40s.

Many told her how fondly they remember her famous line: "Every time a bell rings, an angel gets his wings." For some, the occasion approached meeting royalty. Certainly, it struck close to the heart. One man in his 30s even knelt at her feet as he told of his joy at seeing her.

This was Zuzu, the little girl whose barely six minutes of screen time a half century ago had in recent years brought lumps to the throats of millions of Americans each Christmas. To see her in person felt stirring, and startlingly real.

And Karolyn Grimes served as more than a memory trigger. With a youthful warmth and appearance that belied her 54 years, she carried the magical essence from the uplifting screen tale. Her eyes shining, her smile aglow and her tree-green dress ethereally dazzling, Karolyn revealed no hint of the turmoil and tragedies of her past as she chatted and laughed with the hundreds who sought her out. It was a giant goodwill exchange, enhancing the spirit of philanthropy.

Karolyn is flanked by the co-chairs of the 1994 Hutch Holiday Gala, Suzanne Hight (left) and Mary Beth Barbour.

Before long, Bruce Murdock, a morning-show host from Seattle's KLSY-FM who served with his partner Tim Hunter as roving, amplified masters of ceremonies, located Karolyn and drew her to a small podium to answer a half-dozen questions – some serious and some just as banter – for all to hear. After welcoming Karolyn to Seattle (she had never visited the city before), Murdock, allowing that anyone's memories of 6-year-old days have to be "a little limited," asked Karolyn the question everyone asks her most often – what she remembers from the making of *It's a Wonderful Life*.

"The Christmas tree was especially beautiful," she answered without hesitation, "and Jimmy Stewart was taller than God. I had a lot of fun running up and down the stairs, hanging on for dear life on his back. That was neat."

'I did a lot of movies when I was a little girl.

'I was in bed with everybody – always had nightclothes on!'

Clarence, the movie's angel, could have been whispering the next question in the ear of Murdock, who then brought up a lesser-known Christmas film, *The Bishop's Wife*, released one year after *It's a Wonderful Life*. Both movies feature angels, and both cast Karolyn as a child of troubled parents.

"Yes, I was Debby, Loretta Young's and David Niven's daughter," she responded. "Cary Grant was an angel who comes down and sets David Niven straight."

"Did you do all Christmas movies?" Murdock asked with a laugh.

"Oh, I did a lot of movies when I was a little girl," Karolyn said, adding with a twinkle in her eye, "I was in bed with everybody – always had nightclothes on!"

"I'm going to check you for petals later," Murdock deadpanned, to which a grinning Karolyn responded with a quick whoop.

Then, with no transition, like the events of her life, the interview turned somber.

"You have a special connection tonight because the purpose of this Gala is, of course, to support cancer research, and you have a special feeling about that," Murdock said.

Karolyn made the switch with what seemed to be an eerie quickness, earnestness, and a smile.

"Yes, I do," she said. "I lost my husband to lung cancer in May of this year, so I want to get rid of cancer the best way we can, and I hope we can all get together and fight."

The "fighting" that night took the form of a four-hour auction in the grand ballroom, where 1,000 of the Seattle area's business and professional leaders bid on more than 80 items, raising a record $660,000 for the cancer research center.

When auctioneer Dick Friel reached item number 8, the Zuzu doll, a 60-second scene from *It's a Wonderful Life*, one of the movie's most familiar, began to roll on two huge video screens on either side of the stage.

The scene, of course, takes place on Christmas Eve. George Bailey, played by James Stewart, has entered the darkest day of his life, his family's building and loan having suddenly lost $8,000. The business hovering near certain bankruptcy, George's thoughts move toward suicide. He has stumbled breathlessly back home and up-ended the warmth of family tree-trimming and carol playing, desperately telling his wife, "Everything's wrong! You call this a happy family? Why did we have to have all these kids?"

'Want to give my flower a drink.'

Zuzu Bailey

In the midst of this turmoil, he takes time to go upstairs to check on Zuzu, the second-youngest of his four children, who had caught a cold that afternoon coming home with her coat unbuttoned so that she would not crush a rose she won as a prize at school. The scene then illustrates how even in the depths of despair, the values of family – and of life itself – emerge in countless moments that reflect the worth of every human being:

George tiptoes into Zuzu's room, but she's awake and sitting up in bed. The rose she won at school stands in a glass of water on her bed table.

"Hi, daddy," Zuzu says.

"Well, what happened to you?"

"I won a flower," she says, turning to the rose and starting to get out of bed.

"Wait, now. Where do you think you're going?"

"Want to give my flower a drink," she says.

"All right, all right," George says. "Here, give daddy the flower. I'll give it a drink."

But Zuzu shakes her head and

"Look, Daddy, paste it," Zuzu (Karolyn Grimes) says to her father George Bailey (James Stewart).

pulls the rose to her, causing a couple of petals to fall onto the bedsheets.

"Look daddy, paste it," she implores her father, her clear, strong eyes locking on his weary ones.

"Yeah, all right. Now, I'll paste this together."

As she hands him the rose, George turns his back to Zuzu. His hands nearly out of her sight, he pretends to paste the fallen petals back on the rose, but instead tucks them in the watch pocket of his pants and rearranges the rose.

"There it is," he says, turning back to Zuzu, "good as new."

Karolyn Grimes addresses the Gala crowd from the "Bedford Falls" stage, December 3, 1994.

"Give the flower a drink," Zuzu says, and he places her rose in the water glass.

"Now, will you do something for me?" he asks, leaning closer to her.

"What?" she whispers.

"Will you try to get some sleep?" he asks, returning her whisper, creating a deeper father-daughter intimacy that continues through the scene.

"I'm not sleepy," she whispers, turning her head to the water glass. "I want to look at my flower."

"I know, I know," her father replies with yet another whisper, "but you just go to sleep, and then you can dream about it, and it'll be a whole garden."

With the innocence and love of a little girl, she looks up and, with a hopeful whisper, answers, "It will?"

Then she closes her eyes. Her father pulls up her covers and, for a moment, gently places his hand on her forehead.

As the scene's final image froze on the Gala video screens, the auctioneer bellowed, "Ladies and gentlemen, please welcome Karolyn Grimes! This is Zuzu from *It's a Wonderful Life!*"

Hearty applause showered Karolyn as she walked on stage, and the ballroom's festive hubbub began to subside. Throughout the evening, those competing for vacation packages and other donated merchandise and services had struggled to make their bids heard over the din of constant chatter that filled the cavernous room – constant, that is, until Karolyn took the microphone. With a broad smile and a voice ringing with emotion, she drew the Gala audience to its only hush of the night.

"I know that cancer has touched many of your lives. It has also touched mine," she said. "This year I lost my husband of 25 years. He gave me a Christmas present last year, and I would like to read to you this Christmas present that he gave to me."

Karolyn held up a 14-carat gold bracelet and began to read from what was suspended from it – two heart-shaped gold charms.

"It says, 'For 27 years, soon to be 25 years of marriage, I have never loved you more than I do now, and I hope God lets me spend more time with you. But His will be done, for all our good. There is a small place for you to hang my bells when I earn my wings. My love forever, Mike.'

"I wish you would ring those bells tonight," Karolyn told the crowd, "because deep in your pockets you can do it, like George Bailey did. Every little thing you do touches everyone's lives, and I really want to hear those bells ring tonight!"

Her emotional appeal took hold. Bids for her Zuzu doll quickly soared from an initial offer of $150 to a final price of $1,850.

As the rest of the auction continued into the night, curious guests approached Karolyn, who thoughtfully answered question after question. At one point, she shook her head with a sigh, marveling at the overwhelming affection that a 1946 movie has brought her – and millions of others.

"The outpouring of love is something else," she said. "Everywhere I go, it's incredible. People tell me the stories that they've associated with the movie. It's heart-rending. The way they embrace me in their hearts keeps me in a continuous high.

"It's the most positive energy I've ever felt in my life. People really do get something from this movie. I guess there are not very many people who haven't experienced the feeling that they wish they hadn't been born. When they see this movie, it makes them have hope, and it makes them reflect on their own lives, and they see that what they have accomplished has touched other lives, and they do have something they have done, and it's good. It's uplifting for people."

"What happens to you," one guest asked, "when you yourself watch the movie?"

"Oh, I always cry, like everybody else," Karolyn responded. "And yes, I go to a lot of *It's a Wonderful Life* parties, so I do watch it a lot."

As she always does, Karolyn hastened to credit James Stewart, as both a performer and a human being, for the film's ability to reach people.

"He *is* George Bailey," she said. "He's leaving his mark. I really feel that it's something that no one else could ever do. And I feel so privileged to have been his child, even just in the movie. But it's him. He is George Bailey in real life. He lives like that, always has.

"Last Christmas, there was a reunion of those who are still alive who worked on the movie, and it was held in Mr. Stewart's hometown, Indiana, Pennsylvania. It's so refreshing to see how beloved he is to these people. It's a spirit that grows and grows and grows. He is the most unassuming man. He's a gracious, good person. He's just George Bailey!"

That spirit, Karolyn told another guest, guides her every day. "If I can do something to help people, I try to do that," she said. "But I feel like I'm being guided. Whatever comes my way will come my way. It'll be good."

While some people might feel bothered by such a weight of attention to a childhood film appearance so long ago, "I don't feel that way at all," Karolyn admitted. "I feel special. I really do. I feel touched that for some reason or another I was lucky enough to be involved in the film."

With her seven children grown and her husband gone, she said she feels she's "going where the guardian angels lead me."

Bells rang on the Gala auction floor as Karolyn finished a conversation, looking back on a life full of incidents as low as they've been high.

"I believe there are no coincidences. I had to be chosen to do this for a reason," she said. "For me to have the ability to reach out and touch other lives the way I

'It's the most positive energy I've ever felt in my life.

'People really do get something from this movie.'

do, the way I can – people cry, they're emotional – it's like nothing you can imagine.

"And for me to have the opportunity to have the goodness and great things that have happened to me because of this movie, it's a balance. You know, my life has not always been wonderful. . . ."

Well past midnight on a sultry summer Saturday night in the late 1930s, time meant little in the West Hollywood home of LaVan and Martha Grimes. Their friends Perry and Ruth Vannice were visiting. The four were into what seemed like their 20th hand of pinochle, the two men puffing on cigars and shooting the breeze.

"LaVan was awful bad about needling, and he'd needle me worse than anybody," Perry later recalled. "Well, we're right in the thick of this game, and I call off and play a card. First thing, LaVan lets out a laugh and says, 'Why didn't you play that card awhile ago?' And I answer such and such, and he says, 'Oh, no, no. If you had played it awhile ago, this and this would have happened.' He had it all figured out from one end to the other before I even knew what was going on. Well, that's fine, but pretty soon he starts needling Martha a little bit, and that's all it took. She didn't say anything, but boy, her hair just stood straight up."

As well as any can, Perry's deceptively spare remembrance sums up the differences embodied in Karolyn Grimes' parents. Theirs was a union of complex, opposite traits: brains, looks, an appreciation for refinement, a lack of pretension, a stern persistence, a teasing irreverence, an easy smile, a competitive spirit, a good heart. These qualities, eventually reflected in their only child, have traceable roots in the lives of Martha Octavia Motley and Ernest LaVan Grimes.

'George Bailey lassos stork!'

(Karolyn's parents and non-film childhood, 1909-1950)

LaVan Grimes and Martha Motley during their courting days in the early 1930s.

The two grew up not far from each other outside of Osceola (pronounced oh-see-OH-luh), a tiny, rural hub in west central Missouri that boasted a turn-of-the-century population of 1,100. Nestled along a bend of the Osage River and part of the larger geographic area known as the Ozarks, the town was named for a chief of the Seminole Indians. Positioned 108 miles southeast of Kansas City, Osceola served – and still does today – as the seat of St. Clair County. Though Osceola is considered part of the Midwest, its Dixie proximity gives its residents the tinge of a Southern accent and hospitality. Whether known for farming and ranching in the early 1900s or for its present-day fishing and boating (ever since the nearby construction of Truman Dam and creation of Truman Reservoir from the mid-1960s through late 1970s), Osceola's character has stayed decidedly rural.

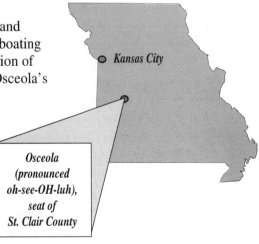

Kansas City

Osceola (pronounced oh-see-OH-luh), seat of St. Clair County

For the well-populated Motley and Grimes families, the flatlands of Osceola were home. The fourth of seven children, Martha was born seven miles northwest in Monegaw Springs on July 9, 1909. LaVan, the third of five children, was born May 6, 1910, in the northeastern Oklahoma community of Bluejacket, but he was reared in Vista, a burg just three miles to the south of Osceola.

Because Osceola served as the center of trade and school life for the surrounding farms, Martha and LaVan got to know each other at Osceola High School and may have met even earlier. Family and friends of Karolyn do not recall when Martha and LaVan started dating each other, but it is easy to pick out the circumstances that brought them together.

Both had families whose solid Baptist religious backgrounds gave them strong moral values. Each shunned liquor, for instance, and embraced the Midwestern work ethic. Yet in some ways they could not have contrasted more.

Fishing from the Osceola Dam was a favorite pastime, before Truman Reservoir was created more than two decades ago.

Martha was small, subdued and not conventionally pretty. A sharp student who earned good grades in all subjects, she grew up gaining an affinity for the traditional homemaking role: cooking, sewing, crafts and gardening.

A whimsical, well-worn 1907 book given to Martha by her grandmother, *How to Tell the Birds from the Flowers: A Manual of Flornithology for Beginners, Nature Series No.* 23, exemplifies Martha's studious and artful disposition. The book's verses and illustrations, both by Robert Williams Wood, delightfully link and compare similar-sounding bird and flower types: the crow and the crocus, the clover and the plover, the parrot and the carrot, the hawk and the hollyhock, and so forth. Poems for each pairing no doubt appealed to the articulate Martha, such as this one for "The Quail and the Kale":

> **The California Quail is said**
> **To have a tail upon his head,**
> **While contrary-wise we style the Kale**
> **A cabbage head upon a tail.**
> **It is not hard to tell the two.**
> **The Quail commences with a queue.**

As perceptively recalled by Lewis Lee Motley, one of Martha's nephews and nine years older than Karolyn, Martha was "a country girl only because she happened to live in the country." She played piano quite well, taking on an appreciation for social graces and the arts uncommon in her region of the state.

Martha was 'a country girl only because she happened to live in the country.'

Lewis Lee Motley, Martha's nephew

Upon her 1930 graduation from Osceola High School and simultaneous receipt of a teaching credential, Martha immediately went to work at Star School, a one-room country schoolhouse serving 20 students from first to eighth grade. Her dignity and sophistication, however, beckoned an eventual departure from her isolated surroundings.

Leaving Osceola also became the destiny of LaVan, though more for economic and social reasons. The son of a carpenter, LaVan lived in Osceola proper for much of his childhood, and friends from outlying farms considered him an outgoing "town boy." As tall as Martha was short, and a year ahead of her in school, he was a math whiz and top student with handsome, attractive features. LaVan also leaped into school sports, developing a lifelong passion, as befit his height, for basketball. Perry Vannice, who befriended LaVan in high school and inspired LaVan and Martha's eventual move to California, recalls that "Grimes," as Perry often called him, tore up the gym floors – both in Osceola and neighboring towns such as Lowry City and Weaubleau – with his basketball wizardry.

"Grimes was the best basketball player we had in Osceola," Perry remembers. "If it hadn't been for him, we'd have never had a team. To look at him, you'd think, 'This guy's awkward. He'll fall over something.' But that kind of favored Grimes, looking awkward to the other guys, because when he went out on that court, these other schools found that he was the toughest guy to guard there was. So right away, they put two men on him. He never went out on that court that there weren't two guys right on his tail. Still, he'd still twist around, around and back, flip that ball up there, and in it'd go. He'd be the highest scorer of everybody."

LaVan's zeal extended to socializing, as he would rather sit and talk with friends than go fishing, the favorite pastime of Osceola men. The Vannice farmhouse became a favorite haunt, as Perry, two years younger than LaVan, was an only child and his parents often encouraged him to bring LaVan home for supper and stay overnight. "I didn't have brothers or sisters, and he just made an awful good stepping stone in that direction," Perry says. Dinner at the Vannices also helped teach LaVan lessons in etiquette he had missed, given that his mother had died years before and his father, while amiable, was fighting a drinking problem. The feasts at Perry's house provided Perry with one of his favorite memories of LaVan.

LaVan Grimes was considered an outgoing "town boy" in Osceola and rural St. Clair County.

"My mother had a huge dining table, and she'd have it loaded," Perry recalls. "If she had a bare spot on it, she felt like she wasn't doing her thing. She had to have something everywhere. So when you sit down to eat, you pick something up, take some and then pass it to the next guy. Well, the food was jamming up in front of Grimes because whoever was on the other side of him wasn't keeping up. My dad was sitting next to Grimes and gave him two bowls to hold and was about to hand him another one, when Grimes said, 'Wait a minute, wait a minute.' There was no room on the table. So he just started setting the food on the floor. If my mother were alive today, that would be the first thing she would laugh about, and my dad, too. They thought that was the funniest thing that ever happened."

LaVan honed his gregarious, easygoing personality in a variety of ways with family and friends. Often, the jokes and conversation came over a checkerboard or a deck of cards. He became a master at poker, pitch, checkers and any other game anyone knew, and he found plenty of players, particularly with contacts he developed in the shopkeeping trade both before and after his 1929 high school graduation. As Perry tells it, LaVan's checker game was rivaled only by his instincts for self-promotion.

"Before he got out of high school, he was working for a little store called the Farmer's Exchange," Perry says. "This place would buy cream and ship it to Kansas City, Clinton or Springfield, and also bought eggs from the farmer. So all the farmers were in there selling eggs and cream, buying groceries and getting pretty well stocked. When Grimes went to work for them, it just wasn't any time until he was the boss. This guy could always sell himself. He just exceeded everybody.

"He could really play checkers, too, and he delighted in playing with me because I wasn't any problem at all. I don't remember ever beating him. We'd start in, he'd move, I'd move, he'd move, I'd move, then he'd say, 'Now, don't move over there.' I'd say, 'Why not?' 'Because,' he said, 'if you move there, I'm going to take this guy and give it to you here, and then I'm going to take these three men right off.' And it would keep going that way. He could see three or four moves ahead.

LaVan and Martha Grimes' formal wedding portrait, taken in 1933 by a studio in nearby El Dorado Springs.

"Well, down at the Farmers Exchange, in the winter when snow gets piled up a bit, the farmers don't come into town very much, so there's not much for Grimes to do. Eventually, his reputation got around that he was an excellent checker player, and every so often a drummer – not a guy who beats on a drum, but a salesman – would come in and say, 'Hey, I heard so-and-so say that you were a good checker player.' Grimes said, 'Oh, I can get by all right.' He never bragged. He'd never even think of such a thing, unless he was doing it to set up somebody. Well, this drummer wouldn't last any longer than I would. Three or four games and he'd be out of it.

"The drummer would get back on the train – there were two different lines that came through Osceola back then – and he'd tell the other drummers about Grimes. His reputation got so big that he hardly had time to run his store because of the guys who'd get off the train, run up there and want to play checkers with him. And he skinned the whole works. Never once did I see him lose a game."

The relationship between Martha and LaVan apparently began with the onset of the Great Depression, which devastated the rural Midwest. Osceola and its surrounding communities could not escape the ravages of severe weather and evaporating employment. Those old enough to work, and their families, fled to greener pastures. Like the desperate Joad family of John Steinbeck's *The Grapes of Wrath*, for many the destination was the Eureka ("I have found it") state – California. Perhaps as an omen, Martha's and LaVan's honeymoon destination, following their May 14, 1933, wedding in Rich Hill, Missouri, was the appropriately named town of Eureka Springs, Arkansas.

Martha Motley and LaVan Grimes were active in First Baptist Church of Osceola, which sits just a block from the Osceola town square.

During their early years of marriage, the two stayed active in the First Baptist Church of Osceola, Martha serving as secretary-treasurer of the church's Women's Home and Foreign Missionary Society. She also quit her teaching, while LaVan kept working at the Farmer's Exchange, his irreverence intact.

In that vein, Lewis Lee Motley recalls that LaVan

once bought a cache of fireworks for $100 (a significant sum in those days) and shot them off for his friends on a bitterly cold Fourth of July evening in Osceola. Younger than LaVan by 21 years, Lewis Lee also remembers staring with awe as LaVan "flew" his Kaiser-Frazer car down a gravel road, called a hay highway, at 80 mph. "He just liked to talk and laugh and have a good time," says Lewis Lee.

Likewise, LaVan's sister-in-law Lilly Motley remembers him as "an awful tease" who gave her the lifelong nickname of Cookie when he and Martha hired her to care for Martha at their home while she recuperated from an operation. "Really, he was a pretty great guy," says Lillian, who now lives just south of Kansas City. "He always thought so much of Martha. He was crazy about her."

As newlyweds, Ruth and Perry Vannice left rural Missouri for the Los Angeles area, prompting LaVan and Martha Grimes to do the same.

As the Depression persisted, Martha and LaVan watched wistfully as several members of Martha's family left Missouri to make the 1,600-mile trek west to California, where newly discovered deposits of oil promised new employment. But their real impetus came when Perry and his recent bride Ruth announced they were moving to Los Angeles. Perry wanted some distance from his father. At the same time, an aunt and uncle of Ruth's had moved west to Selma in the San Joaqin Valley, and they kept insisting that Perry and Ruth join them in California. "So that's what we did," says Perry, who places their move in June 1936.

Through a friend, Perry almost immediately hired on as a streetcar conductor/motorman for the Los Angeles Railway. It was a key step. "My getting a job meant Grimes had a place to come to," Perry says. "We wrote back and forth, and I didn't think they would move. But Grimes was just too smart for Osceola, and it wasn't two months later that they said they would come out." The decision was testimony to the strength of LaVan's friendship with Perry, but the prospect of a fruitful climate and better job opportunities also held potent appeal.

Hollywood represented a land of opportunity for LaVan and Martha Grimes. "It was like the new world," says their daughter Karolyn.

So in the late summer of 1936, LaVan and Martha left their rural roots and moved west, winding up in the suburban city of West Hollywood, whose population and density, while nowhere near as immense and intense as today, nevertheless left them awestruck. "It was like the new world," concludes Karolyn. "They were young, they wanted an adventure, and they got it."

Of course, by the late 1930s, Hollywood already had established itself as the world's moviemaking capital. The glamour and prestige of the film industry had seized and maintained its grip on America for the previous three decades. But for this young couple bred in the sensibilities of small-town virtues, Hollywood was merely a place in which to launch a new, more promising life. LaVan, restless, wasted little time in getting started.

"I've worked a long, long time," LaVan told Perry on the morning that he and Martha arrived in Los Angeles, "and now that I'm here, I'm going to have a couple weeks' vacation. That's all there is to it."

LaVan Grimes (right) and a coworker stand outside one of the Safeway branches at which he worked his way up the company ladder.

"Well," Perry responded, "do as you like about it."

That night, when Perry returned home from work, LaVan had an announcement.

"My vacation's over with," he told Perry.

"What do you mean?"

"I can't take this sitting around. That's all there is to it."

"Well," said Perry, "what do you plan on doing?"

"I could be a merchant. I could follow up on that line."

"Okay," Perry said. "Where do you think we should go?"

"We'll go over to Safeway and find out what they've got."

The next morning, Perry got time off work and took LaVan to an office in Vernon, about 10 miles southeast of Hollywood. Perry waited outside as LaVan entered.

"I'll just leave it up to you now," Perry told him. A half hour later, LaVan emerged.

"Well, they told me it was pretty favorable," LaVan said. "I gave them all my credentials. They told me they'd be able to call me in a short while."

That afternoon, LaVan got the call, and in short order he worked his way up the company ladder, eventually managing his own store. Never once did he tell Perry of any doubts or regrets for having moved west. "He always seemed like he was satisfied wherever he was or whatever he was doing," says Perry. "He was not a complainer, that's for sure."

LaVan did embrace the responsibilities of being a grocery manager, and he particularly enjoyed regaling family and friends with stories of catching shoplifters in the act. His trick was to climb several rungs up a stepladder, nudge the knot out of a high knothole in a plywood partition at the back of the store and surreptitiously view his customers hiding foodstuffs in their clothing, from bottles of beer to bars of chocolate. Once a shoplifter was spotted, LaVan would take over at the front checkstand and confront the offender as he or she was about to leave. "C'mon now," he'd say. "I know you've got it in your pocket. You don't want me to have to call the police now, do you? They'll search you and embarrass the life out of you."

In an impish incident recalled by Perry, LaVan called the bluff of a woman who had lifted a can of cayenne pepper, wearing her down by telling her that the store happened to have a special on cayenne pepper that day and insisting that she should take advantage of it. "Finally," says Perry, "she got so nervous and scared that she let her water loose right on the floor."

Meanwhile, the more serious Martha, like many women at the time, did not seek outside employment. Eager to establish the new Grimes household, Martha set about furnishing and fixing up their home, a garden court rental cottage on North Orange Grove Avenue whose neighborhood sat east of Beverly Hills, southwest of Los Angeles' gargantuan Griffith Park and a short drive, or streetcar ride, from the Pacific Ocean.

The California social life of LaVan and Martha connected closely with that of Perry and Ruth. "Every Saturday night," says Perry, "you could just bet that we were going to be over at the Grimeses or the Grimeses were going to be at the Vannices, playing pinochle until 2 in the morning." With LaVan's steady income and Martha's persistence on the domestic front, the couple's new life began to fulfill the promise of their cross-country move.

Pictured at 6 months, this was Karolyn Kay Grimes, LaVan and Martha's "firecracker," born on July 4, 1940.

And soon the household was to grow. Martha became pregnant in the fall of 1939, a development that Karolyn surmises was at least somewhat accidental. "I think they didn't really mean for it to happen," she says. "My mother was very happy with my father and the life they had. I don't think she really anticipated a child."

Perry perceives the situation differently. The Vannices had given birth to their first child, Beverly Ann, in June 1939, and, like the move to California, this triggered action in the Grimes household. "As soon as Beverly came along, it was just killing Grimes. I was one step up on him,"

LaVan and Martha Grimes cuddle with their first and only child, in the tiny living room of their house on West Norton Avenue.

Perry says with a chuckle. "We were always competitive, but not in a get-even way or in a bad mood. It was always for fun."

Whatever the impetus, at Hollywood's Bellevue Hospital at 5:06 p.m. on Independence Day 1940, a new dependent came into the world of 30-year-old Martha and 29-year-old LaVan – a seven-pound daughter whom LaVan introduced to relatives as his "firecracker." They named her Karolyn Kay Grimes.

Actually, her first name started out as two: Karo and Lynn. "I was named after Karo syrup," Karolyn says her parents told her later. "They wanted me to be called Karo Lynn, with a K, but it didn't quite work. It turned into Karolyn right away, and that's okay with me."

Karolyn at 1 year.

By this time, the Grimes family had moved two blocks east to a one-bedroom rental cottage that sat in back of a larger home on West Norton Avenue. Their tiny brown house, which still stands today, had little space for a third inhabitant, but it sufficed for the threesome for the first seven years of Karolyn's life. The small front porch looked out onto a swing and a small garden that Karolyn soon adopted as her "jungle."

Seven-year-old Nicole Bonilla bounces on a mini-trampoline in front of the tiny backlot house on West Norton Avenue in which Karolyn Grimes spent her first eight years. The house, home to Nicole, her sisters Karla and Vanessa and mother and dad Cenia and Carlos, has not been modified significantly since the Grimes family lived there 50 years ago.

In the spring of 1943, Karolyn, nearly 3, stands outside her house, which is accented by the horticultural talents of her mother.

Inside, an older upright piano dominated the front room. A kitchen, a bathroom and washing-machine nook were sandwiched between the front room and the back bedroom. The entire interior occupied less than 600 square feet.

Karolyn and her parents shared the bedroom. She had no separate space for books or toys, except for a spot on her bed eventually reserved for a Shirley Temple doll. The house was so cramped that the family's tiny Christmas trees each year had to fit on a tabletop.

One of Karolyn's first memories from pre-school days centers on "the only thing I ever stole in my whole life." Karolyn was home alone – her mother had left the house for a short time – when another girl in the neighborhood talked her into pilfering a strawberry from a passing truck that was delivering fresh fruit. "We each grabbed one and ran back to my house just as quickly as we could," Karolyn recalls. "Apparently, the truck driver saw what happened, so he was chasing us and came knocking on the door. I was so scared, I thought I was going to die. He finally left, and then my friend left, and my mother came home, and I was absolutely shaking in my boots. She said, 'Did anything happen while I was gone?' And I said, 'Y-y-e-s-s,' in a long, wavering voice. Then I told her that I'd stolen the strawberry. I didn't get in trouble, but I had to go and apologize to that man.

"But you know why I didn't get in trouble? Mr. Boyd, who lived in the house in front of us, already had told my mother that I'd stolen the strawberry, because the truck driver had gone to Mr. Boyd's house, so she knew it, and because I confessed to it, I didn't get in trouble. She told me, 'I knew that you did this, and I'm very proud.' She made a big deal about it, and it really impressed me. If I'd lied, that would have been the end, but I told the truth. I've never forgotten that lesson. Those were the days – one strawberry. And I don't even like strawberries!"

As full-time homemaker and mother, Martha instilled many such values in young Karolyn. While LaVan worked long hours at the grocery store, Martha provided loving, determined care, even speaking to her daughter in baby talk long after her infancy. "I think she just devoted her whole life to me," Karolyn says. "There wasn't much else but me that she doted on."

Much of Martha's attention took the form of passing on to Karolyn her love of the arts. One way Martha inspired and investigated the talents of her blue-eyed blonde little girl was to pursue film roles for her. With a start as a double at the age of 6 months, Karolyn's work in films (and, later, television) began in earnest at age 4 and continued for 12 years. The discipline of answering questions at auditions and playing child roles helped to foster an appreciation for the performing arts and other humanities that Karolyn still retains.

Martha did not merely shepherd Karolyn through film work, however. She also lavished lessons on her daughter, starting with piano at age 3, supplemented by violin at age 5. Conveniently enough, both were taught by Eunice Boyd, who lived in the larger house out front. "I also eventually had dancing lessons, voice lessons, dialect coaching – you name it, I had the lessons for it," Karolyn says.

Sharing Karolyn's battery of lessons was Beverly Vannice, who recalls that Mrs. Boyd "absolutely loved classical music, especially Mozart, and expected that everybody was going to love Mozart as much as she did." Learning piano, violin and, later, organ, Beverly and Karolyn joined other pre-school students in periodic programs organized by Mrs. Boyd. An undated flyer for a recital announces Karolyn playing "We'll Make Hay While the Sun Shines" and "Mozart's Lullaby." In another program for Mrs. Boyd, a musical skit, Karolyn played the young Marie Antoinette, the 18th century French queen later beheaded for allegedly passing military secrets to enemy forces. The script includes dialogue between Marie and the character's mother, who joyously await a pending children's performance of Mozart.

Beverly remembers Karolyn as a "cheerful, fun, gentle, kind and giggly" 4- and 5-year-old. The two became fast friends due to their parents' closeness and to their shared desire to escape the rigors of music lessons. Together, they played with dolls, arranged and rearranged the furniture of a playhouse and dressed up in their mothers' clothing. One of the girls' favorite fantasies was pretending to be

Martha proudly elevates her daughter on a tabletop.

The Los Angeles Ostrich Farm made for an unusual outing for (from left) toddlers Karolyn Grimes and childhood best friend Beverly Vannice, shepherded by their fathers LaVan Grimes and Perry Vannice.

princesses locked up in a castle, which Beverly now suspects was inspired by their mothers' pressure on them to perform. "I think we enjoyed the music," says

Beverly, who today is a psychologist in Rancho Palos Verdes, south of Los Angeles, "but I think maybe our mothers were a little bit invested in having us do it."

Some of Karolyn's training endured, and some did not. She later dropped piano in favor of violin because her fingers never grew long enough to stretch across an octave on a keyboard. The dance lessons served only to confirm her lack of physical coordination, she recalls. However, Karolyn's voice lessons uncovered a strikingly clear soprano with an extraordinary range in the upper registers.

Karolyn's lessons not only helped prepare her budding acting career, but they also paralleled and enhanced her involvement in nearby West Hollywood Baptist Church, which her family attended. "I was raised to go to church," she says, "and I started singing solos there when I was 6 and joined the choir when I was 7." A written program from the church's Dec. 21,

Karolyn performs at a violin recital, backed on piano by her teacher, Eunice Boyd, who lived in the house in front of the Grimes family home.

1947, Christmas service indicates that 7-year-old Karolyn also performed a solo, "Away in a Manger," on violin.

The churchgoers' plaudits meant more to young Karolyn than the religious meaning of what she performed. "People would come up to me and say, 'Oh, you sang that so well,' and I liked that," she says. "It was part of learning to get up and perform in front of people, like debate and oral interpretation in high school later on, and live theater work after that."

Though the services themselves were onerous at times, the Grimes family's regular attendance helped Karolyn to memorize Bible verses. Today, she values the practice. "One thing that is important in the Protestant religion is that they learn the Bible verbatim," she says, "and there have been times in my life when I've drawn upon the Bible verses that I had memorized when I was a child. They would pop into my mind, and I would get strength from them."

Karolyn's home life, however, was not overly religious, even at Christmastime. What she remembers most about the yuletide season is that she and her parents routinely opened gifts under their tabletop tree on Christmas Eve. The next morning, Karolyn opened further presents left by Santa Claus while she had slept. Her new toys and other gifts remained stored below the tiny boughs for the next week, until her parents took down the tree and its decorations.

Four-year-old Karolyn dons a new hat and purse and wheels a new baby buggy on Christmas Day 1944.

Although performance, family friends and church provided company, many of Karolyn's day-to-day activities were quite solitary. "I used to cut the women out of mail-order catalogues and cut out clothes to fit them," she says. "I loved the pretty dresses and clothes, and I liked to color."

Because she had no siblings, Karolyn often played alone at home. "Today, I do everything by myself because that was the way I was born into doing," she says. "In those days, I entertained myself all the time, and so now, for some reason or another, I have to keep busy. I can't just sit and not do anything. It's extremely hard for me to just sit and watch television. I've always been that way, and it's very difficult for me to be any different. I can go to a theater and watch a movie, but the movie's got to really be good."

Reading books became a treasured pastime, encouraged largely by her mother. The first book that touched Karolyn indelibly, and her childhood favorite, was L. Frank Baum's *The Wizard of Oz*. Unlike many of today's youths who see the famed film version first, Karolyn initially encountered Dorothy and the wizard in written form.

Raised a city girl, Karolyn nevertheless was exposed to rural life during her parents' summertime vacations to the Midwest. Here, she rides a horse at her aunt Myrtle's farm in Independence, Iowa.

"I just loved the story," she says, "maybe because Dorothy was all alone and I felt all alone." Karolyn recalls sitting with the book, devouring the fantastic tale, turning page after page. "I was toward the end, and my mother came over and said, 'It's time to take a bath and go to bed.' I begged her. I said, 'I'm almost at the end. Please don't make me stop right now.' And she let me finish the book. That was the kindest and best thing she could have done, because my momentum was there, and to this day, I love to get to the ends of books."

Her father also influenced the way Karolyn spent her free time. LaVan, the clever strategist, taught his daughter the rummy-based card game of canasta. "He was a gamer," she says. "He didn't gamble, but he was a brilliant man, and any game that there was, he could win. He started me playing canasta when I was 6. He put me in tournaments, and I absolutely loved it."

Karolyn's young world, outside the home, centered on her front-yard jungle. "That was my exploring land, an adventure place," she says. "There were some odds-and-ends bushes, but because my mother was a horticulturist, we also had banana trees, orange trees, fig trees – ugh, I hated 'em – a lemon tree, pomegranates. She liked all that stuff."

When Karolyn ventured beyond her jungle, she often visited a family whose intriguing religion would later play a larger role in her life. "A girl who was a friend of mine was a major Catholic," Karolyn says. "Her sister became a nun, so I wanted to be a nun. I just thought the Catholic religion was absolutely beautiful. You had to wear things over your head, and you had to genuflect. I'd go with them to church sometimes.

"Her family was different, and I liked them. They were really nice, moral, upstanding people, but they all sunbathed in the nude. They would hang blankets out on a clothesline in a square area of their backyard, and the women would lie inside there. I wouldn't go inside myself, I'd just peek in, but they'd say, 'Get out.' They didn't like us kids bothering them, but I got a big hoot out of it."

The drama of ceremony enthralled Karolyn so much that one time, she and a little boy from her neighborhood held a funeral for a dead

Though it is less lush than Karolyn recalls it to have been, the "jungle" along the sidewalk to the Grimeses' home survives today.

mouse in the alley behind her house. "I don't remember how it came about, but we just had to do it," she says. "We buried it in a shoe box. It was during World War II, and we sang a song from the war: 'Bell-bottom trousers, coat of navy blue

Karolyn received a bicycle for Christmas in 1945. She recalls that she was restricted to riding within a two-block radius of her home. (The photo at the upper left is one of several movie-portfolio portraits that Karolyn's parents proudly displayed on their living-room wall.)

. . . Now is the hour, when we must say goodbye.' It was probably the only song I knew. It seemed the right thing to do." Likely it was the first funeral at which Karolyn sang, but it wasn't to be the last.

Although Karolyn never lacked for daytime adventures, her home was dark in the evenings, due to wartime restrictions. "There were only two small front windows that you could see out of, and my mother had long blinds and quilts up over them at night when there would be mock air raids," she says. "We were allowed to use candlelight as long as we had those quilts up on the windows. Everywhere else in the neighborhood, all the cars and other things were covered with Army camouflage canvases and tarps."

Because of California's precautionary exercises, Karolyn, and occasionally her parents, ate dinner early, when it was still daylight. Then, and for years following the war, the favored companion in the Grimes household, as with many other families across the nation, was the radio. Martha and LaVan owned a three-foot-tall console model, and they placed a high value on the programs that filled the air. "I remember that when my mom and dad bought a car," Karolyn says, "they had to decide whether they wanted to get a radio or a heater. They chose the radio, because in California you really didn't need the heater, and it was just really important to have a radio."

The adult Grimeses did not always agree on their radio programming. For instance, despite LaVan's partiality to country-western music, Karolyn rarely heard it. "My mother wouldn't allow it in the house or the car. She thought it was for hillbillies," Karolyn says. "I grew up hating country-western music, and I still don't like it, but I think it wouldn't have hurt me to hear it."

Instead of music of any kind, the Grimes family tuned in to what Karolyn calls "the stories": *Inner Sanctum, Mary Worth, The Shadow, The Green Hornet,* Jack Benny, Abbott and Costello and Fibber McGee and Molly. Besides occupying the evening hours at home, these dramas and comedies helped ease the tedium of long drives in the car. "California is more spread out than most other places," says Karolyn, "so if we wanted to go visit somebody, it'd sometimes take hours, and that was how we passed the time."

Interestingly, while she listened to the radio one night at home with her father, a memorable exchange took place between the two that illustrates the influence that LaVan's gregarious, normally upbeat personality had on his daughter.

"The president was talking on the radio," Karolyn says, "and I was so young that I hadn't put it together in my mind that people stopped growing. I couldn't figure out why people didn't grow on up through the roofs of houses. I was in one of those curious, 'What if?' and 'What happens?' question-asking stages, and I asked my dad, 'Boy, wouldn't you just love to be the president of the United States?' And rather than brush me off and say, 'Oh, yeah, that'd be great,' and that would be the end of it, he said, 'No, I wouldn't.'

"Well, that was like putting gasoline on a fire. I asked him, 'Why? Tell me.' And he explained that he wouldn't want the responsibility. He just wasn't really interested in the kind of decisions that the president would have to make. He gave me the example of whether to go to war or not to go to war, and other things. And it lasted. I decided right there and then, 'I don't like politics,' and I never have been interested since."

Although Martha's proper and artistic tendencies dominated her child's formative years, the more playful and charismatic LaVan influenced Karolyn in many ways as well. She seemed to inherit his gregarious and bubbly personality. She also had other, more active hobbies, such as taking care of a succession of dogs and riding a bicycle throughout the neighborhood, though staying within a two-block radius. Of course, once she turned 6, school became a big part of her life as well.

LaVan and Martha often took Karolyn on long car trips, such as this one in 1944 to a well-appointed park near a friend's house in southern California.

She attended first grade at Gardner Street Elementary School, just nine short blocks northeast of her home. Martha walked Karolyn there each morning and home in the afternoon, except for the occasional days when Karolyn had to work at a studio to film scenes for a movie. At Gardner, Karolyn earned many "outstanding" marks, with an overall B average.

Although summertime was a vacation from school, for Karolyn and her mother it meant a longer, interruption-free opportunity for film work. But summer did not just mean work to the young girl. It also was the time when Karolyn, LaVan and Martha made an annual two-week trek to reconnect with family back in Osceola and other towns in west-central Missouri. The trips were grueling, as the family drove straight through from California to Missouri. The heat in the car during the 1,500-mile drive sometimes would make Karolyn faint. However, her reward for enduring the journey was a more simple, rustic routine with her cousins and other relatives.

Her family stayed most often in the two-floor house on Martha's mother's farm, where Karolyn eagerly explored

LaVan Grimes (left) and his Safeway staff pose for a photo. Teen-aged Don Gates, who became a family friend, is at LaVan's left.

the diversions of rural life non-existent in Hollywood: riding a horse and wagon into town with her favorite uncle Truman, her mother's brother, helping her grandmother make modeling clay and cook aromatic meals, fishing, milking cows, collecting eggs, watching hunting puppies being born, visiting cemeteries and, because of a lack of indoor plumbing, using her grandmother's outhouse, and not having to take a daily bath. Always at one point during each year's vacation trip, everyone in the family piled into cars and drove 40 miles east to spend a couple of days wading and visiting at a resort owned by one of the relatives at Lake of the Ozarks.

On these summer excursions, people entertained and fussed over the young Karolyn because of glowing letters her mother had regularly written about the tot's film appearances. "She wasn't just a regular little girl then," says Marie Barnes, an Osceola resident and childhood friend of Martha and LaVan. "Karolyn had been taught to put her best foot forward. That's what was fascinating to the people who knew her parents." At the same time, however, for Karolyn the vacations meant a welcome break from the movie work that awed Osceolans.

Karolyn cavorts with one of the dogs her parents gave her when she was a child.

One downside of the idyllic family vacations was the closeness to the unpleasantries from which an urban, middle-class California girl is normally sheltered. Karolyn was eaten alive by red chiggers and mosquitoes, and she endured canned-milk treatments for sunburns. One summer, she remembers that, to her shock, she sat down on a potato bug. On another occasion, a rooster pecked her in the face. Yet another time, when she was dressed up and admonished by her mother to stay clean, she ignored the warning and played atop a wagon, only to slip and fall into a pool of feed-lot manure that her mother later scrubbed off beneath an outdoor water pump. Arguably her worst encounter with nature lay only in her mind, however, as she became convinced that snakes, of which she developed a massive fear, lurked in the dark hole of her grandmother's outhouse.

Gardner Street Elementary School (shown as it looks today) allowed Karolyn a school outlet for her singing and violin playing.

On one occasion, the yearly trip to Osceola was prompted by a rift between Karolyn's parents. LaVan, whom Karolyn always considered a "ladies man," apparently had had an affair with a woman in California. Martha, in anger, took Karolyn and moved in with her mother in Osceola for several weeks, and a dark cloud hung over the trip until Martha and LaVan reconciled, and Martha and Karolyn returned.

For the most part, though, the jaunts to Missouri built good feelings in Karolyn for her family and for Osceola, as well as an appreciation of the urban advantages her life offered back in the Los Angeles area.

Although one of those pluses was the availability of many movies, Karolyn does not recall seeing many films in theaters as a young child, ironic given her personal involvement in the industry. The few movies she can name that her mother took her to include the ballet classic *The Red Shoes* and the family memoir *I Remember Mama*, both released in 1948, and a revival showing of 1939's *The Wizard of Oz*, all of which held appealing elements of romance and fantasy.

A typical summertime gathering of the Grimes and Motley families in Osceola, including Karolyn – seen here standing in front at left. Her parents LaVan and Martha are at far right. Karolyn's cousin Lewis Lee Motley kneels in front at right.

The reality of a new adventure soon intervened, though. By the time Karolyn reached third grade, in the fall of 1948, the family's need for a larger home had grown unavoidable. So LaVan and Martha bought a house about 25 blocks south of their old one, on Ridgely Drive in Los Angeles, south of Wilshire Boulevard and near the LaBrea tar pits. The move cost the family the close-knit, smaller town atmosphere of their cozy West Hollywood neighborhood, but it also offered

great advantages. Besides shortening the length of LaVan's daily commute to his store to just seven blocks, the move to the larger home gave 8-year-old Karolyn a bedroom of her own.

Her room in the southeast corner of the house sported a couple of bonuses: a walk-in closet the full length of the back side of the room, and two large windows. Karolyn recalls being so excited about having space to call her own that she spent many a day rearranging her furniture. "I loved to think that I had a room of my own," she says, "My mother made me curtains, and she made a little vanity table with a skirt to match the curtains. My shelf for toys and books was made out of orange crates, and she made curtains to match everything on the orange crates. Everything was pink-and-white-striped, with little bows."

The Ridgely Drive house as it looks today – remodeled but much the same it was during Karolyn's upper grade-school years.

The rest of the house didn't lack for charm, either. Though modest compared with the rest of the neighborhood, it sat on a hill and had the stature of serving as the first farm house in the area. "We had no fans or air conditioning," Karolyn recalls. "You just pushed open the front windows so the fresh breeze from Santa Monica would come flowing through." Inside, the home had a total of three bedrooms (including one with a separate entrance that LaVan and Martha would rent periodically to a single boarder), a living room and dining room, a kitchen, laundry room and one bathroom. Martha delighted in planting flowers out front, buying new furniture covered in green satin and installing several chandeliers. In back was a large, picket-fenced yard with a swingset, plus a small garage adorned with a basketball backboard and rim, where LaVan, who regularly coached church boys' basketball teams, often could be found shooting hoops on weekends and warm evenings.

Many adjacent and nearby lots lay vacant, so the area lacked a certain intimacy. The only family Karolyn remembers knowing well was a couple across the street, only because they owned a television and Karolyn could regularly watch *The Lone Ranger* there.

Despite the distance between neighbors, Karolyn's life in the new house did not want for adventure. Once, just after moving to the house, Karolyn vividly recalls, she atypically became afraid to be left alone. "During that time, I remember that my mother made me stay home while she went to the drugstore," she says. "It probably was just for five minutes or so. She wouldn't let me go with her. She made me stay home because I was so afraid, so scared. She wanted me to get brave. So I sat and pounded on the piano the whole time she was gone, just for noise, I guess."

The new house also was the setting for a memorable, if mysterious, incantation of sorts that Karolyn remembers her mother performing to rid her daughter of an irritating wart. "She did a witch thing, something from an old wives tale," Karolyn says. "She rubbed a potato on my toe where the wart was and buried the potato underneath the driveway. She told me to think that the wart was going to go away, and by God, the thing went away."

Martha Grimes stands outside Cochran Avenue Baptist Church in the family's new neighborhood.

After moving, Karolyn's parents switched their religious membership to Cochran Avenue Baptist Church, just around the corner from their new home. Karolyn attended the church's day school for third and

Cochran Avenue Baptist School (left) and Church, as they look today. Karolyn attended third and fourth grade at Cochran.

fourth grades, then moved to Burnside Elementary, a public school accessible through an underground walkway beneath Pico Boulevard, from fourth through sixth grades. "It was a lot bigger than Cochran, with a major emphasis on sports, and I was always the last person to be chosen for a team," Karolyn says. "I hated that."

Notwithstanding its athletic leanings, Burnside gave Karolyn the opportunity to serve as concert mistress (second in command) for the school orchestra, and her sixth-grade teacher there gave her a confidence boost, albeit temporary, in her artistic abilities. "I always felt like I was less than adequate in art, but one day I drew a picture of a tropical jungle scene with palm trees and flowers. The teacher knew the way I felt, so she put the picture up on the wall, and my God, I was in heaven. I tried for the rest of the semester to get another picture up on the wall. Needless to say, it never got there, but she did the right thing because I tried the entire time to get something back up there."

In these upper elementary years, Karolyn excelled in all areas of citizenship and drew generally good grades. While she drew average marks in math, science and handwriting, Karolyn earned A's and B's in reading, music, art and, unsurprisingly, memorization.

Though Martha maintained Karolyn's lessons with Mrs. Boyd, Karolyn started new pursuits after the move to the new house, such as Girl Scouts and ice-skating. She continued to hone her musical skills with periodic performances at church, such as a vocal solo of "Christ Arose" on April 2, 1950. The proximity to La Brea tar pits – the bubbling natural phenomenon whose quicksand-like properties have lured, killed and petrified all manner of animal life over the centuries – provided a new and fascinating attraction for Karolyn to show to out-of-town guests.

Seated with her violin at front left, next to the conductor's position, Karolyn served as concert mistress for the Burnside Elementary School orchestra.

By all accounts, Karolyn's childhood reflects none of the popular stereotype of young film stars whose lives are traumatized and ruined by abuse and excess. However, it was far from a life of deprivation.

"My mother spoiled me terribly," Karolyn says, noting that she has never been able to shake the example Martha set for presenting a proper appearance by acquiring, making, growing or cooking the finer things in life. And there was no question to anyone who knew the Grimes family closely that Karolyn and her film work were a source of unending pride for Martha and LaVan. Framed photographs from Karolyn's interview portfolio had lined the walls of the front room in the family's tiny Hollywood home, and while Martha upgraded the decor in the second house, a portrait of Karolyn still hung in a prominent spot in the living room. Her parents also loved to display their daughter's achievements and never hesitated to ask her to sing or play a violin piece for visitors.

By the time Karolyn entered sixth grade,, her interests had begun turning to boys, including classmate Billy Swift.

Stability reigned in the Grimes household, in large part due to LaVan and Martha's quest to establish a home underpinned by strong religious and moral values. Don and Nancy Gates, who as teen-agers worked in LaVan's grocery store in the mid-1940s, look back upon the Grimes family as normal and upstanding. Don and Nancy, who now live in Scottsdale, Arizona, became close family friends during Karolyn's younger years, viewing her father and mother as mentors and parental role models.

"Karolyn had a wonderful, wonderful life as a child," says Nancy. "She had a Norman Rockwell life. They enjoyed doing things together. They were very

Karolyn Grimes (back row, left) and her graduating sixth-grade class at Burnside Elementary School. Her best friend at the time, Linda Fukuyama, stands at her left.

Karolyn was her dad's (and mom's) "star" from the beginning, say family friends Don and Nancy Gates.

strong in the church. They enjoyed Karolyn's work. The family itself seemed very lovely. They adored one another, and they adored Karolyn. It was like Karolyn was their star, and anything Karolyn wanted to do, they would see that she got to do it."

To the Gates couple, Martha and LaVan, known in the store as Ernie (the informal version of his first name), proved an unbeatable combination.

"Ernie knew everybody, and everybody knew Ernie," says Don. "I wouldn't say he was loud and boisterous, but he was very enthusiastic, and always, always upbeat." Don fondly recalls Ernie's key role in raising money among store employees so that Don and Nancy could enjoy a honeymoon on Catalina Island in 1950. Ernie also earned the respect and affection of both his employees and higher-ups. "He worked hard. So many store managers thought they were above working, but Ernie always worked, and everybody liked him." Indeed, says Don, when a mid-level supervisor decided to clean house by firing 19 of 22 store managers, Ernie was one of the three who hung onto their jobs.

Meanwhile, Nancy regarded Martha as "the perfect mother" who "would have been totally content to sit at home, bake some cherry pies and keep house. She always had flowers from her garden in her house. She was very plain in a sense, but I would always notice little things she'd done in the house that were quite lovely."

Both Nancy and Don remember Karolyn as a combination of her parents' best qualities: her mother's refinement, and her dad's happy-go-lucky personality.

"She was always nice," says Don, "not a smarty little kid at all, but very respectful and sweet. Being in the movies, you would think she'd be different, but she wasn't. She was just a darling little girl."

Gail Taylor Adams, a cousin of Karolyn's who now lives in Warsaw, Missouri, partly agrees with Don and Nancy's observations of Karolyn's family. A year younger than Karolyn, she developed her first perceptions of LaVan, Martha and Karolyn when they visited Osceola on summer vacations during the 1940s.

"LaVan was a real fun person, laughed all the time, always had tales to tell, and Karolyn was his girl," Gail recalls. "We could just be setting, and all of a sudden he would jump up and say, 'Let's go to Clinton [a larger town 22 miles north] and have a Coke.' It was just spontaneous. Just all of a sudden, he would decide we were going to do something, and everybody would go along. He was a leader, the type everybody followed. Martha was more sincere – not that LaVan wasn't sincere, but I think Martha was a more deeply rooted person, and more concerned day-to-day with Karolyn and wanting her movie career to go somewhere.

"You know, it takes two different kinds of people to balance out and make a good marriage. You draw off of one another. He was the pied piper, and she was the serious one. She was the one who made sure that they were stable financially. He did the work to earn the money, but she saw that everything was on the straight and narrow. They did very well. Martha wanted a lot for Karolyn, and LaVan wanted what Martha wanted for her. He loved Karolyn, so if movies were the route she was to take, that was all right with him."

'Martha wanted a lot for Karolyn, and LaVan wanted what Martha wanted for her. He loved Karolyn, so if movies were the route she was to take, that was all right with him.'

Gail Taylor Adams, cousin

Looking back, Karolyn knows that her home life through her grade-school years was filled with love, but it was a love leavened with limits and high expectations, leveled primarily by the person with whom she spent the most time – her mother.

"I don't think I necessarily had a happy childhood," she says. "I think there was extreme pressure put on me to be this little girl who my mother wanted me to be. She pushed what she really wanted for me into a totally different person. I did feel that."

Karolyn suspects, but cannot remember clearly, that there was sporadic friction between her parents, perhaps in part over what she was and was not allowed to do.

"I don't think I could be with other kids much," she says. "I never could go to parties because I always had my lessons or work or something. I know how much my dad wanted me to play basketball with him, but my mother would never let me do that because I might hurt my hands, permanently damage them for playing violin and piano. I felt like I never could have fun. To play and just think about playing didn't happen much. I always had to be the little lady. I couldn't grow up and be the tomboy that maybe would have given me a little better balance."

Chomping on a cigar, LaVan embraces his wife and daughter.

Semi-athletic pursuits such as ice skating and miniature golf were not out of bounds, however. "That's because those things wouldn't hurt my hands," she says. "My dad used to play miniature golf all the time, and he entered me in tournaments, and I loved it. But even later, when I was in high school, my music teacher wouldn't let me go to games and watch because I might scream and hurt my voice.

Seven-year-old Karolyn poses with the requisite basket on Easter 1948. Today, Karolyn looks back on her childhood and observes that she was raised to be a "cream puff."

"So I was brought up to be this little cream puff, and in a way I am a cream puff, a little froufrou person who's totally uncoordinated and hates sports. Yet we live in a world in which sports are probably the biggest recreation. I don't like them and can't participate, and that's sad, because I probably would have enjoyed something like golf or tennis. I look at sports fanatics, and I can't figure them out. What do they see in it? I wish it were different for me, because it's so good for you physically, mentally and every other way."

In adulthood, Karolyn has discovered how the early influences of her parents shaped her later life. She increasingly recognizes the day-to-day effects of her childhood, from her mother's scorn for country music to her father's aversion to politics.

"Of course, as a child, you pretty much are guided by your parents to do what they tell you to do. But the way that you're raised, boy, you just don't realize how much you learn and how you get impressed, how things get ingrained in you that aren't very movable. Then as a parent, you don't realize what you're molding in this little child, and you really are. You just don't know."

S he's just 4 years old. Her mother has dressed her "picturebook perfect" and she has to stay as clean as possible during the morning streetcar ride.

As the tot listens to the motorman's whistle and feels the vibrations of the streetcar tracks, her mother sits next to her, carrying her portfolio, a notebook-sized, black folder with a bumpy texture on the outside and two snaps that hold it closed. Inside is a sheaf of plastic sleeves protecting 28 professional black-and-white 8x10s of her in an array of little-girl costumes and expressions: happiness, surprise, pensiveness, anger.

They walk inside a building and sit in chairs next to each other outside an office. Scanning the room, she sees other mothers and daughters, some carrying portable roll-up tap-dance boards, but most with portfolios like hers.

Someone calls her name. Without her mother, she gets up and, cradling the portfolio, enters the office. Inside, three other grown-ups sit in chairs in a semi-circle and eye her.

She hands the portfolio to the grown-ups, and they pass it around, flipping through the photos. One of the grown-ups, a woman, addresses her.

"Now, think how you would feel if your dog died," the woman says. "Think if you lost your dog and he was dead. Think about that. Think how you would feel."

Then the grown-ups watch the girl's face as she tries to display sadness.

Another grown-up, a man, tells the girl that she will now play part of a scene. He reads aloud a few lines, asking her to memorize and repeat them. Then he instructs her on when the lines are to be spoken in response to the lines of others, and with what emotions. She gets no script because she can't read yet.

Two of the grownups read from the script and pause momentarily so that she can chime in with her lines.

This continues for about an hour. Then the grownups usher the girl out of the office to her mother, and the two of them ride home on the streetcar.

What is to come of the little girl's meeting in the office – and scores of others just like it? No one in her house knows, until the telephone rings.

Filled with 8x10 photos showing her in various facial expressions, costumes and backgrounds, this portfolio accompanied young Karolyn to countless interview appointments.

Chapter

3

'Nope. Nope. Nope. Nope. Now look, I want a big one!'

(Karolyn's first four films, 1944-1946)

The portraits in Karolyn's portfolio were designed to display how she could show a variety of emotions.

For Karolyn Grimes and her mother Martha, on at least 17 occasions the phone brought good news – that yes, the grownups wanted Karolyn to be part of a Hollywood film.

Today, Karolyn does not recall that her early career had any grand scheme, ideal goal or ultimate measure of success. Martha Grimes believed in the arts, and she made certain that Karolyn had myriad opportunities to develop her performing talents. Yet, the financial rewards of film roles did have some influence on Martha, especially during World War II.

Martha, assuming that LaVan would be drafted, decided to try to get Karolyn into the movies, partly because she feared that she and her daughter could not live on Army pay.

Martha, assuming that LaVan would be drafted, decided to try to get Karolyn into the movies, partly because she feared that she and her daughter could not live on Army pay. She took the young girl to see the agent of a friend of a friend, Lola Moore, who was known for representing young talent. The agent liked Karolyn, and soon the child started going to interviews.

The very day Karolyn's father was to enter the Army, the war ended and the threat of his induction evaporated. Nevertheless, Martha continued to pursue film work for her. Don and Nancy Gates, friends from LaVan's grocery, recall that far from embodying the stereotypical driven, star-struck mother, Martha merely saw that her daughter had talent, was hearing the same assessment from Karolyn's teachers, and therefore wanted to give Karolyn opportunities to express herself.

"I never got the impression from Martha – and we talked a lot about this – that she really wanted a career for Karolyn in the movies," says Nancy. "You have to understand that at that time, everyone in southern California could be an extra at one time or another. When I was a little girl and took dancing lessons, I was in four or five movies myself. It was just something everybody seemed to do.

Opposite: Karolyn was asked to pose with a variety of props. The nightclothes, the doll and the dark chair with its forboding shadow – along with Karolyn's wide-eyed apprehension – combine to create a mood of innocence threatened. (Karolyn's signature is a modern-day addition.)

"There were always people looking around for a kid to fill a void in some movie they were making. If you were in a dance class, there was always someone looking at these classes for a special child. If you were in a class of violin players, there was always someone from the studio looking for a child who showed promise. It was part of our lives. So this activity that Karolyn was involved in, it was Martha's duty to see that she be there for her daughter, but Martha was not one to push it on her."

Don and Nancy say that LaVan expressed pride in Karolyn's film work, but the

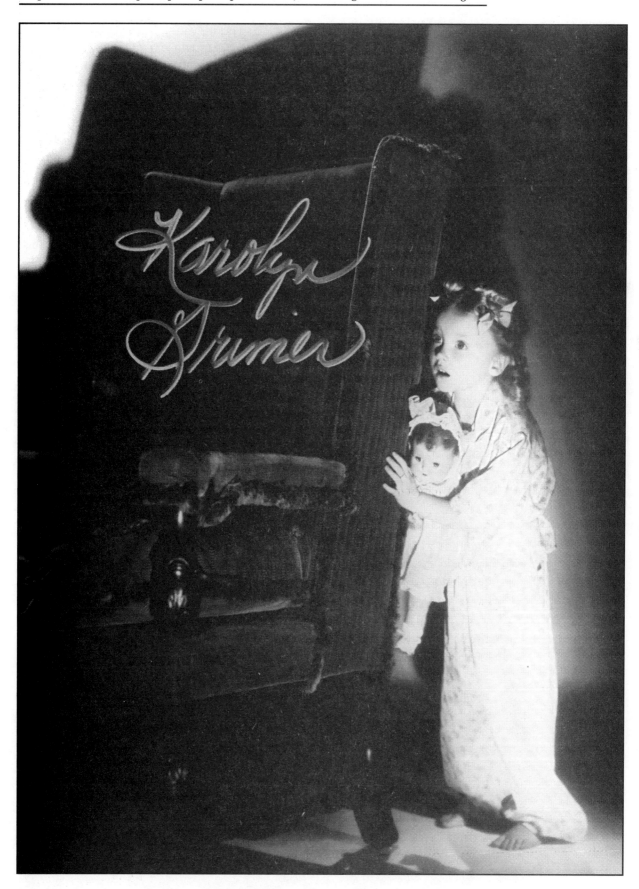

For 2-year-old Karolyn, a bonnet added the right touch . . .

. . . and for 3-year-old Karolyn, a bow did the trick. But often the pose – as with Karolyn's 4-year-old china-doll look above – was the key.

task of getting Karolyn to interviews and accompanying her to the studios fell to Martha. LaVan did not care for the people in the movie industry, and his own work schedule did not permit his getting more involved.

Perry Vannice believes Martha's organizational and managerial abilities suited the uncertain world of Hollywood filmmaking. "She was on top of it," Perry says. "She began to learn people, and learn who you can depend on, who you can ask about this and that, and she didn't mind calling them up to move things along. She could really handle a situation."

To some degree, and contrary to the reflections of Don and Nancy Gates, Karolyn remembers that her mother did show signs of what might be called a "heavy-duty" stage mother. "I think she was pretty good at it," she says. "For a little country girl, she had some pretty high aspirations for me and wanted a lot out of me. I don't think she put that much pressure on me to get a particular part or made me feel bad if I didn't get a part, but very little was left to luck. I knew if I didn't do what [the interviewers] wanted, they'd get someone else who would. I learned what rejection was, and I would do everything I could to please. I was raised wondering what I did wrong when I didn't get the part.

"I do know that my mother was pushy to others, though. She had to be. She had to stick me in front of people. She had to put me in the right places at the right times. There is a rhythm to the whole thing, to get it done."

'I learned what rejection was, and I would do everything I could to please.'

Just how that rhythm played out remains somewhat mysterious to Karolyn. Certainly, she holds a trove of recollections and artifacts from Hollywood features of all types: comedies, musicals, Westerns, biographies, family dramas and the Christmas classic *It's a Wonderful Life*. But she has no way of knowing exactly how many interviews she went to or how many times she was hired. Nor does she possess what she knows to be a complete list of her films. Martha Grimes seemingly saved every still, clipping and pay stub she could lay her hands on, but even that material, stored in boxes for decades, is incomplete. Moreover, most of the adults who worked on or acted in the films Karolyn made as a youngster, and who might have been able to fill in the holes, are no longer living.

As a result, what Karolyn knows of her childhood film career is an amalgam of the materials her mother saved and discoveries that others have made, along with her spotty childhood memories. In many cases, her films themselves, some of which Karolyn has seen only in the past few years, provide the best or only documentation.

Despite her sketchy memory, Karolyn can identify the first time the telephone rang with good news of movie work. She was just 6 months old, and was called to be a "carry-on," off-camera double for the part held by infant Sharon Lynne in Paramount's *West Point Widow*, released June 11, 1941.

Directed by Robert Siodmak and starring Anne Shirley, Richard Carlson, Richard Denning and Frances Gifford, this now-obscure black-and-white romantic comedy interestingly had a string of draft titles ranging from the innocent ("Little Miss Muffet") to the sensational ("Nurses Don't Tell"). The movie tells the good-natured story of a nurse (Shirley) who has consented to an annulment of her marriage so her husband (Denning) can attend the U.S. Military Academy at West Point, which requires cadets to be bachelors. A hospital intern (Carlson) falls in love with the nurse, who has a baby, Jennifer, from her

By the time she was 4, Karolyn was well-practiced in the craft of posing for photos to draw studio attention.

previous marriage about whom the father knows nothing. A scandal erupts when the intern is seen with Jennifer, whom everyone assumes was fathered out of wedlock by the intern. All ends happily when the academy man graduates and marries a socialite (Gifford), freeing the nurse and the intern to marry.

Although the infant is on screen for nearly half the film, stand-in Karolyn does not appear in the finished product. However, her June 30, 1941, pay stub, from Central Casting and issued to "Katherine Grimes," shows that she earned $44 for her efforts. In a letter back home to Osceola in early 1941, Karolyn's mother related details of the experience that shed light on the manner in which Hollywood handled tiny would-be actresses at the time:

The first time the telephone rang with good news after an interview for movie work was when Karolyn was just 6 months old.

On Monday afternoon, Jan. 24, I sent Karolyn Kay's picture and Social Security number to Miss Bernice Saunders c/o Central Casting Corp, Hollywood, Calif. Tuesday, they called

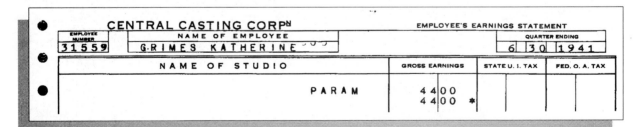

CENTRAL CASTING CORPᴺ			EMPLOYEE'S EARNINGS STATEMENT		
EMPLOYEE NUMBER	NAME OF EMPLOYEE			QUARTER ENDING	
31559	G·RIMES KATHERINE			6 30 1941	
NAME OF STUDIO		GROSS EARNINGS	STATE U. I. TAX	FED. O. A. TAX	
PARAM		44 00			
		44 00 *			

Karolyn's first pay stub, representing four days of stand-in work at $11 a day. She served as a double for infant Sharon Lynne in the 1941 romantic comedy WEST POINT WIDOW.

and wanted Karolyn to report to work at 10:15 a.m. Wednesday morning at Paramount Studio.

Mrs. Kuhn took us to the studio. We got our voucher check and waited for a car to take us to Stage 14. We reached the nursery and learned Karolyn was to double for Sharon Lynne. She was dressed in Dr. Denton's diapers.

At 1:15 p.m., she was before the camera 5 minutes with Anne Shirley and Richard Carlson. She only was there four hours. LaVan called for us at 2:15.

LaVan was on next day. If the weather was pretty, we wouldn't work, but she would get her pay just the same. The weather was nice, so didn't work.

She was called on Thursday to report to the studio at 11 o'clock. Friday, it rained, so we were brought home by studio chauffeur and car.

Saturday, we reported to work at 10:15. Still raining. We were dismissed and brought back home around 10 o'clock. Karolyn was paid $11 for a four-day amount of $44.

> *'If the weather was pretty, we wouldn't work, but she would get her pay just the same.'*
>
> *Martha Grimes*

The *West Point Widow* experience only whetted Martha's stage-mother appetite. Among the scraps saved by Martha is a voucher for 20 cents to reimburse her for carfare to an interview with "Director #129" at Columbia Pictures on July 23, 1941.

Five-year-old Karolyn acts in the live ranchers' drama GENTLEMAN JANE in late 1945 at West Hollywood's Call Board Theater.

While there is no evidence of film work by Karolyn over the next three years, her mother, with the help of her agent Lola Moore, landed the tot in at least a couple of local performing roles. At age 3-1/2, she was one of eight girls "Taking Dolly Out for a Ride" in the Dec. 13, 1943, free Christmas Carnival put on by the Peggy Vanne School of Dancing in the sixth-floor auditorium of the Broadway Department Store in Los Angeles. Two years later, in late 1945, Karolyn played a character named Judy in the stage drama *Gentleman Jane* by Stephen Marek at the Call Board Theater on Melrose Place in West Hollywood. One in a cast of 14, the 5-year-old was mentioned fifth in a brief newspaper review of the show, set on a ranch in southern Idaho in 1889. Karolyn remembers nothing of her no-doubt tiny part, though three promotional photographs showing her acting in the play survive in her memorabilia.

Karolyn's next foray into films is difficult to pin down definitively. In the pressbook for *Pardon My Past*, an amiable 1945 comedy in which the nearly 5-year-old Karolyn held a key role, a promotional article states that Karolyn already had appeared the year before in two movies. They were *The Seventh Cross*, a harrowing, inspirational account of a Nazi concentration camp escapee played by Spencer Tracy, and *The Clock*, a 1945 romantic drama starring Judy Garland as a secretary and Robert

Walker as the lonely soldier she encounters in New York City's Grand Central Station.

Viewings of both films today reveal no trace of Karolyn. It is possible that she served as a double in each movie (particularly *The Seventh Cross*, which has a brief, prominent part for a girl her age), or that her scenes were left on the proverbial cutting-room floor. But the writer of the promotional article may have stretched the truth for the cause of Hollywood hype. The article goes on to say that Karolyn "made her debut" in *West Point Widow*, without mentioning that she did not appear in the film.

If *Pardon My Past* was Karolyn's next step into films, unquestionably it represented a giant leap. Not only was it her first speaking role, but a pivotal one with a firm grasp on the heartstrings that underlie the movie's screwball proceedings.

Released by Mutual Productions under the Columbia Pictures banner, *Pardon My Past* is a breezy, talky, mistaken-identity farce, largely a vehicle for Fred MacMurray, who plays a double role: (1) Eddie York, an amiable, just-discharged World War II veteran eager to start a mink farm in the Wisconsin town of Beaver Dam (not coincidentally, MacMurray's home town),

This promotional photo cleverly uses Karolyn to convey the screwball atmosphere of PARDON MY PAST. In the farce, Rita Johnson (left) and Fred MacMurray (playing Francis Pemberton) are Karolyn's parents. MacMurray also plays Eddie York, who doesn't know he is Pemberton's twin. Circumstances prompt York to impersonate Pemberton and fall in love with Karolyn's "Aunt" Joan (Marguerite Chapman, right).

and (2) Francis Pemberton, an insensitive, wealthy playboy from Great Neck, New York. Neither Eddie nor Francis knows, until disclosed late in the film, that they were born identical twins and separated at birth.

Accompanied by Army buddy Chuck Gibson (an uppity William Demarest, who later co-starred with MacMurray as Uncle Charlie in the TV series *My Three Sons*), Eddie trades in his khakis for civilian duds at a New York City men's store, but he's mistaken for Francis by a bookmaker who insists that he owes a $12,000 gambling debt. Eddie and Chuck wind up spending several days at the Pemberton mansion, with Eddie impersonating the playboy, who has been in Mexico for two years. Everyone associated with the Pemberton house mistakes Eddie for Francis, including Francis' wife, sister (described as a "poor relation"), uncle, grandfather and 5-year-old daughter – played by Karolyn.

In the original, more salacious storyline, MacMurray's character was an international merchant seaman and ex-bookie who impersonates his dead twin brother, whose infant child had been born out of wedlock. The Hays Office, responsible for censoring films according to a voluntary production code, ordered scriptwriters to eliminate any suggestion of "an illicit sex affair." As well as adhering to this admonition, scriptwriters expanded the child's role and raised it to age 5, which producers later would claim was done specifically for Karolyn.

Karolyn's first segment of PARDON MY PAST, with Marguerite Chapman and Fred MacMurray, establishes a pattern for her roles in future films – a youngster who, often in bedclothes, helps to bring a family back together.

On screen during five scenes of *Pardon My Past* that total nearly seven minutes of the 88-minute black-and-white feature, Karolyn plays Stephani, who becomes an innocent but integral catalyst for an immediate attraction between Eddie and the Pemberton "poor relation" sister (Marguerite Chapman), whom Stephani calls Aunt Joan.

The first encounter of the three establishes a pattern for many of Karolyn's later film appearances – she's in a nightgown in bed, her long, blonde hair pinned by her mother into two braids along with a bun rolled up on the front of each side of her head. The dialogue in which she engagingly participates shoots straight for the emotions, as her character unwittingly attempts to heal family scars.

The dialogue in which she engagingly participates shoots straight for the emotions, as her character unwittingly attempts to heal family scars.

"Daddy! It really is Daddy, isn't it?" Stephani cries with joy upon seeing Eddie, whom – because of his likeness to Pemberton – she immediately assumes is her long-absent father. With no hint of shyness, Stephanie eagerly pushes for a reconciled homefront, asking Eddie, "Are you going to live here now?" and "Will you let Momma come to see me?"

A flustered Eddie supplies encouraging answers, and the next day, as he and the little girl play with toy blocks and a wagon in the mansion's lush backyard, Stephani's mother arrives and also mistakes Eddie for Pemberton. Again, the face of Stephani fills the screen with surprise and delight. "It's my Mommy!" Stephani says, running toward her estranged mother (Rita Johnson). And again, she zeroes in – as any child would – on the possibilities for reconnection: "Daddy, could I go and stay with Mommy?"

After Eddie agrees to Stephanie's request, the real Pemberton coincidentally returns from Mexico, and the resulting confusion and maze of which-character-knows-what provides entertaining suspense – not about the predictable matter of who eventually will end up with whom, but how the tangle of relationships will be sorted out.

 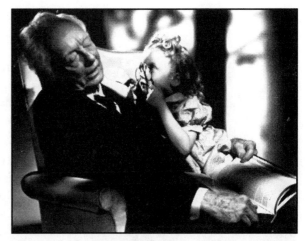

Though Karolyn has no scenes in PARDON MY PAST with Harry Davenport, who plays MacMurray's grandfather, studio publicists couldn't resist pairing the two for an inter-generation photo series.

Karolyn recalls little of the filming of *Pardon My Past*. While most of the movie supposedly takes place on New York's Long Island, it was filmed on a Hollywood set, with the backyard scene shot at a Beverly Hills home. There, an opulent outdoor privy is the only image lodged in Karolyn's memory.

"It was the most magnificent bathroom I've ever seen in my life," she says. "It was like a sultan's palace from the Arabian Nights, satin and gold everywhere, with draped curtains, cloth on the ceiling, giant pillows and mirrors. It was really unusual, incredible, gorgeous, like a fairy tale castle, and it was sitting out in the middle of somebody's backyard."

Karolyn was eighth-billed in *Pardon My Past* and was paid a total of $175 for a week's worth of scenes, shot in May 1945. For each day of filming, the not-yet-5-year-old had to memorize long exchanges of dialogue the night before, coached by her mother. "Kids are really bright at that age, well-trained and obedient and well-disciplined. They can do it," she says. Aiding Karolyn's natural youthful ability was her early Bible school training. Competing in contests during "Bible vacations" sponsored by her family's Baptist church helped the young child become a quick learner. "I had to memorize verses and books of the Bible, and I won one of those prizes once."

The studio pressbook writers also took note of Karolyn's feat of studying and recalling complicated dialogue. One promotional article mentioned that Mutual interviewed more than 500 youngsters before settling on Karolyn. "Casting was difficult," the article stated, "because the child not only had to resemble MacMurray, but also possess the ability to memorize unusually lengthy lines."

MacMurray, Karolyn recalls, was nice to her, as was director Leslie Fenton. "By nice, I mean they paid attention to you," she says. "So many of the stars would ignore you, because as a child you're nothing. You can do them no good, so why should they bother to speak with this person?"

Karolyn later deduced that the stars who shunned child actors off-screen invariably were female. "Any movie I was in, the women weren't very cordial or friendly," she says. "I think it's because the men were the ones who had their

'Kids are really bright at that age, well-trained and obedient and well-disciplined. They can do it.'

name on the marquee. They were the idols who really made the money and could command the salary. But there weren't as many women who were that appealing to the public. The male image was the one that got the top billing. Children were considered scene-stealers, and that was detrimental to the female performer. Children are darling and precious, and sometimes they capture your heart with a look, and that's a threat to someone who wants that scene for herself. You remember the child, not the star."

Karolyn at the water cooler with Fred MacMurray, who said he enjoyed appearing on screen with child actors.

That made plentiful grist for the *Pardon My Past* publicity mill once the film was released on Feb. 8, 1946. Portfolio photos of Karolyn and promotional stills from the film that featured her began appearing in newspapers in Los Angeles and around the country. "Scene Stealer" was the label the *Los Angeles Examiner* and other newspapers used to identify a photo of Karolyn, dressed in a sun hat and plaid dress and holding a like-dressed doll. Another clip, rewritten from the film's press book, employed provocative hyperbole:

> **The sketchiest costume ever worn by an actress in a boudoir scene appears in "Pardon My Past," the Fred MacMurray comedy opening tomorrow. . . .**
>
> **The revealing costume consists only of extremely brief scanties, but the Eric Johnston Office (formerly Hays Office) is not in the least concerned. Wearer of the garment is Karolyn Grimes, 5 years of age.**

With a stereotypical flair for hype, a studio press release drafted for Karolyn proclaimed: "Hollywood discovers one more little star":

> **Always with new discoveries, Hollywood continues to be the main interest of movie fans. Since the rise of Margaret O'Brien, there have been no child prodigies, as was frequent during the times of little Shirley [Temple].**
>
> **The years have passed, and now there is Karolyn Grimes, the newest and most charming baby-star of Hollywood. A tiny person, with golden hair, blue eyes and a lot of personality, as stated by a famous American columnist. To see her is to adore her.**
>
> **Karolyn was born in Hollywood itself. She is the daughter of Van and Martha Grimes, people who never dreamed of the theater or the movies, yet living at the very foot of the great studios which are the great frontier to success and fame.**
>
> **No member of that family has been born with a vocation for the theater, and tiny Karolyn is the first to invade the arts of the theater, and we must confess she has done so with great success.**
>
> **Karolyn . . . has good diction, learns her dialogue easily, repeating with charm the lines mother Martha teaches her, since, as you can imagine, Karolyn cannot read yet. She loves blue dresses. She loves movie books, to look at the pictures, naturally.**

'The revealing costume consists only of extremely brief scanties, but the Eric Johnston Office (formerly Hays Office) is not in the least concerned. Wearer of the garment is Karolyn Grimes, 5 years of age.'

Press clipping

Karolyn drew good reviews for her prominent role, the *Los Angeles Examiner* declaring that she and Rita Johnson, who played her mother, "are splendid in their parts, and do a great deal to add heart to the film." Plaudits in *The Hollywood Reporter* went a step further, singling out Karolyn as "a cute kiddie with a wee piping voice who behaves well in front of a camera."

More significantly, a detailed United Press story, a clipping of which survives from the Aug. 22, 1945, *Salt Lake City Telegram*, heralded Karolyn's first speaking role and confirmed her later conclusion that it was the male actors who did not mind appearing on-screen with children:

> **Starlet Karolyn Grimes, who made her screen debut when she was just 6 months old, has some pretty grown-up ideas for a 5-year-old.**
>
> **"I'm going to be a great actress," she announced. "I'm learning to play the piano and violin, and some day I'll learn how to kiss."**
>
> **Karolyn is taking lessons – in the first two subjects only – at the Boyd School for Actors.**
>
> **The last thing most stars want in their movies is a child actor, but Fred MacMurray and producer-director Leslie Fenton actually wrote a part for Karolyn into Mutual Productions' "Pardon My Past."**
>
> **Kid stars are a lot of trouble. They can work only a few hours a day. They have to be under the care of a school teacher all the time. Their lines and wardrobes have to get special attention. They need lots of rest.**
>
> **It all adds up to bother, and in the end the kids get the oohs and ahs while the star stands in the background looking dramatic and frustrated.**
>
> **"But a moppet always seems to help a picture," MacMurray explained. "I've worked with lots of them. Little Caroline Lee was a doll, until she got too big and had to retire. Karolyn Grimes will be 6 or 7 before long, and she'll have to retire, too. Sounds like a double-talk gag, doesn't it?"**
>
> **Karolyn, who was born in Hollywood, is the first member of her family to go in for acting. . . .**
>
> **The tiny actress leads a normal life off the screen. She plays with the neighborhood kids and tends her own small garden. Her mother makes all her clothes.**
>
> **Karolyn is an ardent movie fan already. She collects fan pictures and sees as many movies as are good for a 5-year-old.**
>
> **"I like Bob Hope and Bing Crosby – and," with an open glance at MacMurray and Fenton, "most of all, Fred MacMurray and Leslie Fenton," she said.**

The article's reference to Bing Crosby could be considered prophetic. Karolyn eventually would collaborate on a segment of a splashy film with the celebrated

'I'm going to be a great actress. I'm learning to play the piano and violin, and some day I'll learn how to kiss.'

United Press story

Karolyn and PARDON MY PAST director Leslie Fenton.

crooner. However, another movie came beforehand, an 84-minute black-and-white musical made by Universal Pictures that summer and released in the fall, called *That Night with You.*

In the film, originally titled "Once Upon a Dream," heartthrob Franchot Tone plays middle-aged Broadway producer Paul Renaud, who is alternately confused and amused by the attempts of Penny Parker (Susanna Foster), a 17-year-old waitress in an all-night diner, to masquerade as his daughter so that he will star her in his stage productions. The film makes a strong case for Penny's talent, as she is shown dreaming herself into several surreal sequences in which she displays a gifted (if dubbed) voice for singing classic opera. Competing for Penny's affections is the diner owner, Johnny (David Bruce), who presses her to shed her career plans, marry him and have six kids. The two men appeal to Penny in different ways, and she struggles with the choice, but it all comes to an agreeable Christmas Eve climax, due to the combination of Johnny's recognition of Penny's talent and his use of six ragged orphans to soften her resistance and convince her of the virtue of domestic life and motherhood.

Karolyn's nameless and unbilled role, running five minutes in two consecutive segments, is as part of the six-orphan ensemble.

Karolyn's nameless and unbilled role, running five minutes in two consecutive segments, is as part of the six-orphan ensemble escorted to Penny by a maid (played by young Irene Ryan, who played Granny in TV's *Beverly Hillbillies* two decades later). Coifed in the same braids-and-buns fashion as in *Pardon My Past,* 5-year-old Karolyn breaks out of the sextet and instantly draws attention. She walks up to a Christmas tree just decorated by Penny and lets her saucer-like eyes roam the elaborately draped boughs. Then, in a vibrant, little-girl voice, she utters the first of her two solitary sentences in the film: "Gee, just like a store window!"

Karolyn is easy to pick out in this line-up of a half-dozen child actors who play orphans at the end of THAT NIGHT WITH YOU. It was the first film in which Karolyn acted, but it was released following PARDON MY PAST.

She reaches out to touch one of the ornaments but accidentally knocks it to the floor, and it shatters. Thinking she has blown their chances for adoption, the other orphans chide her. She turns to Penny, her face filling the camera frame as she apologizes: "I didn't mean to. I won't do it again."

Penny soon warms to the children and has them stay for Christmas Eve dinner, after which the kids sit on a couch as Penny sings them a lullaby. Karolyn cuddles in Penny's lap, her face again filling the frame as her eyes slowly and endearingly blink as she falls asleep.

Her role in *That Night with You* took three days to film: Saturday, June 30, and Monday and Tuesday, July 2-3, 1945. (She was listed as "Carol Grimes" on the assistant director's daily report.) Though small, her place in the plot continued to foreshadow characteristics of some of her parts in future movies. As an earnest example of the preciousness of young life, she helps heal hard feelings of betrayal between adults in tandem with the warm spirit of Christmas. However, Karolyn remembers little of the making of *That Night with You*. Her only recollection, a vague one, is of resting peacefully in Susanna Foster's arms.

The arms of a star soon became a comfortable, familiar place for the young actress, as her next film role was as Bing Crosby's daughter in a popular color musical called *Blue Skies*.

Bing Crosby, whose character hasn't seen his daughter in four years, reunites with her in BLUE SKIES.

With a paper-thin plot, the 104-minute Paramount Pictures release strings together more than 30 Irving Berlin songs performed by Crosby and Fred Astaire (reunited from their teaming three years earlier in the similar, more memorable *Holiday Inn*). Bing plays Johnny, a flighty New York nightclub owner and singer who vies with the more stable Jed (Astaire) for the attentions of Mary (Joan Caulfield). The plentiful tunes make up for the barely plausible story line, ranging from the flashy "Puttin' on the Ritz" to the introspective, low-key "Getting Nowhere," which Crosby sings to Karolyn in her only segment of the film.

As in *Pardon My Past*, eighth-billed Karolyn plays a daughter who has not seen her father for a long time – in fact, her entire, four-year life. Johnny has been separated from Mary since their child's birth. In Karolyn's only scene, Johnny comes to see his daughter, Mary Elizabeth, when Mary is out. The housekeeper lets him into Mary Elizabeth's bedroom, where – also as in *Pardon My Past* – she sits in bed, her hair in the familiar braids and twin buns. It is there that a compelling paternal chemistry ensues.

Johnny introduces himself as "an old friend of your mother's," but Mary Elizabeth quickly senses his real identity. She gets out from under the covers, walks on the bed over to Johnny, stares quizzically at him, then figures it out. "Mommy showed me your picture," she says. "You're my old daddy, aren't you?" Soon, she throws her arms around him and asks him to tell her a bedtime story. Given that the actor is Bing Crosby and this is an Irving Berlin musical, the story turns out to be "Getting Nowhere" (originally titled "Race Horse and the Flea").

Johnny plays the tune in obvious pantomime on a nearby child-size piano, given to Mary Elizabeth by her "Uncle Jed" (Astaire). As pre-recorded, stringed accompaniment swells in the background and Karolyn hugs him from the side, Crosby sings the ballad. Its singsong melody belies an adult lyric that is clearly aimed at persuading Crosby's character to settle down. After references to a greyhound chasing its tail, a squirrel on a treadmill and an all-day carousel operator, the point is driven home by the final stanza:

*The arms of a star soon became a familiar place, as her next film role was as Bing Crosby's daughter in **Blue Skies**.*

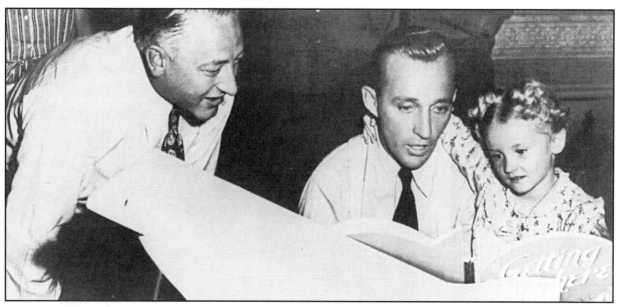

Director Stuart Heisler coaches Bing Crosby and Karolyn as they rehearse their segment at the piano in BLUE SKIES.

Karolyn gets acquainted with composer Irving Berlin on the BLUE SKIES set.

**So concentrate and clear your mind
of schemes that never last.**

**Or you'll wake up some day and find
your chances all have passed.**

**You've been running around in circles,
running around in circles,
getting nowhere,
getting nowhere very fast.**

As Crosby sings the final words, Karolyn kisses his cheek, he kisses hers, and the poignant tone continues through the end of the segment. The dialogue reveals that Uncle Jed (whom Mary Elizabeth adores, in part because he can "kick his heels up in the air") is engaged to Mary Elizabeth's mother. When Mary Elizabeth shows Johnny the invitation and asks if he, too, received one, Johnny avoids a reply, kisses her goodnight and bids her goodbye.

The five-minute segment, a genuine charmer, was filmed two months after her work in *That Night with You*, on Sept. 6-8, 1945, and again Karolyn (this time listed as "Caroline Grimes" in the daily report) was paid $35 a day. Her part serves a purpose similar to that of her scenes in *That Night with You* and *Pardon My Past*, providing an emotional impetus for the adults in the movie to do what they know in their hearts that they should do. In this case, Mary Elizabeth is a key reminder to Johnny of his true love for Mary.

The child's bedroom setting in *Blue Skies* also works as a clever plot device, as in *Pardon My Past*. Attention is focused on her for a few important minutes, generating exchanges that add cuteness and an emotional bond. ("I knew you when you were that big," Crosby tells Karolyn, holding his hands just a few inches apart, to which Karolyn replies, "I must have been very young.") But after the child is sent to bed, the action quickly returns to the adult issues at hand, leaving the grown-up characters to maintain the audience's concern and carry the movie's weight.

With this film's prominence, however, Karolyn was beginning to gain stature of her own, however, at least in her parents' hometown. When the Grimes took a vacation trip to Osceola in October 1945, Karolyn's triple-play of film work from the summer (*Pardon My Past, That Night with You* and *Blue Skies*) netted her top placement on the front page of a community weekly, the *St. Clair County Republican.* "Daughter of Osceola Parents a Featured Player in Hollywood," the bold headline announced, with an equally awe-struck subhead: "Mr. and Mrs. LaVan Grimes' daughter, Karolyn K., is featured in several new pictures with the high up stars." The story quoted several newspaper clippings that Martha no doubt supplied, and went on to say:

> **We were mighty happy to see LaVan Grimes and his wife and daughter this last week. . . . The daughter is now making striking headway in Hollywood pictures. . . .**
>
> **Karolyn's mother had a lot of mighty cute pictures of Karolyn that will be used all over the world to advertise [her] pictures. Osceola will lay part claim to this new Starlet of Hollywood even tho she was born in Hollywood.**
>
> **We wish every success to our Starlet Karolyn, and congratulations to her parents, Martha and LaVan.**

(The same newspaper ran a front-page notice the following summer, on June 20, 1946, when *Pardon My Past* finally made its way to Osceola's Civic Theatre. "I am sure many of us will want to see this picture," the non-bylined item stated. *Blue Skies* arrived in Osceola with similar attention in June 1947.)

Karolyn's early film appearances netted her the lead story in the Oct. 18, 1945, ST. CLAIR COUNTY REPUBLICAN, in Osceola, Missouri.

Soon after her family's return from Missouri, Karolyn fell into the arms of yet another major Hollywood star, this time Rosalind Russell, in a black-and-white RKO Radio Pictures production called *Sister Kenny* that was filmed for three months starting Nov. 8, 1945, and released on Sept. 28, 1946. In this 116-minute biography, which also starred Alexander Knox, Dean Jagger, Philip Merivale and Beulah Bondi, Russell plays the title role of Elizabeth Kenny, a dedicated Australian nurse who is belittled by the medical establishment throughout the early 1900s for her unconventional physical-therapy approach to treating – and, in some cases, curing – childhood polio.

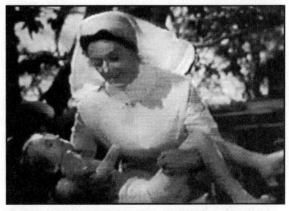

Karolyn's brief part in SISTER KENNY found her in the arms of Rosalind Russell playing the title role.

Unbilled, Karolyn plays one of the children Kenny treats at her clinic. Dressed only in white undershorts, an alert, compliant Karolyn is cradled by Russell, who carries her outdoors to lie face up on a gurney in a sunny courtyard. There, Russell speaks reassuringly to

***Five-year-old Karolyn
poses on the set of
BLUE SKIES.***

*'It took a
scriptwriter to
bring about the
miracle, but Bing
Crosby finally will
have a daughter.*

*'Four-year-old
Karolyn Grimes
will play Der
Bingle's youngster
in Blue Skies.'*

Press clipping

Karolyn as she extends Karolyn's left arm, tells her to roll onto her stomach, then manipulates her shoulders before hearing a doorbell and turning Karolyn over to another nurse. Russell three times addresses Karolyn by her real first name, but Karolyn's part is wordless and lasts just one minute. The role was decidedly smaller and less significant than Karolyn's showy and sentimental role in *Blue Skies*, and Karolyn cannot recall filming the segment.

However, coy notices from the Hollywood press just before the release of *Blue Skies* did etch some memories for Karolyn. Writers sensationalized the human interest of her daughterly segment with Crosby. The singer had four sons at the time, and *Blue Skies* was the first movie in which he was shown as the father of a girl. "Bing finally gets daughter – in film," announced one pre-release headline, followed by the lead of a story:

It took a scriptwriter to bring about the miracle, but Bing Crosby finally will have a daughter. Four-year-old Karolyn Grimes will play Der Bingle's youngster in "Blue Skies."

A caption for a promotional still read: "Singing lullabies to a daughter – even in the movies – is quite an innovation for Bing." Another item, from the *Los Angeles Herald Express*, went so far as to inaccurately predict that Karolyn was to sing a duet with Crosby in the film. Yet another squib, from the *Los Angeles Examiner*, exaggerated:

Did you know that Para was so desperate trying to get a 4-year-old girl who looks like Bing to play his daughter in "Blue Skies" that they almost put a wig on one of the Crosby kids? But a juvenile cutie, Karolyn K. Grimes, popped up out of nowhere – and honestly, she looks like Bing!

When *Blue Skies* was finally released on July 25, 1946, nearly a year after it was made, reviews praised the film highly, especially Crosby's singing and Astaire's footwork. The lone critical mention of Karolyn, however, appearing in *Variety*, was offhand and unappreciative:

It's in a rather corny scene with the baby that one of the three new Berlin numbers . . . is done by Crosby to Karolyn Grimes, a rather self-conscious five-year-old.

Despite the dismissive critique, the rapport between Crosby and Karolyn is obvious. As he sings to her, their smiles gleaming, she chatters at him intermittently like a chipmunk. Amused, he pretends to bite back at her. Though his singing is lip-synched, the comfort between the two suggests a warm, unrehearsed feeling. Karolyn considers it her best movie performance.

"The whole segment looked so natural, and I think the director [Stuart Heisler] made that happen," she says. "It even looks like I spontaneously reach up and touch Bing Crosby, as if it were the real thing. It could be that the sound was off and the director was saying, 'Put your hand up on him' or 'Make a noise like a chipmunk,' but if they were doing that, it seems that I would have looked over at them, and I didn't. I don't know how they got me to do that, but I'm impressed."

Karolyn recalls Crosby as a kind man who liked children and "horsed around" with her and funnyman Jerry Colonna on the set – and their friendship continued after *Blue Skies* was finished. She recalls her own delight, as well as that of her mother, when a package from Paramount Pictures arrived in the mail. Inside was a gift from Crosby, the nightgown that she had worn in the movie. The camaraderie resurfaced a few months later, when she was at an interview on the Paramount lot and spotted him across a street.

"He said, 'Hi, Mary Elizabeth,' using my name from the movie. I went running over, and he started talking to me, and I told him that I'd just gotten a dog the night before, and I named him Bing because he howled all night. He had a big laugh about that."

As studios released her first four films, Karolyn started receiving mementos from Hollywood luminaries. Thanks to her mother's packrat penchant, Karolyn still has period autographs from celebrities ranging from Dorothy Lamour to Jane Withers, a child star older than Karolyn who had acted with Shirley Temple and earned later fame in TV commercials. "You're a very fine little actress," Jane wrote, "and I hope that you'll always have success and happiness."

In addition, because of her *Blue Skies* appearance in particular, Karolyn began hearing from fans – adults and children alike – who wrote to her from as far away as England. The postcards and brief letters sent to her in care of the movie studios (one was addressed only to "Miss Karolyn Grimes, Hollywood, California" and delivered intact) usually asked for a photo and autograph. Her mother, Karolyn recalls, had photo postcards made and insisted that she sit at the kitchen table and reply to every request.

During the BLUE SKIES filming, Karolyn whispers something to Bing Crosby, whom she remembers as a kind man who "horsed around" on the set.

Businesses also began seeking Karolyn's services. To promote Sidney Levitt's Junior Bootery, Karolyn posed for a photograph published April 4, 1946, in the *Hollywood Citizen-News*. A solicitation for the use of her name even came from *Parents* magazine's *Polly Pigtails, The Magazine for Girls*, on Oct. 7, 1946:

> **We enjoyed your work in "Blue Skies" so much that we are particularly anxious to have you join our Polly Pigtails Club. Our club is quite new – just a little more than a month old – but it already has 20,000 members throughout the country, including charter member Margaret O'Brien.**

> **Although we know busy movie stars like yourself won't have much time for club activities, these girls are eager to have you one of them. They are great movie fans, you know, and it will**

mean a lot to them and to the 250,000 other readers we expect to join to know you share their club interest. In joining the club, of course, you won't have to take part in any activities unless you want to. All you do is say you want to be one of us.

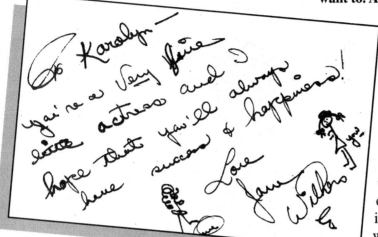

One of Karolyn's mementoes is this postcard from actress Jane Withers, known today as much for her adult-age "Josie the Plumber" TV commercials as for her child film roles.

And of course, her gregarious agent Lola Moore patted her on the back and sent her little gifts when Karolyn finished, as Moore put it, "in the money."

The attention didn't faze Karolyn, however. For her, periodic forays into films were nothing extraordinary. "It was just run-of-the-mill. It was the only thing I knew, so I didn't know that it was special. I had no clue. It was just what I did.

"I really had no burning desire to be an actress. It wasn't something that I hungered to do. It was just everyday stuff. A lot of the girls I knew did it. To be a bit player in the movies was nothing new, nothing great."

Nancy Gates confirms that the budding actress carried a nonchalance about her work, but she says Karolyn also found it fun. "She loved it," says Nancy, "but she loved school, too. Everything she did, she just loved. She was never one to run around and tell everybody what she did in the movies. To her, it was like a game. She'd play the game, and then she'd go back to her home or school. No one ever made a big thing of it."

Karolyn does not attribute what success she had in her first movie roles to talent, but rather to proper behavior enforced by her mother. "In those days, if you didn't do what they told you to do, you were out," she says. "You had to be extremely well-disciplined because you would cost them money otherwise. The equipment wasn't as sophisticated as it is today, so any noise that was made while they were filming a scene would be picked up, and you would be in deep trouble if it was you who caused the noise. You had to be very quiet and still. You couldn't be rambunctious at all."

Karolyn further downplays the effectiveness of her work in *Pardon My Past, That Night with You, Blue Skies* and *Sister Kenny* in speculating on why she was selected for her next film, a Christmastime story made in the late spring and summer of 1946. "I had no redeeming quality," she says. "I didn't have doe eyes or anything special. I just looked like everybody's daughter, just the all-American kid, so I think that's why I got the part."

It turned out to be quite the part.

A fan letter from England.

S ix minutes. That's how long it lasts.

But because of a 1970s revival that shows no signs of abating, it's the role that has defined Karolyn Grimes in the public eye and made her a part of popular American history.

The role, of course, is that of 6-year-old Zuzu, and the movie is the classic *It's a Wonderful Life*. Unquestionably a holiday masterpiece, the film is as deeply rooted in the nation's Christmas consciousness as Dickens' *A Christmas Carol*. But in 1946, the role of Zuzu was no more special to Karolyn than any other she had played. She was merely to be one of four children of George and Mary Bailey, portrayed by James Stewart and Donna Reed. However, the enduring emotional impact of this 20th century parable has elevated its every element – including the essential connection to real-life family heartstrings supplied by Zuzu.

The saga of how the movie came about has been told many times over (most comprehensively, so far, in *The 'It's a Wonderful Life' Book*, a compendium of facts, interviews and anecdotes from 1986 that offers an excellent examination of the film's evolution). The story's humble beginning, as a 24-page Christmas card called "The Greatest Gift" and mailed to 200 people in the early 1940s by its author, Philip Van Doren Stern, represents Americana at its best.

Purchased by Frank Capra, the quintessential "little guy" Hollywood director, for $10,000, the story became a litmus test of relevance and popularity for both Capra and Stewart shortly after the end of World War II. Neither had made a feature film since before the war. Capra had started an independent film production company, and Stewart, his studio contract expired, was a free agent. The question in their minds was clear: Could they pull off the same magic they had accomplished together with the films *You Can't Take It with You* and *Mr. Smith Goes to Washington* more than seven years prior? Their educated, enthusiastic guess was an optimistic "yes."

In the minds of thousands of moviegoers (and a fair number of critics) who viewed *It's a Wonderful Life* soon after RKO Pictures released it on December 19, 1946, Capra and Stewart did just that. Certainly the movie – trumpeted as the pair's first Hollywood film since before the war broke out – benefited from a gale of hype, led by a six-page layout in *Life*, a color photo on the cover of the syndicated newspaper section *This Week* and a Christmas appearance on the cover of *Newsweek*, followed by such prominent fanzine treatments as a color photo on the February 1947 cover of Dell's *Screen Romances*.

The film did not reach hit status in its initial release, however. Its message, that virtue is its own reward and that life indeed is wonderful, was upbeat. Its ending was suitably joyous and inspiring. But its bleak premise – a contemplated suicide and the exploration of what life would be like if a decent, generous Everyman had not been born – apparently did not appeal to the collective postwar sentiment of optimism and weariness. As Stewart put it later, audiences wanted "a little breather" from seriousness and were more receptive to slapstick.

Chapter

4

'He says it's the chance of a lifetime.'

(Karolyn's role in 'It's a Wonderful Life,' 1946)

Reflecting high hopes for Frank Capra and James Stewart, IT'S A WONDERFUL LIFE made the covers of NEWSWEEK (December 30, 1946) and SCREEN ROMANCES (February 1947).

As a result, box-office numbers for *It's a Wonderful Life* didn't live up to the expectations of Capra and others at newly formed Liberty Films. Proceeds barely covered the film's costs. And while it was nominated for several 1946 Academy Awards, including best picture, director and actor, the film was shut out of the winner's circle at the 1947 ceremony. Two years later, the RKO Special Effects Department did carry away an *It's a Wonderful Life*-related Oscar, but in recognition of a technical achievement only: "development of a new method of simulating falling snow on motion picture sets."

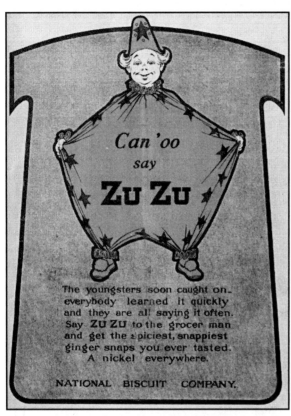

This ad for Zu Zu ginger-snap cookies appeared in magazines in 1904.

Copyright © 1904
Courtesy of Nabisco Brands. Co. All Rights Reserved.

The amount of time Karolyn appears in *It's a Wonderful Life* – just two segments, plus the brief, opening voiceover line: "Please bring Daddy back" – totals just under six minutes of the film's two-hour, nine-minute running length. Her role as Zuzu may seem measurably small (Karolyn is billed 33rd, along with Larry Simms, Carol Coombs and Jimmy Hawkins, the other three kids, at the bottom of the credits), and Karolyn herself describes it as a "bit part." Still, critics gave the Bailey kids favorable notice, *The Hollywood Reporter* calling them "excellent" and *Variety* saying they did a "top job."

Far more noteworthy than the fleeting reviews, however, is the unqualified uniqueness of the Zuzu role. It is crucial, both as an on-screen character and as a symbolic presence in the plot.

The distinctiveness begins with the character's name, which stands apart from the more conventional monikers of Pete, Janie and Tommy used for the other children. "Zuzu" was the name for a National Biscuit Company brand of ginger snaps at the turn of the century. Magazine ads indicate that a girlish clown face served as the cookie's visual identity. The fanciful wording of the ads suggests the spirited temperament of the movie character:

> **Can 'oo say Zu Zu?**
>
> **The youngsters soon caught on. Everybody learned it quickly, and they are all saying it often.**
>
> **Say Zu Zu to the grocer man, and get the spiciest, snappiest ginger snaps you ever tasted. A nickel everywhere.**
>
> **– Collier's magazine March 26, 1904**
> **– *McCall's* magazine, April 1904**

• • •

> **Rain! Rain!! Rain!!! All in vain!**
>
> **If you lack snap and want ginger, use the old established countersign, Zu Zu, to the grocerman.**
>
> **No one ever heard of a Zu Zu that wasn't good. No! Never!!**
>
> **– *Life* magazine, May 1911**

To use "Zuzu" for the little girl's character in *It's a Wonderful Life* was the brainchild of famed playwright Clifford Odets, the third of three writers hired to pen early scripts for the movie before Paramount sold it to Capra. Odets' first draft calls for the movie to open with Zuzu wandering into a "music conservatory" in heaven. She interrupts the harp practice of her dead grandfather (Peter Bailey, George's father) who is an angel and returns her to earth as part of a quest to earn his wings.

As finally scripted and shot, however, Zuzu's role is planted firmly, albeit sentimentally, in reality. Her key, one-minute segment with her father George comes midway through the film, in which he pretends to paste petals back onto a rose she has brought home from school. The scene hints that Zuzu is her dad's favorite child – or that she is at least the most endearing example of how George deeply values his family.

In this segment, Zuzu is in a nightgown in bed after having caught a cold while coming home from school. Letting her believe that he actually is pasting the fallen petals back onto the rose, her father instead slips them into the watch pocket of his pants. The absence of the petals later in the film helps prove to George that his guardian angel (Clarence Oddbody, AS2 – angel second class) has granted his wish to never have been born. Near the end of the movie, after George makes a tearful plea to return to real life, the petals reappear as evidence of Clarence's further intervention and represent the preciousness of George's loving family.

It is only natural, then, that in the movie's five-minute final segment, when an overjoyed George returns to his home and scrambles upstairs to hug his children, Zuzu gets a separate welcome:

> *"Daddy!" Zuzu calls as she runs out of her bedroom.*
>
> *"Zuzu! Zuzu, my little ginger snap!" George shouts as he reaches out to her [the script says he "crushes" her to him]. "How do you feel?"*
>
> *"Fine," Zuzu answers with glee.*

Zuzu's special role doesn't stop there. She's the one hanging on her dad's shoulders and back as he and his family make their way down the staircase, and she's the one cradled in his arms as he stands next to the family Christmas tree to take in his friends' fiscal and emotional bounty.

As the town-sized assemblage of family and friends flows into the Bailey front room, singing impromptu versions of "Hark, the Herald Angels Sing" and then "Auld Lang Syne," George glances at the pile of money on the table before him. On top is a copy of Mark Twain's *Tom Sawyer*, which George picks up and Zuzu opens to Clarence's inscription: "Remember, no man is a failure who has friends. Thanks for the wings." Then, perhaps because someone has jostled the Christmas tree, a tiny silver bell rings. Zuzu closes the book and points to the bell.

There is no mistaking the impact of Zuzu's final words – easily the most memorable line of the movie:

> *"Look, daddy. Teacher says, 'Every time a bell rings, an angel gets his wings.'"*

While the line is essentially a restatement of words uttered earlier by Clarence,

Zuzu's key, one-minute segment with her father George comes midway through the film, in which he pretends to paste petals back onto a rose she has brought home from school.

The scene hints that Zuzu is her dad's favorite child – or that she is at least the most endearing example of how George deeply values his family.

its culminating position in the movie and the eager, matter-of-fact manner in which Zuzu delivers it, make the line her own. Flush with joy, her father gratefully acknowledges Zuzu's youthful wisdom:

"That's right, that's right," George responds with a grin, then looks to the ceiling and winks. "Attaboy, Clarence!"

This image of Mary, George and Zuzu Bailey closes IT'S A WONDERFUL LIFE.

As the voices of everyone assembled rise for the finish of "Auld Lang Syne," the ones most distinguishable are those of George and Zuzu. And it is the life-affirming smiles of Zuzu and her parents that close this intensely soul-shaking film.

All of these elements combine to create an emotional alchemy that lifts the Zuzu role to a level beyond rational description. For instance, how else to account for a seemingly simple error – that countless fans insist upon identifying Zuzu as the youngest of the Bailey children, when in fact she is second youngest? (Tommy, he of the "S'cuse me, s'cuse me, . . . I burped!" line, is Zuzu's younger brother.)

A variety of reasons can be articulated: that she's a girl and that gender stereotypes often call for females to be younger than males; that she has a youngish, high voice; that diminutives such as "little Zuzu," "little ginger snap" and "not a smitch of temperature" are applied to her; and that she is mostly shown in bed or being carried and not standing on her own. But part of the explanation transcends mere words, such as the non-verbal communication between Zuzu and her father as he pretends to "paste" fallen petals back onto her flower. A close look at the scene shows that she momentarily sees him pocket the petals, yet the magic of the moment allows viewers to believe otherwise. Zuzu obviously carries special status.

The innocence of Zuzu, and the simplicity and beauty of her rose petals, are the most compelling earthly representations of the life force that saves her father.

No one would deny that George Bailey's joys, obstacles and ultimate dilemma and resolution constitute the heart of the movie. But it's not too great a leap to also assert that the innocence of Zuzu, and the simplicity and beauty of her rose petals, are the most compelling earthly representations of the life force that saves her father.

• • •

What would *It's a Wonderful Life* have been like as a film had the character of Zuzu received more screen time? Was Zuzu conceived to be different from how she turned out in the finished product? Did her role remain magical in spite of its brevity, or did it become magical because of its truncation?

While there are no conclusive answers to those questions, early scripts for *It's a Wonderful Life* provide a bounty of clues and insights. For instance, opening the film with Zuzu wandering through heaven, as writer Clifford Odets posed, could have turned the initial focus away from the movie's central character, George Bailey. And by linking Zuzu directly to George's father (angel 1163 in search of his wings, instead of the Clarence of Capra's later scripts), Odets may have unduly broadened – and diffused – the scope of the story's central struggle to three generations of Baileys instead of keeping it aimed at a single individual with whom every viewer can identify.

This is but one of the fascinating areas opened up by the film's early scripts. Other portions of the scripts reveal that the evolution of the Zuzu character was not a simple matter. These drafts, however, point to the painstaking work necessary to shaping rough concepts into a sum greater – and wiser – than its formative parts.

• Zuzu's illness

Odets' first script, dated Feb. 12, 1945, opens with George's father Peter Bailey returning Zuzu from heaven to her bed, and a hopeful outlook for her recovery prevails. But in this script, Zuzu lies in bed through most of the rest of the film, her illness repeatedly mentioned in troubled tones. For example, at one point the Baileys' other child, 8-year-old Pete (there are only two children in early versions of the script), enters the bathroom and starts to noisily daub his face with shaving cream in imitation of his father. George shushes and urges him to tiptoe. "Zuzu has to get all the sleep she can," he tells his son. "We almost had a catastrophe here last night."

In Odets' second version, dated Feb. 23, 1945, when George kisses Mary on the front porch late at night as he leaves for his office, he tells her he's worried about Zuzu. "Doctors can be wrong," he mutters.

Later in this draft, George grows increasingly upset about Zuzu's sickness and the attendant doctor and nurse bills – the result of Zuzu having won a flower at school and not buttoning her coat on the way home in attempt not to crush the prize. In the living room late at night, George startles Mary and Pete with a rhetorical outburst: "What the deuce was Zuzu best in class about? Will you tell me that?"

This everpresent, in-the-viewer's-face worry about Zuzu could have complicated the purity of George's desperate thoughts of ending his life. This may explain why Zuzu's illness, and George's response to it, were muted in the final version. In this regard, director Frank Capra may have heeded the following written

Posing for a summertime scenario that never appears in the final film are the Baileys (clockwise from lower left): Zuzu (Karolyn Grimes), Pete (Larry Simms), George (James Stewart) Mary (Donna Reed), Janie (Carol Coombs) and Tommy (Jimmy Hawkins). Early scripts for the film gave the Baileys just two children, Zuzu and Pete.

advice from script consultant Michael Wilson, dated Jan. 10, 1946: "The scenes built around the sick child, Zuzu, are tender and moving; but in a way, they . . . detract from the motive of suicide. George has been revealed as a man who forgets himself and his own troubles when there are troubles around him. Yet he is now contemplating suicide when his daughter is ill. This is a minor inconsistency, but . . . it detracts from the total effect."

• Orange juice

There's an intriguing emphasis on orange juice throughout Odets' scripts that vanishes from the final film. At one point, Mary tries to serve a glass to Pete, who turns his up nose at it. "Lots of boys and girls would be glad of the chance to get fresh orange juice," she tells him.

Later, in a scene in which neither a nurse nor Mary can persuade Zuzu to hand over the flower she has won from school, George comes in, pockets a fallen petal from Zuzu's rose as in the final film, then tells her, "And now . . . the magic orange juice that makes the birdies sing and the rainbows fill the sky! Red, yellow, green and blue!" As she sips from the orange juice glass, Zuzu looks wisely over the rim at her father and says, "Green?" George: "And blue." Zuzu: "Red?" George: "And yellow, too."

A script consultant suggested that segments of IT'S A WONDERFUL LIFE that dealt with the illness of Zuzu (above, cradled by her father George) could detract from her father's suicide motive.

In Odets' second script, the film ends in Zuzu's room, where George reminds her to drink her orange juice. Again with a child's studied seriousness, Zuzu tells him she's decided that orange juice isn't for her. "If I swallow an orange seed, a tree would grow in me," she says. "But I could eat ice cream, ice cream on a stick. There's no seeds in ice cream."

It's possible that the citrus references would have deepened the finished film's legendary status. The prominence of orange juice as a health drink may have skyrocketed, and its connection with the movie probably would have been exploited commercially, with the revival of interest in *It's a Wonderful Life* decades later. Such a turn of events might have trivialized the film, though.

Perhaps, as with Zuzu's petals, the juice could have come to symbolize another life force. However, that would have been unfortunate, as the petals draw much of their power from their clearly focused role. The film didn't need the clutter of another symbol. As with the muting of Zuzu's illness, Capra's genius was at work in the removal of a competing, diverting story element.

• Zuzu's pet name

Many *It's a Wonderful Life* fans fondly recall that George affectionately refers to Zuzu in the final film as "my little ginger snap." However, the reference, which surely stems from the National Biscuit Company brand of ginger snaps sold at the turn of the century, does not appear in any of the film's early scripts. It is not until after Capra bought rights to the story, in a Jan. 14, 1946, script called the Swerling version, that the ginger snap line appears.

Instead of that reference, Odets' second draft offers one that was more aligned with his orange juice theme. It comes in the middle of the story when George talks with Zuzu in her bedroom. "How is the prettiest peach in the orchard?" he asks cheerily. Zuzu's response is certainly little-girl-like, but perhaps more prickly than a viewer might expect or desire: "I'm not a peach. I'm a girl!"

Of course, peaches, oranges and flower petals are all valuable forms of life that originate in Mother Nature, which may have been the underlying reason that Odets included them in his scripts. Removal of the two fruit-oriented references, however, cleared the way for audiences to pinpoint their attention on Zuzu's petals.

• The prize flower

In Odets' first script, George and Mary argue over Zuzu's rose much more overtly than in the final film. While the wind blows through the drafty Bailey kitchen, George spouts off, telling his wife to take the flower out of Zuzu's room because it gives him "the willies." When Mary objects, underscoring its importance as a prize, George slams it as a "pretty expensive prize." Mary, undeterred, responds: "Well, that flower's the pride of her little life, and you leave it right where it is."

Later in the same script, as George and Mary leave Zuzu's room and walk downstairs, "that danged flower" retriggers George's scorn. George: "It's dying, anyway," he tells Mary. "It smells like a fungus." As they reach the kitchen, the argument expands to the education of their younger daughter, who apparently has not attended school for very long. Mary urges that they keep Zuzu home during the next term, while George, professing that he wants Mary to have more time for herself, maintains that Zuzu is not too young for school. Annoyed, Mary insists that her daughter can learn more at home than at school, and George snaps, "Okay, you win!"

In director Frank Capra's first script, dated Jan. 3, 1946, Zuzu's rose is referred to several times as "the hated flower." At one point, describing George's actions in Zuzu's bedroom while she's asleep, the script has George look over at the flower, lift and cock its glass as if to destroy it, then change his mind after seeing more petals fall.

In director Frank Capra's first script, Zuzu's rose is referred to several times as 'the hated flower.'

At one point, describing George's actions in Zuzu's bedroom while she's asleep, the script has George look over at the flower, lift and cock its glass as if to destroy it, then change his mind after seeing more petals fall.

George and Mary's blunt-spoken sparring and George's angry references to the flower would have added credence to the overall desperation that was overtaking him. They also would have enhanced the dark tone of the film's final third. But they also could have changed markedly the life-affirming feelings generated by Zuzu's petals. Though George's bitterness is understated in the finished film, his inner rage is potent. Trimming the vitriol directed at Zuzu's flower in the early scripts did prove the adage that less is more.

• Zuzu's personality

Late in Odets' second script, George, Mary and a character named Aunt Laura sip coffee and discuss Zuzu in a sitting room at Uncle Billy's house. (Aunt Laura is a pivotal character in Odets' second script, for it is her feeble-mindedness in secreting the missing $8,000 in one of her stamp-collecting books that sends George to the brink of suicide, not an accidental misplacement of the money by Uncle Billy as in the final version. By the end of the film, in this and later drafts, Pete discovers the $8,000 gift-wrapped in a stamp book that is opened by the Baileys on Christmas Day.)

A bit of an eccentric herself, Aunt Laura declares that if she had a child, "I'd want her just like little Zuzu – cussed and on the temperamental side." In a dismal tone of voice, George disagrees, but as in earlier scenes, Mary contradicts her husband. With that confirmation, Aunt Laura repeats her assertion: "Yes, she is, just like me. Old-fashioned and cussed!"

From the final version of the film, it is difficult to see how any of the Bailey children could have been conceived as cussed. Their sweetness, a reflection of the souls of their parents, is a key element in shaping the audience's loyalty to the Baileys and engendering its identification with George's joy as he rises out of despair to welcome the outpouring of love from his family and friends. "Cussed" is a quality unwelcome at 320 Sycamore – and, not surprisingly, it does not appear in the movie's final depiction of Zuzu or any of the other Bailey kids.

'I loved the Christmas tree in that final segment. It was so big and beautiful and fully decorated, with beaded ornaments and lots of tinsel. I thought it looked like it should be from a fairyland.'

• The classic line

Zuzu's overarching line from the end of the film – "Look, Daddy. Teacher says, 'Every time a bell rings, an angel gets his wings' " – appears in many of the early scripts. It's a an element that survived many rewrites, though its evolution was far from smooth.

In Odets' second script, for example, Zuzu hears the bell from a small alarm clock and speaks the line in a slightly more awkward fashion: "Every time you hear a bell, the teacher says, it means an angel is getting his wings." In Odets' third version, dated Feb. 27, 1945, it is Mary who utters the line: "My grandmother believed in fairies and elves and leprechauns and – and everything. She used to say that every time you heard a bell ringing, an angel was getting his wings." George tenderly replies: "Gosh, I hope so!"

In Capra's first version nearly a year later, the line returns to Zuzu, still not in its final form: "Every time you hear a bell, the teacher says, it means an angel's got his wings." It is in this draft that the movie's angel becomes Clarence, instead of George's father. So after Zuzu says her line, the whole family looks at a little bell "madly swinging back and forth" on their tree. Pete says: "Look at it, daddy, all by itself!" George smiles and says softly: "Good luck, Clarence."

Script consultant Michael Wilson's written suggestions of Jan. 10, 1946, one week after Capra's first script was completed, pose a different speaker for the classic line. Zuzu points to a ringing bell on the Christmas tree and says: "Look, daddy – the little bell's ringing all by itself." George looks at the bell, then speaks to Zuzu: "You know what? I heard that every time a bell rings, an angel wins his wings."

Surely, much strength was gained – and an angel's vision is reflected – in the final decision to hand the line back to Zuzu.

• • •

By the time shooting began on *It's a Wonderful Life* on May 27, 1946, Capra had finalized the script and assembled his actors. No records apparently exist as to how Karolyn was chosen for her part of Zuzu. However, the movie's two-month shooting schedule does indicate that Karolyn worked on Monday, June 17, and Friday and Saturday, June 21-22, as part of the film's finale, and – nearly a month later, after her sixth birthday – on Tuesday, July 16, for her bedroom segment with James Stewart.

George Bailey (James Stewart) holds Zuzu (Karolyn Grimes) as he is overwhelmed by the generosity of the townspeople of Bedford Falls, in the climactic scene of IT'S A WONDERFUL LIFE.

It's safe to assume that, at the time, neither she nor anyone else working on the film had even the remotest premonition of the phenomenon that *It's a Wonderful Life* would become decades later.

Nor, much as she might like them to be otherwise, are Karolyn's memories of *It's a Wonderful Life* much more fleshed out than those she has of her earlier pictures, *Pardon My Past*, *That Night with You*, *Blue Skies* and *Sister Kenny*. After all, she was just turning 6 when her scenes in the movie were made. Some impressions do remain lodged in her consciousness, however.

"I loved the Christmas tree in that final segment. It was so big and beautiful and fully decorated, with beaded ornaments and lots of tinsel. I thought it looked like it should be from a fairyland," she says, fairly certain that this impression is of the *It's a Wonderful Life* tree and not a similar Christmas tree used in her segment of *That Night with You*, filmed a year before. "At home, we never had that size of tree, because I was an only child and we lived in this tiny place, and our tree would be a small one on a high table."

The fact that Zuzu's bedroom was not really at the top of the stairs that are shown in the movie, but rather on another side of the ground-floor set, is another memory. She also recalls repeatedly riding on the shoulders of Jimmy Stewart as he ran up and down the stairway during take after take in the film's final segment. "He had Tommy under one arm and me hanging on his back, and he couldn't hold onto me, so I was really holding on – probably choking him, if you want to know the truth – and my knees are bearing into him, and my legs are hanging out. I look like a little frog hanging up there. But he was so patient, so nice. He never lost his temper, no matter how many times we had to do that over."

Then there was the "snow." Though filmed from late spring to mid-summer, the movie had several major winter segments, including its entire, climatic final third.

'I was really holding on, probably choking him . . . but he was so patient, so nice. He never lost his temper.'

This culminating scene near the end of IT'S A WONDERFUL LIFE, in which George Bailey (James Stewart) ecstatically reunites with his family, was filmed on a staircase that led to nowhere, inside a huge, hangar-like set. Karolyn observes that she hung from Stewart's shoulders "like a frog."

Capra had just devised a new mixture of fire extinguisher chemicals, soap and water to replace the gypsum and corn flakes typically used in hundreds of other feature films. The result was much quieter, more realistic-looking snow, a nuance not lost on Karolyn. "Being raised in southern California, I had never seen snow before, and this was similar to snow," she says. "I found it fascinating."

Even though her scenes in the Bailey house were filmed entirely inside a huge, hangar-like set, it somehow seemed like a real house to Karolyn.

Even though her scenes in the Bailey house were filmed entirely inside a huge, hangar-like set, it somehow seemed like a real house to Karolyn. "Looking from the outside through the windows, if there was no one around, it was always quiet in that particular room," she says. "I can remember walking on the outside of the windows and thinking of how quiet it was. It wasn't a real house, but you felt like it was. Somehow you really did."

Interestingly, Karolyn's key line from the movie – "Every time a bell rings, an angel gets his wings" – presages plentiful references to bells and angels in several of her later films. But viewing *It's a Wonderful Life* today, as she often does at appearances she makes each fall and winter, when she hears the line Karolyn winces a bit. Though millions would never imagine her saying it in any other manner, she insists she could have – and should have – stated those classic words more expressively.

"Frankly, I don't think I was that good an actress," she says. "I think I was shallow and like a little parrot. They told me to do something, and I did it. I don't think I put an interpretation of my own into it. So it amazes me that they let that line stand the way it was said. It's what you call a sing-song. It's not a good way of saying a line at all, and I'm surprised they left it in. It may have been very little-girl-like, but I think they could have changed it."

Karolyn also feels that someone should have made sure during filming of the final scene that she knew the words to the chorus of "Auld Lang Syne," because it is obvious from the finished product that she doesn't quite get them right on-screen.

"I'm always embarrassed every time I see that scene," she says. "I fluff the line to the song, and Jimmy Stewart hears me and looks at me and laughs. Maybe we both made a mistake and he's looking at me like, 'Neither one of us knows this.' I just know that I didn't know the lines. I'm surprised they didn't try to tell me about it. Apparently Capra decided to keep that in there."

Looking back, Karolyn cannot point to anything that would have clued her in that this film would turn into the one for which she would be best known. "There was no reason for me to think that *It's a Wonderful Life* was anything special," she says, noting that she cannot even remember whether she saw it in a theater at the time.

In fact, hard as it may be for *It's a Wonderful Life* fans to initially fathom, Karolyn's thoughts at the time about the film – and moviemaking in general – centered on its routine aspects, not on the glamour. And for her it was assuredly a routine. "It was like going to school," she says. "You just do it. You don't ask questions. I just did what they wanted me to do. That was my life. I didn't know any different."

The Sunday magazine THIS WEEK, distributed in the Los Angeles Times, ran a color photo of the same composition as the still photo on the opposite page – this one more posed and without the stairway prop.

Parts of that life were fun, she says, but most of it was just hard work that was falling into a predictable pattern by the time she acted in *It's a Wonderful Life*. As a child with relatively short amounts of screen time, Karolyn was hired on a per-day basis, her salary having risen to the level of $75 a day. With only a few pages of script and no concept of an overall plot, she memorized her lines, with the help of her mother, before working on any given film. "I would ride in a limo from the studio," she says, "but it would pick me up at about 5 in the morning, and I wouldn't get home until about 7 at night, and then I'd have to study my lines for the next day."

Karolyn would arrive at work with an outfit picked out for her on a previous day at Western Costume Co., an enormous Los Angeles warehouse with "floor after floor after floor of clothing." Once on a studio lot, she would dress in a wardrobe room, then staff would fix her hair and apply makeup. "It was heavy, what they called pancake makeup, and you wore it all day," she says. "It was very thick, cake-like, skin-color stuff. They put it on with a sponge – just wet the sponge, dip it in and put it on. That's what everybody wore." For her sensitive face, however, the makeup was no treat. "My face would be raw when I took it off, and it would sting when it would go back on the next day. But you learn early to be a trouper. You don't complain."

'You just stood there, and they just primped on you all the time. It was like you were a little queen.'

Then it was on to the set, a place that was formidable. "The sets were in huge buildings," she says. "You always had to be careful where you walked because there were giant cables, plug-ins and cameras everywhere. It was like a little obstacle course."

Added to the physical trappings was the cacophony of people scurrying everywhere. "They had light meters they would run around with and put in your face, and they had wardrobe people who came around and made sure your dress was just right, and they had makeup people who came to splat powder on, so you didn't have a shiny nose or face. They'd just stand you there and say, 'This is what I want you to do.' So you just stood there, and they just primped on you all the time. It was like you were a little queen. Then there was a woman they called a script girl, and it was her job to look at the script and see in the last segment where my hand was, what exactly I had in my hand, or what exactly I was doing. Each braid had to be just so, just the way it was in the scene before."

"Karolyn, what we want you to do is really be excited. Think about if you'd been away from your daddy for a long, long time and you hadn't seen him, and all of a sudden there he was."

At times, however, the frenzied activity slowed to a crawl. Karolyn remembers spending hours under hot lights just waiting. At other times, she recalls, she stood, absolutely still, to one side with her mother while other scenes were filmed. "You're there at their disposal," she says, "and they're going to take advantage of you as much as they can to save money while you're there, but there are other scenes that have to be shot, too, so it's a matter of where they're at in that particular sequence, the sets they're using and whatever is economically feasible for them."

These circumstances, unusual for any child, were the reason for having a teacher/welfare worker assigned to each film, "to be sure that you weren't abused,

Karolyn Grimes (circled above right) and her parents Martha and LaVan (also circled above and at far left) were present for the culminating IT'S A WONDERFUL LIFE picnic for cast and crew, held August 4, 1946. The panoramic group photo, melded from three separate shots, is well-known for star Jimmy Stewart and director Frank Capra appearing at both ends.

that you weren't under the lights too long," says Karolyn. If filming took place during the school year, during breaks the teacher/welfare worker took all the children at work on a movie to a dressing room that served as a one-room studio schoolhouse, where kids of all ages studied. "If we knew it was going to be a long movie, my mother would get assignments from my school ahead of time and we'd take them with us. But most of the time we'd wing it, because you'd get in the middle of something you were studying, and they'd come get you because they were ready to use you for a shoot, and they would lose continuity otherwise."

While studio school was intended as a substitute for regular school attendance, Karolyn thinks being repetitively pulled out of regular school for filmmaking eventually contributed to a drop in her grades. Her report cards bear this out, indicating that as she progressed from elementary to junior high, she slumped closer to a "C" average. The in-and-out-of-school routine also hurt her ability to build friendships with peers. "I missed out on a lot of slumber parties and birthday parties and that kind of thing," she says. "I really didn't form relationships with any of the kids because I was gone a lot."

The actual filming of her scenes Karolyn remembers as cut and dried. While some directors, such as Capra, kneeled on the floor to instruct her at her level, most stood and gave orders, simply and directly. "They would just tell you what they wanted you to do, and you would do it," she says.

For instance, she notes that the top-of-the-stairway scene in *It's a Wonderful Life* calls for Zuzu to burst through her bedroom door with a heart full of emotion. "They would say, 'I want you to run through that door and say "Daddy, daddy!" ' And then if you didn't do it like they wanted you to, they'd say, 'Now, Karolyn, what we want you to do is really be excited. Think about if you'd been away from your daddy for a long, long time and you hadn't seen him, and all of a sudden there he was. Think about that, and then run out there and say, "Daddy, daddy!"

'I missed out on a lot of slumber parties and birthday parties and that kind of thing.

'I really didn't form relationships with any of the kids because I was gone a lot.'

because you know you love him and you missed him.' They do mind stuff with you to get out what they want. And I was a very obedient child. I grew up with direction, and I did whatever anybody wanted me to do. I just wanted to please everyone, so I guess I was a natural for the directors to work with."

'Of course, I never saw the bell ring on the tree. It was a totally separate thing.

'That's the way filming worked – and still does.'

Over and over in the process were reminders that whatever movie resulted from her efforts was an illusion. The ending of *It's a Wonderful Life* provides bracing examples. "People have a hard time understanding that it didn't happen that we were all standing there at the tree and there's all these people dropping money into the basket, and we're all together and doing this like in a play. I probably never saw some of those other people. Much of the time it was a close-up of Mr. Stewart and me. I know for sure that I never saw some of the things that are going on in that scene in the movie. When the high school principal hands me his watch in the movie, he wasn't there when I took it in my hand and looked at it. And of course, I never saw the bell ring on the tree. It was a totally separate thing. That's the way filming worked – and still does."

Despite such techniques that mask the reality of the filmmaking process, Karolyn enjoys watching her movies as a way to scour her memory about her early past. "It brings it all back, sparks memories, triggers things," she says. "It's like part of your childhood. If you see something that happens to somebody else and you remember, 'Wow, that happened to me,' that whole scenario plays for you again. That's what happens when I see *It's a Wonderful Life* or any other movie that I was in. It's like having family home movies. It's like walking into the past for a few minutes."

Immediately after shooting her scenes for *It's a Wonderful Life*, Karolyn stacked up plenty of future opportunities for such glimpses. The next 12 months passed like a blur, becoming the fastest-paced period of her cinematic career. Her number of minutes soared.

By the summer of 1946, a smooth-voiced brunette actress named Catherine Craig had amassed 15 Hollywood credits. The 31-year-old had graced several of the World War II era's crowd-pleasing movies, such as *Louisiana Purchase*, *Nothing but the Truth*, *You Were Never Lovelier*, *Here Come the Waves* and *Lady in the Dark*. In those films and others, Craig co-starred with the varied likes of Bob Hope, Ginger Rogers, Boris Karloff, Madeline Carroll, Fred Astaire, Ray Milland, Jennifer Jones, Fred MacMurray and Betty Hutton. Married to actor Robert Preston (who a decade later rocketed to fame as *The Music Man*), Craig had another 10 feature films in her future.

But for four days beginning on July 31, Craig had signed on to portray the mother in a 19-minute Technicolor short subject called *Sweet and Low*. Her daughter, who innocently engineers the story's happy ending, was played by 6-year-old Karolyn Grimes. This was an unusual pairing for Craig, who typically had not shared the screen with child actors. As it turned out, Karolyn left a lasting impression on her *Sweet and Low* mom.

Chapter

5

'*Still got the nose to the old grindstone, eh?*'

(*Karolyn's next six films, 1946-1947*)

"She wasn't the little baby doll, the little one in Mary Jane slippers and perfect little socks and all. She was just a little natural child," says Craig, one of the few actors still alive who shot movie scenes with Karolyn. Today, Craig lives in Montecito, near Santa Barbara, California, and remembers quite clearly that the youngster was

Two weeks after finishing IT'S A WONDERFUL LIFE, Karolyn teamed with veteran actress Catherine Craig to make the Technicolor short SWEET AND LOW.

Copyright © 1947 Paramount Pictures, All Rights Reserved.

"professional, but not in the way of a show-off or stagy or that sort of thing. When she was in her costume and saying her words, it came out of her so naturally, and you just believed she was that little girl."

The hectic schedule Karolyn maintained during the 12 months following *It's a Wonderful* Life indicate that many in the film industry shared Craig's regard for the 6-year-old. During that period, she played parts in six more feature films, each as different from the other as possible.

But before the six features came her work on the *Sweet and Low* short, two weeks after the filming of her bedroom scene in *It's a Wonderful Life*. Although the UCLA Film and TV Archive owns a negative of the short, apparently no print exists today for viewing. However, among the many papers saved by Martha is a July 22, 1946, script from the production, under the working title of "The Masque Ball." Not only do these 15 pages lay out the short's dialogue and action, but they show that Karolyn's role, third-billed and one of only four main speaking parts, is rather meaty.

The story mostly takes place in the enormous living room of a Fifth Avenue townhouse in New York City. The room is packed with people who are dressed in costumes, dancing and watching several specialty acts. The party hosts are Tom Mather (Richard Webb) and his wife Andrea (Craig), who want to persuade the guest of honor, a nationally renowned composer named Harlan Kane (Griff Barnett), to write the music for Tom's play, "Springtime in Paris." This storyline was the reason for another of the short's working titles, "Words without Music."

Karolyn plays Tammie Mather – changed from Timmie, when the part originally called for a boy. Again dressed in nightclothes (closed-toed sleepers this time), Tammie is supposed to be in bed during the party. Her mother even tries to sing her to sleep. But Tammie will have none of it.

In SWEET AND LOW, Karolyn's character (Tammie) once again is the catalyst for bringing adults together. This time, she befriends composer Harlan Kane (Griff Barnett) on the stairway at her parents' costume party.

"Please stay, Mummy," says Tammie. *"I don't want you to go downstairs."*

"But I must," Andrea says. *"We're having a party."*

"What kind of a party?"

"A masquerade party."

"What's a masquerade party, mummy?"

"Oh, it's a party where everyone comes dressed as kings and queens and cowboys and Indians. You know what make-believe is, don't you? Well, it's a make-believe party."

"Can I go?" Tammie asks excitedly.

"You've got to go to sleep," Andrea says. Then she adds with a laugh, *"Besides, you'd steal all the attention."*

As soon as her mother leaves the room, Tammie's eyes pop open, and she sneaks down a stairway to watch the dress-up revelry from behind a huge potted palm.

Tammie closes her eyes as her mother sings to her, but as soon as her mother leaves the room, Tammie's eyes pop open, and she sneaks down a stairway to watch the dress-up revelry from behind a huge potted palm. Weary of the other guests' fawning, and hurting from the constrictions of too-tight shoes and a wig, the composer eventually hides behind the same plant. There, he encounters Tammie, who nonchalantly suggests a solution:

"Do your feet hurt?" Tammie asks Kane.

"They're killing me."

"Then why don't you take your shoes off?"

Surprised, he says, *"Why didn't I think of that?"*

> *Tammie again suggests the obvious to Kane: "You're not having a good time, are you?"*
>
> *"I don't think so."*
>
> *"Then why don't you go home?"*
>
> *"Not a bad idea," he says. Then, after a yawn by Tammie, he adds, "Why don't you go to bed?"*
>
> *"I think I will," she says.*
>
> *"I'll walk up with you. My hat, coat and shoes are upstairs."*

The two apparently continue their camaraderie in the bedroom, where viewers find out later that Tammie has persuaded Kane to read her to sleep. The reading material is Tom's play, for which Kane eventually agrees to write the music – all thanks to Tammie, of course.

*From indications in the **Sweet and Low** script, Karolyn may be on screen for nearly half of its 19 minutes.*

From indications in the *Sweet and Low* script, Karolyn may be on screen for nearly half of its 19 minutes. This role also is amazingly consistent with many of her previous parts. She plays the child who eases tensions between adults who are confused or at cross-purposes. Most notably, however, the script twice calls for songs by "a small Negro orchestra, members of which include the Willie Mastin Trio featuring Sammy Davis Jr." Released on March 28, 1947, and screened around the country that summer (including a Sept. 9-10 booking at the Plaza Theatre in Appleton City, near Osceola, Missouri), *Sweet and Low* surely marks one of the first celluloid performances of Davis, who was just 20 at the time and whose feature-film debut came nine years later in 1955. Perhaps one day the short will be made available for public viewing.

Although no longer standard staples of movie theaters, shorts such as *Sweet and Low* played a major role in neighborhood moviehouses of the 1940s, before the advent and popularity of television. In those days, feature films rarely exceeded 90 minutes, the same length as a present-day made-for-TV movie. Theater owners, aiming to provide an evening's worth of "product" twice a night, naturally looked to the economical shorts, as well as cartoons and newsreels, to fill out the bill. Shorts cost a small fraction of the capital that it took to produce and distribute a major movie. (For instance, while Karolyn was paid the same $75 daily rate she earned for *It's a Wonderful Life*, the four days of shooting for *Sweet and Low* amounted to one-fifteenth of the schedule required for a full-length feature.)

MOVIE STARLET PAYS VISIT TO APPLETON CITY PEOPLE

Starlet Karolyn Grimes accompanied by her mother visited P. R. Alexanders of Appleton City before returning to their home in Hollywood, California. Having just completed featured roles in "Albuquerque" and "The Bishops Wife" Karolyn has spent most of her vacation in and around Osceola.

Karolyn plays a big part in a technicolor short subject titled "Sweet and Low" which will play at the Plaza Theatre Tuesday and Wednesday September 9 and 10. She also plays supporting role with Jimmy Stewart in "It's a Wonderful Life" coming soon to the Plaza Theater.

Ironically, while Karolyn's billing in the short subject was the highest in her career to that point, in her next film, the bloated, 146-minute *Unconquered*, she dropped to a decidedly bit part. The pre-Revolutionary War saga, starring Gary Cooper, Paulette Goddard, Howard Da Silva and Boris Karloff and directed by the legendary Cecil B. DeMille, was filmed in September and October 1946 and released by Paramount on Oct. 3 of the next year. The color drama aspires to lay out the conflicts among British patriots, American colonists and several Native American tribes over the fate of the unsettled Ohio territory and, by implication, the future expansion of the United States, all with the typical DeMille mishmash of epic and sensational

This item from the September 4, 1947, APPLETON CITY JOURNAL (30 miles from Osceola) reflects the importance placed on short subjects in 1940s movie theaters.

In the 1947 Cecil B. DeMille film UNCONQUERED, Karolyn's role apparently is of the girl carried in the arms of her mother (Nan Sunderland) following a deadly Indian attack.

elements. In call-board records, Karolyn's part is identified only as "little girl," and she appears 133rd in a characteristically enormous DeMille cast of 194 actors and 4,233 extras.

Apparently, Karolyn's part in *Unconquered* consists of a 15-second segment in which she lies lifeless, her voluminous blonde locks hanging from her blood-stained head, in the arms of her mother (played by Nan Sunderland, then-wife of actor Walter Huston), who bursts into a roomful of partying rebels at Fort Pitt and chastises them for ignoring a deadly Indian attack. Karolyn does not remember the filming and, looking at the film today, doubts that she's the one in the mother's arms. But the child in that segment bears an uncanny resemblance to Karolyn as a 6-year-old, and she is nowhere else to be viewed in the final version of this historical fiction.

Karolyn's part is identified only as 'little girl,' and she appears 133rd in a characteristically enormous DeMille cast of 194 actors and 4,233 extras.

Karolyn jumped more than a century forward in time for the setting of her next film, *The Private Affairs of Bel Ami*, based on the Guy deMaupassant novel set in 1880s upper-class Paris. Filmed in the fall of 1946 and released by United Artists on Feb. 25, 1947, *Bel Ami* is a cold, bleak, self-described "story of a scoundrel" that stars George Sanders as the title character (translated as "best friend") Georges Duroy, who attracts and disposes of women with abandon. A lovely young Angela Lansbury plays Clotilde deMarelle, the only woman who truly loves him, and Karolyn portrays her 5-year-old daughter Laurine. On screen for four scenes totaling two minutes, and 17th billed in the credits, Karolyn is the only child in this black-and-white, adult-themed literary adaptation, which used lurid words and graphics to lure viewers. Tall, narrow ads in *Life* magazine and elsewhere pictured a rapt Lansbury clinging to a man's left pantleg, with the accompanying text, "Any man sincerely in love with a woman will find a way to make her wretched."

As in previous films, the role of Karolyn's character in *Bel Ami* is one of innocence and purity, first helping to draw Georges to Clotilde, and later providing poignancy to Georges' disaffection. The role also may constitute Karolyn's only genuine singing part in the movies (besides the unison "Auld Lang Syne" of *It's a Wonderful Life*, and a brief, plaintive "matches" refrain five years later in *Hans Christian Andersen*). Unlike her previous movies, however, Karolyn's hair is coifed in rivulets of curls, not in buns and braids, in the style of the wealthy 19th century Parisian characters.

In Karolyn's first *Bel Ami* scene, Clotilde brings Georges to Laurine's bedroom to see her asleep and clutching a toy soldier dressed in the uniform of the Sixth Hussars, Georges' old regiment. As if to recall *It's a Wonderful Life*, a maid tells the two that Laurine is sleeping "like an angel," and Clotilde asks Georges, "What do you think of my daughter? Isn't she an angel?"

*The role in **The Private Affairs of Bel Ami** may constitute Karolyn's only genuine singing part in the movies.*

The film's next scene finds Georges at a piano singing to Laurine, who sits next to him on the bench, head thrown back, a delighted smile on her face. The song lyrics reek of sentiment that the audience suspects Georges could never have:

The lark sings in the morning.
The robin sings in the day.
The nightingale sings in the moonlight.
But my heart sings night and day.

Clotilde walks in during the song, and when Georges is finished, Laurine turns and says joyously, "He wrote it for me, Mummy, for my birthday." Then Laurine hugs Georges and says, "I love you so much," as tears well in Clotilde's eyes.

A bitter echo of that scene comes later in the film, when Georges tells Clotilde of his decision to marry someone else. During their conversation, in a room visible behind the two, Laurine runs in, sits down at a piano and twice plays and sings the song that Georges ostensibly had written for her. Karolyn faces away from the camera during the song, so it is not possible to tell from watching the film, nor does Karolyn recall, whether it is Karolyn or someone else doing the playing and singing on the soundtrack. Her mother had given her piano and voice lessons by this point, though, and the on-screen voice – strong, clear and in tune – sounds like what might have been Karolyn's singing voice at the time.

Interestingly, Karolyn recalls that a couple of years later, when she was singing solos at West Hollywood Baptist Church, an agent asked her mother's permission for him to have a professional recording made of

In THE PRIVATE AFFAIRS OF BEL AMI, Karolyn's character Laurine sleeps as she clutches a toy soldier on which the words "Bel Ami" are later stitched by her mother, played by Angela Lansbury.

Karolyn's singing voice. "I don't know if it was her decision or my own agent's, but I do remember that the final decision was that I wouldn't do it," she says. "I always wondered how things might have been different if they had decided otherwise, because I would have loved to have been a singer. I was a good singer when I was a child, and as I grew older my voice got better. That was one thing that I knew I could do well."

Karolyn was recognizable but fleeting in her next movie, a period piece placed in the same era as *Bel Ami* but a hemisphere away. Set in the world of 1890s American burlesque, *Mother Wore Tights* was a popular 20th Century Fox color musical filmed from October 1946 through January 1947 and released Aug. 19, 1947. It starred Betty Grable and Dan Dailey as song-and-dance performers who struggle to raise a couple of daughters on the vaudeville circuit. Karolyn's role is incidental and unbilled, lasting 30 seconds in just one transitional segment that shows the girls at a young age (for the bulk of the film, the story's two children are in their teens and played by older actresses).

Dressed in girls' underwear for her scene in a side room of the family house, Karolyn plays 6-year-old Iris, who tries to comb the tangled hair of her 3-year-old sister, Mikey, with no success. Karolyn's repeated lines ("Mikey, don't touch that!" "Stop that, Mikey!") are merely part of a sibling bicker that prompts their mother's admonishment.

Leaping back to contemporary times, and into her trademark buns-and braids hairdo, Karolyn appeared in five fun scenes and logged nearly six and a half minutes in her next movie, *Philo Vance's Gamble*, a 62-minute black-and-white whodunit filmed in December 1946 and January 1947 and released three months later by Producers Releasing Corporation. Nestled squarely in the B-grade detective genre that usually played in small-town, independent theaters, the film was the middle offering in a series of three Philo Vance mysteries produced that year as a revival of the 1930s detective movie serial that went by the same name. In this installment, the title character (Alan Curtis, sporting a suave, pencil-thin mustache) stumbles upon a ring of Los Angeles jewel thieves who have their eye on a $500,000 emerald. As a long night elapses, several murders occur for Vance to unravel.

'I always wondered how things might have been different if they had decided otherwise, because I would have loved to have been a singer.'

Assisting Vance, quite literally, is Karolyn's character, Pam Roberts. She makes an auspicious entrance in an evening segment when Vance rings the doorbell of the house owned by Jeffrey Connor, the thief who triggers the movie's succession of killings. The shadow of a pistol looms into view, the tension of the musical soundtrack rises melodramatically, and Pam, in close-up and using her best mean-voice imitation, snaps:

> *"You're covered, mister. Reach! Hand over the loot!"*
>
> *"Oh, ho!" Vance says as he whirls around. "I know you," he adds in jest. "You're Jesse James' kid sister."*
>
> *"No, I ain't," she replies, losing her sinister tone. "I'm Pam Roberts. I live over the garage with my uncle. He's Mr. Connor's butler. And this ain't a gun. It's candy, see?"*

Pam turns her pistol to its side, revealing it as a see-through container molded in the shape of a gun and holding several pieces of rock candy. Pam's presence and get-up are soon explained by the butler, who points out that because radio dramas have made Pam a fan of private-eye stories, she uses the fake gun to stir things up a bit around the house.

Of course, the scriptwriters couldn't introduce such an unusual prop to let it evaporate. When Vance later discovers the prize emerald, it turns out to be the same size as the candies in Pam's toy, so he surreptitiously slips the gem into the gun, then gets it away from Pam by promising to buy her a leather holster. Along the way, Karolyn gets to engage in some of the movie's cliché banter. When she meets Vance's sidekick Ernie Clark (Frank Jenks), she tells him:

> *"You don't look like a detective."*
> *"That's the reason I'll be a good one," Ernie says with a conspiratorial glance. "Nobody'll ever suspect me of having any brains."*
> *"You'll sure be able to fool 'em, all right," she replies.*

It's all good fun, in the same vein as the classic detective shows of early television. Because the film was put together with tight pursestrings, the performances carry some rough edges. But Karolyn's role – unusual for a stereotypically adult plot – brightens *Philo Vance's Gamble* into memorable fluff.

She gets a chill from the memory of a scene in which Vance wipes her sooty face clean with sticky cold cream from a jar in which he first discovers the emerald.

Not unexpectedly, Karolyn clearly recalls making the film, mostly because of the toy gun. She also gets a chill from the memory of a scene in which Vance wipes her sooty face clean with sticky cold cream from a jar in which he first discovers the emerald. Given the movie's quickie, low-budget feel and small cast, though, it's no surprise that Karolyn's images of making the film relate solely to what ended up on the screen. There probably was little left to hit the cutting-room floor.

Detective Philo Vance (right, played by Alan Curtis) shows his sidekick Ernie Clark (Frank Jenks) and Pam Roberts (Karolyn) the emerald he had hidden in Pam's fake gun, in PHILO VANCE'S GAMBLE, released in 1947.

As the calendar flipped over into 1947, Karolyn's film projects came swiftly, with the expected frenzy and stress. But the diversion of Karolyn's musical aptitude, including her status as the youngest player in her elementary school orchestra, provided Karolyn and her mother some comfort, as Martha indicated in a letter to her own mother dated Jan. 9:

> **Karolyn is up for screen tests for some big roles. Competition is too strong the higher you work up. So I stick to music when we aren't working.**
>
> **Karolyn will play with the Gardner Street School Orchestra**

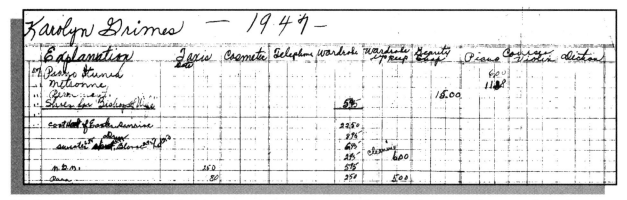

Martha Grimes faithfully kept track of the expenses related to Karolyn's film career, from wardrobe costs to diction lessons.

Tuesday for our PTA meeting. Since she started playing the violin in orchestra, her interests in music have doubled.

She just does extra well. She just amazes the teachers at school with her art and music. She had a private lesson today. It sure keeps me busy.

In the same letter, Martha also alluded to the gradual, inexorable maturation of her daughter:

There's a certain kind of a doll she wants that costs $6. You turn a knob that is the top knot on the doll's cap, and it turns the doll's head to where it cries, then laughs and goes to sleep. So I guess we'll let her get it.

I'd like to keep her playing with dolls as long as I can. Ha!

'When I saw Karolyn on the screen, I said, "That's my little girl," and I was so pleased because I knew it was such a good break for her.'

Actress
Catherine Craig

The same month, January 1947, *It's a Wonderful Life* went into wide release around the country, and contrary to others' reminiscences decades later that it was a flop, thousands took it in and came away from it enthralled. One acting veteran so moved by *It's a Wonderful Life* was Catherine Craig.

"The moment anyone had anything to do with that movie, just sitting in an audience watching it, that marked people for life, I think. It was such a marvelous picture, and everybody I knew raved about it," Craig recalls, insisting that her memory is of the year of the film's release, not of its decades-later exposure on TV.

"I also was absolutely thrilled to pieces to know the little girl in Jimmy Stewart's arms," she says. "After all of his terrible time [in the 'never-born' sequence], to come home to her, I felt that was just perfect. When I saw Karolyn on the screen, I said, 'That's my little girl,' and I was so pleased because I knew it was such a good break for her. It just seemed to mark her career, and I was proud and happy we'd worked together, just for the connection."

Karolyn soon extended that connection in the next film she made, but in a category new to her – the Western. *Albuquerque*, shot from March through June 1947 on the Circle J Ranch in the San Fernando Valley north of Los Angeles, starred Randolph Scott, Barbara Britton, George "Gabby" Hayes, Lon Chaney Jr. and Craig. The traditional good-guy-vs.-bad-guy yarn brings ex-Texas Ranger Cole Armin (Scott) to the frontier town in 1878 to wage a showdown with his uncle John, a hard-bitten, wheelchair-bound heavy, over the transporting of ore from nearby mines. Advertised as a "million-dollar action epic," it is predictable yet lively, thanks in part to Karolyn's giddy presence.

Not quite 7 years old, she plays Myrtle Walton, whom the script describes as "a pleasant chatterbox of 7 or 8." Myrtle arrives in Albuquerque to meet her father and unwittingly becomes embroiled in the conflict of this 89-minute Paramount-Clarion color drama. It was clearly Karolyn's most active and varied role to date. Tenth-billed, she appears prominently in six segments totaling 12 minutes, with not a nightgown or bed in sight. Instead, she rides a stagecoach, testifies atop the judge's bench in a courtroom and tries to spring the hero from prison. In fact, *Albuquerque* was the first of several films in which Karolyn's on-screen action truly excited her. As she puts it, "It's like I never had to go to an amusement park as a child. I had my own real one."

Cole Armin (Western star Randolph Scott) entertains Myrtle Walton (Karolyn) by turning his left hand into a puppet, in ALBUQUERQUE, filmed in 1947 and released the following year.

The opening of the film involves her in a big way, simultaneously kicking off some formulaic old-West bravado. A team of horses and stagecoach driven by Juke (the bearded Hayes) rolls through the southwestern hills toward Albuquerque. Inside, the passengers include Myrtle, stylishly dressed in a green outfit and bonnet and her hands in a muff, and her aunt Celia Wallace (Craig), both of whom are entertained by Cole (Scott), who fashions his knuckles into a face and drapes his hand with a handkerchief to represent a high-voiced, chattering puppet.

When Cole advises Myrtle to get some sleep "so's to look fresh and purty" for her father, the girl pertly responds, "My daddy don't care how I look, just so I get there." Such a simple goal cannot go unobstructed in a true Western, however, and *Albuquerque* is no exception. Mounted thieves show up, halting the stagecoach, ordering the adults to "come out a-jumpin' and reach for nothing but sky." They take $10,000 from Celia and a cache of collections from a pastor. But when the pastor draws a derringer in self-defense, the bandits shoot and kill him, their gunfire frightening the horses, spurring them to run away with the empty coach – empty, that is, except for Myrtle. Cole hops one of the robbers' horses and rides off in pursuit. Wild with fright as the coach lurches and weaves across the dusty terrain, Myrtle leans out of the stage door window and spies Cole galloping behind.

> *"Woah, horses, woah!" Myrtle calls out. "Come on, Mr. Cole! Come on! Woah, horses! Woah!"*

Though Karolyn does her best to impart her character's breathless fear, her shouted pleas to the horses are almost unintentionally comical, as this portion of the segment was obviously filmed with a stagecoach that was artificially jostled on a soundstage. Still, Karolyn's long, curled hair flies back furiously and she

Karolyn rides a stagecoach, testifies atop the judge's bench in a courtroom and tries to spring the hero from prison.

holds on tight to her bonnet and the door window as she tries in vain to urge the horse team to a stop. Finally, Cole catches up with the runaway stage, reins in the horses and saves the day. As he approaches the stagecoach door, Myrtle leaps into his arms, praising his "elegant" heroics and cajoling him to let her ride with him atop the coach as they return to the others.

Myrtle, Celia and Juke ride on the driver's platform in the next segment as the stage rolls boisterously into Albuquerque. There, Myrtle greets her dad and tells

him of Cole's gallantry. It doesn't take long, however, before Cole's evil uncle John falsely charges Cole with arson. In the resulting trial, Myrtle, not understanding the effect of testimony she delivers while sitting on the judge's elevated desk, seals Cole's temporary fate, as the judge sends him to jail.

Loyal to the man who saved her life, however, Myrtle shows up outside Cole's ground-floor prison window with a burro. Her hair done in the braids-and-buns of Karolyn's films gone by, Myrtle means to conspire with Cole on an escape. The resulting dialogue through the prison bars – arguably Karolyn's cutest ever, as she tiptoes on a box to reach the window – illustrates Cole's rock-solid virtue and Myrtle's equally stubborn devotion.

"It was right neighborly of you to come and see me, honey," says Cole, *"but you better run along home now. Jail's no place for a lady."*

"It is, too," she answers defiantly, *"if that lady's best friend is locked up inside."*

"But I've got to stay here until they let me out."

"Oh, no, you don't!"

Myrtle looks up and down the street, scrambles off the box, runs to the burro, fishes a huge horseshoer's file from a pack and runs back to the window.

"Here you are. I've got Clara all saddled and ready. She's watered and fed and can travel four days without sleep. Now, get to work! I'll keep watch while you saw."

Straight-faced, Cole shakes his head and says, "But that would be against the law, and we've got to respect the law."

Cole (Randolph Scott) praises Myrtle (Karolyn) for her bravery in riding a runaway stagecoach.

Myrtle plops down on the box and sits determinedly.

"All right," she says. *"I'm going to stay here until they let you out, if I have to stay till I'm a little old lady in a shawl. I'll be a-sittin' here, a-knittin' and a-waitin'."*

At this point, Juke (played by Gabby Hayes) stops by with sheriff's papers that will free Cole, and he admonishes Myrtle to "skedaddle home" to her "pappy." Myrtle, wary, tells Juke she doesn't trust the sheriff, but finally relents, grabbing the reins of the burro and leading it away. "C'mon Clara," she says. "Reckon Mr. Cole won't be needin' us now."

Sitting on the judge's desk, Myrtle (Karolyn) inadvertently testifies against her hero Cole (Randolph Scott, far left).

The good-natured exchanges gave Karolyn her biggest opportunity yet to stretch her memorizing and acting skills on-screen. Almost 50 years later, in 1996, after seeing *Albuquerque* for the first time ever at the UCLA Film and TV Archive, Karolyn assesses her enjoyable performance as much more natural than her self-described "wooden" work in *It's a Wonderful Life*.

As a major character in *Albuquerque*, Karolyn witnessed a lot of action, including the nighttime burning of a trading company building and a blisteringly realistic fistfight between Randolph Scott and baddie Murkil, played by Chaney. "That fascinated the heck out of me, all that fake blood," she says. "I remember asking how he (Chaney) did it, and he showed me. He was pretty rough." But all was not happy thrills on the set for Karolyn, as the experience etched two unsavory off-screen incidents into her memory.

The first involved a fainting spell. "I was sitting in a makeup chair," she says, "and suddenly everything got sort of black, and I fainted. Boom, I was gone. The next thing I knew, I was lying outside and there were people hovered all around me, including Randolph Scott. They thought I had gotten too hot, because there was a wood stove in there and it was cold outside and the change of temperature or something had done it to me. Fainting later became one of my crosses to bear, but I finally learned after awhile that it always happens at high altitudes, and you know when it's going to happen, so you can avoid it by putting your head between your legs."

Worse, in Karolyn's mind, was a second incident – involving snakes. "They were shooting a scene where they were putting a building on fire, and my mother and I were sitting on a log and watching all this going on. Next thing I know, I saw this little thing on the log. I went to reach down to pick it up, and my mother screamed and jerked me off the log. It was a little baby rattlesnake. She really got mad at me and made such a big scene about it. I think it scared her so badly that she probably passed that fear on to me. She was so upset about what could have happened, and by explaining to me how dangerous that was, she made me

'Everything got sort of black, and I fainted. Boom, I was gone. 'The next thing I knew, I was lying outside and there were people hovered all around me, including Randolph Scott.'

frightened of snakes. The men came and killed the snake, and a bigger one under the log, but from that time forward, I've been scared to death of snakes. I won't even touch 'em in a book."

Equally repulsive to Karolyn was Gabby Hayes' mealtime routine. "They had lavish tables set up outside for lunch, with food everywhere, and the cast and crew and everybody would come eat," she says. "I remember Gabby Hayes' lunch. It was corn bread and buttermilk, every day – yuck. But you know, that was because he really didn't have any upper teeth."

'I remember Gabby Hayes' lunch. It was corn bread and buttermilk, every day – yuck.'

Craig's memories of the *Albuquerque* filming are equally vivid. For example, she regards with no small alarm the early segment in which she, Karolyn and Hayes ride the stagecoach into town. "As I look back on it, this comes to me as a very sudden, much-delayed shock: We weren't tied in to the stagecoach," she says. "Little Karolyn could have been flipped and thrown. She wasn't buckled down. There wasn't even a little toehold where you could put a toe in the floor of the stagecoach. We were riding up there up front, and the horses were running very fast, and we didn't even have sense enough to be nervous about our lives. But that's show biz. While the camera's rolling, you've got to stay in the wagon."

In the segment immediately following Karolyn's wagon-driving scene with Craig and Hayes, she and the others greet a group of Albuquerque townspeople and tell them about the hold-up and resulting excitement. Filming that sequence with Karolyn provided Craig and Robert Preston, who visited the set that day, with one of the more endearing and enduring memories of their lifelong marriage:

"You'd better skedaddle home. . . . Run along, now," Juke (Gabby Hayes) tells Myrtle Walton (Karolyn) in the 1948 Western, ALBUQUERQUE.

"Karolyn is telling her father about the runaway stagecoach, and at one point – it just rings in my ears – she says in that little voice, 'The horses were running away, and they were running so fast, and nobody could stop them, and finally they stopped them,' and then with that slight Southern accent of hers she says, '. . . And I helped!' My husband heard it, and it became a catch-phrase at our house, something you say for the rest of your lives and the two of you get the joke: 'And I helped!' That's one of the sweet things I took away from the picture. She gave me a lovely gift."

To Craig, Karolyn seemed a perfect fit for the *Albuquerque* role of Myrtle. "She was sort of a ragamuffin in that film, just a little girl from the country, and when she spoke, that's what she sounded like, and she played it perfectly," Craig recalls. "You felt she was just a normal, good child in what she did, and you needed those because some of them were pretty bratty. Karolyn knew what the rules were and what good behavior was, but that was just part of her makeup, I think. What you saw was what you got, and that was very lovely, very sweet, very appealing, very natural, and certainly contrasted with the overdone children whom you sometimes found in movies." Craig adds with a laugh, "I didn't act with too many children, so she probably spoiled me."

The promotional material generated about Karolyn at the time she filmed *Albuquerque* generated similar warmth. Quotes from Karolyn in these three news items, obviously assembled by a studio publicist, spiced up the Hollywood movie pages in early 1947:

> **INTERVIEW – Producer Bill Thomas was interviewing a 6-year-old, Karolyn Grimes, for a role in "Albuquerque." "Any other talent in your family?" he asked. "Oh, yes," said Karolyn, "both of my fathers are talented." "Two fathers?" said Bill. "Yes," said Karolyn, "Bing Crosby and Jimmy Stewart." (She played Bing's daughter in "Blue Skies," Stewart's in "It's a Wonderful Life.")**

· · ·

> **JUVENILE DEPARTMENT – Director Ray Enright told 7-year-old Karolyn Grimes how fortunate she was to be enhancing her career in "Albuquerque" at so early an age. "That's true," said she, turning to Barbara Britton, Randy Scott, "Gabby" Hayes and Lon Chaney, "but I'm running an awful risk of being a has-been before I'm 10!!!"**

· · ·

> **On the set of "Albuquerque," Karolyn Grimes pays a lot of attention to Lon Chaney and brings him flowers. "Why is Lon**

'What you saw was what you got, and that was very lovely, very sweet, very appealing, very natural, and certainly contrasted with the overdone children whom you sometimes found in movies.'

Actress
Catherine Craig

Driven by Juke (the everpresent sidekick Gabby Hayes), the stagecoach carrying Myrtle Walton (Karolyn) and Celia Wallace (Catherine Craig) rolls into Albuquerque – actually the Circle J Ranch in the San Fernando Valley north of Los Angeles.

Chaney your favorite, over Randolph Scott, Barbara Britton
and Gabby Hayes?" the director, Ray Enright, asked. "Because
he's truthful," Karolyn replied. "All the other men tell me how
cute they think I am, but Mr. Chaney says I'm ugly and that I
have freckles."

Even more enjoyable was an article about Karolyn cooked up for the
Albuquerque studio pressbook. Headlined "Director Enright on
Collecting End," the fanciful, fabricated story refers realistically to
the challenge of learning lines:

> Karolyn Grimes is a Hollywood rarity – an actress who
> pays to work.
>
> The seven year old movie player has an important role
> with Randolph Scott, Barbara Britton, George "Gabby"
> Hayes and Lon Chaney in Paramount's "Albuquerque,"
> the Clarion Production Cinecolor outdoor thriller. And for
> letting her work in the film, director Ray Enright
> demanded most of the small weekly allowance given to
> Karolyn by her mother.
>
> Enright concocted the revolutionary switch on
> Hollywood salary procedure as a method of getting the
> most out of Karolyn's considerable ability. After each of
> her scenes, Karolyn paid the director two cents if he said
> he could use the sequence in "Albuquerque." If he
> thought the scene wasn't good, Enright refused the
> money. Karolyn would then beg for an opportunity to
> run through it again, so that she would have that much
> more footage in the completed film.
>
> In one sequence, Karolyn had to make a long speech.
> After several rehearsals, she turned to director Enright.
>
> "If you let me do this scene once more I'll be much
> better and I'll even give you three cents, one more than
> usual," she said.
>
> Then there was the shot in which she had to be the only
> passenger in a runaway stagecoach. She was delighted with the
> situation and, after the "take" was completed, handed Enright a
> nickel.
>
> "That's a bribe," she said. "If that scene stays I'll be a hero
> among all my friends." The money must have gone to Enright's
> head, for the runaway coach stayed in the picture.
>
> What Enright really did with the money was to put all the
> pay-offs in a sterling silver bank he bought for Karolyn, and
> present it to the young actress when "Albuquerque" was
> completed.

*Early 1948 ad
featuring Karolyn
modeling a formal girl's
jacket. "Little movie
stars wear Budsters by
Rothschild," the ad
reads.*

The promoters for *Albuquerque* took every opportunity to feature the emerging
young actress. Paramount press materials for the film linked Karolyn with her
famous prior "screen daddies" and identified her as "the delightful little moppet,"
"the engaging little seven-year-old" and "one of Hollywood's most popular screen
children." The still photographer on the *Albuquerque* location even snapped

Karolyn holding "a newly acquired pet" in a glass jar. "Karolyn Grimes captured a moth and immediately made it the company's pet," read the accompanying caption.

Karolyn's image as an up-and-coming starlet was underscored further by her appearance before 50,000 people as the "Dove Girl" who released 200 white pigeons symbolizing the resurrection at the April 6, 1947, outdoor Easter sunrise service at Forest Lawn Memorial Park in Los Angeles. A photograph of a smiling Karolyn stroking a dove appeared in a Hollywood newspaper to promote the service. The *St. Clair County Courier*, a community weekly 1,600 miles away in her parents' hometown of Osceola, also took note of the event, with an article that read, in part:

At the Easter sunrise service at Forest Lawn Memorial Park in Los Angeles, Karolyn was billed as the "Dove Girl" who released 200 white pigeons symbolizing the Resurrection.

> **Needless to say, we are proud of Karolyn, and we are looking forward to seeing her soon. Her mother ... and her father were both graduates from the Osceola high school, and we are so happy that they have such a talented daughter and they are giving her every opportunity, and yet she appears a very normal child and is not spoiled by all the attention she has received.**

When *Albuquerque* was finally released on Feb. 20, 1948, clothing retailers began to use Karolyn in their advertising. One newspaper display ad for Philadelphia-based S. Rothschild and Co. pictured Karolyn, "appearing in her latest Paramount Picture *Albuquerque*," modeling a formal girl's jacket. "Little movie stars wear Budsters by Rothschild," the ad read. "The club checks, double box-pleated back and wonderful, wonderful colors give her the 'right look.' " The ad, stamped with the *Parents* magazine commendation, also appeared in *Parents* and *Good Housekeeping*. Karolyn's mother, in a letter to her mother and a brother back in Missouri, glowingly described the Dec. 26, 1947, modeling session that Paramount Pictures arranged for the ad:

> **They made her a gift of the things she modeled. They are so lovely. And it's really something to be asked to do that, for [child actress] Margaret O'Brien is the only one who does that sort of thing.**

Back in Missouri, Karolyn's films were starting to show up with regularity. For instance, *Mother Wore Tights* played Osceola's Civic Theatre on Feb. 18-19, 1948, and *Albuquerque* was screened there on Aug. 22-23, 1948, with Karolyn's and Randolph Scott's names the only ones appearing in community newspaper ads for the movie. (Two years later, on August 10, 1950, *Albuquerque* returned to the Civic for a one-night encore.) One of those who made a point to see Karolyn's movies was Gail Taylor Adams, a cousin one year younger than Karolyn who had

'We are so happy that they have such a talented daughter and they are giving her every opportunity, and yet she appears a very normal child and is not spoiled by all the attention she has received.'

St. Clair County Courier

gotten to know her from the Grimes' summertime visits and who lived in Clinton, 35 miles north of Osceola, during the 1940s.

Karolyn's movies supplied Gail with an interesting perspective on her cousin – and bragging rights among her grade-school peers. Gail vividly remembers the tenor of her conversations with friends upon leaving Clinton's Uptown and Crest moviehouses after seeing Karolyn on the big screen:

"I know her," Gail would say.

"Oh, no, you don't."

"No, I really do know her. I play with her."

"That's a joke. You don't know her."

Karolyn's performances also left Gail with a sense of awe. "Being small, I'd think, 'How does she remember all those lines? What are they doing to help her with that?' " says Gail. "I can remember being in school plays at the same time, and thinking, 'I'm having a hard time remembering my lines, and I'm just getting up in front of a few people. I'm not in a movie, and Karolyn has all that to remember.' Of course, at a later date I realized that she was just saying a little bit and then she was going off and coming back again. So I was really having a more difficult time than she was!"

With hometown pride (at least for Karolyn's parents), this ad in the August 19, 1948, ST. CLAIR COUNTY REPUBLICAN, in Osceola, Missouri, gave Karolyn equal billing with Randolph Scott.

Gail's feelings toward Karolyn's film work never turned to envy, she says, primarily because Karolyn was a real person to her, not a Hollywood image. "I just thought it was great that she had the ability," Gail says. "Now, I did go home after movies and stand on the back porch and sing 'Singin' in the Rain' and play like I was Betty Grable or Dale Evans, but I never played like I was Karolyn Grimes. I just knew Karolyn as Karolyn, and I knew that that was work. That was what her mother would always say: 'Karolyn worked.' So I never felt that I had to be like Karolyn when I was little. I just knew that was what she did, and her family was very proud of her, and I was, too."

That pride was to deepen with her next film after *Albuquerque*, Samuel Goldwyn/RKO Pictures' *The Bishop's Wife*, which represented a return to Karolyn's familiar milieu of contemporary family drama, the likes of *It's a Wonderful Life*. Ninth-billed, she appears in six scenes for a total of seven of the black-and-white film's 108 minutes. But that kind of measurement cannot fully account for the significance that *The Bishop's Wife* holds in Karolyn's mind.

First, Karolyn was just turning 7 during the summer of 1947 when the movie was made, so her memories of *The Bishop's Wife* are sharper than those of her previous projects. Second, the film stars Cary Grant, who took special interest in her during the shooting (and who, oddly enough, was to have played Zuzu's father in *It's a Wonderful Life* before Capra bought the story). Moreover, *The Bishop's Wife* sports a stellar main and supporting cast (including the Mitchell Boychoir), an uplifting theme and an overall quality to rival *It's a Wonderful Life*.

In fact, like *Wonderful Life*, it was Academy Award-nominated (but didn't win the Oscar) for best picture. Promoted at the time as an endearing holiday fable, its enjoyability still endures.

Two other interesting factors parallel *The Bishop's Wife* with *It's a Wonderful Life*, even linking it to Karolyn's famous Zuzu line: It's an angel picture, and it has a Christmas theme.

Cary Grant plays Dudley, an angel without wings.

Like the actor who portrayed Clarence in *It's a Wonderful Life*, Cary Grant plays Dudley, an angel without wings. Dudley, however, carries himself with a Grant-like urbane demeanor. He is assigned to Henry Brougham (David Niven), an Episcopalian bishop who is unwittingly shunning his family and his principles in an obsessive quest to raise funds to build an expensive cathedral. Dudley also is assigned to Henry's wife Julia (Loretta Young), whose marriage to the bishop seems to be hanging by a thread.

Karolyn plays Debby, the daughter of Henry and Julia, and hers is a pivotal role. While Grant gives Dudley an ambiguous edge in his dealings with other mortals in the film, it is through Debby the audience detects Dudley's divine purpose. As in *That Night with You*, *Pardon My Past*, *Blue Skies*, *It's a Wonderful Life*, and even *The Private Affairs of Bel Ami*, Debby's youthful innocence promotes family harmony and unity.

Karolyn's affection for Cary Grant during the making of THE BISHOP'S WIFE was genuine. "I think he loved to be with children, loved to make them happy," she says.

Grant's debonair Dudley first introduces himself to Henry as the answer to his prayers. Then Henry awkwardly introduces him to Julia as his new assistant. Debby meets Dudley in the entryway of the bishop's house, just as she's about to go out and play in the snow. Dudley's angelic status is not disclosed to Debby. Still, she prods him hopefully ("Mommy told me you came to help Daddy"), and Dudley soon cements a bond with her, confirming for the audience the validity of his intentions.

Out in a city park with her mother, Debby whines that a group of rowdy boys is keeping her from joining a snowball fight because "I guess I'm too little or something." Instantly, Dudley appears, first trying to goad the boys (including Bobby Anderson, who also portrayed the young George Bailey in *It's a Wonderful Life*) into including her in their game, then remedying the situation with a little heaven-based magic. Dudley persuades Debby, who admits that she "can't throw," to hurl a snowball at the boys. Her snowball swerves through the air and (with the aid of one of the movie's angelic special effects) hits the first boy, prompting the whole bunch to take notice and bring her into their game.

The most significant scene involving Debby (and Karolyn's longest of the movie, lasting nearly three minutes) takes place back in the bishop's house on the floor of the drawing-room, with Dudley. Prodded by Debby's eager questions, Dudley weaves a mesmerizing version of the Biblical tale of David and Goliath, emphasizing the illusory role of an angel who helps David.

"Angels come down and put ideas into people's heads," he tells Debby, "and then people feel very proud of themselves because they think it was all their own idea."

As Dudley relates the story, Henry, Julia and others gather one by one in the background to listen. The moment not only echoes Debby's David-and-Goliath confrontation with the boys in the earlier snowball scene, but also becomes a none-too-subtle lesson for Henry on the ethics of cathedral fund-raising.

Near the end of *The Bishop's Wife*, Dudley has vanished, as he has set Henry back on track, helping him to realize that his duties to his small, downtown parish and his own family are more important than impressing an apparently selfish benefactor. When Julia looks in on a sleeping Debby and kisses her, Henry peeks in and the two notice an angel doll hanging above Debby's bed. With no small irony, Julia tells Henry, "I can't imagine where it came from."

As her parents (Loretta Young and David Niven as the bishop) and the bishop's secretary look on, Dudley the angel (Cary Grant) tells Debby the story of David and Goliath.

Perhaps surprisingly, neither did Karolyn at the time. In fact, she insists that all she was concentrating on was closing her eyes and keeping a straight face.

"I remember lying in that bed because when they came to kiss me goodnight at the end of the movie, Loretta Young had horrible breath. I think I lay there a long, long time, because I was threatened with death to stay quiet. 'Don't move!' they'd say. 'Lie real still. Don't smile.' There was a car dealer at the time who had a slogan, something about a smiling Irishman, and it was all I could do to keep from smiling because that ran through my mind."

The Bishop's Wife also gave Karolyn a chance to learn adaptability as a child actress. She can't recall the exact changes involved, but *The Bishop's Wife* marked the first time that she came to work one day and had to learn a revised portion of script on the spot.

"You know, in a movie you don't learn your lines all at one time like you do in a play," she says. "You take them a day at a time. You study for tomorrow, or you come early that morning and you learn your lines for the day, whatever works for each different person. The thing is, you can study the night before, but then you get there the next morning and they've changed it all. They might have even changed the schedule and be shooting something else. They call it giving you a revision, and you have to change, go with the flow. I guess that's where I learned that, because I do that very well. Something bad happens? Well, that's okay. I move on."

As with *It's a Wonderful Life*, winter scenes for *The Bishop's Wife* were filmed in June, forcing the creation of artificial outdoor settings. A soundstage laid with 10 miles of pipes that were flooded and frozen served as a glazed-over lake for skating. The movie's snow resulted from the shaving of 20 tons of ice into tiny flakes, allowing for the creation of realistic snowballs, snowmen and slush. Karolyn cannot remember the filming of her snowball-throwing scene, but she still squirms at the recollection of the wool snowsuit she had to wear, as it itched the sides of her face.

The David-and-Goliath storytelling scene also sticks in her memory, primarily because the director, Henry Koster, and a Saint Bernard named Queenie lay on the floor, out of camera range, as the scene proceeded. "You feel good about a director being on the floor with you because it makes you feel like you're in a cocoon," she says. "It's a good way to deal with children. They don't feel like they're out there alone so much."

Karolyn's most indelible memory from *The Bishop's Wife*, however, is of Cary Grant. In contrast to the distant David Niven, whom she was told was an "untouchable" star and someone to avoid, Grant was kind, fun and prone to loosening up the atmosphere between takes, traits appealing to a 7-year-old girl working in a controlled environment.

TICKETS FOR THE JUDGE—
Karolyn Grimes persuades Judge A. A. Scott, presiding judge of Juvenile Court, to buy two tickets to the benefit premiere of Samuel Goldwyn's "The Bishop's Wife" on Christmas night at Carthay Circle. All proceeds from the premiere will go to Variety Club boy's club fund.

Karolyn and a local judge promote ticket sales for the Christmas 1947 premiere of THE BISHOP'S WIFE.

"I think he was extremely bright and didn't have to work on his lines that much, and he was bored, so he messed around and played and that kind of stuff. When the star makes noise, so can you," Karolyn says. "When they had a real skating rink on the set, he took me on a sled every day at lunch – 'C'mon, Karolyn, let's go!' – and he would pull me around while he was ice-skating. It was so exciting, I loved every minute of it, and I thought he was the neatest guy ever."

Karolyn doesn't believe Grant behaved that way just to build rapport with her. "I think he just really did like children," she says. "I think he loved to be with children, loved to make them happy. He really had a wonderful personality. And I never thought of him as a handsome movie idol, because I was too young to realize that. I saw these people all the time, and I didn't really think too much about it. They were just like everybody else, and he was a friend."

The Bishop's Wife apparently premiered on Nov. 25, 1947, in London, England, at the Odeon Theatre, as a Royal Command Film Performance for Their Majesties the King and Queen, to benefit the Cinematograph Trade Benevolent Fund. In Los Angeles, however, *The Bishop's Wife* opened on Christmas night as a charity premiere at Hollywood's Carthay Circle Theater.

Karolyn was enlisted to promote the event, a benefit for the Variety Club's East Side Boys Club fund. Her long, blonde locks in a ponytail, she posed for newspaper photos with A.A. Scott, presiding judge of the local juvenile court, to sell tickets for the fund-raiser. And when the big night arrived, she recalls, she was interviewed live on local radio. The experience was heady for Karolyn's mother Martha, as she described it in a letter to her Missouri-based mother and her brother Truman:

> **They gave us a police pass, so we drove right up front. Some fellows in white coats parked our car. We got out and walked in on red carpet under the bright lights. They took Karolyn's picture with the captain of the Michigan football team that was here to play in the Rose Bowl football game. . . . Then we sat among the stars in the show.**

'When they had a real skating rink on the set, he took me on a sled every day at lunch – "C'mon, Karolyn, let's go!" – and he would pull me around while he was ice-skating.

'It was so exciting, I loved every minute of it, and I thought he was the neatest guy ever.'

The stars present that night were plentiful, to say the least. In addition to the names of Cary Grant, Loretta Young and Karolyn, Los Angeles newspapers dutifully reported the presence of dozens of luminaries, including William Bendix, Virginia Mayo, Dana Andrews, Teresa Wright, Eddie Bracken, Danny Thomas, Cathy O'Donnell, Shirley Temple, Paul Henreid and Robert Cummings.

The morning-after reviews for the film were gratifying, as well. Karolyn even rated praise from the *Hollywood Citizen-News* for her "vivid characterization."

RKO did not hesitate to use Karolyn to advertise the film in the usual promotional materials. In addition, however, *The Bishop's Wife* pressbook included an intriguing photo picturing Cary Grant, Karolyn and other children from the movie's snowball-throwing scene poring over a just-released children's book, *You and the United Nations*, issued by Chicago-based Children's Press, Inc. Theaters were urged to build window displays around the book, described as "unique in style, containing human interest copy and profusely illustrated." The studio's alignment of the movie with such a political concern as the United Nations was unusual, but it likely reflected the national hopes for world peace following the UN's post-World War II formation – and cleverly reinforced the movie's underlying theme of community harmony.

Karolyn signed autographs at Bullock's Home Store in Los Angeles on December 30, 1947, to promote sales of a "Wee Bit of Heaven" doll inspired by THE BISHOP'S WIFE.

Look and *Modern Screen* magazines prepared *Bishop's Wife* layouts, including photos of Karolyn, for their January editions. In addition, advertisements used a photo of Karolyn, Loretta Young and David Niven from the film to promote sales of "The Lucky Star Doll" marketed by the Hollywood Doll Company as a replica of the angel doll that hung over Karolyn's bed near the end of the movie.

Karolyn also made a prominent personal appearance with the same theme in downtown Los Angeles. Five days after the Christmas premiere of *The Bishop's Wife*, a large ad in the *Los Angeles Times* showed Karolyn linking up with Bullock's Home Store to encourage sales of a "Wee Bit of Heaven" doll, also inspired by the film's angel doll. "Come to Our Autograph Party! In person . . . Karolyn Grimes, child star of Samuel Goldwyn's *The Bishop's Wife*," the ad read. The store set up a throne-like seat for Karolyn to sit in, and for two hours she jotted her name on dolls for a steady stream of youngsters.

'They made a lot of froufrou about that movie.'

"They made a lot of froufrou about that movie," Karolyn says. "I signed dolls and pictures and that sort of thing, so that movie became bigger to me because of that." The autograph-seekers knew her from the film, "but it was no big thing to me at the time. I never had a big head. I think my mother kept me level-headed. She just kept me right on track."

Or at least she tried to. By 1948, as Karolyn approached her eighth birthday, the skein of childhood movie roles threaded largely by her mother began to unravel – in large part because of a mysterious disease over which neither her mother nor Karolyn had control.

Slowly, imperceptibly at first, it advanced. And while no one can pinpoint the precise onset of the Alzheimer's-like disease that became Martha Grimes' death sentence, it probably started wreaking its incremental havoc in her late 30s. Were it not for a painful backyard accident at age 41 in late 1950, it may have progressed at a tamer pace, and Martha's life may have extended past 1954.

Much of the information on Martha's health during this period borders on speculation. What is well-documented, however, is a sharp decline in Karolyn's film appearances. Despite her astonishingly busy schedule of six feature-length films and one short subject from early 1947 to early 1948, Karolyn's output dropped dramatically to just one movie role in each of the following four years.

Martha's condition undoubtedly contributed to this retrenchment, but precisely when its influence commenced is open to question. No doubt Karolyn's slowdown also stemmed from changes churning within Hollywood itself, as the film industry braced for the entrance of television, the dreaded box that was destined to find its way into almost every American home. Martha herself acknowledged, in passing, the coming trend in a Jan. 9, 1948, letter to relatives in Osceola:

> **The studios have closed down. There are very few pictures in production. Where there used to be 50, there are 18 now.**

Accordingly, Karolyn's next film, *Lust for Gold*, was no huge addition to her resumé. Filmed by Columbia Pictures in late 1948 and released May 31, 1949, the self-described documentary Western is a melodramatic treasure-hunt yarn set in hilly, arid Arizona. The 90-minute black-and-white morality tale stars Paul Ford, Jay Silverheels and, in an extended flashback to 1880 that takes up the majority of the movie's running time, Ida Lupino, Gig Young and Glenn Ford. Attempting to emulate more prestigious adventures, the film underscores the futility of greed in the face of an impassive earth reluctant to disgorge its riches. It might be called a poor man's version of *The Treasure of Sierra Madre*, released just a year prior. Studio promoters obviously wrestled with how to sell the picture, saddling it with a plethora of working titles: "For Those Who Dare," "The Secret of Treasure Mountain," "Gold," "Superstition Mountain," "Greed," "Thunder Gods' Gold" and "Bonanza!"

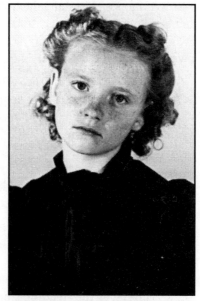

Karolyn's mother Martha wrote on the back of this photo: "Blue eyes, golden blonde hair, very fair with few freckles. Find enclosed full face picture and $2 for paper doll. Yours truly. Like to have by 14 Feb. on Valentine Day." Whether Martha sent the photo off and received a paper doll in Karolyn's likeness is unknown.

Early in the picture, rural rest-home resident Martha Bannister reminisces about her childhood in the tiny town of Florence Junction, east of Phoenix. Martha's recollection of Jacob Walz (Glenn Ford), who owned the legendary Lost Dutchman mine on Superstition Mountain, into which $20 million in gold had been buried, kicks off the film's extended flashback. The unbilled Karolyn (whose

Chapter

6

'Now, if you'll just point me in the right direction . . .'

(Karolyn's final four films, her mother's decline, and her early teens and sexual awakening, 1948-1955)

name is spelled Karoline in the daily production reports) plays the childhood Martha. She has just a single scene lasting 40 seconds, designed to establish Walz' slothful wickedness.

On a dusty street, the youngster wanders up to a drunken, sprawled-out Walz, a shotgun in his lap as he fiddles with a leather strap. She peppers him with questions about what he's doing and the gun. Finally, Walz answers in a slur, "C'mere. Want to have some fun, eh?" He tells the girl to put her finger on the trigger and to pull on it. When she does, the gun fires a deafening blast, Waltz lets out a hideous laugh, and the scared girl quickly backs away and hides behind a barrel.

Karolyn remembers little of the *Lust for Gold* filming. Her part originally had more action, she recalls, but it was cut from the final movie. The two days or so that she worked on the film were not easy for her, either, because the part called for her to cry on cue, something that she had never found easy to accomplish.

'I was supposed to stand there and weep, with tears coming down my cheeks, and to help me do that, they told me they were going to blow onion dust in my eyes.'

"I was supposed to stand there and weep, with tears coming down my cheeks, and to help me do that, they told me they were going to blow onion dust in my eyes," she says. "I was afraid of that, and I worried about it the whole night. Then I went in to do it, they did it, and it wasn't that bad – and then they cut it."

Soon after *Lust for Gold* was released, the relationship between Karolyn's parents and agent Lola Moore soured. Moore had represented Karolyn practically since her birth. Karolyn has no memory of what transpired, but a clipping saved by her mother from the June 18, 1949, edition of a publication called *Talent Review* provides a clue. The article, headlined "Worthless spending," excoriated Moore for charging parents $15 to $75 for their children to appear in her talent directory, with no promise of work. The writer urged parents to file complaints with the Better Business Bureau and the license commissioner against Moore:

> **She is overcrowding the profession with too many children, not talented but of the same size and type as the talented ones. . . .**
>
> **The agent who professes to be the friend of juvenile talent who offers, as the stepping stone to success, a place in their useless catalog, opens the door to disappointment and disillusionment in the minds of mothers and children alike.**

Whether this article had an effect on the decision is unknown, but in 1950 LaVan – not Martha – terminated the relationship with Moore and switched Karolyn's representation to another Sunset Boulevard agent, Sid Gold.

Early that year, as family friend Nancy Gates recalls Martha Grimes telling it, Martha took Karolyn to Republic Pictures for what was termed a casting call. Much different from a one-on-one interview, in this session dozens of girls were herded into one large room to be evaluated en masse.

"Martha had read in the paper that they were casting little girls," Nancy says, "and at the casting call, all these adorable little curly-headed girls were standing around. Karolyn stood to one side and was dressed in a plain little school dress with her braids." Martha apparently took one look at the assemblage and told herself, "Well, this is one we'll miss." Instead, the opposite occurred. "Karolyn was exactly what they wanted," says Nancy. "They wanted a little girl who didn't look like Shirley Temple – and that's how she got her part in *Rio Grande*."

If Karolyn had wanted an extraordinary experience in moviemaking, she could not have asked for more than her *Rio Grande* assignment. The third in director John Ford's so-called trilogy of calvary pictures, this black-and-white, 105-minute film, whose working titles were "Rio Bravo" and "Rio Grande Command," explores the tensions between U.S. soldiers and Native American tribes along one of the great Southwestern rivers after the Civil War, and the similar tensions between a military colonel and his wife and grown son.

By turns stately and silly, rhapsodic and raucous, *Rio Grande* teams for the first time two actors at the peak of their popularity – John Wayne and Maureen O'Hara, playing Col. Kirby Yorke and his wife Kathleen – as well as a collection of crotchety character actors supplemented by the Sons of the Pioneers singing group. Released on Nov. 2, 1950, the film was shot the previous June and July on a private ranch along the Colorado River near Arches National Monument and the city of Moab in eastern Utah, some 600 miles away from Hollywood.

'They wanted a little girl who didn't look like Shirley Temple – and that's how she got her part in **Rio Grande***.'*

Nancy Gates

Twelfth-billed, Karolyn appears throughout the film in a dozen scattered shots totaling about a minute and a half, plus one climactic segment of about four and a half minutes. Her character, Margaret Mary, appears to be the oldest child at Fort Stock, where Yorke's regiment is stationed. She is the daughter of the fort's schoolteacher and the niece of an Irish sergeant named Quincannon (played by Victor McLaglen), to whom she refers several times as Uncle Timmy.

For Karolyn, Moab, Utah, the location for the filming of RIO GRANDE – Moab, Utah – became a Western adventure land, as depicted on this postcard from the time.

While Karolyn seems ever-present in *Rio Grande*, her part, unlike many of her previous roles, eschews plot advancement and relationship building. Instead, it serves mainly to bring some color and warmth to the dry, bleak environment of a military outpost.

Margaret Mary's few lines are either throwaway statements ("Uncle Timmy, you're going to be a good boy, now, aren't you?" "Travis sure swiped your horse, General!") or shrieked exclamations made while recoiling from a pair of Indian attacks. She is more memorable for her physical presence and action: running out of a schoolhouse, fishing from a dock, riding a runaway wagon and sitting with a parasol on a podium during a commendation ceremony.

Intriguing nowadays, though, is the fact that Karolyn's *Rio Grande* props provide an uncanny reminder of Zuzu's most famous line. In four of her short scenes in *Rio Grande*, ostensibly to identify her as the schoolteacher's daughter, she is shown continuously ringing a large school bell. And in her extended climactic segment, in which Margaret Mary and the other children are rescued from an old mission held by a tribe of partying Indians, she not only rings a school bell, but also clangs a calvaryman over the head with it. Later in the segment, it falls to her to send a decoy signal to the tribe by yanking the long rope of the mission's huge church bell, up and down, over and over again. The accumulation of Karolyn's bell-ringing scenes, perhaps remotely symbolic of Americans' thirst for liberty, seems to communicate an additional, subliminal message – as if, throughout *Rio Grande*, her character is imitating the cash-register antics of Nick the bartender in the "unborn" sequence of *It's a Wonderful Life* and "giving out wings" to angels.

Sending a decoy signal, Karolyn yanks the long rope of a huge church bell in RIO GRANDE.

The accumulation of Karolyn's bell-ringing scenes seems to communicate a subliminal message, as if her character is 'giving out wings' to angels.

Whatever the rationale for all the bell action, Karolyn clearly had the time of her young life while making the movie. Along with the acting and production crew, she spent a full three weeks filming in Utah, an adventure that began a week before school formally let out in June. The filming offered Karolyn a number of unique experiences, from her first plane flight to a recurring intrigue about quicksand. "I was fascinated because they said there was quicksand there, so I was always looking around, wondering where it could be," she says.

Her enthusiasm rang clearly from a postcard she sent to her father back in Los Angeles on June 10:

Dear Daddy,

I am fine. Did not go to location today. Having lots of fun. Had my hair washed today. Loving the food. I just adore the Indians.

Love, Karolyn

By two and a half weeks later, in a June 27 letter to LaVan, Karolyn's upbeat spirit prevailed, if sullied slightly by the travails of the wild:

Dear Daddy,

. . . I worked today. Got a mosquito bite on my cheek. Swelled up bad and had to get to hospital. Doctor told me to put ice pack only, and check and see if it's down in the morning or my eye would be swelled up.

But I slept on it, and eye was all right. Also, the doctor gave me medicine to drink and salve to put on. Fine now.

Well, I have to go to bed soon. Good night.

With all my love, Karolyn

Looking back today on *Rio Grande*, Karolyn recalls a nasty sunburn that resulted from the hot day on which the fishing scene was shot, and splinters on her rear end from landing on a wooden ledge during filming of the mission scene. But all was not painful for her on the set. Karolyn liked the desert terrain, explored the fort's elaborate setup of tents and thrilled when the time came to shoot the movie's ferociously agitated chase scenes.

"Riding in a covered wagon with the Indians chasing you – and a truck speeding alongside of you shooting it – is pretty exciting," she says. "You're going up and down and hanging on for dear life, and you're looking at the Indians all around you. Of course, a wheel could have fallen off and a lot of things could have happened, but you take your chances."

Karolyn also remembers a family-like atmosphere on the location. On hand to help oversee the proceedings were Karolyn's mother, whose pending debilitation was starting to reveal itself in her unsteadiness, plus the usual teacher/welfare worker. Karolyn and Martha were lodged with the other actors and crew at a Moab motel and ate their meals in a huge community hall. Wayne's sons Mike and Patrick were visiting their divorced father during the filming, and both managed to snag bit parts in the movie. During off days, Patrick, who was Karolyn's age, and Karolyn pored over comic books in the Waynes' motel room, and on Sundays Karolyn and her mother became immersed in the ways of a religion that was new to them but not to the area.

"The ranch where the film was made was owned by a Mormon family, and I'd never been exposed to Mormons before," she says. "We got to know their beliefs and their lifestyle, and it was fascinating because they wore the clothes that were in the times of the movie. The men had beards and worked as extras, as did their children. My mother got to know some of the children and their parents, so we were invited to their homes for Sunday dinners. It was different to walk into their worlds."

The nearly all-male *Rio Grande* cast made for interesting observations as well. The Indians, brought in from a nearby reservation, "sat around and played poker and drank red and orange pop," Karolyn says. "We were warned to stay away from them, not to bother them." On the other hand, the actors playing calvary members essentially were "a bunch of good old boys," including Wayne. "There were J. Carrol Naish, Chill Wills, just old crony men. It was fun hanging around them."

Karolyn found the Sons of the Pioneers, who harmonize on four prairie songs during the movie, to be kind, especially their leader Ken Curtis, who was the director Ford's son-in-law and resembled Karolyn's favorite uncle Truman back in Osceola. But an innocent off-screen contact she had with one of the singers led to a sharp rebuke from her mother.

"We went to a restaurant in town one night, and as I came out, one of the Sons of the Pioneers came out. I hugged him around the waist because I was so happy to see him. But when I got in the car, my mother really got after me because I hugged this man. She said, 'Don't ever do that.' I don't know exactly why. Maybe she was trying to protect me from being taken advantage of, or maybe it was part of her sickness. But I have a hunch she taught me not to touch people." Whatever

'Riding in a covered wagon with the Indians chasing you – and a truck speeding alongside of you shooting it – is pretty exciting. . . .

'Of course, a wheel could have fallen off and a lot of things could have happened, but you take your chances.'

the reason, Karolyn feels the incident contributed to her reluctance to engage in "touchy-feely" contact with others for much of her adult life.

Besides her mother, the only significant contact Karolyn recalls having with an adult woman during the *Rio Grande* filming was with Maureen O'Hara, in a memorable limousine ride along the Colorado River from the fort set back to the motel. "The road ran along a bluff that the river was etched into, and I was looking out the window because I was afraid the car was going to fall into the water," she says. "All of a sudden, Maureen O'Hara was cursing like a sailor, getting mad about something, I can't remember what. Normally, I wouldn't have paid any attention, but her hairdresser, who was riding with us, really dressed her down because she was cursing. This hairdresser said, 'Be quiet, there's a child in the car.' Naturally, I was all ears and listened as hard as I could from then on, but I didn't hear anything more."

'I was afraid the car was going to fall into the water.

'All of a sudden, Maureen O'Hara was cursing like a sailor.'

The culminating experience for Karolyn on the *Rio Grande* shoot came on her 10th birthday – July 4, 1950. Filming had been completed, but because the Korean War had just begun, the production crew could not easily get flights back to California. So John Wayne, who Karolyn feels was "truly a special person, the man who had time for everyone," arranged for a huge birthday cake to be brought into the town hall and bought $300 worth of Independence Day fireworks to shoot off over the river bluff for the benefit of the cast and crew.

"It was really a neat deal," Karolyn says, "and it was awfully kind of him to do that." The fireworks were set off and seen mostly by the drunken revelers, she says, leaving only a few sparklers for her and Patrick Wayne. "We were kind of bummed out about that, but we were just kids. Overall, it was fun. We had a good time."

Karolyn's *Rio Grande* adventure didn't end with the fireworks, however. On a DC-4 flight back to California, the aircraft encountered a severe storm. The plane bumped and rocked, scaring Karolyn mightily.

This was soon-to-be 10-year-old Karolyn's look during RIO GRANDE, in which she played Margaret Mary, the military post schoolteacher's daughter. As when she was much younger, the photographer who shot these pictures aimed to depict Karolyn in a more than one facial expression.

"I wasn't afraid we would crash and die or anything," she says. "I was afraid of getting sick." It was a fear she had developed at a younger age after a car trip to the mountains during which she had thrown up on the lap of a friend and her dad had become livid. "It just became the most horrible thing in the world for me to throw up." So on the California flight, she sucked on a lemon, which she'd been told prevented motion sickness. Taunting her, Pat Wayne "ran up and down the aisles eating chocolate candy bars and oranges. Then he threw up all over his dad and John Ford, and I had the last laugh."

In August 1950, just weeks after returning from Utah, Karolyn was slated to begin work on her next feature. But the death of the mother of the movie's lead actress, Judy Canova, delayed filming until November. In the interim, as the *Rio Grande* filming receded into Karolyn's memory, the reality of her mother's disease lurched into view.

On an early autumn day, 41-year-old Martha walked out of her house on Ridgely Drive to hang a basket of wet wash on a clothesline. As her small frame negotiated the steep back steps, however, she slipped and landed on her tailbone – hard.

The fall sent shooting pain through her body. She apparently had jolted the nerve center of her spine. In a Nov. 9 letter to her sister Myrtle in Iowa, with an uncharacteristic wavering hand, punctuation errors and other lapses, Martha's low-key description of the fall and its aftermath is chilling:

> **No one was around so I finally got my breathe and hobbled in house and went to bed for one week I went around like I was punch drunk doing things so crazy I thought I was losing my mind.**
>
> **The next week I went to a Ph.D. He said I almost broke my spine in tow and I was suffering from a nervous shock to the my nervous system.**
>
> **I have had two treatment and he said I would have to have 2 more $10 a treatment I'm feeling much better. He said I'm amazed I could walk after a blow to my spine I injured the cord and have had fever in my spine for weeks. He said if I wasn't better that week he would send me to hospital I was better thought Guess I'm lucky not be be in a cast. . . . I'm slowly coming to my sences.**

Whether the early effects of Martha's illness contributed to the fall, or whether the fall hastened the march of the deadly disease, or both, the gradual decline in Martha's physical and mental capabilities – including what she could do to advance her daughter's film career – had begun.

Martha probably tried, successfully at first, to hide from Karolyn the signs of her weakened condition. But the severity of Martha's injury was immediately clear to Don and Nancy Gates, grocery workers and family friends who recall playing a round of miniature golf with Karolyn's parents about a month after the back-porch accident and returning to the Grimes house for dessert.

"We had heard about her fall, and we were really afraid," says Nancy, "When we were back over at their house, Martha cut us all a piece of pie, but when she carried the plates in to us, her left thumb was right in the pie, and she didn't even know it. I thought that was so strange, and when I told her, she said her whole hand was numb. There must have been nerve damage."

While they knew there was "something very wrong with Martha," the Gates could not persuade her to see anyone other than her general practitioner. "So we just watched her gradually deteriorate," says Nancy.

Martha's debilitation did not prevent her from chaperoning Karolyn during that November's filming of *Honeychile*, a homespun musical comedy produced by

On an early autumn day, 38-year-old Martha walked out of her house on Ridgely Drive to hang a basket of wet wash on a clothesline.

As her small frame negotiated the steep back steps, however, she slipped and landed on her tailbone – hard.

Republic Pictures, the same studio that made *Rio Grande*. The movie represented a step down in prestige, but it also offered Karolyn a part longer than any she would ever experience again, billing her sixth and putting her on the screen for 15 scenes that fill more than 20 of the film's 90 minutes.

A jelly sandwich in one hand, Karolyn, as Effie, talks to Judy Canova's boyfriend Joe on the phone, in HONEYCHILE. Joe is played by Alan Hale Jr., better known decades later as the Skipper in the television comedy GILLIGAN'S ISLAND.

The movie is largely a vehicle for Canova, a popular comedienne, yodeler, radio star and actress during the 1930s and World War II years, whose zany characterizations were a precursor to those of Martha Raye and Carol Burnett. Canova plays herself in this amiable effort, set in the fictitious town of Cactus Junction, Wyoming, but filmed on a studio backlot. The writer of the color movie's title song, the Canova character is pursued by Eddie (Eddie Foy Jr.), a New York music publishing executive whose firm has mistakenly pressed 200,000 records of "Honeychile" under another writer's name. The company hopes to avoid trouble by buying the song from Canova for a paltry $50, as the executive tries to win Canova's favor by undermining her romance with fiancé Joe Boyd (Alan Hale Jr., the skipper of later *Gilligan's Island* fame), for whom the song is written. By the end, after a string of Canova songs, a barrel of slapstick gags and puns and a frenetic horse-drawn wagon race between Boyd and Canova, every character in this predictable cornball flick is happy.

Karolyn's role is that of Effie, Canova's efficient, if absent-minded, niece. Her main function is to help keep things on track for the household of her whirlwind aunt.

Karolyn's role is that of Effie, Canova's efficient, if absent-minded, niece. Her main function is to help keep things on track for the household of her whirlwind aunt: wrapping a birthday present, announcing the arrival of Eddie the "city dude," answering the phone, fighting over a guest's hat and seeing that a blacksmith fixes a crooked horseshoe. Unfortunately for Canova, however, at one point Effie hands her aunt a brand-new party dress to use in cleaning up a mess on the kitchen floor. Along with Larry, her on-screen younger brother, Effie also listens and gazes contentedly at Canova during each of the star's four song sequences, including, predictably, a nightgown-in-bed scene.

Honeychile contains a couple of other coincidental, oblique references to Karolyn's previous film roles. At one point, Eddie, the publisher's executive, comments on Canova's perfume, which she identifies as "Albuquerque #5." Later, Joe Boyd lets on that he once acted in a school play, as an angel.

The most substantial segment for Karolyn, one that explicitly influences the course of the action, comes mid-way through the film. In this turning-point scene Effie persuades Canova to intentionally lose her impending race with Boyd, for reasons rooted decidedly in the pre-feminist era:

> *"Aunt Judy," Effie says. "You remember when you beat Joe in the wagon race last year? He got so mad, you and him didn't speak to each other for a month. I just been thinkin'."*
>
> *"He just said he wanted me to enter," offers Canova.*
>
> *"But I'll bet he doesn't want you to win," Effie responds. "You know, what he said was right, Aunt Judy, I mean about wearing the pants in the family. Men don't like for women to beat 'em at anything. If you win again –"*
>
> *"But he's liable to beat me, fair and square," Canova says.*
>
> *"You better see that he does – that is, if you still want to marry him."*
>
> *"You know something, Effie," says Canova, breaking into a grin, "you're a pretty smart young-un!"*

As Karolyn now notes, at age 10 in that film she was quickly turning into a not-so-young-un. "I developed early, and I'd started to hit the awkward stage by that film," she says. "The baby fat starts going away, you get big hips and you don't fit anywhere. I was starting to shape up, shall we say, and my mother had made a binder for my breasts. In fact, I'll never forget the first time she took me shopping for a bra. She didn't really want to, but she knew it was to the point where she had to, because I couldn't wear those little dresses anymore. Even the binder didn't help."

Not only were her physical changes problematic, but roles also started drying up for girls entering their early teen years.

"I was getting a little old to be in some parts, and too little to be in other parts," she says. "They wanted either little kids or adults. Today, even the television sit-coms have pre-teens, and that's great, but in those days, they didn't have that. You were either too old or too young, and that was before girls were allowed to wear pants. They wore dresses all the time. Well, at that age in a dress, you looked like a big cow – and yet you weren't really old enough. You go through the uglies. You've got these big teeth. For boys, the voice changes, and then there are the pimples. It happens. It's just a really bad stage in life."

Playing a farm girl in *Honeychile*, Karolyn, like her "Aunt Judy" in the film, got away with wearing pants in some instances, including a scene she remembers well in which she and Canova try to pry a pail off the head of her screen brother Larry. "I think we probably did that 30 times before we got that right." Karolyn also recalls camera operators catching the action from "20 different angles" as she and her screen brother listened to Canova sing the mock opera tune "R-a-g-g-m-o-p-p" and an ice-cream-truck ditty called "Tutti Frutti."

The singing scenes required extra concentration, she says, because her attention was mandated to be rapt. "I was taught not to look at anything but the star or what I was supposed to do," she says, "I can't remember seeing the camera crew and equipment, because if you look at what's going on around you, you lose your focus and forget your lines, and you don't remember what they tell you to do. You have to be disciplined not to do that, so I never did, not ever."

Her hair mostly braidless but nevertheless coifed in her trademark pair of buns, Karolyn appears in five different costumes through the film, ranging from a frilly dress to a country combination of plaid shirt and gabardine riding pants. Though it barely shows up in the movie's final scene, Karolyn fondly recalls a fancy

'They wanted either little kids or adults. Today, even the television sit-coms have pre-teens, and that's great, but in those days, they didn't have that. You were either too old or too young. . . .

'You go through the uglies. You've got these big teeth. For boys, the voice changes, and then there are the pimples. It happens. It's just a really bad stage in life.'

cowgirl outfit she donned. Decked out in scarf, boots and a white broad-brim hat, she wore a green suede dress with white fringe – a get-up that, despite her "uglies," became her favorite costume from the film.

Karolyn's work in *Honeychile* netted her favorable comments when the film was reviewed upon its release on Nov. 12, 1951. *The Hollywood Reporter* said she and nine others "stand out in a commendable supporting cast." *Motion Picture Daily* stated that Canova received "good support" from Karolyn and six others, and *Variety* listed her among half a dozen also-rans who offer "effective contributions."

But what was visible to the public masked the private reality of Karolyn's family life. Martha was going downhill fast. In another letter to her sister Myrtle, dated Jan. 17, 1951, Martha announced, in shaky lettering, their purchase of a first television set, adding:

> **As you can see, I'm not over my fall I can sew a lick my hand don't cooperate at all when we get caught up. . . . I guess trying some more treatments on my spine. . . . I don't know whether you can read this or not I find it so hard to do my back gets so tired.**

For Don and Nancy Gates, Martha's decline became painful to witness. "Each time we saw her, it got worse," says Nancy. "At first, she was limping. I would say, 'What did the doctor tell you?' and she would say, 'Oh, he just says that I bent my tailbone.' Then I noticed when she'd sit down, she sat to one side, so she definitely had a very sore spot there. Then when she had no feeling in her fingers and her whole arm was numb and she wore it in a sling for awhile, it worried me to death that she wouldn't get a second opinion."

While Martha's ordeal was to touch her daughter indelibly, Karolyn knew little of it at the outset – or at least she didn't allow herself to acknowledge it.

While Martha's ordeal was to touch her daughter indelibly, Karolyn knew little of it at the outset – or at least she didn't allow herself to acknowledge it. The following story, told to her years later by relatives, reveals much about how Karolyn coped with her mother's illness.

In the spring of 1951, following Martha's accident the previous fall, Myrtle drove out from

Martha, clearly in her horticultural element, stands with Karolyn in a fair garden in Pomona, east of Los Angeles, during an October 1950 outing with LaVan. It was just three months after the filming of RIO GRANDE, one month before the shooting of HONEYCHILE and about the same time that the 41-year-old mother took the fall that hastened a decline in her health.

Independence, Iowa, to visit her sister in California. While Myrtle was present, Martha underwent a series of medical tests. The results were not good. A written diagnosis, dated May 3, 1951, confirmed the worst: "cerebral atrophy." Myrtle and LaVan talked over the situation, then sat Karolyn down on a bed and out of the earshot of Martha to tell her that her mother was going to die. Karolyn doesn't remember any of the conversation. She thinks she blocked it out of her mind.

Nevertheless, it was clear to LaVan and Myrtle that Martha's health had deteriorated to the point where the inevitable conclusion also was unavoidable. In order for Martha to see her family one last time while she was marginally coherent and physically able, LaVan lined up a five-week family vacation to Osceola from mid-May to late June, much longer than the two-week annual excursions to Missouri that Karolyn and her parents had taken during previous summers. A one-paragraph story, headlined "Movie Actress Here," appeared with a photo of Karolyn on the front page of the May 31, 1951, *St. Clair County Courier*. It mentioned Karolyn's recent films and the family's five-week visit but avoided any reference to Martha's sickness.

When they returned to California, LaVan brought back the first in a series of caretakers who looked after Martha at home on weekdays while LaVan did his grocery work and coached their church's boys basketball team. While Karolyn occasionally attended to her mother, most of the duties were the job of the caretaker.

Karolyn knew that her mother deserved compassionate treatment, and today she regrets not having made a serious effort at the time to tend to some of Martha's needs. "I should have waited on her, hand and foot," she says.

But as a pre-teen in the presence of her mother's debilitation, Karolyn understandably felt jealous of the attention LaVan increasingly paid to Martha. One example of LaVan's well-meaning indulgences for Martha was his making sure during each December that Martha had at least one more present under the family Christmas tree than did Karolyn, which infuriated their daughter. Embarrassed at the prospect of friends seeing Martha, Karolyn steered them clear of her home. When she interacted with her mother, Karolyn sometimes made fun of her, asked her to repeat sentences and acted as if she couldn't understand her.

In part, Karolyn's mixed emotions toward Martha stemmed from frustrations over the absence of attention she needed and wanted from her. As Martha's condition worsened, Karolyn's clothing and hair became unkempt. At one point, a neighbor across the street who had watched her walk to and from school every day and had noted her unattended clothing, stopped her one day and offered to hem her skirts.

Inexorably, Martha's attention became more sporadic and less intelligible. That much is clear to Karolyn when she recalls dealing with her first menstrual periods. It was at the relatively young age of 11, when Karolyn was going into sixth grade. One night, scared she was bleeding to death, Karolyn ran to her mother. She took Karolyn into a closet, closed the door and told her that this was a woman's curse, during which a woman could not eat mayonnaise or fish and could not help during the canning of fruits and vegetables because the food would become contaminated.

How much of this "advice" her mother truly believed and how much was a result of her illness Karolyn doesn't know. Whatever the answer, Martha never taught Karolyn how to use sanitary napkins, so at first Karolyn ran around unprotected during school recesses, her flow often staining her dresses. When she came home in bloody attire, her mother's caretaker chastised her, but Karolyn didn't really care.

One night, scared she was bleeding to death, Karolyn ran to her mother.

She took Karolyn into a closet, closed the door and told her that this was a woman's curse, during which a woman could not eat mayonnaise or fish and could not help during the canning of fruits and vegetables because the food would become contaminated.

"Maybe I resented the fact I didn't really have a mother anymore," Karolyn says. "It wasn't her [Martha's] fault, but there was just so much in me that never got played out. We didn't talk about it. Everything was taken for granted, and you just went on with life. That's how life was from then on. I just sort of had to stumble through and find my own way."

That remained the case with her film acting, too, as apparently Karolyn was not getting enough help from her agent, Sid Gold. A letter saved by Martha indicates that she terminated Karolyn's contract with Gold on Aug. 2, 1951, because Karolyn had not been offered work during the previous six months. Eventually, Karolyn returned to Lola Moore's representation.

It was as Karolyn approached the age of 12 that she interviewed for *Hans Christian Andersen*, the semi-biographical fairy tale starring Danny Kaye. "Before I tried out for that part, my mother had me take German accent coaching," Karolyn says. Over and over, Karolyn remembers repeating for the coach, "Giff me, please, a piece of choe-coe-LATT." Whether that training impressed the filmmakers at the time is unknown. "I just don't think I was that good," Karolyn says modestly. "I think I was cute as a little kid, but I think it stopped there."

This certificate of Karolyn's from 1952 was typical of the kind of records the schools were required to keep on underage actors.

Whatever her adolescent shortcomings may have been, Karolyn did win a role in the fanciful musical, a color children's tale filmed in May 1952 and released by RKO the following Nov. 25. Karolyn has an unbilled, self-described "blink your eye and you miss me" part, as an unnamed waif – visibly more mature than in *Honeychile* – who lyrically tries to sell her wares to the mythical storyteller on the streets of Copenhagen. In her 10 seconds of screen time, she walks past Hans and his protégé, looks into their eyes and sings in a melancholy minor key, "Matches, matches, please buy my matches, matches . . ."

So closed a moviemaking career that might be called meteoric. It spanned 12 years and at least 16 films whose themes, actors and settings could not have been more diverse. The innocence of Karolyn's face and voice darted into several of the best-regarded American movies from the mid-1940s through the early 1950s, only to depart abruptly from the big screen.

While the strain of her mother's illness ended Karolyn's acting in feature films, Karolyn managed to keep her hand in the trade via the rapidly growing field of television. But the records of Karolyn's appearances on the small screen are the sketchiest of all her Hollywood artifacts, most likely due to her mother's deteriorating condition.

The July 10, 1952, script for a one-minute TV commercial that the 12-year-old made on July 24 and 25, 1952, does survive, however. It's a typical early-TV spot for a then-new breakfast cereal. The commercial stars Karolyn, a boy named Jimmy Bates and none other than actor George Reeves, who played television's Man of Steel:

> *"Now," says an announcer, "Sugar Smacks invites you to meet Clark Kent, the star of 'Superman.'"*
>
> *Clark, holding a box of Sugar Smacks at the back of a house, speaks to the camera: "My friends inside are having a very interesting talk – interesting because it's about my favorite subject, Kellogg's Sugar Smacks. Listen . . ."*
>
> *In the kitchen of the house, a boy and girl are at the breakfast table, where sit three bowls and a box of Sugar Smacks.*
>
> *"But sis," says the boy, "what's the extra bowl for?"*
>
> *"It's for Superman," says the girl, "in case he stops in for breakfast!"*
>
> *Clark opens the door, pokes his head in. "Hi, kids!"*
>
> *"Hi, Clark," says the boy.*
>
> *"Come in, Clark!" says the girl. "You're just in time for Sugar Smacks!"*
>
> *Clark approaches the table. "I see you have a place all set," he says. "Were you expecting me?"*
>
> *"Naw," says the boy. "Sis here decided to set a place for Superman."*
>
> *"Well, what's wrong with that?" asks the girl. "After all, Sugar Smacks is the cereal Superman says is best!"*
>
> *"That's right," says Clark. "Say, do you suppose it'll be all right if I sit here?"*
>
> *"Sure, Clark," says the boy. "After all, even Superman couldn't be in every home that has Kellogg's Sugar Smacks!"*
>
> *Clark picks up the box and turns to the camera. "He's right," Clark says, "all over the country, kids and grownups are discovering the most exciting new cereal ever made, Kellogg's Sugar Smacks! You'll like it, too."*

Karolyn was paid $140 for her two days of work on the commercial, but this was not one of Karolyn's better performances, as she recalls. It came at a time when her mother no longer was able to accompany her to such appointments. With her dad, a reluctant, replacement stage "mom," watching from the side, Karolyn uncharacteristically flubbed her lines flat-out, take after take. "The boy playing my younger brother asked me, 'Aren't you embarrassed at what you're doing?' 'No,' I said flippantly. 'No, I don't care.' I remember that well, because even though I didn't say it, I really was embarrassed that I'd done so badly. My father, who got time off work to take me to this one, never said a word, but I knew he was embarrassed, too. I really felt bad."

Owing to her father's disinterest in the Hollywood scene and his inability to simultaneously work as a grocery manager, care for Martha and spend any significant time looking after his daughter, Karolyn's acting stints dwindled during the next couple of years. The disintegration of her career didn't trouble her in the least, however. Contrary to today's glamorous image of idolized, sought-after child actors, life at the big studios was mainly work to Karolyn, something she had done since before she could remember, nothing unusual or vaunted for a child in Hollywood, and something she felt no hunger to continue. Her attentions

So closed a moviemaking career that might be called meteoric.

It spanned 12 years and at least 16 films whose themes, actors and settings could not have been more diverse.

The innocence of Karolyn's face and voice darted into several of the best-regarded American movies from the mid-1940s through the early 1950s, only to depart abruptly from the big screen.

and cares had turned to her relationships with other teens. The shedding of her ties to screen acting amounted to a shrug.

"I didn't think about it much one way or the other," she recalls. "By then, I had friends, and I'd gotten into a social group because I wasn't working very much, and I kind of liked that. Besides, I had discovered boys."

Her mother's deterioration indirectly touched off Karolyn's involvement with the opposite sex at a much earlier age than she now thinks it should have begun. Because of Martha's plight, LaVan became less attentive to and more lenient toward Karolyn. By the fall of 1952, when Karolyn entered seventh grade at Louis Pasteur Junior High School, he allowed her to date boys in cars, and it was only a matter of months before she lost her virginity to the son of the head of a studio makeup department.

"I started having relations because it seemed like everybody was having relations in those days in California," she says. "The pace was fast, and that's the way it was. I was a normal teen-ager, and it turned out that I loved sex."

Karolyn says she "petted and necked a lot" as an early teen-ager. But while she sometimes likes to let people think she was intimate with hordes of boys then, she says there were only three such partners – an approach that today might be called serial monogamy. "There was a relationship of sorts with each one," she says. "It wasn't like 'with the football team,' you know what I mean? But I was loose. In a small town, it would have been terrible, but in California, it didn't make any difference. I had boys everywhere."

The favorite setting for teen-age romance, as in any town, big or small, was wherever a car could be parked in a secluded spot. The preferred lover's lanes for Karolyn and her succession of boyfriends quickly became Baldwin Hills and Mulholland Drive, both of which provided lots of winding roadways and scenic turnouts from which the lights of the city could be seen. There, under the moonlight in a variety of vehicles, Karolyn and her dates experimented with the ways of physical love.

LaVan's role in Karolyn's early extracurricular sexual education was one of benign neglect. Not that he didn't care, but LaVan, ever the "ladies man" himself, certainly didn't try to halt his daughter's behavior. As Karolyn puts it, "I'm sure I didn't quite fulfill my dad's dreams for me, but he hardly ever said anything," she says.

Her father's stance toward her liaisons surely stirred some confusion in Karolyn's mind. "Sometimes he would even help me out," she says. "There would be two boys I was interested in. I'd get a date with one, and then somebody better would call me. So I'd say yes to him, too – I was terrible – and they'd both come to my house at the same time, and I'd make my dad take care of it for me and get rid of one.

"It was awful, but he was always real good about it. I can hear him warning me, 'Karolyn, I'm not going to do this for you anymore.' But he kept on bailing me out. He probably should have made me deal with my messes, but he was a very kind man. He wasn't a fool, either. He knew that I was having sex with these boys."

Because of Martha's plight, LaVan became less attentive to and more lenient toward Karolyn.

By the fall of 1952, when Karolyn entered seventh grade at Louis Pasteur Junior High School, he allowed her to date boys in cars, and it was only a matter of months before she lost her virginity to the son of the head of a studio makeup department.

One boy in particular (the only one of her three junior high lovers whom she would like to see again), apparently triggered LaVan's generosity to the same degree that he touched Karolyn's heart.

"He was an Italian boy who was already out of school," says Karolyn. "He was part of a Catholic family with a lot of kids, and his dad got hurt in an accident. It was in the day before disability insurance and workers' compensation, so my father gave them special deals at his grocery store. They used food stamps because they had to go on welfare, and my dad kept it a secret. He was just that kind of guy.

"Well, the boy I was going with from this family had to leave and go back east to Rochester, New York, and work for the family so that he could support his dad and all the kids. My dad knew that I'd be broken-hearted that he was going to leave, so the day before he left, my dad told me I didn't have to go to school that day, and I could spend the day with him, knowing full well what we were going to do. It didn't turn out quite like that, though. We ended up having a car wreck."

School photos of Karolyn at 12 (left) and 13.

Fortunately, no one was hurt in the accident, but the boy did move away. "I mooned over him and wrote him letters every day for awhile," Karolyn says. "I liked him a lot." Soon, however, Karolyn's letters came less frequently. This prompted the boy to make and send to her a 78-rpm record, which Karolyn still has. On the 10-minute recording, the boy, unaccompanied and in his best imitation-Dean Martin voice, sings "Young and Foolish" (which he labels "our song"), "Kiss Me" and, in Italian, "The Butcher Boy." In 1950s fashion, he touches on cars and hairstyles, but he also "moons" over Karolyn:

> **Hi Kay, this is your dear, departed "husband." . . . Gee, I haven't got mail from you for the last two days, and then I just got one today, and it's only a page. What's happening? You getting lazy or something? Gee, it seems when I get home from work, . . . even before I eat I have to write you a letter. . . .**
>
> **Do you remember when we were going up to the hilltop there, over Laurel Canyon? Gee, I'll never forget that day when we had to get a hamburger in such a hurry, and taking that turn about 80 and missing that rock. Sure glad I missed it. Most of all I miss you. . . .**
>
> **What I said about me coming back to L.A., well, it depends on my father, because if I treat him good . . . he'll treat us good by giving us his blessing. . . . I know I will be coming back when work slows up, but we'll just have to wait to make it. . . .**
>
> **I'll send this record special delivery. You know I love you, and I hope you love me, too.**

'Gee, I'll never forget that day when we had to get a hamburger in such a hurry, and taking that turn about 80 and missing that rock.

'Sure glad I missed it. Most of all I miss you.'

Boyfriend, in a message to Karolyn on a 78-rpm phonograph record

The boy's recorded sentiments did reach Karolyn's soul. "I would have married him," she says today, with a sigh, "but I was a teen-ager, he was gone, and somebody else came along. You know, out of sight, out of mind? So I had my dad call him long distance and tell him that I couldn't go with him anymore.

"In some ways, I was just mean to my dad. I was just a teen-age witch. It was

As the child of a large metropolitan area, 13-year-old Karolyn was well-accustomed to large groups of teens as she attended the Los Angeles County conference of Junior High Christian Endeavor, held August 8-15, 1953, at Tahquitz Pines.

like I was living on PMS. I can remember telling him things like, 'Everybody else is doing it. Why can't I go?' He'd surely end up letting me go. It was stupid. He should never have let me do any of that."

Along with her mother's disease and boys, Karolyn occasionally occupied her junior-high mind with academics. From the solid B's of her elementary years, her academic performance dipped to the B-minus/C-plus level. Despite her love of music, Karolyn fluctuated between A's and C's in orchestra, although she did serve as the group's concert mistress. She continued to earn lesser marks in math, physical education, science and social studies, and she fared no better in typically all-female home economics.

Outside of school, Karolyn remained active in her church's Christian Endeavor activities and kept her interest in ice skating, but opportunities also arose occasionally for jobs on TV shows and commercials. Swamped at the store, her father sometimes asked Don Gates or a church friend to take Karolyn to the tryout appointments.

Because Karolyn recalls little of her television work, the scraps that Martha saved, corroborated by fleeting references from library archives, provide only incomplete glimpses of the teen's TV acting.

In the half-hour show, she was reunited with Thomas Mitchell, who played Uncle Billy in It's a Wonderful Life.

Twenty-one pages of a May 9, 1953, script from Frank Wisbar Productions include a major role for a 10-year-old girl named Cassy, the daughter of a well-read drunkard and an uneducated mother who reveres him. Whether Karolyn acted in this domestic drama – identified as "Production No. 5314" and titled *Jason* – is unknown. The same is true for four tattered pages of undated, unidentified script that Martha preserved from another production.

Karolyn did act, however, on Dec. 1, 1953, as a character named Mary Burke in an acclaimed Ford Theatre TV drama called *Good of His Soul*, which aired in March 1954. She was sixth-billed and paid $70 for a day's work. And in the half-hour show, she was reunited with Thomas Mitchell, who played Uncle Billy in *It's a Wonderful Life*. Mitchell stars as an aged priest who gives up his office to a younger man and, likewise, loses his last companion, a collie dog named Spot, to a boy played by Tommy Rettig (who later starred as the boyhood master of a more famous collie in the *Lassie* TV series). A critic for *Daily Variety* called Mitchell's "the best telepix performance of the year" while offering perfunctory praise for Karolyn and the other supporting actors, noting they were "more contributory than functional."

A baffling $35 pay stub dated Nov. 4, 1954, is evidence that Karolyn worked in another TV program, a production for Cincinnati-based Ziv Productions labeled only as "Fireside #132," presumably part of the Fireside Theatre anthology. Also, a federal tax withholding statement from 1954 indicates she was paid $39.50 by the Lever Brothers Co., presumably for work in a TV commercial.

Today, Karolyn remembers no details of these television jobs. Nor can she summon what it was like to audition for a continuing role on the popular Walt Disney children's television show, *The Mickey Mouse Club*, other than the fact that she did.

Her blanked-out memory of the TV work reflects not only her waning interest in acting and her dad's heavy work schedule, but also – and most important – her mother's rapidly worsening situation. As it quickened and steepened, the drop in Martha's health complicated every aspect of Karolyn's life.

"Early on, my mother was cognizant of things. She would laugh when we laughed," Karolyn says. "Then there was a period when she screamed, and then one when she would grit her teeth. She wore diapers, there were odors, the house smelled all the time, and I'm not sure she knew what was going on."

Beverly Vannice, Karolyn's childhood friend, recalls that on her occasional visits with her family to the Grimes house, Karolyn was "really loving and kind toward her mother when her mother was acting a little strange or just being completely tuned out to everything. I certainly picked up from Karolyn that that was a hard position to be in. She would cover for her mother by saying, 'Mom hasn't been feeling so good today, and she was better a little while ago.'"

Karolyn's memories of her own behavior toward her mother are not quite so charitable.

"I didn't do the right things. I said hurtful things. I didn't get up and run her into the bathroom when she needed it. That was a rotten thing to do. I seldom had friends over because I was embarrassed. It's terrible to say, but it's true. I should have felt differently, but I was raised in California, and nothing is ugly there. You don't want to have anything ugly around you. Plus, I was a teen-ager, and teen-agers are pretty uncaring sometimes, and I was no worse than any other teen-ager."

On Sept. 22, 1954, doctors determined that Martha had fallen into spastic paralysis. By this time, and for the next three months, the daily routine at home wrenched Karolyn's emotions. Each morning, LaVan woke up, placed Martha in a living room chair and went to work at the grocery while his wife watched television all day. LaVan was the only one who could get Martha to eat, so when he returned home from work, he fed her baby food. Then he and the caretaker cleaned her and put her to bed. In Karolyn's teen-age eyes, her mother had become a thing – no longer a person, a vegetable.

LaVan took his wife's situation "just as sincere as anybody could under the circumstances," says his friend Perry Vannice. "He knew that her chances were nil, and I'm sure what was running through his mind was, 'Why is she having to stay so long?' It was a real bad time."

Martha lived her last days at home, withering to what Karolyn recalls as a few dozen pounds and spending every night with LaVan in the bed in which they had always slept. On Dec. 19, 1954, doctors' diagnosis was cardio-respiratory

Her blanked-out memory of the TV work reflects not only her waning interest in acting and her dad's heavy work schedule, but also – and most important – her mother's rapidly worsening situation.

As it quickened and steepened, the drop in Martha's health complicated every aspect of Karolyn's life.

insufficiency. Then, two days before Christmas, at age 45, Martha died.

The somber funeral for Martha at Forest Lawn Memorial Park, where Karolyn was the "Dove Girl" seven years earlier, drew family members from 1,800 miles away in Missouri. It represented the final punctuation mark for a woman's life cut short – a life once fast-paced that had relentlessly evaporated over the past seven years. The mood around the Grimes house was downbeat. The normally gregarious LaVan set the tone, and as Perry Vannice puts it, "When Martha passed on, Grimes just kind of put everything away. Around me, it just seemed like he had a problem and he was able to cope with it. Instead of letting everybody know how bad he felt, he just kind of sealed it up."

Still, LaVan retained his affable personality, especially with the opposite sex. Karolyn recalls that during her mother's last years and after her death, LaVan did not lack for female attention. "Women hung off of him all the time," she says, adding that she has no doubt that her father engaged in more than one affair while Martha was in the final stages of her disease.

LaVan's penchant for joking stayed intact as well. Perry recalls that one night not long after Martha's death, LaVan showed up on the Vannices' doorstep. Perry was working, and his wife Ruth was alone in the house. "He came to the door and knocked big and loud. Ruth said, 'Who is it?' and Grimes said, 'Aw, it doesn't make any difference. Open the door.' Well, that just about scared the tail off Ruth. Then finally, she peeked out through the window and saw that it was Grimes. She was about to skin him alive. She told him, 'Don't you never do that again, Grimes!' LaVan shot back, 'Well, I didn't know it was going to scare you, and I thought you would know who it was if I knocked that big and loud.' He was always such a clown."

After Martha's death, life also went on for Karolyn – and for Karolyn, life meant boys. Nothing else was a close second. Her teen-age obsession is obvious from several so-called "slam books" that Karolyn has saved from her ninth-grade year. A slam book was a steno notebook with each page graced with a question or topic at the top and a series of numbers down the left-hand side. Friends allocated numbers to each other and answered each question on each page on the assigned line. Looking at any one page shows the most popular answers for any one question, and collecting all of one person's answers from multiple pages produces a verbal snapshot of the participant. Questions and Karolyn's answers from a slam book from February and March of 1955 reveal a Karolyn stuck on boys but coveting a bit of privacy and discretion as well:

After Martha's death, life also went on for Karolyn – and for Karolyn, life meant boys. Nothing else was a close second.

Nickname? Katie

Boyfriend? Dominick Anthony Scira, Jr.

Steady? Yes. I love him.

Want to break up? No, no, no, no, no, no.

Dreamboat? Marlon Brando.

Want to marry? Yes.

How many children do you want? Four.

Where do you want to live? New York.

What kind of house to live in? Chinese modern.

School? Stinks.

Karolyn's ninth-grade class at Louis Pasteur Junior High School, gathering on the front steps in September 1955, numbered more than 430 students.

Hobby? Ice skating.

Favorite song? "The Little White Cloud that Cried."

Favorite color? Blue.

Worst color? Pea green.

A penny for your thoughts? CENSORED.

How far have you gone with a person of the opposite sex? Far enough! (I am a prude.)

For all her raging hormones, Karolyn retained a sense of innocence and fantasy during her junior high years. While she listened faithfully with her friends to popular disc jockey Wolfman Jack on the radio, she also enjoyed classical music such as "Scheherazade" and the instrumental ballet "Slaughter on Tenth Avenue." The 78s and 45s she played on her tiny, suitcase-like record player in her room leaned more to the slow ballads of Johnny Ray ("The Little White Cloud" of her slam book, and "Cry"), Doris Day ("Secret Love") and Nat King Cole ("Mona Lisa") than anything uptempo.

For all her raging hormones, Karolyn retained a sense of innocence and fantasy during her junior high years.

"My friends could dance, and they did the be-bop, the hop and all the different things," she says, "but I never was a dancer, so I didn't like fast music. I went for the schmaltzy stuff. To me, it was the emotion. I liked to feel love and romance and fantasize into another world, even for just a minute."

The same sense of escape was reflected in the movies that enthralled her in junior high. However, besides Flash Gordon serials and a 1953 science-fiction cult classic, *The War of the Worlds*, Karolyn cannot recall the names of her favorites of the time, largely because when she went to films, most often it was on single or double dates to a nearby drive-in theater. "It was always a massive petting session, and we never saw a film through to the end," she says with a laugh.

Like any teen, Karolyn idolized her share of celebrities, including the Indian film actor Sabu, the turbaned organist Korla Pandit ("His eyes could mesmerize me") and teen actor Sal Mineo. But the one who sent her pulse off the register was the young Tony Curtis, who had broken into the movie scene in his 20s as Karolyn was going through junior high. "It was his looks," she says. "I used to buy movie magazines and cut out his pictures and slap them up on my bedroom walls. It was him forever. Even when he married Janet Leigh [in 1951], it didn't break my heart. I just thought she was an awfully lucky woman."

Perhaps surprisingly, given this otherwise typical teen-age star worship, Karolyn did not think of movies in the context of her own film work over the past decade. It was as if she were almost trying to convince herself that it never happened.

"I was so self-centered about having a normal life and having friends that I didn't want to think about that other stuff," she says. "What was important to me at the time was that I have friends and that I was looking for love."

The celebrity who sent Karolyn's pulse off the register was the young Tony Curtis.

'It was his looks. I used to buy movie magazines and cut out his pictures and slap them up on my bedroom walls. It was him forever.'

More underlay the gradual deadening of her connection to film and TV work, though, including her lessening ability to get a role and the embarrassment of doing a poor job when she did land one. "Maybe I didn't want to be put under that kind of pressure, so I put it out of my thoughts," she says. "I became afraid to want the parts. You couldn't want them badly because you might not get them, but you still had to deal with the pain of rejection. Because of the pain, I couldn't love it, so I had to quit.

"Rejection is not really fun, and all my life as a child I strove to please others. I still do in everyday life. It's a bad habit, and I get into a lot of trouble trying to do that, but I was raised that way, always striving to make somebody smile or to do good. There's nothing really wrong with that, but the problem is that I don't know how to put limits on it."

Two months after Karolyn's June 1955 graduation from Louis Pasteur Junior High, she and LaVan took the traditional vacation to Osceola by themselves. This summer trip, more than any of the others, deepened her distance from the movie life.

Along with the usual family visits in and around Osceola, Karolyn befriended her 14-year-old cousin Gail Taylor, who helped Karolyn get to know a few of the local boys their age. As might be expected, LaVan's goofy personality enlivened the proceedings. "He would deal these boys fits every time they'd come by," Gail says of LaVan. "He'd tell them, 'The girls aren't here. You can't go with the girls, but I'll go with you boys, and we'll just have a gay old time.' He was just real jovial, real spontaneous and a lot of fun to be with."

So, too, was his daughter Karolyn. "She was giggly and vibrant, and she could act silly," says Gail, whose family had just moved to Osceola from Independence, just outside of Kansas City. "She and I were both from metropolitan areas, so we made up names for a lot of the guys in Osceola because, to us, they were kind of hickish."

During that trip, Karolyn became strongly attached to a boy who was to figure prominently in her later life, Hal Barnes, son of Marie and Marion Barnes, childhood friends of Karolyn's parents. Her crush came from a rural thrill the two shared one night. Hal, who at 16 was a year older than Karolyn, took her for an exhilarating, late-evening ride on an old horse he owned, the first time Karolyn had ever ridden such a swift, graceful animal. "I was in front with Hal holding me," Karolyn says, "and goodness sakes, I was on a horse with a boy, and we were running that horse so fast in the wind at night. It was the most exciting feeling, and he made me feel like an expert horsewoman."

Overconfident as a result of the heady episode, back in California that summer at a church camp, Karolyn volunteered to ride the camp's fastest horse solo down the side of a mountain. She lost control of the horse's ever-increasing pace, a tree branch knocked her to the ground and the horse trampled her legs. Karolyn was rushed to a hospital by ambulance, and her recovery took months.

While at church camp, Karolyn received a keepsake in the mail – a charming letter written by her father. Despite her waywardness and his inattention at that point in their lives, the letter, dated Aug. 23, 1955, paints a homey picture, complete with Karolyn's Chihuahua named Cisco. It also reflects the warm father/daughter love that remained between LaVan and Karolyn following Martha's death:

LaVan hugs his 15-year-old daughter in the Grimes front yard, early 1956.

> **Dear Darling Daughter:**
>
> **Just received your letter. Sure was tickled to hear from you, as Cisco and I were very lonesome. We were watering the front lawn when the mailman came so I sat down and read Cisco your letter, but he is so drunk I don't think he absorbed much of it.**
>
> **Bet your trip up was fun. Too bad about your purse, but guess the good Lord saw to it that you had money anyway.**
>
> **Sunday I stayed home except to go to church in the morning and out to Harry's and Violet's for supper and Harry's for one o'clock dinner.**
>
> **Monday cleaned home and repaired cleaned and waxed your cedar chest.**
>
> **Today, Tuesday, am planning on going out to get your picture. Then I can have you on the TV set or anywhere I want you all the time.**
>
> **Linda is the only one who has called for you. Several people have called me. Even Guy came by last night and left me a note on the door as I was out eating supper.**
>
> **Andy and Rich came by for a while to visit last night. Gil has been here almost every night since you have been gone.**
>
> **This is as long a letter as I have written for 10 years, but it is to a very, very sweet, nice girl, so have fun, honey, and I will see you sometime Saturday.**
>
> **With my love, Daddy.**
>
> **P.S. Don't forget, I have more letters coming.**

'This is as long a letter as I have written for 10 years, but it is to a very, very sweet, nice girl, so have fun, honey.'

LaVan, writing to Karolyn

By this time, Karolyn had been supervised almost entirely by her father for several years. As her dad's lack of strictness continued, she further lost interest in acting, checking into potential parts only sporadically.

Late in 1955, Karolyn, then 15, went on her final tryout interview, this time for a plum TV role as the girlfriend of Ricky Nelson on *The Adventures of Ozzie & Harriet*. Oddly enough, Jimmy Hawkins, who played Tommy, the youngest Bailey child in *It's a Wonderful Life*, won a part on the popular family sitcom at about the same time, to play Ricky Nelson's friend.

Karolyn never did find out whether she, too, would be hired for the show. A different kind of call intervened. It sent her away from Hollywood for decades.

With terrible force, the telephone call pierced, twisted and lodged in her soul. It changed everything.

Just five months before that Sunday afternoon in February 1956, Karolyn had entered Los Angeles High School, part of a 10th-grade class of 900. Though most of her friends from junior high attended Hamilton High to the west, she was happy and settling into her huge, new academic environment. With a more flexible class schedule, she could take both choir and orchestra. No longer bouncing from public school to studio school to private school and back again, the 15-year-old also was building friendships with other girls and relationships with boys that seemed more meaningful. Her mother had died a little more than a year before, but the effects of that loss were passing with each day, and the discipline forged in Karolyn's childhood film work kept her moving forward with confidence and hope. Her life had begun to stabilize – until the phone call.

Karolyn's father had asked her to accompany him that Sunday on a day trip 120 miles east to Palm Springs in his brand-new 1956 Buick. The outing was tempting. LaVan had just bought the sedan largely at the behest of Karolyn, who had grown tired of the 1945 Kaiser-Frazer he had driven for many years. Along for the ride were four others: a family friend named Helen who clerked in LaVan's Safeway, Helen's husband George and their two children.

More compelling to Karolyn, however, was a pledge tea put on by 'Cajon, the high school sorority she hoped to join. So she and her dad chose to go their separate ways that day. LaVan left in the morning, and in the afternoon Karolyn's then-boyfriend Ray Snodgrass drove her to the tea, held in one of the posh homes in an exclusive neighborhood just off Wilshire Boulevard and near Los Angeles High. While Karolyn recalls little of the tea, what happened afterward seared her memory.

This is the 1956 Buick that LaVan Grimes and four others drove to Palm Springs on the last day of his life.

Ray, several years older than Karolyn and already a high school graduate, picked her up at the tea and drove her home. Waiting for LaVan to return, they sat on the couch and watched television in the living room.

The phone rang, and Karolyn got up to answer it. It was Helen, calling from a hospital east of Los Angeles.

"I have some really sad news," she said. "Your father is dead."

Karolyn thought the phone call must be a prank. Her father, after all, made practical jokes a way of life. In Karolyn's younger years, he liked to clown about his Missouri roots at restaurants by removing the bridgework in his mouth and playing like he was "Mr. Hillbilly." Once, when Karolyn and her mother stood outside a neighborhood Sears store waiting for LaVan to pick them up, he donned

'Just remember that this thing isn't as black as it appears.'

(Karolyn's father's death, her move to Osceola, her late teens, and the beginning of her first marriage, 1956-1959)

an artificial nose and glasses and drove by six times before they figured out who he was. And he often roped others into his antics. Helen, talking of a crash on the highway, surely was a willing participant in a similar spoof.

"Oh, yeah," Karolyn responded dryly. "Sure, right. . . . Tell me another one."

Helen obviously wasn't getting through. She asked to talk to Ray, so Karolyn handed him the receiver. Immediately his face fell, his expression ashen. Karolyn watched as he took down instructions to telephone Karolyn's uncle Clyde, LaVan's brother, in Osceola. The reality began to sink in.

Ray handed the receiver back to Karolyn, and Helen's voice once again imparted the fatal news. Helen, who had broken her arm in the collision, told Karolyn that she and George would arrive as soon as they could and promised to call another of LaVan's employees, Virgil, to come over to wait with her until they arrived. Karolyn hung up the phone and sat stunned.

Her dad was gone.

LaVan – for all his faults and absences, the backbone of Karolyn's life – was now, without warning, a mere memory. (The week before, Karolyn and LaVan saw a movie together, something they rarely did. Eerily, the film was *The High and the Mighty*, an emotional nailbiter starring John Wayne as the pilot of a California-bound airliner full of passengers that is destined to crash.)

Ray picked up the receiver, called his mother and asked her to come over. One by one, people arrived. The first was Virgil who, mistakenly thinking LaVan was still alive, tried to console Karolyn, telling her everything was going to be fine. But Karolyn looked into his eyes and earnestly told him, "My father is dead," and Virgil went to pieces, crying and apologizing. Somehow Karolyn stayed calm for the moment – and for the remainder of the day, even comforting Virgil and others who tried to comfort her.

When George and Helen finally arrived after Helen's broken arm was set, Helen carefully conveyed to Karolyn the circumstances of the accident: With George driving the Buick and LaVan sitting across from him on the passenger side, they were cruising back from Palm Springs. All at once, they hit bumper-to-bumper traffic, George pounced on the brakes, and the Buick inexplicably slid into the oncoming lane and slammed head-on into another car. The impact threw LaVan out of the Buick and onto the road, where another car ran over him. LaVan lay bleeding and, in his last words, told George and Helen, "Take care of Karolyn."

Listening to Helen's recounted details, George paced, fidgeted and agonized, but Karolyn told him, "These things happen." Still, distraught over his role in the collision, George could not understand how Karolyn could not be upset with him or blame him.

"I was probably in a state of shock, but I knew then that I had some kind of guidance," Karolyn says. "I didn't come unglued. There was something within me that let me help them more than they helped me, because I really didn't need it. It was a strange thing."

Her mental state may not have been strange as much as born of experience. The death of a parent was not new to her. Clearly, Karolyn had built inner strength she didn't realize over the seven-year decline and death of her mother.

All at once, they hit bumper-to-bumper traffic, George pounced on the brakes, and the Buick inexplicably slid into the oncoming lane and slammed head-on into another car.

The impact threw LaVan out of the Buick and onto the road, where another car ran over him.

LaVan lay bleeding and, in his last words, told George and Helen, 'Take care of Karolyn.'

Soon, relatives were on their way to Los Angeles. However, Martha's death already had complicated the politics of the Grimes and Motley families, bearing ultimate consequences that no one foresaw.

Upon Martha's death on Dec. 23, 1954, a $2,500 share of the estate of her mother (Karolyn's grandmother), transferred to Karolyn. The grandmother had died in Osceola just a few years earlier. Because Karolyn was underage, she needed a guardian in Missouri to represent her. LaVan called Osceola to ask Martha's brother Everly Motley, the administrator of Martha's mother's estate and one of Karolyn's favorite relatives, to serve as Karolyn's representative. But Everly declined, saying other family members already were angry with him over his handling of the estate. He told LaVan it would not look good to the rest of the family for him to represent Karolyn as well.

Marsha and Clyde Grimes, Karolyn's aunt and uncle, of Osceola, Missouri.

So as a distant second choice, LaVan called his brother Clyde Grimes, asking him to serve in the role of Karolyn's guardian for her grandmother's estate. Clyde, a building contractor, lived in Osceola with his wife Marsha and their adopted daughter Marsha Ann. Clyde agreed to LaVan's request and represented Karolyn's share of the estate. This direct link to Missouri came into play ominously for Karolyn a year later with the sudden collision that killed LaVan.

On the afternoon of her dad's death, Karolyn's first thought about her future was a fearful one – that she might be forced to leave her school and friends and move to Osceola to live with Clyde, Marsha and 8-year-old Marsha Ann. Karolyn's parents, thinking that they were out of their daughter's earshot, had frequently and derisively talked about Marsha and her apparent command over Clyde. So Karolyn, who had become accustomed to the far more lenient guidance of her father, looked upon their imminent arrival with dread.

"I saw the handwriting on the wall," Karolyn says. "I wanted to stay in California, and I was scratching every post I knew how to scratch to see that I could stay there."

'I wanted to stay in California, and I was scratching every post I knew how to scratch to see that I could stay there.'

Karolyn had always liked Helen, whose pet name for the teen-ager was Snowball, stemming from a wintertime trip the families had made to the mountains. So Karolyn asked Helen to become her guardian. Helen turned her down. While she would have liked to have taken Karolyn in, she predicted correctly that the court would side with Karolyn's remaining family.

Her calm exterior hiding an inner desperation, Karolyn found occasion to confront a legal representative handling her case: "Do I have any voice in this matter at all? Can I say who I want to live with? Do I have any choice?" The reply was short, firm and memorably devastating: "Your feelings and wants will be like a drop in the bucket."

The night of LaVan's death, Clyde immediately drove to Kansas City and boarded a plane to Los Angeles. Marsha – along with Marsha Ann, Marsha's sister Margie Taylor, Margie's husband Dale and their 14-year-old daughter Gail – wasted little time jumping into the Taylors' Buick sedan and driving to California.

During the two days between Clyde's flight and the arrival of the five other family members by car, Karolyn did not return to school. Instead, she cleaned the house with Ray's mother, who stayed with her part of the time. Karolyn also asked Clyde to have the brakes checked on the new Buick. "George had said there was something wrong when he had put his foot on the brake," she says, "and this was a new car and power brakes were fairly new." Clyde later reported, however, that a mechanic had found nothing amiss.

Karolyn spent the entire time at her father's service staring at a wall, not glancing even once at LaVan or his coffin.

This did not sit well with Clyde and Marsha, who tried unsuccessfully throughout the service to get her to look.

Clyde scheduled LaVan's funeral for Forest Lawn Memorial Park on the day following the arrival of the other family members. Those attending included family friends Perry and Ruth Vannice and Don and Nancy Gates. As they sat through the service, each couple, stunned by the news of LaVan's death, had thoughts and had talked separately about seeking to adopt Karolyn, in spite of the guardianship held by Clyde and Marsha. The Vannices discussed having Karolyn join their household and become a sister to her childhood friend Beverly Ann, "but we just didn't think our pocketbook would quite take care of it," says Perry. Don and Nancy, on the other hand, were despondent about their own unsuccessful attempt to have a child and, at first blush, looked favorably upon the prospect of adoption. However, they didn't advance their thoughts about Karolyn publicly, as the 15-year-old was swept out of town before the Gates couple could gather sufficient information.

Karolyn spent the entire time at her father's service staring at a wall, not glancing even once at LaVan or his coffin. She remembered seeing her mother lying in a casket during her funeral a little more than a year before and could not get that image out of her mind. She decided that she wanted to recall the way her father looked when he was living, not dead. This did not sit well with Clyde and Marsha, who tried unsuccessfully throughout the service to get her to look.

Over the next two days, Clyde, Marsha and the other family members from Osceola pored over the belongings of Karolyn's father and mother. LaVan had hardly been in financial straits, but he left no will, so a probate court took a significant amount of his savings. The rest was up for grabs, and the relatives packed up LaVan's and Martha's valuables, including a silver-dollar collection, a carnival glass collection, crystal chandeliers and a set of quilts handmade by Martha's late mother, as well as not-so-valuables such as LaVan's clothes.

Agitated about her impending loss of boyfriend, girlfriends and school and home life, Karolyn watched as her parents' belongings seemingly evaporated. Her father's attorney told Karolyn that she could retain for herself only the items that were absolutely hers, such as a portable record player and a few pieces of clothing. "No one," Karolyn says, "looked out for me to say, 'Now, you need to keep this because you'll want this someday.' " As a result, all that Karolyn has today of her father's are three small items: a tobacco pouch, a wooden box puzzle and a Polly Ann perfume atomizer that LaVan was bringing back to her from Palm Springs on the day of the wreck.

The funeral's aftermath moved with a speed beyond Karolyn's comprehension. But the romantic activity she had become accustomed to did not escape the attention of the visiting family members from Missouri. Before leaving California, Clyde – whether at Marsha's behest or on his own is unclear – had a serious talk with Karolyn's boyfriend Ray about his intentions, and Clyde contacted Karolyn's doctor to determine if she was in good health. Apparently satisfied with the responses, Clyde and Marsha pushed toward a speedy departure.

On Saturday, March 3, 1956, just six days following the fatal car crash, in the driveway of the Ridgely Drive house that became the foundation of her inheritance, Karolyn said goodbye to her boyfriend Ray. Minutes later, she found herself in tears in the back seat of the Buick, sharing space with six Missouri relatives, her Chihuahua Cisco in her lap, all heading 1,800 miles east for Osceola.

"It hurts, even today, to think of that time," Karolyn says. "As we pulled away, I knew I'd never be back, that that was the end. I knew my life would never be the same again. Things had been going well, and it was heart-wrenching to leave. It was goodbye to my life. Everything was gone. I couldn't even look out the windows of the car. I just wanted to look at my dog and hold him, and that's what I did. He rode on my lap for three days. It was a really awful, awful thing to have to go through."

Karolyn almost didn't have Cisco to accompany her, for Marsha had told her before leaving California, "That dog's not coming back. You're going to have to leave the dog." Clyde managed to intervene, however, and told his wife, "You cannot take everything away from her, and she is going to be allowed to take the dog."

Gail, whose father Dale packed the rooftop luggage carrier of the Buick so full as to crack the roof, recalls the ride – and Karolyn's glassy-eyed demeanor – vividly.

"The seven of us, plus Cisco, were cramped up in that car," says Gail. "I knew the people I was with, and I knew the circumstances and the way they talked and bickered. But Karolyn wasn't used to that, and she sat there cuddling Cisco or holding him on her lap. It was a very uncomfortable trip, and she showed no emotion – none, like she was almost in a trance. She walked here, she walked there, she did as she was told. She ate when she was supposed to eat. She slept when she was supposed to sleep. If they told her, 'Here's a drink of water,' she'd drink it.

"It was terribly hard. At the time, I realized she was in pain, and I felt sorry for her, but now, looking back, I think she really went through hell. She had lost her mother and father and was on her way to changing her lifestyle completely, going into a household with a smaller child who had been an only child, moving to a rural area. She had to leave a lot behind that was of importance to her. Her life was just washed away."

As Karolyn rode to Osceola in the back seat, a myriad of thoughts passed through her mind. Chief among them, she wondered why, of all her Midwestern relatives, only Clyde and Marsha sought to take her into their care. Later, she learned that LaVan's older brother Orrin and his wife Eva, who were not well-off financially, had thought Karolyn would have been unhappy with them. Martha's sister Myrtle said later that she had gotten sick at the time of LaVan's death and couldn't take Karolyn. Martha's brother Everly considered offering to take Karolyn, and even wrote a letter to that effect, but after envisioning a possible fight with Marsha, never mailed it.

Karolyn also pondered in the car why Marsha and Clyde so eagerly sought to maintain guardianship, for while she was legally under their care, nothing

Karolyn and her dog Cisco.

'Everything was gone. I couldn't even look out the windows of the car.

'I just wanted to look at my dog and hold him, and that's what I did. He rode on my lap for three days.'

prevented them from cooperating with an adoption by a third party. The couple probably had feelings of family responsibility, and there is little doubt that Karolyn's "loose" lifestyle provided plenty of motivation for the church-going Clyde and Marsha to set their niece straight. But Karolyn also notes that the arrangement supplied a court-regulated means to augment their income, and it turned out later that the judge presiding over Karolyn's case in Missouri required little justification for drawing money from her inheritance, which totaled more than $45,000. As Karolyn rode toward her new life, however, such insights naturally were not fully fleshed out in her mind.

'I thought I was going to die. It was a horrible culture shock.

'Given where I had come from, I thought Osceola was hell, the end of the earth, the end of my life.'

As the miles rolled by on the nonstop trip, Karolyn tried to picture what lay ahead in Osceola. The scenarios in her mind drawn from her family's annual summertime vacations in years past were quite pleasant. But those sweet memories turned into bitter reality as Clyde and Marsha pulled their car into Missouri and Karolyn settled into the prospect of living in a town that by 1956 had slimmed to a total population of 800, smaller than Karolyn's 10th-grade class at Los Angeles High School.

It was not just the size difference that was disquieting. Nor was it simply the abrupt change of terrain and weather, from the sparkling mountains and ocean beaches of California to the endless flatlands, snow, river flooding, hail and tornadoes of the Midwest. It was the entire situation.

"I thought I was going to die," she says bluntly. "It was a horrible culture shock. Given where I had come from, I thought Osceola was hell, the end of the earth, the end of my life."

As if to confirm her foreboding, a sour memory leaped to mind as she stepped through the front door of her new home. The only time Karolyn had stayed in the house of her uncle Clyde and aunt Marsha was one night the previous summer, when Karolyn experienced her first thunder and lightning storm. An uncommon occurrence in Los Angeles, the storm frightened her terribly, she remembers, "but they just laughed at me."

At the all-grades Osceola School, which Karolyn entered in the middle of 10th grade, no one laughed. In fact, as her high school years progressed, Karolyn's feelings about Osceola and its residents gradually became more accepting and affectionate.

Word of the deaths of Karolyn's parents had spread quickly through the small town and its high school. Her tragic status as an orphan meant much more to locals than her Hollywood past. Osceola in 1956 had one tiny theater where movies played two or three days and moved on. Local newspapers carried frequent references to Karolyn's acting work during her most prolific periods, but had not reported on any of her work since 1951. As a result, most treated Karolyn as just another teen-ager, but one who had met the unthinkable misfortune of losing her parents.

"The whole town poured out their hearts for me," Karolyn says. "They never used me. I was just Karolyn, and I liked that."

Neither seeking nor coveting fame from the movies, Karolyn soon became known in Osceola for the interests she pursued there, mainly any activity that allowed her to present or perform before a group.

The beginnings of that reputation came, incredibly, not three weeks after arriving from California. Leaping into Osceola School's musical opportunities, Karolyn was featured in a March 23, 1956, music program, singing Fred Morris' "Night Song" as part of a girls trio and Schubert's "Avé Maria" as a soprano solo. Two weeks later, she participated with other students in a regional music contest,

singing the same selections and earning two of Osceola's 13 first-place performance ratings. At the April 28 state music competition, her work as part of the girls trio won top honors.

Osceola School, which housed grades 1 through 12.

In line with her religious upbringing, Karolyn soon began singing solos at First Baptist Church of Osceola, where she also taught Bible school. While her mother had fostered Karolyn's development of a musical aptitude in Hollywood, Karolyn honed her voice – a trained, two-and-a-half octave soprano that could hit high C – in Osceola by learning chords, phrasing and arrangements from the church organist, Beryl Keifer, who accompanied Karolyn on dozens of occasions. "She was just there to sing whenever I wanted her," Beryl recalls. "She had the ability, of course, but somebody had to bring it out."

Sacred music, the only type of music Karolyn had been exposed to in any depth since performing her first church solo at the age of 6, became her specialty in Osceola. Requests flowed her way, from Lions Club programs to memorial services at Goodrich Funeral Home, where she was a regular standby performer. "I loved being on stage," Karolyn says, "I loved making people cry and changing their emotions."

Through her sophomore, junior and senior years at Osceola School, Karolyn found teachers in the smaller environment more caring than those in Los Angeles. Although she never did conquer algebra or find an interest in social studies or physical education, she raised her overall grades to the B-plus/A-minus level and landed on the school's honor roll, a far better academic performance than the B-minus/C-plus average she had maintained at Louis Pasteur Junior High in California. "In Osceola, I could study and enjoy it," Karolyn says. "The teachers were way backward, but they were sincere, and they loved you and helped you."

Sixteen-year-old Karolyn in her junior-year photo in the Osceola School annual, the Indian Scout.

Plunging into extracurricular activities such as Glee Club, Future Homemakers of America, the Pep Squad, Safe Drivers Club and the school paper (as the literary editor) and annual (as production manager), Karolyn found her real niches in music, drama and speech classes. Like her father 30 years before, Karolyn's special talents were recognized outside of her own small town. She excelled as a singer, soloist, orator and solo violinist in regional and state contests in

Members of the Future Homemakers of America club at Osceola School included Karolyn (front row, above "ers" in sign).

Contest ribbons came her way as her voice soared through such pieces as 'O, Holy Night' and 'Black is the Color (of My True Love's Hair).'

Warrensburg and Columbia. Fern Lyons, the drama teacher, and Blanche Remington, music teacher (and the school superintendent's wife), accompanied Karolyn to such events, where she consistently earned top rankings, in no small measure due to the novelty of someone with her gifts and Hollywood experience.

Contest ribbons came her way as her voice soared through such pieces as "O, Holy Night" and "Black is the Color (of My True Love's Hair)." Karolyn's soprano was "clear as crystal," recalls her cousin Bill Grimes, who was a year older than her. Contest judges tended to agree. "A very lovely voice. A fine job on this," wrote a district judge on the latter song on March 27, 1958. "You are very successful in presenting your songs. A voice of excellent promise."

Her oral interpretations of poetry, monologues and political essays also earned her medals. For instance, representing St. Clair County in a Jan. 6, 1958, seven-county district American Legion oratorical contest in the city of Butler, she spoke on the subject, "Do American Citizens Understand Democracy?" A story and accompanying photo atop the front page of the Jan. 17 *St. Clair County Courier* heralded this effort:

Blanche Remington (left) and Fern Lyons, the two teachers who encouraged Karolyn most. Osceola School's Double Mixed Quartet, 1958. Karolyn is fourth from right.

**She is a talented, outstanding student in both music and
speech. . . . She is a leader in her class and in the student body.**

However, of all her performing abilities nursed carefully by her mother in
California, Karolyn's skill with the violin was the rarest in rural Missouri. She
won judges' honors for her intonation and musicianship by playing classical
solo compositions obscure to Osceolans such as "Meditation" from Jules
Massenet's "Thaïs."

"They'd never seen a violin, let alone had anyone to play it," Karolyn says.
"Little towns in the Midwest did bands big-time, but stringed instruments
were unheard of, there was no orchestra, and nobody could even give me
lessons because no one knew how to play, so it was open range for me.
Blanche Remington really helped me keep my music alive. She'd give
me the music, and I'd go from there. I'd just practice and practice in
front of her, and I would be a star because I was the only one who
could do it."

These extracurricular exploits undoubtedly contributed to Karolyn's
selection in July 1957 as the Osceola high school representative in the
regional Golden Valley Queen Contest in nearby Clinton. One of 18 candidates
for a crown representing beauty, charm, poise, intelligence and personality,
Karolyn was described with local understatement in the *Clinton Eye* newspaper as
having "a dramatic quality and gentle allure that Hollywood would be glad to
find." She considered it an honor to participate, but she soon blew any chance of
winning. Ironically, considering her views of rural backwardness at the time, she
committed a faux pas during a meal at which nominees were judged on their
social graces. "They served us fried chicken, and I truly didn't know how to eat it,
so I ate it with my fingers," she recalls with a laugh. "It was all over after that."

*The musical letter that
Karolyn earned at
Osceola School.*

At Osceola School, Karolyn shone socially. "She was very popular," recalls Bill
Grimes, "very outgoing, friendly and considerate. I don't think she ever met a
stranger."

Karolyn quickly struck up close friendships with six other girls in her class of
40. One of the six friends, Wanda Lyke Firestone, today a bank employee still
living in Osceola, vividly recalls the day she met Karolyn. That's because
Karolyn dressed in nylon stockings, or "hose," instead of bobby socks. The
difference in legwear formed no barrier to their attachment, however.

*Karolyn (seated fourth from right) was literary editor of The Totem Pole, Osceola School's student newspaper, during her
senior year, 1957-58.*

Wanda Lyke, 1957, one of Karolyn's close friends at Osceola School.

"First time I laid eyes on her, I liked her," Wanda says of Karolyn, who soon came to be known by her middle name of Kay because of the emphasis on middle names in the nearby South. In fact, if Karolyn ever carried the mantle of a newcomer when she entered Osceola School, she quickly shed it. "I think it was her outgoing personality," says Wanda. "You put Kay in a room, and she was just not an outsider. It might have been the training she had as a child, but I'm a believer that there are only two classes of people in the world – givers and takers – and she is a giver. As a group, we were all givers."

The group – Karolyn, Wanda, Judith Garrison, Emmalou Eslinger, Marsha Casteel, Lila Bauer and Ruth Ann Wilson – held somewhat divergent interests. Two were straight-A students, absorbed in earning good marks. One was in the band. Wanda was a majorette and cheerleader. And most of the six latched onto the school drama program. "We all just blended together," says Wanda. "We were comfortable together, and we were not jealous of each other. If one excelled at something else, we were glad."

Their friendship transcended the connections they had to others and to the past. So Karolyn's childhood movie career, which Karolyn found unimportant at the time and didn't mention to her friends, made as little difference to the group as it did to Karolyn. "It's just like in any small town when a new child comes in," says Wanda. "Everyone knew her history, but it was mainly that she was a Grimes, she'd visited in the summers before, and she'd lost her parents. Once she was here, she was just us. The movies weren't any big deal. They didn't matter one way or another. It was just like with our friend Ruth Ann: I didn't really care that her dad was a professor. Big deal – you're just who you are. You get along with them, you accept them."

Karolyn's base of friends lay in Osceola School's all-girl drama program. Karolyn is in the front row, second from right. Her friends included Ruth Ann Wilson (back row, second from left), Marsha Casteel (back row, fifth from left), Judith Garrison (back row, far right), Beaulah Noakes (front row, third from left), Wanda Lyke (front row, fourth from left) and Emmalou Eslinger (front row, far right). Fern Lyons, drama teacher, is in the back row, third from left.

Karolyn and her friends shared an affection for Fern Lyons, the only teacher who served as a credible sounding board for the girls' ever-present teen-age plights. One of those perennial issues was the shortage of desirable males in their class, especially for Karolyn, who found most of the tiny crop to be unintriguing farm boys. "There was a world of difference between California guys and these boys," Karolyn says. "It was like being 16 and going out with 12-year-olds."

This situation only deepened the girlfriends' bond. Like any group of teen-agers, they built camaraderie from shared secrets and mishaps – such as a date with a boy during which Karolyn wore underwear accented with a hidden picture of a mouse and its cheese, and a school play in which Wanda, playing a track star, ran out from the wings to pick up a shot put and accidentally knocked a pitcher of water clear across the stage.

Osceola School's yearly high school plays were all-girl productions (no boys were ever interested), and, beyond her scant pre-school-age stage roles, they became Karolyn's first real opportunity to plunge into live theater, which she seized eagerly. In drama, she not only forged friendships but also discovered another natural fit for her performing talents. She played the lead role of Bonnie in *Family Tree*, a three-act comedy about a young woman whose grandmother is a fanatic about ancestors, and she won the attention-getting villain's part of Mary O'Ryan in *Nine Girls*, a college sorority murder mystery.

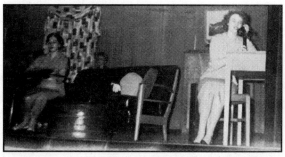

Karolyn, 17, talking on the phone at right, as Bonnie in Osceola School's FAMILY TREE, performed February 7, 1958.

Uncannily, as any good drama can do, the script for the latter play gave Karolyn lines that reflected facts and feelings about her own life at the time. Early in the play, her character Mary notes in passing, "I don't see much of Ray anymore, you know," and at another point says, "It's my family, such as it is, and I'll manage somehow." At the close of the two-act production, when an exasperated Mary fails to kill a sorority sister as part of a cover-up for her murder of two rival girls, she sums up her motivation: "I was afraid . . . and fear drives people to madness sometimes. . . . Try not to think of me like this. Think of all that happened as a bad dream – that's it, a bad dream. And maybe we'll both wake, presently."

Karolyn wasn't contemplating any crimes at the time, but she did wish that her circumstances were merely a bad dream from which to wake.

Karolyn wasn't contemplating any crimes at the time, but she did wish that her circumstances were merely a bad dream from which to wake. While her school activities, church involvement and friendships were all positives, they could only narrow, not eliminate, the swath cut by what Karolyn – and many others in town – saw as the unnerving control over Karolyn's life by her aunt Marsha. Over time, despite her successes in music and other performing arts, Karolyn's home life became a succession of restrictions. Perhaps some were appropriate for a teen-ager who had lived a fast, loose life. Karolyn weathered them all with resignation and the moral support of her friends and teachers, plus the understanding from her California youth that the potential for a different future lay ahead.

Strictness permeated Karolyn's day-to-day life with Marsha. Upon Karolyn's arrival, Marsha situated her in the center of their mid-sized house, in a tiny room with just enough space for a bed, flanked by two doors that made the bedroom more of a hallway than a place for privacy. "If you wanted to get from their bedroom to the kitchen, you'd go through my bedroom," Karolyn says. "You could have gone another way, but everybody went through my bedroom."

Marsha enforced a household regimen far different from Karolyn's California past. She gave Karolyn one towel that had to be folded precisely after each use, and she allowed Karolyn to sit in only one chair in the living room. She required Karolyn to ask permission each time she wished to get food from the refrigerator, and she admonished Karolyn never to leave the toilet seat lid up. In a context of love, those rules might have seemed understandable as discipline, but they were merely a foundation for Marsha's control. What bothered Karolyn far more was

Marsha's insistence that Karolyn kiss her hello and goodbye every time Karolyn entered and left the house. This produced an aversion to kissing that took Karolyn decades to reverse. "I wasn't raised like that," says Karolyn. "I'd never kissed my own parents, and for me to force myself to do it was awful."

In other ways, too, Marsha took charge, driving the 15-year-old to and from school every day and picking out her clothing ("She loved brown and made me

This is the house of Clyde and Marsha Grimes as it looks today. Moved to a new location in Osceola when Truman Dam was built in the 1970s and 1980s, it has different occupants today.

wear brown. I hate brown. Hated it then. I hate it worse now. It's a color that isn't a color, the color of dirt, of bland nothingness."). Marsha required her to stay home and do homework every afternoon without exception instead of joining friends at the local bus-station cafe, and only once in three years allowed her to bring friends to the house.

No doubt Marsha had pictured vividly the promiscuous life Karolyn had led in Los Angeles and was, in part, trying to keep her from setting an undesirable example for Marsha Ann, seven years younger. But Karolyn found Marsha's approach mean-spirited, overshadowing any higher purpose.

No doubt Marsha had pictured vividly the promiscuous life Karolyn had led in Los Angeles and was, in part, trying to keep her from setting an undesirable example.

For instance, Marsha allowed Karolyn to go out on dates, but at first only to Osceola's lone moviehouse, the Civic, and straight back home again. Few boys to Karolyn's liking dared ask her out, because they did not wish to encounter her aunt. Only three – including Hal Barnes, the boy who had given her the magical horseback ride in the summer of 1955 and even mailed a gift to her in California the following Christmas – were up to the challenge.

From Marsha's subtle emotional control, Karolyn quickly got the message to cut her ties to California, despite a steady flow of letters from family friends there. From the first months following her arrival in Missouri, Karolyn still has about two dozen letters mailed from California friends and well-wishers. One, sent March 19, 1956, by Gerry Trapps of San Bernadino, is representative of the sentiments:

> **You have been in our thoughts. . . . I think you did remarkable at the funeral. I know if you have half the good qualities your dad and mother had, you are getting along fine and will make the best of life and take it as it comes.**
>
> **. . . I feel there was never a child loved any more in all their lifetime than you, Karolyn, in the short time you had your parents. I feel as much as they loved you while they were here in body, they are still with you and must have a guarding angel looking over you somehow. They wouldn't have it any other way.**

However well-meaning the letters were, "I was not allowed to answer them," Karolyn says. "Marsha didn't tell me this outright. I just knew that I would have to write to people and tell them not to write me anymore, or I just wouldn't answer their letters. I knew that was the only way to please her."

In her first weeks in Osceola, Karolyn quickly discovered the stakes for not pleasing Marsha. Missing her California boyfriend Ray, with whom she had been intimate, Karolyn wrote him explicitly of her desire to lay her naked body next to his. The letter came back with insufficient postage. To Karolyn's horror, Marsha opened and read it and, as Karolyn puts it, "I was dead." Marsha banned Karolyn's Chihuahua Cisco from sleeping in Karolyn's bed. When Karolyn protested, Cisco was confined to the basement. Then, as a final punishment, she says, Cisco was shunted to an outdoor shed, where, in the cold Missouri winter, the tiny dog soon died.

That incident and others – such as a time when Karolyn sat in her chair in the living room not looking particularly unkempt, only to have Marsha walk in from the kitchen, grab her by the scruff and yell, "Go fix that damn hair. It looks like hell." – taught Karolyn to "go with the flow" of Marsha's household, a practice familiar from her days on Hollywood back lots.

'That was the worst that she could ever do to me, to have someone else hurt because of me.'

For Karolyn, contravening Marsha also ran the risk that someone else, including her uncle Clyde, would be reprimanded. Once, when Karolyn became ill, Clyde expressed concern. "Then my aunt started railing on him that he loved me more than he loved her," Karolyn says. "She'd make my uncle suffer, and he'd pay dearly. She'd start in on him about when he stayed with an Italian family during World War II and there was a single woman there. She always accused him of having an affair with this woman, and she never let up."

Marsha's tendency to punish someone else when she was angry at Karolyn proved demoralizing. "She would be so cruel to other people, and I knew I had caused it," Karolyn says. "That was the worst that she could ever do to me, to have someone else hurt because of me. It's the guilt you carry around, whether it's justified or not. I knew it wasn't right for her to do that, I knew it wasn't right for me to feel guilty, and I knew that other people knew it wasn't my fault, but I still felt responsible for their pain, and I didn't want that. I didn't want to cause trouble.

Christmas 1957 in Osceola: (from left) Karolyn, Marsha, Marsha Ann and Clyde Grimes.

"All my childhood, I'm quite sure I was a very well-disciplined little girl, because you can't be non-disciplined and be in the movies. You can't be a rebel. You have to do what you're told and do it well. So I feel relatively sure that I was capable of doing what I was supposed to do. But in Osceola I was a normal teen-ager, and sometimes I would get in trouble. At first, I tried talking back and being ugly and all that sort of thing, but that wasn't going to fly. It just made it worse. I had no guts, so I became a worm, a mouse."

Karolyn's cousin Gail observed that Karolyn became mousy in more ways than one. Around Marsha, the Karolyn with a bubbly personality and long, blonde hair gradually evolved into a reclusive stoic in darker, short, tight curls. "She went within herself," Gail says. "She wasn't as open, because she couldn't be."

The transplanted teen complied with her aunt's wishes, even when they reinforced her worst fears. Marsha turned Karolyn's bedroom closet into a general storage space, forcing Karolyn to dress every morning from a basement closet, but during the warm months of spring, summer and early fall, greeting Karolyn in the basement each morning were snakes – real, not imagined.

"It was a stone house with an old, concrete foundation, so the snakes could get in anywhere," Karolyn says. "She knew I was deathly afraid of snakes, and she knew that I knew there were snakes down there. But every morning I would get up, go downstairs and open up that closet door. I wouldn't look down or around. I'd look straight ahead and I'd psyche myself up. I would steel myself so that if I saw a snake, I wouldn't react or overreact. I would control myself. I'd pick out quickly what I was going to wear from the closet, go in the bathroom there and jump on top of the toilet seat. That's where I'd dress."

The Osceola School Girls' Sextet, 1957. Karolyn, 17, stands third from right.

Karolyn's attempts to oblige her aunt pulled her through some trying times, but this approach backfired on one occasion in which she represented Osceola High in a state music contest.

"I woke up that morning with diarrhea," Karolyn says, "but I never said a word. I just went right on. I was so sick that whole day, and my teachers were so good to me. My feet hurt, too, because I had to be on my feet for the contest because I was in a lot of ensembles and had some solos. So after I got home that night, I just went to bed. I never said a word about anything. Then one of my teachers called and asked my aunt how I was feeling, and of course I hadn't told her I was sick. Man, did I get punished for that. It embarrassed her that she didn't know."

The transplanted teen complied with her aunt's wishes, even when they reinforced her worst fears.

Often accompanying Karolyn to the singing contests was another student, Mary Tucker, daughter of a Methodist minister. "We would walk and be on our feet for hours at these things, sometimes for two days. My feet hurt so bad. They just killed me," Karolyn says. "One time Mary told me that her father had rubbed her feet that night, and that little comment really left its mark. I never forgot it because there was no one to rub my feet. I thought to myself about how good it would have been to have someone do that."

The crowning touch to Karolyn's life with Clyde and Marsha was a strange ritual that the Grimes couple practiced some weeknights and on Saturday evenings. With Karolyn and Marsha Ann in the back seat, often assigned to their homework, Marsha, sometimes with Clyde and sometimes alone, drove the family car to the one-block square that makes up downtown Osceola, and parked at the northwest corner of Chestnut and Second streets. For hours, they sat, stared and commented on the town's nightlife: who drove and walked by; who went into and came out of the Civic Theater, the bus-station cafe and the bars; who was doing what with whom and where. Rarely did the family frequent those places. They only observed the behavior of others.

To Marsha and Clyde, these forays apparently served as entertainment, but Karolyn perceived them as bizarre information-gathering sessions for the gossip in which Marsha engaged with neighbors the next day. Although news is generally expected to spread quickly around small towns such as Osecola, the park-and-watch routine seemed excessive. It was a procedure Marsha did not hide. Many in town seemed to dismiss it as harmless, if odd. Wanda and other teens, finding it humorous, on occasion went so far as to park and watch Marsha.

Sometimes, Marsha's watch over the square extended into school hours. One day, late for a typical senior-year lunch with girlfriends at the bus-station cafe, Karolyn hurried down the hill from the school. One of her girlfriends drove up in her boyfriend's car and offered her a ride. She had no clue at the time, but a girl whom her aunt had warned her not to associate with was behind her, and also hopped in.

"We drove down to the square, got out of the car, went inside, and she sat with her friends, and I sat with mine," Karolyn says, "but Marsha happened to be in the square picking up the mail, and she saw me get out of the car with the gal. So she came into the restaurant, jerked me up, got me outside on the sidewalk and lit into me, up one side and down the other, in front of the whole town."

As punishment, Marsha forbade Karolyn from eating lunch off campus and restricted her to eating by herself in an empty history classroom on the high school's third floor for the remaining two months of the school year. Karolyn, the "mouse," complied.

"She could tell you that something red was black, and you know, you'd eventually believe it?" Karolyn says. "She had that power. She would tell people something, and I knew it wasn't true, and they knew it wasn't true, and yet they saw it the way she wanted them to see it. It was scary. She had a real talent. It's too bad she couldn't have used it in a positive way."

As might be expected, Marsha's version of the years that Karolyn lived with her and Clyde differs markedly from those of Karolyn and others. Today, at 76 and living alone (Clyde died at age 79 in November 1994 after 54 years of marriage), Marsha fiercely and bitterly contradicts many of her niece's harrowing remembrances. But for this biography of Karolyn, Marsha is willing to share only a brief, diplomatic summary.

"We loved her," she says. "Our hearts ached for her when her home was broken up. We were glad to help her when we could, and we tried to raise her in a Christian home, and we were proud of her music and her singing, and we always wished the best for her."

Those who knew the situation thought differently. "I don't think Marsha wanted her," says one, "and Karolyn couldn't help but sense it."

Marsha Ann, who now lives in Chouteau, Oklahoma, was not directly involved in many of the conflicts involving Karolyn, as she was a grade-schooler during Karolyn's high-school years. However, she was quite aware of the tensions in the household. On one hand, Marsha Ann, adopted at age 5 after several years in

For hours, they sat, stared and commented on the town's nightlife: who drove and walked by; who went into and came out of the Civic Theater, the bus-station cafe and the bars; who was doing what with whom and where.

Rarely did the family frequent those places. They only observed the behavior of others.

foster care, felt Karolyn was lucky to have a home and family immediately after the deaths of her parents. However, Marsha Ann recalls that this particular home was far from ideal. "You couldn't be your own person" as a child of Marsha, says Marsha Ann. "Mother [Marsha] was very controlling and intimidating. She ruled. She could see only one vantage point or side – hers."

How did Karolyn cope inwardly with Marsha's control? Karolyn recalls that she voraciously read from the school library ("Very few people owned books in Osceola except for the Bible, and there weren't bookstores like there are now"). Her reading included such escapist fare as the 1953 best-sellers *The Silver Chalice* by Thomas B. Costain and *Désirée* by Annemarie Selinko. She also created a fantasy world, a process that today would be called positive visualization. "Each night," Karolyn says, "I would lie in bed and think about what I wanted in life and what good would happen to me. I was old enough to know that I'd have to get out and make a life for myself pretty soon, so I would visualize what would feel right for me, and what would make me happy."

This habit was borne, quite naturally, from Karolyn's Hollywood filmmaking experience. "I was raised in a world of fantasy at the studios," she says. "You went into a house that wasn't a real house. It's just a façade, and for a few minutes you are that person in that world, and then you're not."

Karolyn's fantasies included her fervent hope and belief that someone she had known in Hollywood . . . soon would come to Missouri and take her back.

During her first months in Osceola, Karolyn's fantasies included her fervent hope and belief that someone she had known in Hollywood – a friend of her parents, one of her boyfriends or girlfriends, or one of their parents – soon would come to Missouri and take her back to Los Angeles. "I would picture them rescuing me," she says, "and I never really knew if anyone tried. Marsha's mother told me once that at two different times two different people came for me, but they were told that I wasn't there and that they couldn't see me."

As time passed, though, the fantasies turned away from an imagined rescue. "I wanted to sing in Broadway shows," she says, "so I visualized that, along with the domestic housewife and picket fence scenario. In those days, that was the only thing you were supposed to do, marry and have kids. The woman wasn't out in the work or corporate world where she is today, and there was something perhaps wrong with you if you didn't get married and have babies, and God forbid you should be an old maid. It just wasn't right. So, I thought of that and took it one step at a time.

Karolyn as she represented Osceola in the July 1957 Golden Valley Queen Contest. At the time of the contest, she was 17, but this photo – taken when she was 14 – was all she had to submit.

"I would visualize myself learning how to drive and getting my driver's license. That would be the happy thing for that day to think about – just baby steps. Somehow, I had a natural inclination to take care of myself that way, and I think it was very healthy. I didn't eat. I lost tons of weight. But other than that, I was pretty healthy."

Although Karolyn determinedly pictured her own future in her mind, she had few present-day images of herself in Osceola. Unlike Karolyn's mother, who had shot hundreds of photos of her daughter as a small child, neither Clyde nor Marsha took photographs of Karolyn or paid to have them taken. This proved awkward in the summer before Karolyn's senior year when she became a finalist in a local beauty and talent pageant. The only photo she had of herself to submit to the Osceola newspaper had been shot more than two years earlier when she was 14. Few noticed the discrepancy, however, as she looked years older in the portrait.

Helping Karolyn contend with Marsha's control was the unspoken support she perceived from nearly everyone in town. "My teachers, all the kids, the vendors in the stores, people in church – everybody knew the situation I was in, and everybody was so kind to me," she says. "It wasn't obvious or flashy. It was just subtle confirmation that, 'Hang in there, and you'll be all right,' and I knew it."

As Karolyn's relationships with teachers and friends deepened, she started sharing her troubles, but not without attendant vows of secrecy. One of her earliest confidantes was her one-year-younger cousin Gail, who attended Osceola School with Karolyn during the last half of Karolyn's sophomore year, and then, after her family moved back to Independence, sought Karolyn out on her visits to Osceola and double-dated with her.

The two shared both their clothes and a bond of trying circumstances, as Gail, also an only child, had grown up in a household of physical abuse. Some days the pair sat on the sidewalk outside their grandmother's home and talked for hours. Their conclusion about

Karolyn and her cousin, Gail Taylor (left), 1956.

Karolyn's situation, Gail says, was that Karolyn would never be allowed the freedom she wanted from Marsha and Clyde, but at the same time, Karolyn would forever remain an outsider in their home. "She was a guest, a longtime guest," Gail sums up.

School became something of a refuge for Karolyn, but even there she chose carefully the confidences she kept. It certainly helped, though, that her group of six girlfriends never came into direct contact with Marsha.

"Of course," says Wanda, "everybody in town knew that Marsha had this complete control, and everyone covered for Kay to a certain degree so she would not get into trouble. If she was having a bad day at home, we all knew about it. We all tried to comfort her, and if anything was going on in our lives, she did the same thing for us. We all covered for each other. It was a bond. I don't know what more we could have actually done for her."

'If she was having a bad day at home, we all knew about it. We all tried to comfort her.'

Wanda Lyke

"There wasn't anything any of my friends and teachers could do, other than listen," Karolyn adds. "I knew I could count on them for anything, and they would keep secrets. They rallied around me, and I grew from that experience. But I didn't dare talk to anybody else, because it'd get back to Marsha. For the most part, I think people knew. They just didn't want to know. They'd just as soon pretend it wasn't there."

Once, Raymond Grimes, Clyde and LaVan's brother, visited and took Karolyn in his car to drop her off on an errand. While talking about Marsha, Karolyn broke down and begged him, "Please, get me out of there." "Oh, she's not that bad," he replied. Nothing came from Raymond about her plea until another night sometime later when Karolyn was watching a movie at the Civic. Her uncle Orrin came into the theater, tapped her on the shoulder and said, "You better come. Marsha wants you to come because Clyde is very ill." So she got in the car with him and they drove home, where Clyde was suffering a mental breakdown. As Karolyn walked out of the car and up the front walk, Raymond emerged from the house, looked at her, shook his head and said, "Karolyn, you're right." Then he left, and Karolyn never saw him again.

A postcard shows the roadside park overlooking the Osage River to where a disconsolate Karolyn was taken to walk off her inebriation.

To Karolyn, Clyde was an enigma. She never could figure out why the soft-spoken carpenter and respected homebuilder married Marsha. Gradually, Karolyn lost respect for him, as did others in town, whose consensus was that he was kind-hearted but "henpecked." Karolyn understood her own subservient role as a ward, but the weakness of a grown man, particularly given her father's example, bewildered her.

"Uncle Clyde was never free to just go to town and have coffee with the guys or anything like that," Karolyn says. "I think he was a bit of a tortured soul."

'She was just drowning in tears. . . . She was crying about the loss of her mother and the loss of her dad. She was very emotional and distraught, an unhappy person, and I felt so sorry for her.'

Gail Taylor

Karolyn's own soul waged an internal battle, even when she spent time with those closest to her, such as Gail. Often, Karolyn would display a breezy confidence, and the two seemingly had no fear. As Gail puts it, "She really thought she was classy, and I thought she was, too. Boy, we thought we were something else. She was a blonde and I was a brunette, and we'd get in the car, and we thought that Osceola couldn't hold us." But at times Karolyn's inner emotions took over.

A planned double date to a dance in Nevada, 45 miles southwest of Osceola, became one such instance, and the agent was alcohol. Gail's date surprised the other three by bringing along a pint of bourbon for the drive. Neither Gail nor Karolyn's date, who was at the wheel, drank the liquor, and Karolyn characteristically was not a drinker. But by the time the foursome reached Nevada, Gail's date and Karolyn had downed the pint and neither one could climb out of the car unassisted. Karolyn's date and Gail decided to turn the car around and head back to Osceola. On the way, Karolyn launched into a vomiting and crying jag the intensity of which Gail had never seen.

"She was just drowning in tears. It was about her whole life," Gail says. "I really saw the deep hurt that she had, because she was crying about the loss of her mother and the loss of her dad. She was very emotional and distraught, an unhappy person, and I felt so sorry for her."

To rectify the situation, Karolyn's date drove the group to a roadside park where he and Gail walked Karolyn up and down the road. Next, they took her to an Osceola restaurant called Pete's and plied her with coffee. When she felt better, the next destination was Karolyn's house, where Marsha was waiting. Gail tried covering for Karolyn, but the next day Marsha discovered Karolyn's soiled skirt. Controversy then erupted about "who got Karolyn drunk," when, in fact, says Gail, it was Karolyn who made the choice and "probably thought she was going to get away from her problems."

As her high school years proceeded, Karolyn generally tried to nourish her soul in a healthier way, by mentally preparing for graduation and the eventual end of her life with Marsha and Clyde. Unlike what graduation meant to many others in her class, for Karolyn the imminent departure from high school spelled a probable transition to college.

In her younger days in Los Angeles she had been raised to believe she would continue her education, and in Osceola she knew her father's estate held funds to make it possible. Vocal and instrumental scholarships she earned from Central Missouri State College (now University) 50 miles north in Warrensburg and from the University of Missouri 120 miles northeast in Columbia – places she'd visited during music contests – supplied additional incentive. Strong but solitary moral support also came from drama teacher Fern Lyons and music teacher Blanche Remington, who ignored rural expectations for women as they counseled Karolyn. They told her unequivocally that her musical talents and performance skills made her college material.

In her younger days in Los Angeles she had been raised to believe she would continue her education, and in Osceola she knew her father's estate held funds to make it possible.

"Not one person in Osceola encouraged me to go to college except Fern Lyons and Blanche Remington," Karolyn says. "College education didn't really mean a whole lot to most of those people. They worked hard, they were farmers or had a job, had children, and that was it."

Karolyn narrowed her sights on Central Missouri, in part because Remington favored smaller schools over larger ones, but also because Karolyn had little encouragement to build her musical aptitude at more specialized, faraway institutions. Years later, Karolyn realized that her voice might have landed her in a prestigious fine arts program thousands of miles away. But back then, she didn't possess the stamina or passion for such a pursuit. "I wasn't smart enough to know what school to go to, and I didn't think about finding that out as well as I should have. It never occurred to me." Central Missouri, an hour's drive away, represented a move that was desirable enough. "It was my way out," Karolyn says.

Karolyn and the 1953 Chevrolet that Marsha and Clyde allowed her to drive during her junior and senior years in high school.

Fueling her move to independence on a different front during her high-school years was her intensifying relationship with Hal Barnes, which also produced enduring ties to Hal's parents, Marion and Marie. The Barnes family lived on a farm just outside of Osceola. In Karolyn's eyes, Marion and Marie – who had known Karolyn's parents as children and teen-agers and whom Karolyn admired as loving parents – eventually took on the roles of Karolyn's surrogate dad and mom.

Some of Karolyn's dates with Hal ended up at the Barnes farm, where the whole family played pitch, a bridge-like card game enjoyed by many at the time. Karolyn, who had absorbed her father's love of cards, eagerly joined in. Marie also worked at Knight's dress shop in the Osceola square, where Karolyn and Wanda occasionally stopped in and spilled their troubles to Marie. "They'd come into the store, they each had a woeful tale to tell me, and I sympathized with them," Marie says. "Karolyn was a sweet, refined girl, and I felt quite motherly toward her."

Marie often heard an earful about Karolyn's home life and became particularly irked at the park-and-watch routine on the square. "Karolyn couldn't do her homework unless she did it in the back of the car," Marie says. "I resented that as much as everybody else did."

One time while Hal and Karolyn dated, Marie recalls that Hal came into the dress shop and picked out a turquoise suede frock skirt and matching jacket to buy for Karolyn. "I tried to say it wasn't an appropriate thing for him to buy a garment for his girlfriend," Marie says, "but Hal wouldn't have it, and he bought it for her, and it was cute on her. Well, Marsha came in the next week and bought one just like it for herself, only in red. I was so angry."

Hal's looks and personality appealed to Karolyn, for he was considered a handsome country boy with an easygoing manner.

He also was reckless in a way that's attractive at a young age.

Hal's looks and personality appealed to Karolyn, for he was considered a handsome country boy with an easygoing manner. He also was reckless in a way that's attractive at a young age. The 1957 Osceola School yearbook revealingly quoted him as saying, "It's not what you do, it's what you get away with." In that vein, Gail recalls seeing Hal and two other Osceola teen boys mounting a slow-moving truck and stealing watermelons from it as it struggled to reach the crest of a hill outside of town. "He was just the ordinary 1950s teenybopper," Gail says, "a fun type who would do lots of little ornery things that teen-age boys do." Overall, however, Hal's biggest value for Karolyn was his family and its connection to hers. "He had known my dad," Karolyn says, "and that was important to me."

Karolyn Grimes and Hal Barnes, 1956.

That is not an unusual sentiment in a small town, says Jim Naylor, who has served as the elected St. Clair County clerk for the past 15 years and who grew up as a younger friend of Hal's. "Hal was a nice-looking young man and he enjoyed a good time," Jim says, "but I think a person's family sometimes can have as much to do with anything as the individual, and the Barneses were really nice people."

In one sense, Hal represented the family relationships for which Karolyn desperately pined. "When we would talk about what we wanted to do with our lives as we grew older," says Gail, "Karolyn would always say, 'Hal is my future.' She saw him as the light at the end of the tunnel. She thought, 'If I can stand this life until I'm 18, I can marry Hal, I can get away, and that's my salvation.' "

What Hal saw in Karolyn is more open to speculation. Karolyn was considered attractive and more sexually sophisticated than many of the girls in her class, and despite Marsha's attempts to clamp down on her, Karolyn eagerly engaged in what she calls "the only real recreation in town" with more than one boy. Hal was drawn to Karolyn by more than sex, however, as by all accounts, including Karolyn's, she held a sincere spot in his heart.

But Gail, who was so close to Hal that he called her "Sis," saw opportunism in Hal's approach. She was fully aware, first-hand, that Karolyn and Hal had often been intimate. On a double date once, Karolyn and Hal had driven to a secluded spot and walked off into the nearby woods to make love. After a long while, Gail and the boy she was with resorted to honking the car horn to get Karolyn and Hal back so the foursome could return home by the time Gail had promised her parents.

Karolyn Grimes, Hal Barnes and Gail Taylor, 1956.

"I accused Hal of using Karolyn sexually," Gail says, "and I accused him of knowing that she had a dowry. 'That's not true, Sis, that's not true,' he'd say. And I'd say, 'Yes, it is, I know that's part of it. You are a user. You're using her in more than one way.' I think he truly cared for her, but you also have to realize, in a little country town like Osceola, someone coming in from Los Angeles who's been in the movies, she was a novelty."

As with most teen-age couples, the courtship of Hal and Karolyn ebbed with arguments as it flowed with passion, and as Hal graduated from Osceola High and Karolyn started her senior year, the two parted for the time being. "I broke up with him because I wanted to date his best friend, and he wouldn't forgive me for that," Karolyn says.

"He would come crying on my shoulder," says Gail. "He'd say, 'Will you go to the show [the Civic movie theater] with me on Saturday night? I don't want to go by myself.' And I'd say, 'Yes, Hal, I'll go with you.' So I'd go and sit in the show with him, and then we'd go to the bus station cafe, and there would be Karolyn with someone else. I told him, 'Hal, I can't help what she does. She's just trying to hurt you.' "

Even when Karolyn wasn't dating Hal, she maintained contact with his mother Marie, who served as a welcome repository for her woeful stories and her desires to get away to college. "I almost hated to think about Karolyn leaving," Marie says. "I was glad for her sake, but I wanted to see her around more. It was like sending my own kid away."

Her desire to move away from Osceola growing by the day, Karolyn received a pre-graduation gift from Clyde and Marsha – a gleaming, new, automatic-shift 1958 Chevy Impala, solid black with turquoise accents, that turned every head in Osceola. (Two years before, when Karolyn had obtained her driver's license, Marsha and Clyde let her drive a used, standard-shift 1953 Chevrolet they had purchased from a teacher, but they also severely restricted when Karolyn could

'I accused Hal of using Karolyn sexually, and I accused him of knowing that she had a dowry.'

Gail Taylor

drive it.) It is possible that Clyde and Marsha proffered the new car as a safer vehicle in which Karolyn could eventually travel to and from college, but to Karolyn it simply represented the potential for more freedom.

Karolyn, 18, senior-year portrait, 1958.

Karolyn, who graduated fifth in her class of 38, decided she couldn't wait until fall quarter and instead enrolled in Central Missouri's summer session.

Karolyn also did not consider the new Impala an act of generosity from Marsha and Clyde, since the cash for the purchase came from her own father's estate. Her inheritance and the associated guardianship checks, Karolyn recalls, also had bought Clyde and Marsha items of their own, including a basement remodeling, clothes, Christmas presents and other items ostensibly for Karolyn but actually for their personal use.

Despite questions about her guardians' disposition of her inheritance, Karolyn focused on college for the time being. In her eyes, the day to leave couldn't come too soon. In June 1958, Karolyn, who graduated fifth in her class of 38, decided she couldn't wait until fall quarter and instead enrolled in Central Missouri's summer session. She packed up the Impala and moved into an upstairs room in Houts Hall, a just-opened dormitory, with her friend, sports-minded Marsha Casteel. For all its newness and separation from home, life in Houts Hall carried strict rules of its own.

"Those were the days when you had a housemother," Karolyn says. "They came around with white gloves and checked to see if you had your room clean, you couldn't have boys upstairs, you had to sign in and sign out and be in at a specific time, you had curfews, and you had to say where you were going and when you'd be back." Except for breaking curfew occasionally, Karolyn says she obeyed the rules to the letter.

Turning 18 that summer, Karolyn found the college environment nurturing, and her role in it pleasingly anonymous. She earned decent grades in her classes, including "Communications 1B – The Use of Mass Media," for which Karolyn chose to write a paper on "The Responsibility of the Motion Picture." The essay surveyed the pressure groups that influenced movie studios' self-censorship in the 1940s and 1950s, from glass blowers who protested the showing of canned beer, to police groups that objected to cops being portrayed as buffoons. Though Karolyn does not recall writing the paper, and while it did not advance any particular opinion of its own, it nevertheless was an interesting academic analysis, given her Hollywood background. Here is an excerpt:

> **. . . There is a saying in Hollywood that villains should be unemployed, white Americans, without religious, professional, labor union or other affiliations. The public of every class resents the suggestion that members of its group could be anti-social or unethical. Many fine dramatic source materials have been abandoned for the reason that these might give offense to the groups portrayed.**
>
> **When in dangerous area, producers must scrutinize carefully every line of dialogue in any story to avoid any statements which might imply that all members of a given profession or other group are unethical or untrustworthy. As a further safeguard, in most cases where dramatic honesty requires that a professional man or a member of some group be characterized as a villain, a formula of contrast is used. This means that in the same story,**

another member of the same professional or occupational group is presented as showing the best ideals of that group.

. . . Patrons go to motion pictures to be entertained, and on the economic side, producers endeavor not to offend these potential customers. There is, however, no other business watched so closely and subjected to so many negative suggestions. However, the pressure groups will remain as potent factors for either the retardation or the continued development of the motion picture industry.

Karolyn spent most of her college days in her dorm room, at the local Baptist church or in the campus music hall, where she played violin in the school orchestra. Although Central Missouri was hardly a Mecca of social life, Karolyn also started dating new boys, including one from Costa Rica.

Karolyn at 17, in a yearbook photo in which she is identified as the annual's production manager.

Her letters to her friends from high school reflected a euphoria of sorts. "I really love it here," she wrote Lila Bauer. "I am having so much fun, and I even think I am learning a few things. Ha ha. . . . Our rooms are very modern, and we have lots of closet and shelf space. Everything works just fine."

"The people, the teachers were just great," Karolyn recalls. "They were caring and kind and sincere and honest, and they didn't know me from Adam. I never told a soul that I was in the movies. I didn't think it was that important and that it would really impress anybody, and it might ostracize me. I didn't want to be different. I wanted to be like them. Nobody ever knew, and they accepted me."

Perhaps nothing illustrated Karolyn's acceptance more than the results of her quest to pledge a sorority, a process echoing the one that her father's accidental death had aborted at Los Angeles High four years earlier. At Central Missouri, she ached to join Sigma Sigma Sigma, the most coveted sorority on campus, "but I didn't have the social background. They didn't know anything about me, I didn't have the old blood lines and, of course, nobody in my family had ever been to college, so I didn't get in."

The same photo appeared with this angel cartoon in Karolyn's senior-year annual in June 1958. Is it a reference to her line in IT'S A WONDERFUL LIFE from 12 years before? Doubtful. It more likely is a pointed reference to Karolyn's less-than-angelic reputation.

However, Karolyn eagerly pledged a sorority that did welcome her, Theta Sigma Epsilon, and soon rewarded the house by winning the lead singing role in an operetta that the Sigma Nu fraternity planned to stage. "It was pretty much a coup for my sorority," she says, but a short-lived triumph. Before production of the operetta could progress to serious rehearsals, the college canceled it as a punishment for the Sigma Nus' violation of campus rules against drinking.

While life at Central Missouri held its own high and low points, in some respects Karolyn remained tethered to Marsha's emotional control. For example, when the mother of her high-school music teacher Blanche Remington died, Blanche asked Karolyn to sing at the funeral. "My aunt didn't want me to, so she told me she didn't think I should, and I didn't because she said she didn't think I should, and I'll regret that till the day I die," Karolyn says. "There was no reason I couldn't sing for her mother's funeral, but it was just a quirk on Marsha's part."

And despite Karolyn's physical separation from Osceola during weekdays, she also participated in a weekend routine eerily similar to that of her high-school years with Marsha and Clyde. As guardians, they still controlled Karolyn's finances, and they encouraged her to return on weekends to their house. During her weekends in Osceola, Karolyn did schoolwork, occasionally ironed clothes or helped Marsha and Clyde can fruits and vegetables, and endured their Saturday night park-and-watch ritual in the square. At least Karolyn could count on the weekday refuge of Central Missouri – or so she thought.

Soon, Marsha began showing up unexpectedly on Karolyn's doorstep at Houts Hall. "It would be a spur-of-the-moment thing," Karolyn says. "I'd never know, and there she'd be." On one occasion, Karolyn's roommate had been smoking in their room. "I never smoked. I never had a cigarette," Karolyn says, "but Marsha was downstairs all of a sudden, so we tried to get the ashtrays and the stale air out. When she came up to the room, she didn't say a word." Two days later, however, Karolyn received a scathing letter from Marsha. In it, Marsha accused Karolyn of smoking and cut off her spending money for a month.

The pattern of Marsha's unannounced weekday visits and Karolyn's weekend trips to Osceola had no end in sight. "I thought I would never be free," Karolyn says. But on a Saturday night in late October, midway into Karolyn's second quarter at Central Missouri, while she sat in her "usual entertainment seat" in the back of Clyde and Marsha's car in the Osceola square, the end came.

Hal Barnes and Karolyn, high-school dating days, 1956.

Driving up alongside the car was Hal Barnes. While Karolyn had seen Hal around town occasionally, the two hadn't dated in a year and a half. "He got out of his car and just sat in and talked with us for awhile," Karolyn says. "He asked me if I wanted to go for a ride with him. I got in his car and we went for a ride, and the next thing I knew, he asked me to marry him – right then, that night. I came back and told Marsha that he'd asked me to marry him, and she said, 'Well, I think you should.'"

In the midst of sororities and music at Central Missouri, this prospect – of marrying, of marrying Hal, of moving back to Osceola to live with him – hadn't crossed Karolyn's mind in recent months. But she also felt she had labored long under a cloud. Hal's proposal offered the sunshine of a new life.

'He asked me if I wanted to go for a ride with him. . . . and the next thing I knew, he asked me to marry him – right then, that night.'

Karolyn remembers thinking that night, "It's a fluke, but he's got the courage to stand up to Marsha, and tomorrow she'll change her mind." She also naively thought she loved Hal. "There were a lot of things in his favor," Karolyn says. "He was still the only one my age who had ever known my dad, and his parents I was in dear love with."

For Karolyn, as was typical for rural, college-age women at the time, getting married meant dropping her life and becoming part of Hal's. In fact, it was an unspoken assumption. "He didn't give a rat's bone whether I went to college," Karolyn says. "Why would he want me to be smarter than him?" So in weighing whether to marry Hal, Karolyn had to decide whether she was willing to forego her education.

Her Osceola girlfriends and former teachers Fern Lyons and Blanche Remington strongly advised Karolyn to put off marriage and continue at college, but Karolyn didn't listen. "I knew I was letting my teachers down," she says, "but you know how you have a way of blanking out things you don't want to hear?" While dropping out of Central Missouri later became one of Karolyn's major laments, on the night that Hal proposed marriage, Karolyn could see only freedom. "So I quit school the next week, and we got married."

For Karolyn, as was typical for rural, college-age women at the time, getting married meant dropping her life and becoming part of Hal's. In fact, it was an unspoken assumption.

Looking back, Gail acknowledges the loss Karolyn experienced by leaving college, but she feels that given the dynamics of her cousin's relationship with Marsha, marriage to Hal was a positive change. "She did the right thing," Gail says. "If she had stayed in that situation, she truly would have lost her mind."

The Nov. 8, 1958, wedding of Hal Delbert Barnes and Karolyn Kay Grimes was a relatively simple affair. Held in the same basement where Karolyn had dressed atop the toilet to avoid snakes during warmer weather, the event drew just a handful of people, including Hal's parents and grandmother, Marsha, Clyde, Marsha Ann and the Rev. Cecil Haines, the minister from First Baptist Church of Osceola, who officiated. Karolyn had driven 100 miles north to Independence to buy a relatively inexpensive white formal dress for the event, and she and Hal had stopped in Clinton, 22 miles north of Osceola, to pick up wedding rings. Much more than that Karolyn does not remember.

Though Marsha and Clyde tried to persuade the newlyweds to use part of Karolyn's inheritance to buy a house that Clyde had just completed, instead Karolyn and Hal rented half a duplex a few blocks from the square, and their married life began. An itinerant truck driver, Hal did not keep jobs long, and he rarely brought home money for joint expenses, preferring to spend his earnings on his expensive hobby of motorcycling. These factors – plus the unhappy but obvious reality that making music to produce a livelihood was not realistic in rural Missouri – told Karolyn that she needed to get a job.

A friend worked as a medical assistant in the small-town-sized Osceola Medical Hospital, and such a people-oriented occupation appealed to Karolyn as a way to earn a living. (Interestingly, in a letter 11 years prior, her mother Martha had clued relatives in to Karolyn's medical interests as a 7-year-old. Thanking her mother and brother for sending Karolyn a doctor-and-nurse set for Christmas, Martha wrote, "It was something she really wanted. It has come in so handy. Her doll has Virus X right now. Ha!")

Soon Karolyn was at work full-time in the Osceola hospital's laboratory, drawing and analyzing blood samples and informally advancing her knowledge of blood chemistry and pathology. The medical world fascinated and challenged her, and each success of her on-the-job training provided a needed boost to her self-assurance.

Hal Barnes and Karolyn, high-school dating days, 1956.

"The day they taught me to draw blood was the day they had about 20 or 30 boys in from a work program who had to pass physicals," Karolyn says. "I think they had to see if they had syphilis, because it was for the state. These young men had fabulous veins, and I went through them like a dose of salts, because they were so easy to hit. That built my confidence up, and from then on I could draw blood from anyone."

The medical work led to a 20-year career as a laboratory technician and physician's assistant (essentially a nurse without the title), but when she began just a half year out of high school, she had no idea it would last that long. Stability – for herself and her new marriage – was the immediate goal. Securing the hospital job, and quickly moving on to a newly built Osceola medical clinic, was a good start. Even more important, however, Karolyn finally felt old enough and sufficiently motivated to unleash herself mentally and financially from the guardianship of Clyde and Marsha. And she did so, with the kind help of the county's public administrator at the time, the appropriately named Helen Hart.

A present-day portrait of Karolyn and Helen Hart, the St. Clair County administrator who agreed to become the teen's guardian and handle her finances when Karolyn turned 19.

A longtime friend of Marion and Marie Barnes, Helen had served in her elected post since 1948, typically assuming guardianship of citizens such as those confined to state hospitals and incapable of handling their affairs. In that context, Karolyn's case was unusual, for she was not incompetent, merely under the age of 21.

Karolyn was no stranger to Helen, who remembered when LaVan, Martha and Karolyn visited Osceola on summer vacations. "She was always a sweet girl – outgoing, pleasant, friendly and nice to everyone," Helen says. Karolyn's teen-age musical talents also made a lasting impression on Helen, as had her film career 10 years prior. "Everyone knew about it and thought an awful lot of Karolyn," Helen says. "It's a small town, and for the daughter of a local person to be in the movies and to have her picture in the paper, that was something."

'All I could think was, "Oh my," but I was glad to try to help her.'

Helen Hart

But while Helen liked Karolyn well enough, Karolyn's petition for a new guardian carried its share of small-town awkwardness. "I never turned away anybody when they asked," Helen says, "but this case was strange." If she were to assume guardianship, Helen would take the place of someone who not only was a good friend to her but also was a blood relative to Karolyn. Helen did her best to approach the matter objectively.

"Karolyn's folks had worked hard and kept an estate for her and wanted her to have it," Helen says. "The court thought Karolyn wasn't getting a fair deal. They figured that her money wasn't being kept and she needed a different guardian. All I could think was, 'Oh my,' but I was glad to try to help her. So Clyde just resigned, and I was appointed and took over."

This monumental break in Karolyn's tortuous connection to Marsha came on June 30, 1959. As word-of-mouth about the appointment of a new guardian traveled from the public court records around town, confirmation of Karolyn's closely monitored life as the ward of Clyde and Marsha soon came to Helen. "I had a lot of people say to me, 'I'm so glad that you've been appointed Karolyn's guardian,' so I knew what they were thinking, because people just don't come up and say those things very often," Helen says.

Karolyn's case proved noteworthy to Helen in an additional respect. Throughout the petition process, Helen perceived in Karolyn a wisdom beyond her years. "Most kids at 18 would never do what Karolyn did," Helen says. "They'd just go on and tell themselves, 'I lost my mother and dad, and this is the way I'm supposed to be,' and just take it. But Karolyn knew what was happening. She was smart and could see that, and she was strong enough to do something about it."

Delighted with Helen and happy with her steady job at the clinic, Karolyn nevertheless faced another major challenge in her husband Hal. Not only was he unwilling to support their household financially (Karolyn had to use her inheritance money to buy furniture and a washer and dryer), but Hal also was accident-prone. Eight months into the marriage, in the summer of 1959, Hal rode his motorcycle down a hill just one block from their duplex, and the brakes failed. The resulting collision with a car made for a grisly street scene.

"Somebody came to the door to get me," Karolyn says, "and when I got to where he was, one of the electric utility people was holding his head up because he was unconscious and choking on his blood. Since I worked at the hospital, I went with him into the operating room. We put a catheter in him, checked vitals and called an ambulance to take him to St. Joseph's Hospital in Kansas City. There wasn't a lot more we could do."

Hal lay in a coma for a week with head injuries and a collapsed lung. In just six weeks in the hospital, his six-foot frame shrank to 140 pounds. "He was like a skeleton," Karolyn says. "For the longest time, we didn't think he was going to make it."

In fact, by his own account shortly thereafter, Hal almost didn't survive. He told Karolyn, Marie and Gail that he had a near-death experience, complete with a peaceful, green setting, a white-hot light and a conversation with a judge-like figure who told him it was time to leave his life behind. But Hal said no, telling the specter that he wanted to come back to life because he could hear the voices of Karolyn, Marie and others. "All the time he was unconscious, he said he knew we were there, even though we didn't think he knew," says Marie.

When the hospital finally sent Hal home, he and Karolyn hired an attorney to sue the motorcycle manufacturer. The attorney told them they had ample grounds but added, "I'll take the case on one condition, that Marsha Grimes doesn't have anything to do with it." Of course, Marsha no longer was Karolyn's guardian. Karolyn and Hal wound up winning a settlement. Soon, the couple moved out of their duplex and rented a small, white cottage with a living room, kitchen, bathroom, two bedrooms and a basement laundry room.

By this point in her life, her teen-age years coming to a close, Karolyn had persevered through several major life changes, some involuntary and some not. To this day, as everyone does, she ponders "what might have been" if she had made different choices or if fate had not intervened during those years.

'Karolyn knew what was happening. She was smart and could see that, and she was strong enough to do something about it.'

Helen Hart

The worldliness of the big city and the discipline of the self-control on soundstages ingrained in Karolyn while she grew up in Hollywood gave her the presence of mind that allowed her to survive her home life in Osceola and mature into a young adult. But she also feels fortunate to have been plucked from California, despite the tragic circumstances, just in time to avoid the drinking, drugs and superficiality that plague Los Angeles teens and to develop an appreciation for the values, friends and "real people" of rural Missouri. While she wishes she hadn't given up on college and a resulting career in the performing arts, her decision to marry provided a foundation for the final escape from Marsha's grip and brought her back to a down-to-earth life that she had come to hold in high esteem.

In the aftermath of Hal's motorcycle wreck, however, as the calendar turned to the new decade of the 1960s, Karolyn's thoughts were not so reflective. They simply focused on the next event in her life – something both concrete and ethereal, something partly the result of her own choice and partly the result of the way of life in Osceola and every American small town.

She was going to have a baby.

A s her 20th birthday approached, Karolyn Grimes Barnes had faced enough upheavals to last a lifetime. She had undergone orphan shock, culture shock and guardian shock. She had even experienced nature-shock, living without mountains and an ocean, and learning how to cope with tornadoes, floods, snow, hail and thunderstorms. But another jolt was just around the corner: baby shock.

Settling into their Osceola cottage, Karolyn and Hal did not talk much about serious topics, including whether to have kids. And the concepts of birth control and family planning weren't part of the newlyweds' vocabulary. "It just happened," Karolyn says. "Everybody did it. In those days, there wasn't much you could do to prevent it from happening except for using condoms, and that wasn't really fun, so we really didn't think about it one way or another."

Moreover, soon after Karolyn became pregnant, during Hal's motorcycle accident recovery, she came to realize that she knew little about how to care for an infant. With her own mother and father gone, and having escaped the control of her aunt Marsha, for guidance on such a personal pursuit Karolyn felt most comfortable turning to Hal's parents.

Marie, in particular, became Karolyn's domestic mentor. An experienced, loving mother, having raised a girl and two boys, Marie opened her arms to Karolyn, and the elder Barnes farmhouse became a schoolhouse in the arts of cooking and child-rearing. Karolyn carefully observed Marie while she cared for her grandchildren, and she benefited from Marie's one-on-one help when her own child came due. In fact, it was Marie who drove Karolyn to the hospital in Clinton, 22 miles north, for the delivery of her firstborn.

"Where was Hal? I had no idea," recalls Marie, "but when Karolyn started needing to go to the hospital, she didn't know where he was, so I just picked her up in the car and went ahead and took her up to the emergency room." Marie's moral support at the hospital came in handy, as Karolyn's physician arrived late. "I was quite upset with the doctor," says Marie, "because the nurses were delivering the baby, and the doctor showed up only in time to say hello. I was about ready to hang him."

Karolyn visits with Marie and Marion Barnes at their farmhouse outside of Osceola, 1995.

The new Barnes child, a girl, was born on June 12, 1960. The baby's name was the result of a pact Karolyn had made with a friend from high-school days, Wanda Lyke. The two had married at about the same time, they lived across the street from each other, and they agreed that their first children would be named after their husbands' first names, even if the children were girls. So Wanda's first child,

'*You call this a happy family? Why do we have all these kids?*'

(*Karolyn's first marriage, motherhood, a medical career, the start of her second marriage, 1960-1980*)

also a girl, became Pauline, while Karolyn gave her daughter the first name of Haleen, along with her own middle name, Kay.

Once Karolyn returned home with Haleen, she spent most of her Sundays at the Barnes farm, Marie teaching her everything from how to bathe a newborn to how to deal with teething and projectile spit-up a few months later. Marie's daughter and other daughter-in-law visited with their children, too, and Karolyn soaked up every tip she could. "I didn't know what babies did," Karolyn says. "It was a place where the other women and I bounced off each other about raising kids. I was maybe 10 years younger than everybody, but we all learned a lot."

Karolyn and Marie also spent a lot of time in Marie's kitchen, trying new recipes on themselves and the kids. "We experimented with every cheesecake we ever heard of," Marie recalls with a laugh.

On occasion, Marie and Marion cared for Haleen while Karolyn and Hal slipped away on short weekend outings and a couple of longer car trips by themselves. Marie liked to take her grandchildren on river walks to find Native American arrowheads and other earthly treasures.

"Family's very important to me," Marie says. "I've had more fun with my grandchildren. Summertimes, I'd keep five or six. I thought that if they could all just be here for the summer and enjoy each other, I could go about the cooking and things, and they could make their own fun. But I got involved, too. We used to take sandwiches and go up the creek, and they'd pick up round rocks and so forth. Then after they got older, I'd take 'em to the swimming hole."

Such rural pastimes were second nature to Marie, and although Karolyn never lost her city-kid aversions to fishing, worms and snakes, she did appreciate and adopt many of the values Marie found important.

Another family member Karolyn connected with as a young mother was Lewis Lee Motley. "A lot of us were young, and we all had little kids," Karolyn says, "and you couldn't really go anyplace because you had to watch the kids." So when Karolyn got together with her older cousin and his family, they created their own fun, most often with a deck of cards. And "the only kind of cards anybody played," Lewis Lee says, was pitch.

"In that game," says Lewis Lee, "you had an ace, two jacks – one of them the jack of trumps and the other was what I called the off-jack – and the joker and the deuce. You'd play each hand trying to catch or save the trump. You played partners, and you had to have four people. Then we got to playing six-handed. It was just fun to do."

Such activities were typical of unhurried, young adult life in Osceola in the early 1960s. "It was more of a slow lane," Lewis Lee says. "People around here had their own ideas and, to me, were more honest. They're just a different kind of people. I found the same thing in the service. You would weed out your buddies who came from the sticks, and they made better soldiers. The only ones I really had problems with were the ones from New York, the smart-alecks. They knew it all and they didn't know anything. The country people were for me."

This attitude grew on Karolyn. While circumstances out of her control had thrust her from her big-city sensibilities into small-town life, by her early 20s she

Once Karolyn returned home with Haleen, she spent most of her Sundays at the Barnes farm, Marie teaching her everything from how to bathe a newborn to how to deal with teething and projectile spit-up.

Karolyn soaked up every tip she could.

was making it her own. "I'd come to know Midwestern people a lot better, and they're real people – not pretentious, just more straightforward," Karolyn says.

She did, however, want for a husband to share life's challenges with. While she and Hal were married in deed, he was often an absentee parent and mate. "He was a bit of a rounder," Karolyn says delicately. For example, she and her friend Wanda recall finding a pair of women's panties beneath Karolyn's car seat and driving in Wanda's car 55 miles west to the town of Butler with the aim of confronting Hal. "I remember thinking, 'Did we really want to find him?' " says Wanda. "I don't think we really wanted to face it."

What kept Hal away from home most, however, was his attraction to motorcycles. "Hal was a motorcycle nut before the time of real motorcycle popularity," Karolyn says. The hobby meant a string of accidents for Hal. One cost him the cornea of one of his eyes. Another, a smash-up with a Ford sedan on August 22, 1960, in downtown Osceola, hurled Hal 24 feet from his cycle, fractured his right wrist, injured his back and left knee and landed him on the front page of the *St. Clair County Courier* newspaper.

His mother witnessed another of Hal's wrecks 90 miles north in Sedalia. "He would go to hillclimbs, and one time I just had to go see," Marie says. "The hillclimb was man-

Karolyn and Wanda Lyke Firestone, shown in 1995, have maintained ties since their high-school friendship. The two shared the challenges of marriage and motherhood in Osceola.

made, right straight up, and, of course, my heart was in my mouth seeing my son up there being so dumb. Several motorcycles started up the hill, and when they got to the top, somehow or other he lost his balance, tipped over, and fell back down the hill. He broke his ankle that time. He had broken bones for everything he did."

Hal's accidents eventually affected his mental and emotional stability as well as his physical health, Karolyn says, and they didn't help the family checkbook, either. Besides laying out cash for expensive cycling equipment, Hal ended up needing lengthy recuperations from his wrecks, making it difficult for him to hold steady work. He once tried delivering dairy products with a milk truck he bought with Karolyn's inheritance money, only to sell the vehicle a year and a half later. He worked at a gas station for awhile, and later he sporadically drove a truck for his brother, delivering mail to regional drop spots around western Missouri. "But I never saw a dime – ever," says Karolyn. "Nor did he pay a bill. All of his money went to buy motorcycles or to play, just to do whatever he wanted to do."

Consequently, Karolyn had weighty financial incentive to improve her own employability. At Osceola Medical Hospital, she took courses in pharmacology and radiology, then switched to a position as a laboratory technician in the town's Tri-County Medical Clinic. The knowledge and experience she gained boosted her confidence, but Hal's habitual absences gnawed away at her home life.

She and her friend Wanda recall finding a pair of women's panties beneath Karolyn's car seat and driving in Wanda's car 55 miles west to the town of Butler with the aim of confronting Hal.

Finally, in the fall of 1961, after she had turned 21 and shed the guardianship of Helen Hart, Karolyn decided she'd had enough. She threatened to separate from Hal. "He had started playing footsies with some women," Karolyn says, "so I told him that I was moving to a different town, and if he wanted to come along he could. Otherwise, he could forget it."

The house in El Dorado Springs that Karolyn bought, and that she and Hal lived in with their children, as it looks today.

Karolyn found a job 25 miles southwest at a hospital in El Dorado (pronounced with a long "a") Springs, the seat of adjacent Cedar County, with a population roughly twice that of Osceola. Then she pulled up stakes from Osceola and moved to El Dorado Springs with Haleen. "By then, I had saved some money, and I bought a house and moved in," she says. Hal tagged along but never really improved his on-again, off-again relations with Karolyn, who had to hire a babysitter for Haleen while she worked full-time at the hospital.

'In those days, it wasn't like it is today. Men didn't change babies' diapers. Men didn't do anything with the kids, especially in the country.'

"In those days, it wasn't like it is today," Karolyn says. "Men didn't change babies' diapers. Men didn't do anything with the kids, especially in the country. That was just the bottom line with babies. The women cooked, cleaned and took care of the kids. That was your role. And if you had to work on top of that, that was just tough luck. So that's the way I lived."

Karolyn did find time in El Dorado Springs to develop friendships, become involved in amateur variety productions and sing and direct the choir at the local First Baptist Church. Still, Hal's lack of contribution to the household and to the marriage left a big hole. Emptiness washed over her late one summer night as she sat on the back porch of her house, a recent-vintage rambler at 323 Poplar, and looked longingly at the brand-new house on the lot behind. "It was dark, and the couple who ran the pharmacy downtown and were new in town had just built this home. I saw them standing there inside their home, and they held each other and kissed, and I thought about how nice it would be to have someone really love you."

It was during this time, a little more than five years since her dad's death, that recurring dreams triggered a desire in Karolyn to return to Los Angeles for a visit. "Every night I dreamt of my life and my home out there and going back – every night – and I'd wake up sad, and it was kind of getting to me," she says. "I wanted to touch that life again, just to maybe ease my pain, because I knew I was in a situation that probably wasn't the best. I wasn't real happy with the choices I'd made by marrying Hal. I said something to Marie about the dreams, and she said, 'Well, you need to go out there.' "

So, taking a reluctant Hal, Karolyn followed that advice. The couple took an extended car trip that rattled Hal once they reached southern California. "He was terrified," she says. "He was a country boy, and he was scared to death of driving there, so I drove. But it wasn't just the driving. He didn't like the city. He was frightened."

In Los Angeles for just one day, they passed up studios or other movie-related locations. "I couldn't have cared less about that," Karolyn says. Instead, they drove to three spots connected to her previous family life: the Ridgely Drive house, her father's Safeway store and her parents' Forest Lawn graves. Then the two took a breather at Sea World before turning the car east to return to Missouri.

○ *Kansas City*

○ *Osceola*

El Dorado Springs (Dorado pronounced with a long 'a'), 25 miles southwest of Osceola

"I had to see it myself, and I had to let it go," Karolyn recalls, in a measured tone. "I was still hanging on to a little thread of my life in California, and I had to sever it. I looked at it, I realized that it was a part of my past and that I could never capture what I had before. By then, I had a lovely little girl, and I had parents again, sort of, and I could make myself happy, so I decided I would."

To that end, Karolyn was determined to maintain steady employment. "I had a responsibility to my child, and I had to work to maintain that," she says. "That was the bottom line. I brought her into the world and had to be responsible for her regardless of whether Hal was going to be or not. I didn't have a choice. It was pretty obvious he wasn't." Job stability just was not in the cards for Karolyn over the next year and a half, however, for she changed work environments in seemingly swift succession.

'I didn't know what the heck I was doing, but I needed to work, so I just applied for the factory jobs.'

First, she left the El Dorado Springs hospital for a better-paying position in the same town, assisting a Dr. Shepard, whom Karolyn considered a gentle and knowledgeable physician. But he was a troubled man who stayed up late at his second-floor office typing random, disconnected thoughts on endless sheets of paper, occasionally staying there overnight. A few months after Karolyn took the job, Dr. Shepard was found in his office, dead of an apparently self-inflicted gunshot wound. "It was horrible, particularly because he had little kids," Karolyn says. However, she did not know the doctor well enough to feel a special loss. Her main thought at the time was that she would have to find new work.

The only places to turn were El Dorado Springs' shoe and shirt factories, both located just a few blocks from downtown. "I didn't know what the heck I was doing, but I needed to work, so I just applied for the factory jobs," she says. "I was not talented in that regard. This was just rote work." At International Shoe, which employed 100 people, Karolyn was a sock liner, gluing linings into an endless succession of shoes. A few

The El Dorado Springs buildings for International Shoe (above) and Dunbrooke Shirt Co., as they look today.

months later, she was laid off, so she turned to the Dunbrooke Shirt Co., where she wielded an industrial sewing machine to sew buttonholes on shirts. "It was boring work, but I really got into the competition there," she says. "The more buttonholes you did, you made more points. There was some incentive to do it faster than everybody else. It gave me incentive and made it fun."

Marie's experience was Karolyn's inspiration once she was able to go back to work.

Karolyn decided to go into business and operate a dress shop in downtown El Dorado Springs.

The buttonholing job lasted nearly a year and might have gone on longer had it not been for another unplanned pregnancy, during the summer of 1962. Ironically, Karolyn and Wanda Lyke had been awaiting the availability of over-the-counter birth-control pills in their region. "She got the first ones," Karolyn says, "and when she called to tell me, I said, 'Oh, no,' because I was already pregnant. I had just missed them by three weeks."

Karolyn eventually delivered her second daughter Ideena Ann (Deena, for short) on Jan. 25, 1963, in the El Dorado Springs hospital. Hal was present at this delivery along with Marie, whose kind gift still stands out in Karolyn's memory.

"We didn't have much money, and because the new baby was a girl, she was going to get hand-me-down clothes," Karolyn says. "Marie brought a pile of boxes all the way over to the El Dorado Springs hospital, and inside was a layette of new clothes. It was the best thing, because you want to take the little baby home in fresh, new stuff and dress her in new stuff for awhile, and I really couldn't afford to buy anything, so that meant a lot. It was the kind of special thing Marie always did."

It also was right up Marie's alley. While Marie was a dedicated homemaker, mother and grandmother, she also had commuted for years to work at an apparel store in Kansas City, then had worked closer to home at Knight's dress shop in the Osceola town square. Marie's experience was Karolyn's inspiration once she was able to go back to work. Karolyn decided to go into business and operate a dress shop in downtown El Dorado Springs.

ANNOUNCING
Friday, June 28

Grand Opening

The Style Shop

215 South Main—El Dorado Springs, Mo.

FREE DOOR PRIZES
Awarded at 3:00 P. M. for
Pearl Necklace — Whimsie Hat — Kayser Slip
Dress by Sy Frankel

FREE ORCHID PINS
Given to first One hundred purchases

SPECIAL—
Big savings on several styles of Career Makers.

JUST IN—
New dresses, hats, purses. Beautiful and unusual Tear-Drop Necklaces.

FIRST SHOWING—
Fall Sports Clothes. Queen Casuals. Mix and match.

The Style Shop's grand-opening advertisement on page 2 of the June 27, 1963, EL DORADO SPRINGS SUN.

Investing the last of her inheritance, Karolyn hired Marie part-time and in May 1963 opened The Style Shop, across from a funeral home at 215 South Main Street in the center of town. The concept was to provide "better ready-to-wear clothes for women," primarily dresses, but also seasonal complements of hats, jewelry and lingerie. "It wasn't mod," says Karolyn. "It was just better dresses, simple-type things." In fact, simpler was better for business, Karolyn found. The shop's biggest selling items became jersey dresses in half-sizes, for heavier-set women, and pillbox hats, as First Lady Jacqueline Kennedy had popularized.

The store's formal grand opening on June 28, 1963, was an upbeat affair, with an ad in the El Dorado Springs Sun promising free orchid pins to the first 100 customers and door prizes of a pearl necklace, a Whimsie hat, a Kayser slip and a Sy Frankel dress. Later ads said the shop featured "the fabric, the style, the size you want," free gift wrapping and sales on "better quality merchandise." The optimistic attitude did not always carry over into sales figures, though.

Operating the store was largely a 9-to-5 one-woman pursuit for Karolyn, whose daily routine included enduring long periods without customers. That was due, in part, to competition from Mack's, an established dress shop run by an El Dorado Springs native. It gradually became apparent that this town of 4,000 wasn't big enough to support two upper-end dress shops. Karolyn didn't worry overly about the competitive aspect, however. "I just figured if I did snappy window dressings and had a nice personality and had a good stock and variety that I could make it work," she says.

As her filmmaking career was long past, Karolyn didn't give a thought to using her parts in movie roles as a way to promote The Style Shop. "I was raised to think that that would be like bragging, and you didn't do that," she says. Moreover, she felt she hardly had celebrity status. "I'd been a bit player," she says. "I was a nothing."

To her daughters, however, Karolyn was everything. Between caring for them and running The Style Shop, she paid little attention to the tumultuous social changes that were rocking the rest of the country during the mid-1960s. She had little time to think about issues of racial discord or about the politics of the Vietnam era. It was while she was in her car on South Main Street of El Dorado Springs, for example, when she heard the news over the radio of President Kennedy's assassination. But even that jarring act of violence registered in Karolyn's mind only remotely.

Hal and Karolyn Barnes and their two girls, Haleen (left) and Deena, in a formal portrait taken in mid-1963 in El Dorado Springs.

"That kind of thing didn't even touch me," she says. "When you live in a little town in the heart of America and have two little kids to make a living for, you are protected from that. It's not a part of your life. It was almost like fiction. I was too absorbed in my own life, worried about survival. I didn't have time to worry about the world."

Nor did Karolyn's taste for music stray much from the romantic strains of her teen years, despite the raucous incursion of Elvis Presley and the Beatles into American culture. Crooners such as Roy Orbison and the Everly Brothers were more her style – and certainly that of The Style Shop customers.

For two years, Karolyn labored to keep her store afloat, and she did find some satisfaction. She loved creating displays and dressing windows, and seasonal

markets in Kansas City, where Karolyn and Marie were able to sift through the latest styles, were a high point. "I'm a girl and I love clothes, so it was exciting to go and try to figure out what might sell in your town," Karolyn says.

Main Street in El Dorado Springs, as it appears today. It looked much the same in 1963, when Karolyn opened The Style Shop in the storefront at far right, behind the two pedestrians.

'Stupid – stupid, stupid, stupid' is how Karolyn looks back on the venture.

'It probably would have made it fine if I hadn't had to live off it. It needed four or five years to establish itself, but I needed money right away to live on.'

Marie looks back on The Style Shop as a success because Karolyn managed to pay all her bills, and the store brought the two of them even closer together. She has fond stories from those days. "We had some of this fine lingerie, and Karolyn would take home and try the highest-priced lingerie we had and the baby doll pajamas," Marie says. "I was over at her house once, and one of the baby doll pajamas was just in shreds. I said, 'Honey, you know you're supposed to wash those in low or by hand,' and she said, 'Oh, I didn't have time. I just threw them in with Hal's work clothes.' "

On the whole, though, Karolyn found the shop an exercise in frustration. It required her to work longer hours than she ever had, keeping her away from home life with preschool-aged Haleen and the younger Deena. Worse, it never turned a sustained profit, draining her hard-earned savings and forcing her to use store proceeds to pay her household expenses instead of plowing profits back into the business.

"Stupid – stupid, stupid, stupid" is how Karolyn looks back on the venture. "It probably would have made it fine if I hadn't had to live off it. It needed four or five years to establish itself, but I needed money right away to live on. Hal wouldn't watch the kids, so I had to pay a babysitter – a lady named Suzy Carouthers whom the girls loved dearly. When I realized the shop was going down the tubes, I tried to bail it out by borrowing on the house and putting more money into it, but that didn't help." Marie considered buying the shop from Karolyn, but was discouraged by the prospect of a daily commute to and from Osceola. "So I just closed the doors," Karolyn says, "took the poison pill, the loss, and went back to work in a medical office."

This time, the only medical job available was in the office of a Dr. Wray, in downtown Nevada (pronounced with a long "a"), the seat of Vernon County, near the Missouri/Kansas border. Karolyn maintained her El Dorado Springs residence and drove 20 miles to and from Dr. Wray's office every day for the next year.

A large, heavy-set surgeon with two fingers missing from his right hand from a shooting accident, Dr. Wray, who drank Jack Daniel's and smoked cigarettes every night in his office, represented the rough-and-tumble practice of a rural doctor. Karolyn received a graphic education from this burly man as he matter-of-factly treated grisly emergencies that clinics in a large city rarely saw.

A 1964 gathering of the Motley side of Karolyn's family in Osceola. Karolyn is in the middle of the back row, holding 1-year-old Deena in her arms. Lewis Lee Motley is to Karolyn's right, and her aunt Myrtle is to Deena's right.

"Once, we had a woman who had caught her arm in a wringer, and her arm was mangled with massive hematomas under the skin. They hadn't absorbed. They were just huge clots," Karolyn recalls. "In Kansas City, you would send somebody like that to the hospital. Not Dr. Wray. He would take care of them right there in the office. We opened her arm up, and he pushed out these clots and put 'em in a dishpan. It was quite a deal. I'd never seen anything like that. There was another woman who had been bitten by a black widow spider as she sat on a privy, and the bite had rotted part of her bottom off. I saw a lot of unusual trauma. We even circumcised babies in there."

Hal, a year older than Karolyn yet still living the irresponsible life of a teen-ager, remained unproductive and unreliable during his wife's latest turn of employment. "He was always on one of his 'mail routes,' " Karolyn says. While it had become clear to her that the marriage would not last, she hung on nevertheless. "I loved his mother and dad and his sister and his brother," she says. "It was like they were my family, so I just put up with the rest."

It was a medical crisis of her own that became the last straw. Her uterus required a surgical cleaning, and Dr. Wray performed the operation. "I was in the hospital for three days, and Hal never came to see me. I didn't tell anybody that Hal didn't come, but Marie ended up coming and was there when I came out of surgery. The only reason she came was that one of my neighbors called her. I wasn't going to bother anybody."

Soon after leaving the hospital, Karolyn knew it was past time to end the eight-year marriage. On a weekday morning in July 1966, before going to work, she

Kansas City

Osceola
El Dorado Springs

Nevada (pronounced with long 'a')

It was a medical crisis of her own that became the last straw.

'I was in the hospital for three days, and Hal never came to see me.'

telephoned Hal and told him that she wanted a divorce and that she had made an appointment with a lawyer that day at 11. "You can be there or not be there," she told him. "Doesn't matter to me, but I'm going to do it."

Karolyn met the attorney at the appointed hour, Hal showed up a little later, and they reached an amicable agreement on all issues. The settlement gave Karolyn custody of Haleen and Deena and ownership of the house, the car and other items she had paid for, but required no child support from Hal. "We had lunch afterwards at a drive-in restaurant, and I hardly ever saw him after that," Karolyn says. "Once in a while he'd pick up the kids, but that was pretty rare."

To obtain a divorce in Missouri at the time, a petitioner needed a character witness. Karolyn's was Charlene Broughton, an electrical cooperative bookkeeper whom Karolyn had met through the local First Baptist Church and whose daughter played with Karolyn's children. Charlene's memories of Karolyn are fond and filled with esteem.

"She was refined, clean, hardworking," Charlene says. "She had a polish that we all admired, and she fit in about anyplace she went." Karolyn's steely determination, particularly with regard to her job changes and her divorce from Hal, sticks in Charlene's mind as well. "I think she's to be admired, really," she says. "There was just something about her. She always had a spirit to keep going. She wouldn't let things get her down. Anybody else would have given up, but she just kept trying, and she was always cheerful and sweet. She could do about anything that she put her mind to."

Looking back on her marriage to Hal, Karolyn doesn't think he really loved her. "It was an impulsive thing," she says. "Hal was too much of a kid. Actually, neither one of us was very adult, but I supported him for our whole marriage. He didn't like to work too well, and he was a philanderer and a few other things." What Hal did provide her, however, was independence from her aunt Marsha, and an in-law family and two girls she adored. The prospect of being a newly single, working mom didn't daunt her, as her married existence had not been much different. "I just took it for granted that this was what was going to be. I didn't have any choice," she says.

Besides, Karolyn retained the support of Hal's parents. While the divorce came as a surprise to Hal's parents, their home stayed – and remains to this day – a refuge for Karolyn and her kids. "The only reason I stayed married to Hal as long as I did was because I loved his parents," Karolyn says. "I was constantly looking for parents after mine died, and Marion and Marie were wonderful. I just loved them, and I still do. We are really best friends. Marie calls me, tells me she loves me, checks on me. It's just really good."

Soon after the dissolution of Karolyn's marriage to Hal, something else in her life fell apart that changed the course of her life – her car.

"My car shot craps and died," she says. "I didn't know what to do, because I needed a car to get from El Dorado Springs to work in Nevada every day. Dr. Wray offered to buy me a car, saying that I could pay him out of my paycheck, but I knew that kind of arrangement would lock me into that job for five years, and I didn't know whether I would like the job well enough to stay that long."

She had recently visited Hal's brother, who lived 90 miles north in Kansas City.

'The only reason I stayed married to Hal as long as I did was because I loved his parents.

'I was constantly looking for parents after mine died, and Marion and Marie were wonderful. I just loved them.'

Immediately, Karolyn's affinity for the urban environment, particularly the concentration and greater availability of the arts that it could afford her and her children, awakened from its dormancy.

"I got all homesick for city life, and I really wanted to move back to the city," she says, "and so when I had another few days off, I went up there again and applied through an agency for a position as a medical technologist for a doctors' clinic. Before I got back home, they called and offered me the job."

The quick response by the clinic was no accident. Karolyn's bubbly, beaming presence and personality emerged in the job interview, recalls Dr. Otto Spurny, one of the clinic's founders. "She was almost radiant when she walked into the room. That smile just sort of lit the place up," he says.

"She'd had a bad experience, and she had to prove herself. She was coming to Kansas City without any backup system – two little kids and no husband – and usually anybody like this is a terrible liability. When the kids get sick, the person can't come to work. At least nine times out of 10 when you try to hire someone like that, it's bad all the way around. But she made such a good impression that we thought we would give her a try."

The job offer was good fortune for Karolyn, but she wanted time to think. She also wanted to give Dr. Wray two weeks' notice. So she negotiated a potential start date three weeks hence. A week later, she gave her notice to Dr.

Dr. Otto Spurny, the Kansas City clinician who hired Karolyn as a medical assistant, says her smile "lit the place up."

Wray and called Dr. Spurny's clinic to accept the job. The forthcoming schedule promised to be hectic. She would need to move to Kansas City, and there still was the problem of transportation. In her mind, there was only one solution.

"My neighbor drove me over to Osceola, to Marion and Marie's farm," Karolyn recalls. "I just looked at Marion and said, 'I need a car. My car is gone. It's too much to fix it. I've got to take care of my kids, and I've got to work.' He got me a car, a used Chevy that had belonged to a teacher and didn't have a whole lot of miles on it, and it was fine. I eventually paid him back, plus interest, but the important thing was that when I needed it, they were there."

A few days later, Hal her to Kansas City and amazingly, in just one afternoon, they found Karolyn a small house along State Line Road plus a babysitter who lived up the street. Her new life, and that of Haleen and Deena, was set and full of optimism. "I would have acclimated to El Dorado Springs, but 'happy' was in the city," she says.

Karolyn started at the clinic in Kansas City's Midtown section in August 1966 and stayed there for the next 15 years, enjoying both the intricacies of laboratory medicine and the one-on-one contact with patients. It was a career that had begun as a fluke back in Osceola in 1959, when a friend had told her that the local hospital needed another worker. At the time, she had no clue that the medical field

'She'd had a bad experience, and she had to prove herself. . . .

'She made such a good impression that we thought we would give her a try.'

Dr. Otto Spurny

would suit her so well for so long. "I didn't even know if I could stomach it," she says. "I never would have thought of it as a career, but it turned out to be a real challenge, and I liked it. Before it was over with, I was doing IVs and assisting in minor surgeries and everything else."

It was hard work, with a never-ending flow of patients and their attendant needs for precise lab procedures and tests. The job pulled in just enough to cover the expenses of her household.

The four-physician team for whom Karolyn worked: (from left) Drs. Jack Wolf, Otto Spurny, Shu-Min Wu and Malcolm Shalet.

Karolyn easily recalls the basics of her monthly budget during her first year in Kansas City: "I grossed $400 a month, and I paid the babysitter $100 a month," she says. "The house payment was $95, and then I had food, car, gas and clothes. I didn't have medical bills because everything was courteous for me in those days. If you worked for a doctor's office, you had free medical care, really. But overall, I barely eked by. My ex-brother-in-law brought me up a deer that year to put in my freezer so I'd have meat. It was hard to make it, but I did."

The babysitter, whom the kids called "Mee-mom," became a godsend, Karolyn says. "She was wonderful. She'd feed them dinner, which really helped, because I wouldn't get home until 7 most nights, sometimes 7:30 or 8."

'I grossed $400 a month, and I paid the babysitter $100 a month. The house payment was $95, and then I had food, car, gas and clothes.

'I didn't have medical bills because everything was courteous for me in those days.'

Karolyn tried to compensate for her weekday absence from her girls by taking them on weekend outings to see relatives and explore new places. "I'd always try to plan a free day, to go someplace where it wouldn't cost us anything. We did museums because they were pretty much free, like the Nelson Art Gallery, the Indian Museum, or places in other towns, like the Jesse James Museum. Or we'd do state parks. I'd pack a breakfast with cereal and fruit in a cooler, and we'd go to the park and have breakfast – just spending time together, doing stuff together. It was worth it, because they got exposed to a lot of art and things that many kids never really did. That was my bag, and I wanted to teach them my bag."

Part of her "bag" was her workplace, and Karolyn didn't hesitate to bring Haleen and Deena to the clinic for social visits. "They had a blast seeing the things that I worked with," she says. "They used to run up and down the halls in wheelchairs, and take home bandages and work with some of the chemicals and litmus papers that weren't dangerous."

When she started at the clinic, Karolyn worked for a team of physicians: Drs. Spurny, Jack Wolf, Malcolm Shalet and, soon, Shu-Min Wu. While she served all the clinic's staff and patients, Karolyn became the primary assistant to Dr. Spurny, an internist and heart specialist whose background as an immigrant enriched Karolyn's work routine.

About 10 years older than Karolyn, Otto Spurny had grown up in Austria, enrolled in medical school there, hid in an attic from the Nazis during World War II and was rescued by Allied soldiers. He served as a houseboy for a U.S. colonel, who cleared the way for the young Austrian to finish his education and come to

Chapter 8   *"You call this a happy family? Why do we have all these kids?"*   *Page 151*

America to work as a physician. It was his chosen vocation, and his dedication and work ethic heartened his assistant.

"His first love in life, his reason for living, was – and is – his practice and his medicine," Karolyn says. "His wife and twin boys were secondary. He's the only doctor I've known who makes hospital calls twice a day, morning and evening. His wife realized this early on, and she was off on her own, doing her own thing. They've led separate lives, because his job is his life. It's what he's liked to do, and he's good at it. To me, he's always been a father-brother figure, but never lover, just sort of a mentor. He's the most caring man I've ever met."

Dr. Spurny, a short man who speaks with a heavy Germanic accent, returns Karolyn's kind evaluation with one of his own. Karolyn, he says, "turned out to be the best employee we ever had – and an individual whom you could consider your friend." She was skillful, dependable and personable – particularly important traits in the practice of Dr. Spurny. Because he could read and write German fluently, he served as the area's German Consulate representative. As a result, the clinic dealt with many patients who had survived the Nazi prison camps of World War II. "A lot of these people are chronically suspicious," says Dr. Spurny, who notes that the adversity Karolyn had undergone made her better able to empathize with and help such patients.

She was skillful, dependable and personable – particularly important traits in the practice of Dr. Spurny.

For Karolyn, interacting with these survivors of the Holocaust subtly helped her build a survival mindset of her own. "The German government paid us to examine these people and assess their condition to see if they were permanently disabled and, if so, how badly," she says, "so I was able to see the numbers on their forearms and hear the stories. It was a fascinating experience."

Because he could read and write German fluently, he served as the area's German Consulate representative.

Over time, Karolyn became quite close to Dr. Spurny, choosing him as her own physician, even house-sitting for him during his vacations. "It got to the point where he didn't want anybody to help him but me," she says. "I could read his mind. I knew what he wanted before he wanted it."

As a result, the clinic dealt with many patients who had survived the Nazi prison camps of World War II.

Her job held what she considered a wellspring of variety. She escorted patients to examination rooms, drew their blood and analyzed it manually (before the use of computers), conducted pelvic exams, x-rays and electrocardiograms, okayed prescriptions, assisted in minor surgeries, even made house calls – "just everything else that needed to be done." The patients themselves provided human interest, as well. "You got to follow their progress and get to know them," she says. "It was always a challenge because no two days were alike.

"One of the doctors was a hematologist, so we had a lot of people come in with blood diseases. The doctor may have suspected a disease, but I was the one who would actually find it and say to him, 'Look.' I would get to be the one who actually sees it before the doctor diagnoses it, or at least could tell him there was something abnormal, and that's pretty interesting."

Another of the physicians who assisted in the hiring of Karolyn, Dr. Wolf, says she possessed "the right stuff" to handle the clinic's demands. "She always took care of everything she was supposed to do, she made the patients happy, and I think all the doctors and staff liked her," Wolf recalls. "She was pretty much everything you wanted in an employee."

"We were like a family," Karolyn adds. "They were good to me, and it was fun.

Then there were the regular patients who came in and tipped me – they'd stick a buck in my pocket after I'd draw their blood – and that was kind of a thrill.

"The only thing I didn't like about the job was the long hours, just being away from the rest of life. I would have liked to leave at 5 o'clock every day, but it usually went an hour or two later. The doctors gave of their heart, gave it all they had. Patients would end up waiting for two hours into the evening in the waiting room because the doctors ran late, and you had to see them. They were sick, and you couldn't really say no. I didn't like it, but I didn't really see any way of fixing it."

In one sense, though, given Karolyn's professional and personal turmoil before coming to Kansas City, a regimen of long hours served almost as a welcome relief. Karolyn's turbulent life finally had begun to settle down. Her job was fulfilling, and the doctors for whom she worked liked her. Her children – Haleen, the quiet one, and Deena, the chatterbox – were growing up with loving care and fleeting tastes of the arts that were dear to their mother's soul. Karolyn managed to stay within driving distance of the family, friends and "real people" she trusted and loved, and she was finding out quickly that people in Kansas City weren't far removed from the small-town sensibilities and values she had come to embrace.

The only two loose ends were her yen to perform and her yearning for romance. Both of these needs would soon get attention.

'We were like a family. They were good to me, and it was fun.

'Then there were the regular patients who came in and tipped me – they'd stick a buck in my pocket after I'd draw their blood – and that was kind of a thrill.'

Soon after moving to Kansas City, neighbors across the street from Karolyn had set the 26-year-old up with a man in his early 30s named Richard, whom she remembers as both kind and frugal. "He lived with his mother and father, and he'd never been married," she says. "My kids loved him, and he would have been good material – a hard worker and good for the kids." Karolyn dated him for many months, but the sexual spark wasn't there. "I just didn't think he was for me," she says.

Meanwhile, Karolyn sought urban venues for singing, hoping to find solo opportunities. She began by trying out for a Kansas City organization called Youth for Christ, but while the group liked her voice, she was considered too old for a paying position. Next, she joined the choir of a Baptist church in an upper-income area near her home. Although the choir director valued the clarity and range of her soprano, he never asked her to sing a solo. "I thought it was really strange, because I didn't think the people I sang with were as good as I was," she says.

Soon, she spotted an announcement of auditions for a volunteer production of the Broadway musical *The Boy Friend* at the local Jewish Community Theater. Karolyn told herself, "I'm going to try out, because maybe I really am not that good." It was a way to find out where she stood. She auditioned for the play, and to her surprise and delight, she was cast as Polly Browne, the lead character. "They were going nuts over my voice, so I thought, 'I'm okay.'"

Winning the part was all the more satisfying since Karolyn said nothing about her Hollywood past during her audition and the subsequent strenuous rehearsals. "Nobody knew who I was or what I'd done in the past, so to them I was this little thing who didn't know anything, a country bumpkin," she says. "The director watched me develop, and I did learn, and in the end I did the part very well, but it took me a long time. I almost gave him a heart attack because he was thinking I wasn't going to put it together."

Set at a "finishing school" on the 1920s French Riviera, *The Boy Friend* is a dancing/singing fest and love story in which girls learn to be "perfect young ladies" and, as Karolyn puts it, "everybody hooks up with everybody." (The Sandy Wilson play was the basis for an affectionate Ken Russell movie released three years later, in 1971, with the British model Twiggy playing the lead.) As Polly, Karolyn played a wealthy young woman in love with a passionate, rich young man disguised as a poor messenger boy. Because she wants to be loved for herself and not for her money, Polly, also disguises herself as the school's secretary. The scheme succeeds until her millionaire father arrives along with her suitor's lecherous dad and blue-nosed mother. It's all good fun, as well as a spoof of the music and manners of the Roaring Twenties.

Shortly before the Kansas City production of *The Boy Friend* opened on March 23, 1968, the company's publicist had to assemble a written program, and Karolyn was asked to list her credits. At this point, she opened up about her childhood movie roles. When the director found out at a cast party, "he was absolutely beside himself. He was off the wall, he was so excited." Not only did the disclosure boost the director's confidence, but his response gave Karolyn a big lift.

Encouragement was just what she needed, as Karolyn had encountered several health problems during rehearsals, including a chest X-ray that indicated a suspicious spot on her lungs.

Encouragement was just what she needed, as Karolyn had encountered several health problems during rehearsals, including a chest X-ray that indicated a suspicious spot on her lungs that Dr. Spurny said could be tuberculosis. "I could have been exposed because Hal's grandma had TB off and on over the years," Karolyn says. "Dr. Spurny could have given me some kind of preventive medicine, but he made a judgment call and said, 'Let's watch it for awhile and not worry about it.' But in the meantime, I'm thinking, 'I may have TB, and I have all these kissing scenes.' So I was reluctant to kiss this guy during rehearsals, and I didn't want to tell him what was going on. Then Dr. Spurny told me he thought it was fine, so I was all right."

In the lead role of Polly Browne in a March 1968 community theater production of THE BOY FRIEND, Karolyn sings, dances and swoons over Michael Owen (her love interest Tommy).

The three-week run of the play was successful, and Karolyn laughingly remembers an incident during one performance that brought down the house. At one point, her character Polly and her intended's mother, Madame Dubonnet, sit down and talk, and Polly pulls a letter from her bosom and shows it to her. On this night, however, the letter wasn't there. It had slipped. "I started winging it, and she realized it wasn't there, and so she started winging it, and all the time I was feeling around my body looking for the letter," she says. "Finally, I figured out where it was and reached my hand under my dress to pull it out. I thought the audience was going to die, and everyone who was part of the play was just hooting and hacking, it was so funny. I got a standing ovation that night."

As rehearsals and performances of *The Boy Friend* proceeded, Karolyn was the object of a different, more personal ovation.

In idle conversation during the past year and a half, a co-worker of Karolyn's had kept her up to date about the marital problems of a young couple she knew. Eventually, the couple divorced. Then, in early 1968, the co-worker set up a blind date for Karolyn with the divorced man – Mike Wilkerson, a tall, gregarious, heavy-construction contractor who, at 26, was two years younger than Karolyn. A native of Oklahoma, he had grown up and worked in Peoria and other Midwestern cities, finally settling in the Kansas City area as part of his father's culvert and bridge building business. A Catholic who lived temporarily with his parents, Mike also was a single father of three: a 5-year-old boy, Michael Christopher, who lived with him, and a 3-year-old girl, Carey Eloise, and 2-year-old boy, Matthew Craig, who were in their mother's custody. A heavy drinker and smoker, Mike carried himself with the back-slapping brashness and hot temper of a high-roller, both professionally and personally.

'He had these gorgeous eyes and this booming voice, and he just commanded the stage.

'He was domineering, and I liked that.'

The evening started as a double date at a fancy restaurant, but because the other couple got into an argument, Karolyn and Mike moved on by themselves to a smaller eatery, then to a seedy bar for a few games of pool. It became a fateful night.

"He wowed me. I mean, he wowed me," Karolyn says, with awe-stricken emphasis. "He was a very handsome man. He had these gorgeous eyes and this booming voice, and he just commanded the stage. He was domineering, and I liked that. And the son who lived with him, he loved more than he did himself. He was a Catholic, and he was devout. He just bowled me over."

Mike Wilkerson, 1969.

Mike was a handful, but he intrigued Karolyn to no end. From the blind date onward he pursued Karolyn, growing ever more sure that she was the right mate for him. Dr. Spurny, who soon came to know Mike, observes, "Being a successful contractor is not easy, because those people are always on the edge of either making a lot of money or going bankrupt. It was the same in his personal life. I could tell he was good dealing with people, but he had had a bad marriage, and he sort of felt Karolyn was his lifesaver, to pull himself together."

The fact that Karolyn regularly fixed Sunday dinner for Mike and his son Chris symbolized Karolyn's lifesaving role. "I never asked for any money or help for that dinner each week, and he knew I didn't have enough money to do it, but I always did it," Karolyn says. "That really impressed him."

To Karolyn, Mike's free-spending nature served as a reminder of the pleasant aspects of growing up as a doted-on child in California. Also, Mike and his family represented a stark contrast to Hal and to her Spartan late-teen and young-adult years in Osceola and El Dorado Springs.

"I had been raised never to have to look at the prices on a menu when I went into a restaurant," she says. "Then after my father died and I was moved out to Missouri, it felt like I was going to live like a guest the rest of my life. My aunt Marsha and uncle Clyde, and the whole situation, made me feel uncomfortable with the inheritance money. They made me feel guilty. I was afraid to eat anything because I'd hear about how much it cost them. Not only that, but Osceola was farming community where nobody ever dressed up.

"Well, Mike enjoyed dressing up. Even though he was in the construction business, he loved to dress and go to fine places. And it didn't matter, I could order anything I wanted to on the menu. He was a very, very generous person, and he could still be comfortable with the lowliest of the low, and I liked that trait. He introduced me to a whole other world."

For Karolyn, unquestionably, the spark was there. She had fallen in love. "I just thought he was the most wonderful thing in the world. I liked his mom and dad, and I knew that his family and the company he worked for were respectable, and he just seemed like he could do anything. I was crazy about him. The chemistry was there."

The obvious passion between the two grew fast. "He just snowed me so, dated me every night, wanted to be with me every night. He really turned it on," says Karolyn. "I was moralistic, I didn't drink or smoke, I was a good person. He introduced me to smoking and drinking, and I sort of changed, but he still liked me, and his kids liked me, and he liked that, and his parents liked me, and everybody in his family did. So he ended up wanting to get married. I did, too."

Karolyn and Mike Wilkerson on their honeymoon in the Colorado Rockies, July 1969. (This is a composite of two photos.)

However, Karolyn had learned from her first marriage the dangers of marrying on impulse. Besides, her demanding job at the clinic and her fast-growing daughters took up most of her time. What to do about Mike could not be a hasty decision.

On the other hand, she faced the stigma of having had a failed marriage. "In the Midwest, you were a real outcast if you were divorced," she says. "During that time it was almost as bad as having the scarlet letter painted on you. It really was." And Mike was not about to give up his pursuit.

So after a courtship of one and a half years, Karolyn finally decided to make Wilkerson her last name. The day before the July 19, 1969, ceremony, however, a distraught Hal visited Karolyn and begged her not to go through with it. But Karolyn was not to be swayed. Hal went on to marry several other women. Tragically, he died five years later at the age of 34 when he accidentally was shot in the head in a hunting accident near Osceola.

The Saturday afternoon wedding was not a big affair. It was held in the city hall of Kansas City instead of Mike's church because according to Catholic doctrine he was still married to his first wife. The two came back to Mike's parents' house for a reception, then hopped in a car and drove to Denver, Colorado, for a honeymoon. The next night, after motoring through the surrounding mountains, they came back to their hotel and had a memorable dinner in the bar, watching the history-making ". . . one small step for a man . . ." moon landing of Apollo 11 on TV.

Mike was a handful, but he intrigued Karolyn to no end.

From the blind date onward he pursued Karolyn, growing ever more sure that she was the right mate for him.

Mike Wilkerson, February 1970.

Karolyn's life with Mike was bound to carry its challenges, not the least of which was becoming, as Karolyn puts it, 'an instant big family.'

Karolyn's life with Mike was bound to carry its challenges, not the least of which was becoming, as Karolyn puts it, "an instant big family." Karolyn had gone from a household of three to a full-time clan of five, which expanded to seven on weekends when all three of Mike's children were present. Karolyn took to the motherly role with obligatory fervor, and during the first years of the marriage, at least, felt that her union with Mike promised a brighter and happier future for everyone involved.

Therein lay a contradiction, however. In a sense, her marriage recalled the days of her youth in performance lessons, church choirs and Hollywood films, when she was rewarded for following the decisions of others. "I think the real reason I married Mike was that I wanted somebody to direct me and take care of me," Karolyn says. "He had a commanding personality, and he was a boss, and I was looking for that." But the reality of her high-school years and her marriage to Hal had proved exactly the opposite. At several key points in her late teens and early 20s, righting Karolyn's life demanded not turning herself over to the direction of another, but taking action on her own. It was a contradiction that was to resolve itself in the years to come. As Karolyn puts it, "I fell in love with Mike, but love is blind, and I didn't see all that there was at the time."

Typical of Mike's dominance was his admonition that Karolyn forgo further community theater work. "He didn't like me being around the dancer-musician crowd," she says, "and it took away from our time together. It takes about six weeks of pretty intense rehearsing to put on one of those plays, and he didn't like that. So that was the end of that."

Mike also displayed his command by insisting that Karolyn and her children join and attend his Catholic church. Karolyn had always enjoyed singing in church, and the slogan, "The family that prays together stays together" was a part of her permanent mental makeup. "I thought it was good for a family to do things together, and this was one way they could be together, through religion," she says. The fact that Mike was Catholic was not a negative to her. "I was raised Baptist, but I had been in love with the Catholic church from day one, and I have always felt that it doesn't matter what your faith is – Catholic, Protestant, Buddhist – if you worship God. It's all one world. So what if you do it a little differently?" Karolyn's compliant attitude paved the way for Mike's Catholicism to prevail in their new family. "There was never any discussion, and I couldn't have cared less," she recalls.

Over time, though, Karolyn began to care more. Whereas before she married Mike she had only two kids to look after when she went to church, she now had as many as five at one time, with no tangible help from Mike. "It became a chore to get all those kids ready for church," she says. "They'd all try me, and Mike wouldn't help. Rather than straighten pants, comb hair and that sort of thing, he'd just yell at me or them. It was so awful that I began to hate church."

Complicating her feelings about attending Mike's church was its music. "During that time, the Catholic church was coming out of this cocoon that had been monophonic chants, more or less," Karolyn recalls. "That's all they ever did. They didn't do what I had known to be music. It was the blossoming of an era for them to discover and know what anthems were available to sing. For the longest time, though, it just was boring. You sang responses, and that was it."

The topper came after Karolyn realized that she could not formally convert to Catholicism. To do so "would have condemned my soul to hell for living in adultery or fornication," she says, because according to the church, Mike was still married to his previous wife. For nearly 10 years, Karolyn resisted conversion. Then, in the late 1970s, after Mike had donated significant sums of money and a van to the church, "the strangest thing happened – the Church let him off the hook, and his divorce was absolved," she says. So they married in a Catholic church ceremony and had Karolyn simultaneously become a Catholic, a step which, for Karolyn, had become less than enchanting.

Another way Mike took charge of his new family soon after his marriage to Karolyn was to take her and the kids on recreational vehicle trips during summer weekends to Hermitage Lake, Stockton Lake and other resorts in central Missouri. On these outings, water-skiing quickly became the preferred activity, as Mike, with Karolyn in the boat beside him, towed all five of their kids both singly and simultaneously. As years passed, the Wilkersons bought jet skis, boats and, finally, a four-bedroom home at Tan Tara resort in Lake of the Ozarks, about 100 miles southeast of Kansas City. There, Mike and the children played hard, often damaging expensive equipment, to Mike's impatient chagrin.

Karolyn – 30 years old and eight months' pregnant with Johnathan Ted, the first of two children she had with Mike Wilkerson – attends a birthday party at the Spurny-Wolf-Shalet-Wu clinic on December 2, 1970. Others (from left) are the birthday celebrant Mary Nicholas, as well as other staffers Gladys Goza, Linda Baum, a nurse named Jan, and Mary Ann Brown.

"There was always something to keep him in a continuous uproar," Karolyn says, "because it seemed like everything broke down, and he wasn't a fix-it kind of guy, and he would make everybody miserable because he was mad at himself. It was frustrating, to say the least."

Though she was not a "water person," Karolyn participated in these summertime trips and enjoyed parts of them. "It was a charming time in a lot of ways," she recalls. But she dreaded the abrupt shifts between hurrying to the resort and driving back home in time to open the clinic on Monday mornings – not to mention tackling the countless tasks and issues that come with such a large, together-at-all-times family activity.

Mike held firm family feelings about the celebration of holidays, including a troublesome one, the Fourth of July. While it was also Karolyn's birthday, she found no independence in it. "It could never be a birthday when I could go out to dinner and have fun," she says. "We always had to have family things, and it was always involved with other people, and it could never be just a little, private birthday. It had to be a big thing, and I didn't care for that. And it got more complicated as the kids grew older, because they wanted to do their own things on the Fourth of July, and Mike wouldn't let them. They had to stick around because it was my birthday. They resented the fact they had to do it, and I felt bad because they had to do it. It wasn't a good thing."

The topper came after Karolyn realized that she could not formally convert to Catholicism.

To do so 'would have condemned my soul to hell for living in adultery or fornication.'

While both Mike and Karolyn maintained their full-time-plus jobs, the wife was still expected to direct most of the domestic proceedings for their burgeoning bunch of grade-school-age and teen-age kids.

Through the 1970s, as Mike's construction business grew, the Wilkersons moved twice to larger homes in suburban Kansas City. For Karolyn, work and family life raced by, but not without at least two momentous occasions: the births of Johnathan Ted on January 15, 1971, and Kylan Kay on November 15, 1974. Also, by the end of the decade, Mike's other two children, Craig and Carey, had come to live with their dad and Karolyn, bringing the household total to nine. The ups and downs of raising an ever-growing "yours, mine and ours" family dominated the Wilkersons during these years.

It did not take long for the situation to dissolve into discontent. While both Mike and Karolyn maintained their full-time-plus jobs, the wife was still expected to direct most of the domestic proceedings for their burgeoning bunch of grade-school-age and teen-age kids. Thanks mostly to booming bridge-building work and a buyout deal engineered by Mike and his brother, both of whom built the family business six-fold over the decade to an annual income exceeding $10 million, the Wilkersons did not lack for finances to boost the standard of living for their nine-member family. But instead of being a cure, money mainly irritated a deepening wound.

Karolyn's clinic job became one casualty. While her family needed the money she was making when she first married Mike, the relative financial benefit of

An informal Wilkerson family portrait from 1976: (clockwise from Karolyn) Deena, Craig, Carey, Mike, Chris, John, Haleen and Kylan.

Karolyn's work rapidly diminished over time. "After he became so successful and his business was in the millions, he thought it was just stupid for me to make these little $5-, $6-, $8-, $10-an-hour wages," she says. But it wasn't just the money that bothered Mike. "I don't think he liked for me not to be a part of his world," Karolyn says. "He didn't know anything about medicine, and that was all I knew and could talk about. When I came home from work, I couldn't share anything that happened during my day. To me, it was exciting work. You have severe medical problems, and you get involved with your patients. They become a part of your life." Mike, she says, was indifferent. "Who wants to hear it?" was his attitude, as he chose instead to watch TV or stay out late.

"After about a year or two of marriage, I began to see the flaws" of Mike's domineering approach, along with the toll taken by his alcohol consumption, says Karolyn. "I was raised a Baptist and hadn't been exposed to really habitual drinking up until then. I honestly didn't know what it did to a marriage or a family." Braced by her own domestic responsibilities, Karolyn gave up the smoking and drinking habits that Mike had prompted in her. Another couple of years later, Karolyn decided that she once again had reached a marital crossroads. "I felt that I had to make a choice, so I wrote down the pros and cons," she says. "I felt like I either had to get out or make it a life of my own and make my own happiness."

For the sake of the children, both hers and Mike's, she chose the latter. "I didn't have time to worry about self-pity, because I had all these kids, and the only stable thing those children had in their day-to-day lives was me," she says. "I could have gotten out of the marriage, but I thought I was doing the best thing for those involved. I had made a commitment. So Mike and I had sort of an arrangement. He did his own thing, I did my own thing, and that's the way it went."

Mike and Karolyn Wilkerson pose for a 1977 portrait with four of their seven children: (clockwise from upper left) Deena, Haleen, Kylan and John.

This arrangement included an unspoken physical distance from Mike that Karolyn imposed. In part, the culprit was Karolyn's revulsion from Marsha's forced affection during her late teens, now carried over to her relationship with Mike. "At first, I wanted to love him to pieces," she says, "but later I would draw away. I could not stand to be touched – by him, and then by anyone, even my kids. It is sad, and I regret it so much, but I just couldn't handle it. I just couldn't accept that physical touch, because I think I would be afraid that I'd figure out that I missed it." She would not regain the joy and comfort of a hug, or a hand held, for another two decades.

As the years passed, Karolyn says that she took her commitment to Mike's children as seriously as she could, perhaps even further than she should have. Caring for seven kids "was a lot to do," she says, "but I told myself, 'I can do it.' I gave Mike's kids so much of myself and took my own kids for granted. I assumed that because they were mine and they came from me they would know I loved them, whereas with the other ones I had to constantly affirm the fact that I loved them and that they had a place in my heart and a home. I tried to give them a balance I figured my own kids wouldn't need. That probably wasn't the wisest thing to do."

Part of her feeling that Mike's children needed more of a balance stemmed from Mike's dominant personality, which translated to a child-rearing approach of put-downs and physical punishment. "His kids knew he loved them, but he wouldn't always express that love so well, particularly with the boys, who were always getting in trouble. When he would yell at one of them, I would try to say, 'What

'I didn't have time to worry about self-pity, because I had all these kids, and the only stable thing those children had in their day-to-day lives was me.'

you did just now made him feel so bad about himself that it really didn't teach him anything. Is this what you want?' And he would tell me, 'Goddamn, I'll raise my kids.' It was never 'our kids.' It was always 'mine' or 'yours.' "

In their own ways, Karolyn and Mike persevered in this less-than-ideal family

situation. Soon after their Catholic wedding, in the fall of 1979, as 19-year-old Haleen contemplated marriage, Mike proposed one last family trip while the nine were still nominally together. To accommodate school schedules, they set the getaway for the break between Christmas and New Year's Day 1980. The destination, proposed by a travel agent and accepted by the Wilkersons, was a resort in Jamaica. It was an exotic endpoint, but not overly awe-inspiring for a family whose members had taken several earlier well-financed trips around the world. Well-intentioned as it was in theory, the week-long journey turned out to be a comedy of errors, magnifying the pressures produced by a turbulent marriage.

Their smiles belying the distance growing between them, Karolyn and Mike Wilkerson pose for a portrait at the close of the 1970s, with five of their seven children (clockwise from lower left): Kylan, Craig, John, Carey, and Deena.

Arriving in strife-torn Kingston, the Wilkersons were surprised to have to drive for three hours, in two vans, starting at midnight, to their villa in Port Antonio. Once there, they found the food rank and nearly inedible, cleanliness lacking and children's activities absent. They encountered drug solicitation, "hate whites" signs and ominous indications of a civil uprising in progress. Five of the seven children became sick – ranging from infections in one's ear and fever blisters on another's mouth to wasp stings and shingles on one's eye and beach tar in another's crotch. Restless, Mike decided to fly back early to attend the Orange Bowl, leaving the rest behind, but he was

stymied by a rule forbidding travel without 45 days' notice. Frustrated further by Cuban-only radio broadcasts, he tried unsuccessfully, while Karolyn nursed the kids' ailments, to get through by long-distance telephone to follow the football game. The vacation did produce a few positive memories, including a notable afternoon of river rafting. Overall, however, it left an unpleasant aftertaste.

As the decade of the 1980s began, and Karolyn neared her 40th birthday, several transitions were in store for the Wilkerson family.

First, as befit the success of Mike's construction firm, they moved in July

Mike Wilkerson and his crew ease a concrete beam into position during construction of a highway overpass.

This 11,000-square-foot home in the Berryhill subdivision of Stilwell, which the Wilkersons purchased and moved into in 1980, sat upon the highest point in Johnson County, Kansas.

The front of the Berryhill rambler featured several entries, while sunset views over an 800-square-foot pool (right) graced the rear. The size and location of the huge home befit the success of Mike Wilkerson's construction business.

1980 from a 3,500-square-foot home in Kansas City to an enormous Country French-style house that Mike had built in the Berryhill subdivision of Stilwell, a southwestern suburb just over the Missouri state line in Kansas. Fronting on a five-acre horse pasture and four-acre yard, the two-level, 11,000 square-foot rambler with seven bedrooms and bathrooms, two dining rooms, living room, card room, exercise room, office, game room, recreation room, concrete storm shelter, swimming pool and three-car garage was expansive, to say the least. While its low profile did not dominate the surroundings, its girth capped a rolling swell, the highest point in Johnson County, supplying a dramatic view in all directions, including north to the Kansas City skyline. Karolyn wasted little time adorning the house with art ranging from French watercolors to Dali prints, the accouterments all in blue, her favorite color. "I think we'll be here forever," Karolyn optimistically told the local *Sun Newspapers* chain, which ran a feature story on the distinctive home a year later. "Everything we want and need is right here."

'I think we'll be here forever,' Karolyn optimistically told the local newspaper.

The coming of the new decade also marked the end of Karolyn's job at the medical clinic, at the behest of Mike. To please him, she already had scaled back to a part-time schedule, and further to a vacation relief role. "Then the computers came into being in a major way, and I became obsolete," she says. While her houseful of growing children no doubt benefited from her being home more often, Karolyn missed the clinic. "I was good at what I did, and I knew it, and I felt good about it," she says, "and there's a lot of difference between that and being a mother at home and trying to solve all the problems of the world, you know?"

The most significant change of all for Karolyn, however, could not be marked with a specific date or act. It had been gradual, something perceptible in joy and tears as much as in measurable terms. It was both close to home and far away. It was a movement that had taken hold across the continent, a surge of interest in a multitude of living rooms. It was a rebirth – and a new, revered status – for the 1946 film *It's a Wonderful Life*, the one in which Karolyn had played the magical role of Zuzu.

For Karolyn, this nationwide resurrection could not have come at a better time.

The saga of the Bailey family of the small burg of Bedford Falls never lost its joy, poignancy and emotional appeal. It merely languished in obscurity for nearly three decades.

It's a Wonderful Life was shown occasionally on the TV late show through the 1950s and 1960s. But as the nationwide nostalgia craze moved into full swing in the 1970s, it was other films from Hollywood's golden age – including dozens of classics made by Frank Capra and James Stewart – that fueled the country's fondness for simpler, more respectful times.

Into this welling reservoir of affection for the "good old days" fell *It's a Wonderful Life*, and a legal oversight transformed it into not only the quintessential American holiday classic, but also what many consider the best movie ever made.

The fluke that triggered widespread exposure for *It's a Wonderful Life* came in 1974. The legal period for copyright of 28 years had elapsed, and it was the time for RKO Pictures to renew. But no one bothered.

With no copyright, under federal law at the time, the film fell into the unprotected status of "public domain." Thus, it became fair game for television network affiliates and independent stations to show whenever they liked. Stations started to screen the movie in December, to tie its culminating Christmas Eve setting with the holidays.

To many people who thought they already had seen the best work of Stewart, Capra and others, *It's a Wonderful Life* came as a welcome shock, a newly discovered Christmas present beyond compare. It was the mid-1970s, several years before taped movie rentals became affordable and video shops popped up on every street corner, so TV stations across the country responded to viewers' raves for the royalty-free movie by screening it two, three and more times a year as each Christmas season came and went.

Hollywood wasted little time trying to capitalize on the surge. In 1977, ABC aired a color remake produced by MCA/Universal called *It Happened One Christmas*, a gender-reversal version with Marlo Thomas as the George Bailey character. As in its 1946 predecessor, there is a daughter with a cold, a prize flower and, word for word, the

The societal affection for the life-affirming message of IT'S A WONDERFUL LIFE *is shows clearly in this painting inspired by the film's joyous final segment. Todd Karns, who played George Bailey's brother Harry in the movie and now lives in Ajijic, Mexico, painted this image and markets a series of greeting cards with this and other "Wonderful Life" scenes he has created.*

"Every time a bell rings" line. But the girl – dark-haired, not blonde, and named Suzy, not Zuzu – is argumentative instead of charming, and the fallen petals that her mother tucks away carry less punch than they do in Capra's film. While this TV retelling was a typically commercial form of flattery, it nevertheless was well-intentioned and has some nice touches. (Sadly, it is not available today on video.)

Chapter

9

'You have no idea what's happened to me!'

(The resurgence of 'It's a Wonderful Life,' and the suicide of Karolyn's son John, 1980-1990)

However, critics and audiences at the time understandably maintained their strong preference for the original.

By the end of the 1970s, as a natural outgrowth of its new-found popularity, *It's a Wonderful Life* had taken on the attributes of a grassroots cult film. People wanting to share with loved ones the movie's themes of hope, friendship, family and the worth of every human being started throwing *It's a Wonderful Life* parties scheduled during one of the film's many TV screenings. The trend was legitimized further by lengthy analyses in the media, including *The New Yorker* and *The Wall Street Journal*.

The new life that came to *It's a Wonderful Life* took Karolyn Grimes Wilkerson by surprise. She had long ago put her Hollywood career behind her. Had she been asked to name the best film she had worked in, or the one she had the most fun making, *It's a Wonderful Life* would not have shown up in her answers. Her moviemaking memorabilia – photo stills, pay stubs, newspaper articles, script pages, all saved by her mother, transported to Osceola in 1956 and hauled from place to place thereafter – had sat virtually undisturbed in boxes in the basement.

"Every once in a while, one of the kids would use some of the photos for show-and-tell at school, but it wasn't any big deal," Karolyn says. "Certainly I didn't try to make it a big deal for them. It was a part of my life that I had written off. It wasn't special. It was nothing. It was absolutely nothing."

But in late 1980, at Christmastime, Karolyn's telephone started ringing. The calls came from reporters sniffing out a new angle and wanting to know more about everyone involved in the making of this extraordinary film. The first call came from a suburban newspaper south of Kansas City, near the Wilkersons' new home. The resulting article, headlined "Salty tears from onion dust" (a reference to how Karolyn was made to cry during the filming of *Lust for Gold*), ran on Jan. 21, 1981, in the Overland Park *Sun*. It read, in part:

> **Natalie Wood, Margaret O'Brien and Shirley Temple were the
> big child stars during the forties, under contract to a major
> studio.**
>
> **But there were other roles for a cute little girl who wept on cue
> – a child who didn't upstage the adult leads.**
>
> **Those roles usually went to Karolyn Grimes.**

By then, the revival of *It's a Wonderful Life* was still formative. The movie had not yet become a household word. So it's understandable that the newspaper story inadvertently referred to the film as "It's a Great Life." Despite this now silly-looking error, the article prompted another phone call to Karolyn, this time from a radio station. Then the next year, another newspaper called, and so on, one by one.

Never one to be shy, Karolyn served as a good interview subject, replying to questions as best she could with details and quips, interspersing earnestness and flourishes of laughter. In one early interview, perhaps because of the lust of her own teen years, she enjoyed recounting the telephone conversation scene between James Stewart and Donna Reed because of the passion between the two characters. "What a dilemma," she told the reporter. "He knows what he wants, but his hormones are just going crazy. There was so much chemistry."

Never one to be shy, Karolyn served as a good interview subject, replying to questions as best she could with details and quips, interspersing earnestness and flourishes of laughter. . . .

But no parents, friends or former co-workers were readily available to help her flesh out the skeletal information.

Some questions, of course, she could not answer, as all that she had to go on were her early childhood memories and the clues provided by the photos and clippings in her memorabilia boxes. No parents, friends or former co-workers were readily available to help her flesh out the skeletal information. "When my parents died and I was shipped to the Midwest, I lost a lot of reference points – basically, I lost my life – and I had to start over," she says. She contented herself with the limitations of her recollections and materials, although every once in awhile a new detail surfaced from her memory, almost as if to tease her own renewal of interest in her past.

With the media coverage came the return of fan mail, after an absence of some 40 years. The typical request was the same. Most people asked for an autographed photo. An obliging Karolyn would dig through her boxes of artifacts, find a promotional still

When fans first asked Karolyn for autographed photos in the early 1980s, she signed her name (as above) on original stills and sent them off. Later, she learned to make copies to send.

from a film, sign it and send it off. "The first two or three times, I sent them original stills," she says. "I had no idea that you could make copies. I didn't think. I just thought it was really special that people would write and ask for my signature on a photo. Then I began to realize that, oops, it was a mistake to do that. So I started having copies made to send out."

As the early 1980s progressed, Karolyn dealt with queries about *It's a Wonderful Life* as they cropped up, then moved on to more mundane pursuits. However, Karolyn's identity was transforming. People were beginning to associate the wife and mother with Zuzu Bailey, a symbol of the goodness that each life can create. Each phone call or request for an autograph quietly bolstered her self-esteem, unwittingly building her inner strength.

She even became so bold as to look into recovering royalties for her part in commercial uses of *It's a Wonderful Life* that kept surfacing. In July 1984, the Wilkersons' attorney sent a letter to Steven Spielberg, inquiring about the use of Karolyn's likeness in several clips from the movie that turned up in Spielberg's *Gremlins*. In February 1985, their attorney wrote a similar letter to a maker of collectors' plates. The correspondence produced no proceeds, however, because the classic film had fallen into the public domain.

As Karolyn's self-confidence about her Hollywood work grew, she tentatively brought it to light at home. She had a few of her movie stills framed, and she hung them on the walls of the downstairs card room in the new house, figuring that they would prompt some interest from Mike and his drinking buddies who came over monthly to play poker. The photos drew little notice, however. "He couldn't have cared less," she says.

Karolyn's identity was transforming.

People were beginning to associate the wife and mother with Zuzu Bailey, a symbol of the goodness that each life can create.

Exemplifying the growing craze for IT'S A WONDERFUL LIFE is this undated lobby card from Mexico, which advertises the film with a photo depicting the key Zuzu's petals segment. Translated, the title of the movie appears as "How Beautiful to Live," and it is billed as "The greatest film of genius Frank Capra!" The smaller text reads, "An impact to your heart. The history of two souls filled with love that only death can separate. An outpouring of human emotions that only those who have loved will never forget!" The film is a "strictly exclusive" presentation of Agresanchez Films.

To Mike and the rest of her family, the attention Karolyn was starting to receive for her moviemaking past was bewildering, even silly. The kids' stance was somewhat understandable. Most of Karolyn's films were in black-and-white and, to them, ancient and irrelevant, and most of her children were entering their teens, the typical age for rejection of parents. "They went through periods where they supported me," says Karolyn, "but the majority of the time, they didn't care. It was just one more thing that their mother was doing. It was an embarrassment sort of thing."

The attitude of Mike was more difficult to explain, however. He didn't hesitate to disparage the burgeoning *It's a Wonderful Life* phenomenon, Karolyn says. "His exact words were, 'It's bullshit. It's just bullshit.' He thought it was small beans. He didn't like that I chose to spend time on something like an interview instead of being with him. To him, he was important, and what he did was important. He was the breadwinner, he supported everybody, he was the king, and nobody should even be trying to get attention but him. He felt he was working hard and not getting much notice for it, and here I was getting this attention. In his mind, I didn't do much to deserve it, and he did deserve it and didn't get it."

'He thought it was small beans. He didn't like that I chose to spend time on something like an interview instead of being with him.'

Karolyn says that to Mike, her film career was so insignificant or threatening, or both, that he never asked about her younger years. "He knew absolutely nothing about my childhood," she says. "He was never curious, never wanted to know anything. I think he loved me, but he was too interested in himself and his work and his kids. That was paramount in his life.

"He and I never sat down and watched *It's a Wonderful Life* together one time. Never. Or any of the other movies I was in. He would tell people, 'Oh, of course, I've seen it,' but he never had. We'd watch the part I was in, and that would be it. He loved to go to movies and could tell you anything you'd want to know about history, but he just didn't like old movies. I'm not an old movie buff, either, and I never watched old movies, so it was something we just didn't do in our home. So my kids were never raised that way. For them to sit down and watch something in black-and-white would have killed them. So I didn't press it.

"I'm just sorry I didn't take the initiative and sit them down to watch *It's a Wonderful Life* every year like other people do. I didn't do it because I thought it

Chapter 9   *"You have no idea what's happened to me!"*   **Page 167**

was the wrong thing to do because they would think I was making them watch it because I was in it. I thought it was part of my childhood and it was different from other people. But so what? My life had been different from other people's in so many ways."

At times, even Karolyn didn't know quite what to do with her Hollywood heritage. Should it become a larger part of her life, something to encourage? Or should it remain a sporadic sidelight? Because of her role as an active mother of seven and caretaker of an enormous home, her choice consistently was the latter, at least for the time being.

Rolling with the yo-yoing fortunes of her husband consumed a great deal of Karolyn's attention as well. As part of the buyout of the Wilkerson construction firm, Mike had signed a five-year non-competing contract. The settlement left him with a multi-million-dollar payment, plus a generous yearly dividend and salary, so that by the early 1980s as he was turning 40, Mike had accumulated enough wealth to retire and to launch a series of wishful investments, each of which eventually soured. There was a restaurant, then a drug store. There were commodities market stabs into cotton and bales of hay. None was a financial winner.

Often, Mike asked Karolyn's advice on these ventures, and Karolyn gamely responded. "Then he'd do exactly the opposite and take risky advice, bet on the market and lose," she says. "I got to the place where I'd say, 'Why ask? You're going to do what you want to do anyway.' Then, in the end, he'd throw his hands up, turn around and tell me, 'You do it.' I told him, 'I don't know anything about the stock market,' and I tried investing like he wanted me to, but I made bad judgments and lost money, too."

Furious with himself and with the dwindling resources, Mike resolved to bring Karolyn even more directly into the financial picture, creating a corporation for her called Second Union (a reference to the fact that each had married before). The company's first undertaking was a late plunge into video games, as she and Mike bought Pac Man and Star Trek machines and installed them in restaurants and sports centers in and around Kansas City and at the Lake of the Ozarks resort where they had just purchased a summer house.

"He wanted to do these machines, and I said, 'You're getting in the end of the phase. Just rent them and have somebody else put them in your restaurant and you take a piece off the top.' But he went ahead anyway," Karolyn says. "I'll never forget, I had just had a hysterectomy, and he brought home four cloth sacks full of quarters and dumped them down on the bed. I had to sit there and put quarters in rolls. He wanted me to get started, because it was my company, and that was going to be my job, and I was going to do it."

Karolyn soon became known as "the quarter lady" as she periodically drove to various sites and emptied the machines of change. She also was responsible for fixing those needing maintenance. "It wasn't really that great for me because I have no technical abilities," she says. "The machines would break down a lot, and I wouldn't be able to repair them. I'd have to have other people do it, and that was expensive. Eventually, when the newer machines came out, I sold the ones I had, except I kept a few for the kids for the basement of the house, so they had a lot of

At times, even Karolyn didn't know quite what to do with her Hollywood heritage.

Should it become a larger part of her life, something to encourage?

Or should it remain a sporadic sidelight?

play and fun with them. In the long run, it was probably worth it, but I wouldn't do it again."

Finally, after Mike's five-year no-compete period had passed and he had given up on ancillary investments, Mike returned to what he knew best – culvert and bridge building. He poured the remainder of the family's funds into starting his own firm, MTW Construction. Over time, the firm acquired a net worth of several million dollars, but the growth reflected Mike's willingness to siphon money from personal coffers more than it did the success of the business.

Mike Wilkerson pilots one of the family's boats in 1986. While the construction chief always wanted to be in charge, he also prodded Karolyn to shed her stereotypical subservience, she says.

Karolyn is quick to point out that Mike's errant financial forays, while frustrating in the extreme, paid her dividends down the road. By thrashing about for ways to make big money, and inducing her to join in that quest, he set her – perhaps inadvertently, no doubt painfully – on a course of independence.

"Mike turned me around," Karolyn says in blunt hindsight. "He forced me to learn about business. He forced me to learn about people, and he forced me to learn about interacting and demanding what's justly yours. I had never heard of amortization and stuff like that. I had no clue. He made me come into the financial world. I was no longer the little domestic housewife who cooked and ironed and cleaned. He made me come out and do things, and when I saw that I could, it gave me self-confidence.

"I don't know if he did it to me to be mean, or to make me change, or to take things off his back. I really don't know. But in the end, he prepared me for the worst that could ever happen to me. Even little things, like making me make long-distance phone calls when I was nervous about it, or making hotel reservations, or calling up an airline to make a flight reservation – he made me do those things, and all of them came to be tools that I use now all the time.

"The way I was raised, the woman was to kowtow to the man and be taken care of by a man in every sense of the word. But he made me take care of myself, plus the kids and him, and it became a whole different kind of life. It was the best thing he could ever have done for me, because he turned a mouse into a lion, and I'm very comfortable with who I am today. In the end, he said he'd created a monster, and he had. He awoke this little fire inside of me that says, 'I like to control situations,' and that grew to be a big flame."

Part of that flame was red-hot anger over Mike's everpresent boss-like behavior. "I used to get so mad at Mike, I'd just die," Karolyn says. However, the women she befriended in her new neighborhood became an outlet for her exasperation. "With my friends, I would talk it out, get it out of my system and end up laughing about it."

Shopping, particularly for gifts for their seven children, was no laughing matter, however. "I was raised an only child, and I used to get tons of stuff for Christmas, so that's what I did with our kids," she says. "Mike thought I went way

'I don't know if he did it to me to be mean, or to make me change, or to take things off his back. . . .

'But in the end, he prepared me for the worst that could ever happen to me.'

overboard, though, and he would get frustrated. At first, we tried shopping together, because that was the kind of thing I'd always wanted to share with a husband: shop with him, go to church with him, go to the grocery store together. That was important to me. It was our life together. But the way I shopped upset him, and I did spend too much money, I'm sure. Eventually, like so many other things, I decided I wanted to do it my way, so I started taking control, being sure everybody had everything I thought they needed. Several times, he told me that I'd taken the fun out of Christmas for him. It always bothered him. We went through a lot of attempts to shop together, but it ended up that I'd do it totally."

An unspoken remoteness continued to divide Karolyn and Mike. They tried counseling, but without success. At times, despite their sporadic fireworks, Mike took pen in hand and tried to express understanding toward his wife. At one low point, he wrote her:

> **You have never gotten over the hurt and sadness of your parents being taken away from you at such a young age and then being put in an environment that was totally strange to you. You adapted very well considering everything, then as you grew you looked for the love and security you missed, without trying to let the hurt or disappointment show.**

Mike also periodically wrote Karolyn of his love for her:

> **You mean so much to me in my life, for I am fortunate beyond anyone's normal right to have a wife and mother of my children and a giving person like yourself. Without question you provide the anchor by which my life runs. I know that sometimes you get fed up with the kids and me, but please remember that you are, after all, all that we have, and all of our love runs deep for you. There are a lot of uncertainties in our future, but the one constant, unchanging, lasting thing is my love for you and my respect for you as a wife, mother and a person.**

However, as Karolyn points out in retrospect, words and actions are two different things. "It got to the point where I wouldn't go out with him socially at all, mainly because of his drinking," she says. "If he wanted to go someplace, I would say, 'Go on your own.' So he would do his thing and I would do mine. It was kind of a cooperative thing." To his credit, Mike finally joined Alcoholics Anonymous and quit drinking in 1983. But while that in itself was a positive step, Mike "became a hermit and wouldn't go anywhere," Karolyn says. He smothered her with attention as *It's a Wonderful Life* was rebounding and making her increasingly busy. As the decade proceeded, the two gradually but ever more deeply carved separate routines.

This evolution was not entirely difficult for Karolyn. In part due to her 15 years at the medical clinic, plus her lifelong aversion to idleness, she could not find it in herself to be a stay-at-home mom. In her Berryhill neighbors, Karolyn found company and intriguing conversation, notably in the presence of Barbara Karnes, a hospice organizer and self-published author on the death experience. She introduced Karolyn and others in her neighborhood to a body of thought called Shusta, a Sanskrit word from India meaning "footsteps back to truth." A philosophy, not a religion, Shusta was originated in Florida as a metaphysical

'You have never gotten over the hurt and sadness of your parents being taken away from you at such a young age and then being put in an environment that was totally strange to you.'

Mike Wilkerson, writing to his wife Karolyn

study of colors. It is based on the belief that there are beings – what Karolyn has come to label guardian angels, just as in *It's a Wonderful Life* and *The Bishop's Wife* – who watch over mankind.

Given her increasing marital disaffection, Shusta arrived in Karolyn's life at a good time. "It was a way for me to get to know some of my neighbors, and I liked the women there," she says. "I've always been interested in things that are challenging, and I was at a stage of my life when I needed to learn more about everything. It gave me a new direction of thought and affected me in many ways. Instead of black-and-white, it made gray walk in."

Trouble walked in with another of her neighborly pursuits, however. It was the popular card game of bridge, which soon led to an unhealthy obsession.

Karolyn's love for bridge had started innocently enough, when her father taught her card games as a child. It had continued with the favored game of pitch she played with Lewis Lee in Osceola. The flame re-emerged in the 1980s when Karolyn, as a homemaker in her huge Berryhill house, joined a local women's bridge club that met two afternoons a month. Pam Yarbrough, a longtime friend of Karolyn's who lives in the Kansas City suburb of Overland Park, recalls meeting Karolyn while substituting in the bridge group.

"It was at a house in my neighborhood, less than a block away, and when I got there I didn't know a soul," Pam says. "Seven of us were sitting around waiting for number eight, because we couldn't do anything until number eight came. I was listening to the chit-chat of people I didn't have anything in common with when, all of a sudden, in the door flies this woman like a bat out of hell saying, 'Deal the cards!' It was Karolyn. Scared the heck out of me at the time, but we became friends pretty quickly."

Bridge, says Pam, served as the catalyst for their friendship to bloom. "For people who don't have a lot in common, it's a mental exercise," Pam says. "Bridge played well is a quick mind, and bridge played poorly is a social experience. This bridge group was social, and most of the players weren't very good. Karolyn and I were more competitive and took it more seriously, so I think we connected as total strangers just over the philosophy of cards."

'One day I took a look at myself and I thought, "I'm in my 40s, and I am sitting at a table playing a game with my life. What a waste of time and energy!"' '

Two of Karolyn's friends, Pam Yarbrough (left) and Karen Treschl, sort and price items for the annual Rockhurst High School Sale-o-Rama, the event that spurred Karolyn's interest in antiques.

That philosophy, both Pam and Karolyn came to realize, can feed upon itself. Soon, at Karolyn's initiation, the two went beyond the bridge club, competing in duplicate tournaments with "men who played bridge with their life," as Pam puts it. The compulsion, at least for Karolyn, had taken off with no end in sight.

"It became a real serious thing for me," Karolyn says. "I didn't like party bridge. I liked playing with men. I liked playing serious, competitive bridge. I wanted to win. I learned to count cards, all the different conventions. I was really adept. But I got to the point where I didn't have time to think about myself or my needs or interests. Everything just went on the back burner. The only thing I did was play bridge, and it seemed like that was the only fun I had in life except for my kids."

By the mid-1980s, Karolyn had come to find that "there are bridge studios all over the world, and you can find a game anywhere you want to. I got to playing at the studio and traveling in the tournaments, and one day I took a look at myself and I thought, 'I'm in my 40s, and I am sitting at a table playing a game with my life. What a waste of time and energy!' "

She tried to quit the game for extended periods, but she relapsed twice. "I was sneaking around trying to hide it. It was really sick," she says. "Mike ended up helping me to get off it, maybe not for the best of reasons. He said it was just something else that was taking attention away from him, and he made that very well known. He was so insistent that it was a decadent thing to do with my life. So the third time I quit, I

Karolyn prepares antiques and other items for Sale-o-Rama with friends (from left) Kathy Williams, Beth Johnson and Kay Sipel.

made it – cold turkey. I never went back. I said, 'This is it, I'm done, I will never do this again.' "

And she hasn't – except for an annual social game with friends. Like an alcoholic who speaks of the craving for booze as an addiction, Karolyn speaks of bridge in the present tense. "It's a real bane, a thorn in my side," she says. "I would rather play bridge than eat or do anything else in the world. So I can't play bridge. If I play more than one game, I'm liable to get hooked again. It's like a potato chip. I love it that much. I love to challenge my brain, but I don't play cards anymore. It's a worthless way to spend your life, in my book. When I'm 80 and can't do anything else and my brain's still alive, maybe I could try it again more seriously, but it's not a cool thing to do with your life when you're active."

Karolyn with her Sale-o-Rama mentor, Father Mario Puracelli.

In addition to bridge, Karolyn became involved in property investment, including the purchase and (and later sale to a friend) of a tiny 1910-era bank building in nearby Stanley. In part, these forays served as attempts to find meaningful ways to spend her time and express herself, particularly given the growing distance between her and Mike. One other vocation of Karolyn's from the mid-1980s also fits that category, and it continues to fulfill her today – the buying and selling of antiques.

In her young-adult years, she never would have guessed that she would later become fascinated by older furniture, knickknacks and collectibles. "I hated antiques," she says. "Anything that was old, I hated." What turned her head, though, was her involvement in Rockhurst High School, which her children attended. "If you're a Catholic parent, you have to participate in fund-raising for the school. That just goes along with life," she says. Unsure of which project to choose, she asked to work in the antique department of a giant rummage sale called Sale-o-Rama that raises $75,000 to $110,000 for the school each year. "I was scared to death because I knew nothing about antiques," she says, "but I started learning, and after the first year they put me in charge of that department."

'I hated antiques. Anything that was old, I hated.'

What turned her head, though, was her involvement in Rockhurst High School, which her children attended.

All of Karolyn's seven children encountered problems of varying degrees during their young lives, but none of the seven reacted as desperately as John.

In that role since 1985, Karolyn has been one of several dozen parents who work at least one day a week for six months each year to prepare for the mammoth fall event. The key skill, Karolyn found quickly, was pricing. She not only bought reference books and studied the antique market, but also enlisted the help of a priest, Father Mario Puracelli, who was seasoned in fund-raising, and a neighbor who ran antique shops of her own, Karen Treschl, who, despite her move two years later to the Chicago area, has become Karolyn's best friend.

The camaraderie of working with a group of women on a common goal kept Karolyn participating in Sale-o-Rama, but she found the main attraction to be discovering what she calls "the treasures." "You always look for that little thing that costs $2 but it's worth $5,000, you know? It's the eternal treasure hunt. That's what it's all about," she says. "It's wonderful, it's exciting, and the more you know, the more you can find."

That excitement soon made her feel that involvement in the Sale-o-Rama was more of a joy than an obligation. It also led Karolyn, in late 1988, to open a stall of her own in an antique mall in Stanley. Her space covers about 75 square feet, in which she displays an eclectic, constantly changing mix of merchandise.

"It just keeps me on my toes," Karolyn says of her interest in antiques. "It keeps me up on what's out there, what people are getting rid of, what the trends are. For instance, when I first started, we'd get fabulous costume jewelry, but now that people are making all of these funky-junk jackets and decorating Christmas trees with it, we're not getting any jewelry at all. It just comes in phases. Some years, some colors are different than others. You know, it'll be the year of avocado or the year of orange.

John Wilkerson, son of Karolyn and Mike, opens a gift on his 18th birthday, January 15, 1989.

"You also want to recognize different types of glass and pottery. You want to be able to look at it and say, 'Okay, that's a Rookwood.' It's something to learn, to broaden your scope. I watch prices and changes in what the public wants, and it's a constant test of your ability to provide that for customers and do it for the sales that you work for. It's a great mind challenge."

"Challenge" is a word that flows freely in Karolyn's vocabulary, and a concept that permeates her life. By the end of the 1980s, she had faced the deaths of both her parents, a wrenching move to Missouri, a trying first marriage, a rocky series of job changes, a bout with bridge addiction, a household with seven kids and a waning relationship with her husband. But the decade soon was to yield her most profound challenge of all – the suicide of Karolyn's and Mike's second youngest child, John, at the age of 18.

All of Karolyn's seven children encountered problems of varying degrees during their young lives, but none of the seven reacted as desperately as John. His death continues to affect each member of the family and their relationships with each other. It is a topic about which Karolyn is quite sensitive. "It's the only thing in the world that can make me cry," she says. Yet she talks freely of the events leading up to the incident, and of its aftermath, largely because she has come to accept that John is at peace.

The last full year of his life, 1988, was hardly peaceful for John, however. A Rockhurst High School student with average grades, John was fascinated by computer games and earned extra money by working part-time as a janitor in Mike's office. The 6-foot-2 teen-ager had a reluctant attitude toward sports, a painfully shy personality and a strong-willed father, but, at least on the surface, John seemed like he could manage. "He wasn't aggressive," says Karolyn. "He couldn't fight back. He couldn't hurt anybody. He couldn't be mean. He couldn't get mad. He was just a nice guy." Underneath, however, hid a deep turmoil.

On a spring day that year while meeting with the school priest, John threatened to commit suicide. Later the same day, though, he insisted to his family that he didn't mean it. The problem, as he described it at the time, was his love life. John anguished over the reluctance of girls to explore relationships beyond friendship, despite the special attention, flowers and other gifts he would offer. John also felt he was overweight. To his face, his dad likened him to the portly Jabba the Hut character from the *Star Wars* trilogy. Later in the year, using a liquid commercial diet unsupervised by a doctor, he shed 40 pounds in three months. Karolyn now wonders if the rapid weight loss may have caused a chemical imbalance in his brain that sent him from despondence into depression. At any rate, John was not the only one in his family with problems that year. The lives of several of his siblings were hardly stable, Mike's construction business had entered a tumultuous period, and the atmosphere in the Wilkerson household at times approached chaos.

'My life from then on has been split – before John and after John.

'It's probably the worst thing I've had to go through in my life.'

The first week of February 1989, Mike took a hesitant Karolyn on a spontaneous horse-race betting vacation 300 miles south, in Hot Springs, Arkansas. While they were away, John, then a senior, was summoned to court regarding a car wreck in which he had been involved in mid-January. A few days after their return, hurt again over being rejected by yet another girl, John bolted early from an afternoon piano lesson, called his parents to say he wanted to consult with their priest the next morning, then left by car to play basketball with a friend. It was the last time Karolyn and Mike heard his voice.

Karolyn called the friend's house later and learned that John had just gotten a speeding ticket. Upset as a result, John had told his friend that he wasn't going to come to his friend's house, but he refused to say where he planned to go. Sensing the need for a search, Karolyn slipped into her car, drove the Kansas City area half the night, then waited up the other half. She tried to cover all of John's haunts, but it turned out that he was uncharacteristically "in the one place he said he wouldn't be." A neighbor found him the next morning in front of his friend's house, at the wheel of his car with the motor running. Karolyn's handgun, which no one had any idea John had taken, lay on the floor of the car. He had shot himself in the mouth. It was Feb. 16, 1989, and John was dead.

"My life from then on has been split – before John and after John," Karolyn says. "It's probably the worst thing I've had to go through in my life."

She feels she had two signs the next night – one from the sky, and one from a person – that John's tortured soul was finally at rest.

"It was like the whole sky was in a circle, and the light in the very center was the moon, like a giant star," Karolyn says. "It was absolutely stunning. I've never seen it like that, before or since. It was like John was up there saying, 'It's okay,' and I really got the message. I really feel that's what was happening."

The second sign came from Barbara Karnes, the neighbor who had introduced her to the Shusta philosophy.

'I have no doubt that when I die I will see John again. He may not be the way that I knew him, but I think our souls interact in some way with each incarnation.

'I have such a faith that that is the way things are. . . . It's not just, "Could it be?" I really believe it.'

"The night after John's death, all the neighbors, people, friends, everybody was coming over to our house," Karolyn says. "Barbara walked in the door, and I walked over and hugged her. She's a big, tall woman, and I just stepped back and looked up at her and said, 'Will I ever have another chance to try and make it right again?' She looked at me straight in the eye and said, 'No.' She could have softened it. She didn't. She just said, 'No.' I knew that was true, but I needed her to tell me that, so I could be in touch with reality and not wish in my mind that I'd have another chance with John, that I could work it differently. I knew that was the finalization right there.

"I had the immediate sense that if John was that unhappy, I had to think of him and what was best for him, not me. And God, I miss him so bad. To this day, I die when I think about him. But when Barbara told me what she did, I knew that I had to deal with it, and I knew that he had made the choice. Even though he was a troubled teen-ager, his soul had made the choice, and he had to live with that choice, and perhaps I do, too."

As might be the case for anyone, Karolyn's thoughts often return to John's truncated life. She readily comes up with things she could have said or done differently that may have made a difference. "In retrospect, I can see all kinds of things. They stick out like a sore thumb. But I couldn't see them at the time, or elected not to see them," she says. "I should have seen the red flags, but given everything, given all the circumstances in our family, I think I did the best I could.

"I have no doubt that when I die I will see John again. He may not be the way that I knew him, but I think our souls interact in some way with each incarnation. I have such a faith that that is the way things are. It's another thing that helps me get through it. It's not just, 'Could it be?' I really believe it."

Karolyn's ruminations on her son's suicide reflect a rare ability to cope with adversity. Just as Karolyn comforted others who were distraught at the time of her father's death, she likewise found ways, such as setting up a scholarship fund for Rockhurst seniors in John's name, to move on from her grief over John's death. "I know I'm unusual in that respect," she says. "I can handle things. Maybe it catches up with me later, but not really. I'm able to take what life hands me and deal with it. I've always been like that."

Karolyn's friends served as amazed, admiring witnesses to her forward-looking response to John's death. "The day that John died, I just about moved in with her and ran her kitchen, and I was astounded," says Karen Treschl. "Somehow, she just bounced back. She's resilient in a way most people never have to be."

Pam Yarbrough agrees, characterizing Karolyn as unsinkable, unflappable. "With Karolyn, it's an indomitable spirit," she says. "No matter what happens to her, things that most people would find a living disaster, things that would disable most people emotionally, she gets through them with poise and determination and pretty serenely. She's a survivor."

*L*osing her son John jolted Karolyn as nothing had before. But her adaptation to the grief of his suicide was hastened by the ever-rising interest among media and fans in *It's a Wonderful Life*.

She could not foresee the avalanche of attention rolling toward her Zuzu persona. As she moved into the 1990s and the fifth decade of her life, however, Karolyn shed anyone's lingering doubts about the validity and satisfaction to be gained from reveling in the role. It was only natural, then, that Karolyn jumped at the opportunity to spend a morning with the man who played her father in *It's a Wonderful Life*, James Stewart.

The opportunity came on April 23, 1990, at a tribute to Stewart by the Film Society of Lincoln Center in New York City. Nancy Dillon, a writer whose affectionate cover story on the venerated actor had appeared in the December 1989 edition of *Modern Maturity* magazine, called Karolyn just the day before with an invitation to meet with Stewart at his New York hotel at 10 the next day. It had been 44 years since Karolyn had worked with Stewart on *It's a Wonderful Life*, she had not seen him in the interim. Given his advancing age (82 at the time), it was possible she would never have such a chance again. So Karolyn dropped everything, rushed to make plane connections and arrived at the hotel with only a few minutes to spare.

Their meeting took place on a couch in the hotel lobby, where for a couple of hours Karolyn, Stewart, and a longtime Stewart fan and family friend pored over a scrapbook the friend had brought that detailed his 60-year film career. He and Karolyn chatted about *It's a Wonderful Life* and about how they both had lost a grown child (Stewart's son had died in Vietnam),

Karolyn reunited with James Stewart on April 23, 1990, in New York City, 44 years after they filmed their memorable scenes in IT'S A WONDERFUL LIFE.

but the scrapbook took center stage, and Karolyn was satisfied to witness the warmth of his reminiscences. "He was very nice," she says. While other stars such as June Allyson and Janet Leigh milled about in the lobby, Karolyn fixed her

Chapter

10

'*Zuzu, my little ginger snap!*'

(*The death of Karolyn's second husband, and the birth of her alter-ego, 1990-present*)

attention on Stewart. For her, it was a large step toward reconnecting with her moviemaking past, memorable not for what was said but for the grace of the experience.

Karolyn ignored Mike's years-old admonition to stay away from community theater, and the experience became a catalyst for her to move further into the local spotlight.

As a guest at that night's Stewart tribute, Karolyn received star treatment of her own, manifested not so much in her treatment inside the theater as outside the back entrance. Like the many famous actors who attended the event, Karolyn and Nancy Dillon had arrived in a limousine, and as they emerged from the theater following the tribute, they overheard the limo drivers talking about whom they had squired.

"I had Robert Stack," said one.

"I had Kim Novak," boasted another.

Karolyn's driver, a short man, piped up and said, "Well, I had Zuzu."

For a moment, it was silent, as if E.F. Hutton had spoken. Then the hubbub ensued: "Oh, what does she look like?" "What is she like?"

"It was wonderful," Karolyn recalls. "My little driver, a very sweet man, was by far the biggest attention-getter because he had Zuzu."

At the same time, a young man in a wheelchair looked up at Nancy Dillon and asked her if she thought James Stewart would sign his autograph book. "There were so many people," says Karolyn, "that Nancy told him, 'I don't think so, but do you know who this person is?' and she pointed to me. When she told him I was Zuzu, he was just overwhelmed with emotion. He said that *It's a Wonderful Life* was his very favorite movie and that he seldom got out of his apartment. The tears just streamed down his face as I signed his book, and he told me it was the most wonderful night of his life."

The GIRL CRAZY Dudettes in July 1990: (clockwise from top right) Debi Schultz, Millie Sampson, Genie Greenburg and Karolyn Wilkerson.

Photo courtesy of *The Sun Newspapers*, Overland Park, Kansas

Shortly after returning from New York, Karolyn received a call from the director of the local Blue Valley community theater group, who, like many in the Kansas City area, was a fan of *It's a Wonderful Life* and Karolyn's role in it. The troupe was putting on the musical *Girl Crazy* for a three-day run that July, and the director asked Karolyn to audition for a part. "She thought that because my son had died the year before, it would probably be good for me to do it," Karolyn says. It was 22 years since she had performed on the stage, as the lead in *The Boy Friend*. But the part she was given in *Girl Crazy* – one of the saloon girls, called the Dudettes – was a small, workable one, with only a handful of solo singing lines. Karolyn ignored Mike's years-old admonition to stay away from community theater, and the experience became a catalyst for her to take a three-year term on the theater's board and move further into the local spotlight. Certainly, the local newspaper promotion of the play was as provocative as it was complimentary. Noting Karolyn's childhood moviemaking, one review said, "She does look a bit like a sexy Donna Reed or a tiny Donna Mills."

In November 1990, Karolyn's fame began to move up another notch, prompted unknowingly by her *It's a Wonderful Life* father. She had agreed to sign autographs as a promotion for the mall in which she operated her antique stall, and flyers for the event were distributed at a movie memorabilia show in nearby Overland Park. There, Ted Warner, a trucking company worker and cinema collector from St. Joseph, Missouri, picked up one of the flyers. He telephoned Karolyn, then came to her house for what became a six-hour interview for an article he later prepared for *Child Star Magazine*. He came away perceiving a kinship of spirit between Karolyn and her movie dad.

"Jimmy Stewart," says Ted, "is the man who has eaten with kings and presidents, and yet he's still the man next door. He is shocked that people love him and recognize him, and he doesn't understand why people think he's special. I see the same quality in Karolyn. She really is the girl next door – a lovable, kind, sweet person."

Ted already had obtained an autograph from Stewart on a still from the *It's a Wonderful Life* scene in which George Bailey "pastes" petals onto a rose for Zuzu. With Karolyn's signature on the photo as well, Ted obtained a unique collectible. Impressed by Karolyn's friendliness, Ted soon became a sporadic volunteer secretary for Karolyn, organizing her Zuzu-related mail, helping her get reprints of the movie stills for fans and digging up the details of some of Karolyn's lesser-known films.

Their contact led Karolyn and Ted to cook up a surprise, 400-mile visit the next month to Aurora, Illinois, a suburb of Chicago. There, they dropped in on Jerry Baker, the principal of a Christian school who for the previous 10 years had held *It's a Wonderful Life* parties, during which family and friends gathered to watch the movie on TV. Jerry, who also had corresponded with James Stewart, had located Karolyn earlier in the year and talked with her by phone, but had no idea that she would drop in on his party. When she knocked on the door of his apartment, Jerry opened it but didn't recognize her. He told her that she must have knocked on the wrong door. With an ear-to-ear smile, Karolyn handed him a red rose and said only, "These are Zuzu's petals." Everyone present began to laugh as Jerry stood speechless. "She brought photos, signed them for everyone, answered questions and left us in a mist of wonderment and awe," he said later. "It is one of my most special memories."

The visit was the first of many *It's a Wonderful Life* parties Karolyn would attend. Besides launching a friendship between Karolyn and Jerry Baker (whose birthday, like Karolyn's, is July 4), the trip fused an interest shared by Ted and Jerry that would play a key role in Karolyn's not-so-distant future.

On the same trip, Karolyn ventured to the Chicago suburb of New Albany, Ohio, to see her friend Karen Treschl, who seized the occasion to engineer Karolyn's first interview by a newspaper outside of Kansas City, the *Chicago Tribune*. Well-timed for the interview was a project Karen had worked on since moving away from Kansas City – a polished scrapbook of Karolyn's movie paraphernalia. Before then, when Karolyn showed her movie stills, clips and other papers to a reporter or a group, "they were in such disarray," Karen says. "She would load these things up in a terrible-looking cardboard box that was the most pathetic thing I'd ever seen." To remedy the rag-tag appearance of the

'Jimmy Stewart is the man who has eaten with kings and presidents, and yet he's still the man next door. He is shocked that people love him and recognize him, and he doesn't understand why people think he's special.

'I see the same quality in Karolyn. She really is the girl next door – a lovable, kind, sweet person.'

Ted Warner

memorabilia, Karen organized the best pieces into a thick notebook that covered Karolyn's film career in a chronological, almost self-explanatory fashion.

The new scrapbook came in handy because back in Kansas City, Karolyn received more and more requests for newspaper, radio and TV interviews, as well as invitations by schools and organizations to speak and sign autographs. Two of these appearances, in 1991 in classrooms at Indian Trail Junior High and Overland Trail Middle School, went so well that teachers Eva Lee March and Kim Manka asked students to write thank-you notes to Karolyn. Excerpts of the students' sentiments reveals an affection for not only *It's a Wonderful Life* but also the vivid anecdotes, unpretentious personality and youthful looks of Karolyn:

During her 1991 appearance at Indian Trail Junior High School in Olathe, Kansas, Karolyn visits with seventh-grader Arland Bruce. Karolyn stays in touch with many of the groups to whom she speaks.

You seem to be a nice person and a good friend. . . .

When you were talking about having a stage mother, I thought you meant they gave you a mom that lived with you and everything! . . .

That really seems like fascinating work, except you don't get many friends. But still it would be neat to have worked with so many neat people. . . .

I have watched *It's a Wonderful Life* every year since I was about 8. I love the movie so much, I about have it memorized. I think you were pretty lucky to have a career at such a young age. I would love to star in a movie. Everyone thinks I should be an actor in the next school play, but I don't know. I just don't think I'm really actor material. But deep inside, I really think I'll be able to do it. Just like you did. . . .

Are you sure you are 50 years old? You look like a teen-ager. I like your stories about all of the movies that you have been in. It sounds like you had a rough childhood. . . .

You said something I never noticed before – in most of your movies you were always in your bed. When you told us about how the kids had to stand on stage all day and the stars didn't, I thought that was unfair. . . .

When you talked to us about how you did not have too many friends, I felt sorry for you, but then when you told us all the neat things you did, I thought that it would be neat to be a movie star. You are a neat person. . . .

Most black-and-white movies I don't really enjoy a lot, but I liked this one. I've wanted to be an actor all my life. Now that I have heard what you said, it doesn't sound that easy, but I like to work hard and I will always want to do it. . . .

The only thing that sounds bad about being in a lot of movies is never having time with your friends, getting up early and always working. Another thing was waiting and redoing for the

'I would love to star in a movie. Everyone thinks I should be an actor in the next school play, but I don't know. I just don't think I'm really actor material.

'But deep inside, I really think I'll be able to do it. Just like you did.'

Middle-school student, in a letter to Karolyn

As an attempt at "family healing" after John's suicide, the Wilkersons take a raft trip on Lake Tahoe: (from left) Mike, Carey, Chris, Craig, Karolyn, Deena and Kylan.

perfect shot. I get very impatient sometimes. But I still want to be an actress. . . .

It's not every day we get to see a child star who was so much like ourselves. You are a living example that those petals of life are the most important thing to anyone. . . .

Such enthusiastic interest surely was an ego boost for Karolyn, and it compounded her interest in moving forward with her Zuzu activity. The backdrop of her home life was increasingly trying, however. John's suicide continued to reverberate through the thoughts and interactions of the Wilkerson household. Recklessness was getting the better of some of the other grown children, and the distance between Mike and Karolyn kept widening. "When they went to a psychiatrist together," says Dr. Otto Spurny, Karolyn's physician and former employer, "they were told that 90 percent of marriages in which a teen-age suicide occurred did not survive. Karolyn more or less absorbed the tragedy, but it didn't help the marriage any."

It also didn't help that in July 1991, Mike was diagnosed with prostate cancer. Then, during a routine X-ray following the successful removal of his prostate gland, a malignant spot was discovered on Mike's left lung. Five weeks later, the upper lobe of the lung was removed. Fortunately, for the time being, surgeons reported they had "gotten it all."

While Karolyn believed in the worth of her Zuzu activity, some might say that it, too, exacted a toll on her worsening relationship with Mike. Eventually, in the fall of 1991, the two separated, Mike moving to an apartment in Kansas City and Karolyn staying in their enormous home in Stilwell, along with their two children who were still living there.

The Wilkerson family still undertook some activities together, even attempting an ill-fated vacation to Amelia Island, Florida, during the Christmas vacation of 1991. But Karolyn stopped attending Mike's church. Further, Mike's departure from the house marked a tangible turning point in Karolyn's growing desire to embrace the Zuzu role. As soon as Mike moved out, Karolyn changed how she

While Karolyn believed in the worth of her Zuzu activity, some might say that it, too, exacted a toll on her worsening relationship with Mike.

Karolyn's IT'S A WONDERFUL LIFE "shrine," in the Berryhill home, fall 1991.

handled her boxes of movie-related clips and photos. She discarded her previous routine of hauling out, unpacking, repacking and re-storing the boxes for each event and interview. Instead, she unpacked them a final time and created a room in the house dedicated to *It's a Wonderful Life*, displaying her many photos, posters and other memorabilia from that film and the others in which she had appeared. "It became my shrine," she says.

Calls kept coming to Karolyn from teachers, fund-raisers and other organization leaders, requesting her for events that she came to label as "Zuzu gigs." The format for these presentations varied slightly, but they boiled down to a display of photos and a question-answer session with one of the few recognizable people still living with a direct connection to the classic movie.

At the same time, the wellspring of affection for *It's a Wonderful Life* continued to flow broadly, throughout the United States and beyond. During each successive Christmas season, it seemed that the movie was everywhere, around the clock. In some television markets, the film aired more than 100 times a year. It was even shown halfway around the world, in Moscow, on Jan. 1, 1992, the first day of the new Russian commonwealth status.

During each successive Christmas season, it seemed that the movie was everywhere, around the clock.

Still photos from *It's a Wonderful Life*, particularly of the closing Christmas Eve segment with James Stewart holding Karolyn in his arms, showed up in publications with quite diverse readerships – from the Christian journal *Guideposts* to the infamous *National Enquirer* to the obscure *Chile Pepper* magazine.

Foreign-film fans discovered a lengthy clip of the same *It's a Wonderful Life* closing segment as the backdrop for an emotional climax to *Splendor*, a 1989 Italian film by Ettore Scola (director of the Academy Award-winning *Cinema Paradiso*) which starred Marcello Mastroianni and Massimo Troisi (later nominated for an Academy Award for *The Postman*, his final film). *Splendor* lovingly recounts the blooming and withering of a small-town movie theater whose retractable roof gives the structure a distinctive charm. At film's end, the

ONE BIG HAPPY

Zuzu's bell rings in the final panel of this syndicated cartoon that ran in newspapers nationwide on December 21, 1991.

theater near-empty, the owner (Mastroianni) and his projectionist (Troisi) tearfully watch the Italian-dubbed close of *It's a Wonderful Life*, and as if by magic, the ceiling opens up, allowing snow to drift gently down upon them.

Stories popped up in news columns about the power of *It's a Wonderful Life*: Former National Security Adviser Robert C. McFarlane told of how the film gave him the inspiration to go on after a failed suicide try. A judge in Broward County, Florida, sentenced a 77-year-old murderer to 30 days in jail, two years' house arrest, five years' probation and a mandatory viewing of *It's a Wonderful Life*. And upon the Sept. 9, 1991, death of Frank Capra, the famed "little guy" director of the film, obituaries zeroed in almost exclusively on what they termed his masterpiece.

This editorial cartoon by Scott Willis of the SAN JOSE MERCURY NEWS ran in newspapers around the country in December 1992.

Reprinted by permission of Scott Willis

That the film would reach the status of cultural icon was perhaps inevitable. A Hallmark holiday greeting card showed a rotund reindeer with a toothpick in its mouth, sitting at a table after having polished off a huge dinner and dessert. Inside, the greeting said, "It's a Wonder-how-I-got-so-full Life!" A cartoon from the *San Jose Mercury News* depicted a man settling into his easy chair with a remote control and a large book marked "TV." In the first panel, a delighted look on his face, the man exclaims, "Wow! 500 channels!" His face winces in the second panel, however, as he notes, " . . . simultaneously broadcasting *It's a Wonderful Life*."

Even the famed, offbeat Seattle artist Gary Larson, who for years penned the popular strip *The Far Side*, paid tribute to *It's a Wonderful Life*, with a one-panel cartoon published nationally on Jan. 20, 1992. It's a scholarly scene, in which a bearded, robed, pipe-smoking botanist shows off a framed specimen to a colleague and proclaims: "And here's the jewel of my collection, purchased for a king's ransom from a one-eyed man in Istanbul. . . . I give you Zuzu's petals." Larson later gave the original drawing to Karolyn, with the inscription: "To Karolyn, a.k.a. 'Zuzu', with best wishes from another *Wonderful Life* fan. Gary Larson."

It's a Wonderful Life caught on in even the tiniest of circles. Tabetha Dunn, a 25-year-old movie theater inspector who published a literary journal from Allentown, Pennsylvania, with a press run of just 130, named her publication *Zuzu's Petals Quarterly*. Noting that her December 1992 edition would have relationships as its theme, Tabetha sent Karolyn a request for her autograph and a few words about *It's a Wonderful Life*. "What particularly struck me about your film," she wrote Karolyn, "was its emphasis on loyalty, honor and close-knit relationships."

While Tabetha suspected that the *Zuzu's Petals* name would be an attention-grabber, she also recognized in *It's a Wonderful Life* a strong undercurrent

The exposure of IT'S A WONDERFUL LIFE knew no bounds in the early 1990s. Karolyn, James Stewart and Donna Reed made the cover of the December 1992 issue of CHILE PEPPER magazine.

Courtesy of *Chile Pepper*, 1-888-SPICY HOT

Zuzu doll, introduced in 1993, was the brainchild of Karolyn's friend Beth Johnson.

befitting a literary publication. "People see the movie as upbeat and heartwarming, but George and the other characters really have to go through a lot to get to the happy ending," she says. "It made me think of experience formed through the loss of innocence, and the value of friendship and family. Zuzu had such hope. She thought her daddy could do anything, and that's really what literature is about. Great literature comes from small things examined."

Such an artistic sensibility was hardly beyond the appreciation of Karolyn, who had in recent years lent her time and money to a variety of cultural endeavors. Besides volunteering at the Catholic Sale-o-Rama and for local cancer and hospice organizations, she sang with the Shawnee Mission Women's Chorale, chaired fund-raising efforts for Blue Valley arts groups and joined the Film Society of Greater Kansas City, the Women of the Motion Picture Industry and the area's arts council. No doubt tapping wisdom from the way her mother raised her, Karolyn grew ever more insistent that the arts will always need a boost.

"I'm concerned about the cutting of the funds for the arts, and that's one of my soapboxes," she says. "People are raising their children with this sports thing. The schools, alumni, everybody, they'll dig in their pockets and get out the megabucks for sports, and that's all that a lot of kids are ever exposed to. How can they become well-rounded characters if they're never exposed to the sensitivity of the world of fine arts? It's just lacking so much, and we're going to have this generation of children who are all one-sided. So I try to do as much as I can to help people out in the arts. That's where my heart is."

THE FAR SIDE   By GARY LARSON

"And here's the jewel of my collection, purchased for a king's ransom from a one-eyed man in Istanbul. . . . I give you Zuzu's petals."

The year 1993 became a watershed for Karolyn's relationship with both her husband and *It's a Wonderful Life*. As fan mail and requests for Zuzu gigs grew, so did people's desire for keepsakes when they met Karolyn. One of her friends from the Sale-o-Rama, Beth Johnson, dreamed up having a doll made in the likeness of Zuzu. "Given what was going on in her marriage, she needed a push," Beth says, "and I think it was her time to blossom, to bring it out." Karolyn contracted for 1,800 of the dolls to be made in Taiwan and began taking them along with movie stills on her Zuzu gigs. The dolls became a popular part of her visits, especially those she made out-of-town. (By 1996, the dolls had become a collector's item, as Karolyn had sold nearly all of them and had autographed the right leg of each one with "Karolyn Grimes – 'Zuzu.' ") It was yet another step toward Karolyn's full acceptance of the Zuzu persona.

However, Karolyn's homefront remained as troubled as ever. The massive Midwestern floods of July 1993 devastated Mike's construction business, leaving the

To Karolyn (a.k.a. 'Zuzu') With best wishes from another 'Wonderful Life' fan Gary Larson

The impact of IT'S A WONDERFUL LIFE and Zuzu's petals on the nation's consciousness was gently and cleverly kidded in this January 20, 1992, edition of THE FAR SIDE. The strip's creator gave Karolyn a reproduction of the panel, inscribing it with a personal message.

family's finances in disarray. Even more devastating were his health problems, which had re-emerged a month earlier. His abdomen aching, Mike was taken by Karolyn to a hospital emergency room, where a doctor diagnosed his sharp pain as mere indigestion. Two days later, however, after several medical tests, Mike was throwing up and having trouble breathing. After he was admitted to the hospital, a CAT scan prompted a new, deadly diagnosis. Mike, a heavy smoker for most of his life, had a massive lung cancer pressing on his heart. He was just 52.

In tears, Mike asked Karolyn if he could come back home, and Karolyn acceded. So Mike returned to the house in Stilwell and within weeks began spending much of his time in bed. With Dr. Spurny's steady moral support, Karolyn became Mike's primary caretaker – if not with the intimacy of her father during her mother's gradual decline, at least with the seriousness of a marital commitment.

It was an extremely grueling time emotionally for both Mike and Karolyn. John's suicide affected Mike deeply. Unlike Karolyn, he continually faulted himself for the tragedy and repeatedly pronounced to Karolyn his blame. "Mike was never the same after John's death," she says. "I think he had such guilt, and the stress from that guilt ate him alive. I really think it caused him to get cancer. He felt guilty because he knew I was hurt so badly, and because he felt he had let his son down and hadn't done the right things with him."

Karolyn sings with the Shawnee Mission Chorale in 1992.

In addition, although Mike knew his cancer was inoperable and terminal, the topic became taboo in his presence. "We could never talk about him dying," says Karolyn, who was never able to elicit his preferences for the eventual disposition of his body. "We couldn't even think that there was a possibility that he would die because he insisted that he was going to beat it, so there was no way we could make any kind of arrangements. It was really hard. I would ask him, 'Why not be realistic about the whole thing and at least think "If . . ."?' But he couldn't do that. He kept saying, 'Aren't you on my side? Don't you want me to live?' The kids couldn't talk to him either. They tried. He just wouldn't do it."

In that light, the timing of the next development of the *It's a Wonderful Life* phenomenon could not have been more difficult.

The Target discount store chain, headquartered in Minneapolis (as close as any big city is to middle-of-the-road, mainstream America) hatched a promotional campaign for its Christmas 1993 season, to mine the country's ever-surging attachment to the charmed film. Donna Reed had died of cancer seven years before, and James Stewart's health had deteriorated badly, but the unavailability of these stars did not deter the family-oriented retailer. With blown-up, sepia-tone movie stills in the shape of ornaments and a new line of miniature porcelain

'Mike was never the same after John's death.

'I think he had such guilt, and the stress from that guilt ate him alive.'

The Bailey kids, as reunited by Target in November and December 1993: (from left) Larry Simms (Pete), Karolyn Grimes Wilkerson (Zuzu), Carol Coombs Mueller (Janie) and Jimmy Hawkins (Tommy).

Printed by permission of the *Star Tribune*, Minneapolis Minnesota

buildings from the film's town of Bedford Falls, Target decided to use the movie as its merchandising theme for holiday sales. Photographs of Stewart, Reed and the four Bailey children were to appear everywhere, from newspaper ads and shopping bags to wrapping paper, glass ornaments, coffee table books, calendars, snowglobes, cookie and popcorn tins, coffee mugs, tissue boxes, chocolates and picture frames. "It's a Wonderful Night" shopping evenings for seniors and the disabled were scheduled, and a new program co-sponsored with Habitat for Humanity called "Building a Wonderful Life" took flight.

The crowning touch was Target's plan to reunite the actors who played the four Bailey children and to send them on a national tour that November and December.

The crowning touch was Target's plan to reunite the actors who played the four Bailey children and to send them on a national tour that November and December. "It was based on a hunch," recalls Becky Bailey, a Target events organizer with a last name that could not have better fit the promotion. "We reasoned that if we felt so strongly inside Target about the popularity of the four kids from the movie, others would, too." To flesh out this hunch, the discount chain's public relations staff telephoned producers of talk shows in Target's largest markets to see if they would interview the Bailey children 47 years after making *It's a Wonderful Life*. The responses resounded with unqualified enthusiasm. As Becky Bailey puts it, "The four kids were a perfect match."

Just as with her James Stewart meeting three years prior, the Target tour was potentially a once-in-a-lifetime opportunity for Karolyn. She warmed to the idea immediately, as did two of the other three: Carol Coombs Mueller, who played Janie, and Jimmy Hawkins, who was Tommy, the youngest. The fourth, Larry Simms, who portrayed the oldest, Pete, took some persuading, but eventually signed on.

Karolyn agreed to participate in the tour before Mike was toppled by lung cancer. Fortunately for her, Target agreed to schedule the tour in separate segments, so that she would be gone from home for just three to five days at a time. During Karolyn's absences, she called frequently to check on Mike while their daughter Carey looked after him.

Stops on the tour spanned the country, starting in Denver, Colorado, then to Portland, Oregon, Tampa, Florida, Los Angeles and Minneapolis. At each locale, the foursome did TV interviews and signed autographs at Target branches for hordes of *It's a Wonderful Life* fans. Most were overjoyed to see the reunited Bailey kids. One couple displayed wedding rings inscribed with, "I'll love you . . ." and ". . .till the day I die," – a line early in the movie that the young Mary Hatch whispers into young George Bailey's deaf ear. One man in Florida earnestly informed the foursome he had considered suicide, and the movie had saved his life.

'The camaraderie was wonderful.

'It was like we had a bond because we had been brothers and sisters in the movie.'

Remarkably, these four "Baileys," who had led quite separate lives, managed to get along amicably, perhaps better than might have been expected. They shared details from the movie that had brought them together, including the revelation that while they were paid different amounts (Larry's daily rate was $100, Carol's and Karolyn's was $75 and Jimmy's was $50), all had the same agent, Lola Moore. "The camaraderie was wonderful," says Karolyn. "It was like we had a bond because we had been brothers and sisters in the movie." Of course, each of the four had a distinct role and personality on the tour.

Jimmy Hawkins, who had stayed in Los Angeles his whole life, appeared in 80 films in the 1940s, won regular character roles in *The Charlie Ruggles Show*, *Annie Oakley* and *The Donna Reed Show* on television in the 1950s and 1960s, co-starred in two Elvis Presley films, headlined a USO tour of Vietnam in 1968 and went on to produce a half-dozen television movies and specials. He was clearly the Hollywood insider of the group – "our schmoozer," as Karolyn puts it.

WARD'S WARM, FUZZY CLEAVER   BY WARD SUTTON

This cartoon in the Twin Cities Reader – a weekly newspaper based in Minneapolis, Minnesota, the headquarters of the Target – poked good-natured fun at the reunion of the Bailey kids and their tour on behalf of the discount chain.

"Usually, we let Jimmy lead the way and talk for us, but he expected us to jump right in there, too." While Jimmy played the youngest child in *It's a Wonderful Life*, he nevertheless shared vivid memories, such as the scratchy roughness of the Santa Claus mask he wore during the segment in which James Stewart tearfully clutches him to his breast in despair.

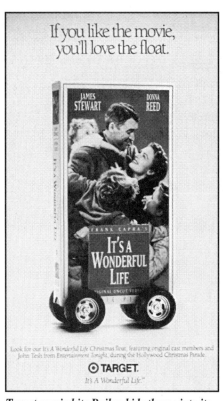

Target carried its Bailey-kids theme into its fanciful ads for the 62nd annual Hollywood Christmas Parade, on November 28, 1993.
Reprinted courtesy of Target Stores

Carol Coombs Mueller, a resident of Crestline, California, whose Janie character is known most for endlessly practicing "Hark, the Herald Angels Sing" on the piano, also had *Wonderful Life* recollections to spare. James Stewart's shouted command to stop playing "that silly tune" so startled her, she said, that the tears she shed in the movie were real. Retired after a 31-year teaching career, the mother of three and grandmother of five made her biggest splash on the tour whenever a piano was nearby. Just as in the movie, she haltingly pounded out the angelic carol, joking that she never had learned the song any better than she played it in the film. But reviewing her own brief film career, she also boasted of twice playing Stewart's daughter, the second time in 1947's *Magic Town*.

Larry Simms, a reclusive engineering consultant and father of three, was the most "high maintenance" of the four Bailey kids, says Karolyn, because he was not eager to join the tour. Only after an in-person appeal from Karolyn and others, which followed a lengthy, backwoods drive to his mountain retreat in the Columbia River country in southwestern Washington state, did he come around. A busy child actor (he played Baby Dumpling in the *Blondie* film series), Simms had turned his back on Hollywood at a young age, although he did credit his interest in the mechanical workings of a motion-picture camera during the filming of *It's a Wonderful Life* with launching him on a career in technology.

On the Minneapolis leg of the tour, Larry kidded Karolyn about the Zuzu doll that she had just begun to market. Laughing at a brochure that stated, "You love the movie, now cherish the doll," he turned to her and said, "You ought to have a string on the back of it. When you pull the string, the doll could say, 'Every time a bell rings, an angel gets his wings.' " Karolyn, according to a newspaper account, would only smile civilly in return. But she considers Larry "a caring and giving person" in whom she "found many lessons about reliance on oneself and about the obsession of worshipping material things."

Karolyn gets a hug from singer Lou Rawls before the 62nd annual Hollywood Christmas Parade, 1993.

Karolyn, of course, because of her distinctive Zuzu role, drew special attention throughout the Target tour. Women, sobbing, brought her roses, and poured out how much the film had meant to them. Karolyn also displayed a knack for humor as she greeted well-wishers, such as a man who brought her a few fallen petals, just as in the movie. "Oh, you found my petals," she told him with a smile. "I was looking for these."

Through it all, the tour inspired Karolyn, making her ever more deeply aware that the messages of *It's a Wonderful Life* apply to everyone, including herself. "I draw from the movie all the time," she

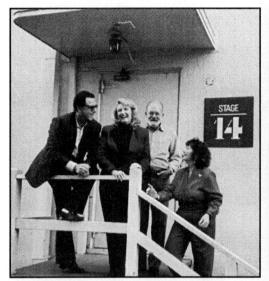

The Bailey kids – (left) Jimmy, Karolyn, Larry and Carol – tour the soundstage where they filmed IT'S A WONDERFUL LIFE 47 years before. Then they mount the Target float, fashioned after Bedford Falls' Bijou Theater from the 1946 film, for the 62nd annual Hollywood Christmas Parade.

told one reporter. "It gives me the strength to go on, and it makes me realize that in everything you do every day, you touch people's lives."

Unquestionably, the high point of the tour for the foursome was the 62nd annual Hollywood Christmas Parade on the day after Thanksgiving. Sharing a float with musician/TV host John Tesh, and hobnobbing with Bob Hope, Mickey Rooney and dozens of other entertainers, the quartet of Baileys was greeted by a teeming mass of 750,000 that lined Sunset and Hollywood boulevards. "It was amazing," Karolyn says. "When we turned the corner to begin the parade, people in the bleachers started chanting, 'Zuzu, Zuzu, Zuzu . . .' I almost cried, it was so touching. It really was. I felt like I was close to being home."

Larry, Karolyn, Carol and Jimmy pose for a PEOPLE WEEKLY photographer in front of the famed Hollywood sign.

And she was – literally. Her parents' first one-bedroom house on Norton Avenue, where she lived when she had first seen the yearly Christmas parade as a child, was just a few blocks away. The Los Angeles stop of the tour marked the first time Karolyn had returned to her native city in the 32 years that had passed since her brief 1961 trip with her first husband Hal. This time, the circumstances were far more pleasant. The Target chain allowed Karolyn a full day's free use of a limousine, and she shared it with her father's best friend Perry Vannice,

Karolyn visits with Perry Vannice, her father LaVan's best friend since their days in Osceola, Missouri.

Reuniting in Indiana, Pennsylvania, in December 1993, are five cast members from IT'S A WONDERFUL LIFE: (from left) Carol Coombs Mueller (Janie), Jimmy Hawkins (Tommy), Karolyn Grimes Wilkerson (Zuzu), Todd Karns (Harry Bailey), and Virginia Patton Moss (Ruth Dakin Bailey).

A larger group of IT'S A WONDERFUL LIFE cast and crew gathers in December 1993 at the James Stewart statue, erected in 1985 in Indiana, Pennsylvania. They are (from left) Ruth and Bob Lawless (who manufactured the "snow" used in the film), Karolyn, Argentina Brunetti (Mrs. Martini), her companion, Chet and Carol Coombs Mueller (Janie), Todd Karns (Harry Bailey) and his wife Kate.

with whom she had recently reconnected by mail and telephone. Perry, who had lost touch with Karolyn decades before, tracked her down after listening to a radio talk show featuring Richard Lamparski, author of the *Whatever Happened to . . .* book series, who had corresponded with Karolyn. "It was so good to talk with Perry and travel around my old neighborhoods because I got to hear about my father and mother," Karolyn says. "If it had not been for *It's a Wonderful Life*, he never would have found me."

Along with her three childhood movie siblings, Karolyn also revisited what might be called one of her old work neighborhoods – the huge, hangar-like set where *It's a Wonderful Life* was filmed. As they walked inside, Karolyn and Larry experienced the same olfactory memory. "There were wires and lights everywhere, and I don't know how to describe it, but the whole place had this wonderful smell," she says. "Both of us noticed it, and it was the first time I'd smelled that smell for almost 40 years. It smelled so good, it felt like home, too, just like the parade. I would have loved to have sat in that set for more time just to smell that smell for awhile longer."

The California portion of the tour also produced high-profile media exposure that further cemented the *It's a Wonderful Life* craze and Karolyn's significant role in it. *People Weekly* ran a two-page spread on the Bailey kids, Vicki Lawrence had the foursome as guests on her TV show, and *Inside Edition*, *American Journal* and *Entertainment Tonight* aired affectionate segments. In the same month, Karolyn wound up on the cover of *TV Guide* in one of the stills from the climax of the 1946 movie, and was the subject of an in-depth profile in the newspaper of the nation's capital, *The Washington Post*.

It was a heady time. And without skipping a beat, immediately after the tour's Los Angeles leg, the Bailey kids (minus Larry Simms) took a significant sidetrack to a celebration in Indiana, Pennsylvania, the hometown of James Stewart, which hosted a reunion of cast and crew from *It's a Wonderful Life* on the weekend of December 3-5. While Stewart's health kept him from attending, both the assemblage – including Argentina Brunetti (Mrs. Martini), Todd Karns (Harry Bailey) and Virginia Patton Moss (Ruth Dakin Bailey) – and the reaction of the city of 18,000 were impressive. The group rode in a holiday parade and took in a

Karolyn and Mike Wilkerson and five of their children – (from left) Kylan, Haleen, Chris, Deena and Carey – in July 1993 after Mike's lung cancer diagnosis. (Right) Karolyn and Mike two months later, after chemotherapy had begun.

new musical version of *It's a Wonderful Life* (written by Sheldon Harnick), drinking in the small-town values embodied by a beloved giant in the world of film acting.

Karolyn returned home from this frenzy of Christmas activity to a shell of the man who had aspired to be the giant of her household. Aged in appearance beyond his years, weak and mostly bedridden, Mike no longer could command obedience from anyone. Instead, he begged for sympathy for his assertion that he could "beat" the cancer that was ravaging him. Karolyn and Mike came to terms about some of their differences during their final interactions, but there is no doubt that their tumultuous 25-year marriage stirred a maelstrom of intense emotions inside her as he lay dying.

The end came May 14, 1994. Lucid and headstrong to the end, Mike died in the evening after a day of breathing "the death rattle," as Karolyn calls it. Three days later, a wake was held, following a long-scheduled auction of the assets of Mike's construction firm.

There were no instructions for Mike's burial, as he had avoided the topic assiduously. Karolyn made the arrangements after the fact, including an adjacent plot for herself as well as a double gravestone with an inscribed "Zuzu" next to her name – perhaps a symbol of the independence in her that had been wrought by Mike. "Only because I married Mike, who made me do things on my own, did I ever develop any independence," Karolyn says. "At the time, I thought it was a horrible cruelty, but it really was a gift, because I learned to stand on my own two feet and survive by myself."

Karolyn returned home from this frenzy of Christmas activity to a shell of the man who had aspired to be the giant of her household.

'Zuzu's Petals' music is punchy with a bunch of attitude.

'They find irony and humor in getting hit on by scums in bars, those who want to be 'artists' and the joys of socializing with friends and lovers.'

News clipping

Karolyn also can look back and see other, more tangible positives from their marriage. "He taught me the world of construction, we went traveling and got to see the world, and he supported me very well," she says. That financial support did not continue in the same fashion after his death, however, as Karolyn's only means of support became Mike's life-insurance policy, whose provisions require that she forfeit income from a resulting trust if she remarries. But even this example of Mike's control Karolyn took in an optimistic stride. "It may sound horrible," she says, "but even though I have to watch every penny now, Mike's death freed me to use what I've learned, in investments and everything, to make my own way."

The grief and details that made up the aftermath of Mike's death might have been daunting, but fortunately for Karolyn, the *It's a Wonderful Life* mania and the public's support for her and her Zuzu character only ballooned in 1994, propelling her forward. This was due largely to the landslide of publicity and goodwill produced by the Target tour of the previous year. Groups spanning the country sought Karolyn for gigs during the coming Christmas season, and she began filling her year-end schedule with appearances. Her mail volume stepped up considerably, Karolyn finding dozens of fan letters in her post-office box each month. And then there were the delightfully quirky discoveries and developments.

Karolyn perused a Kansas City entertainment weekly in July 1994 to find that performing in town was a Minneapolis-based, three-woman rock band billing itself as Zuzu's Petals. "Instead of focusing on the rage and anger which many women in the music biz choose to perform about, Zuzu's Petals takes a more cynical, yet equally biting view of music," said the paper's brief profile. "Zuzu's Petals' music is punchy with a bunch of attitude. They find irony and humor in getting hit on by scums in bars, those who want to be 'artists' and the joys of socializing with friends and lovers."

Zuzu's Petals, (from left) Laurie Lindeen, Coleen Elwood and Linda Pitmon, a rock band based in Minneapolis, Minnesota.

The article's final reference to the band's approach, if crude, came closest to capturing the spirit of its namesake character: "This isn't music to piss off the audience. It's music which makes the body smile."

Indeed, the music created by Laurie Lindeen, Coleen Elwood and Linda Pitmon on the band's 1992 album *When No One's Looking* (TwinTone Records), jars listeners' ears with a barrage of electric guitar chords, through which it's barely possible to discern the enigmatic, sometimes profane, lyrics. The chorus of "God Cries," written by Lindeen, is an apt example:

God cries three times a day.
She's everywhere I look – I wish she'd go away.
Oh, God, I can't forsake you.
Just living my life, my sins weren't meant for you.

The next month, in August 1994, writer Nancy Dillon wrote Karolyn to say that while she was strolling a mall, she bumped into a woman wearing a T-shirt with the word ZuZu on it. It turned out to be the logo for a Texas-based restaurant chain by the same name that specializes in homemade Mexican food.

It seemed that Zuzu was popping up all over – even on stage. That fall, thinking that she would like to get back into some kind of singing, Karolyn began taking voice lessons. Soon her teacher told her the local Olathe Community Theater was casting parts for an offbeat, newly written production called *Dracula – The Musical?* directed by Don Carlson, an illustrator for cartoonists Garry Trudeau and Gary Larson. On a lark, Karolyn auditioned and won the hefty part of Nelly the maid, who is on stage through most of the play, keeping a psychologist's family in balance and running a household that includes several mental cases. "I'm a smart-aleck, but I've really got a big heart," she says of her part. "I love the nuts, but I'm sarcastic and make snide remarks behind people's backs." Singing a solo, a duet and portions of several other songs, she also winds up as the love interest of the thirsty title character in this goofy spoof, which drew enthusiastic crowds during its early November run. "It was really a funny play, and I was proud to be in it," she says. "I hated to see it end." And ironically, while everyone in the production knew of Karolyn's childhood cinematic connection, it wasn't used to promote the play, except in after-the-fact notices.

Karolyn as Nelly the maid in the fall 1994 Olathe Community Theater production of DRACULA – THE MUSICAL?

Her *Dracula* participation came at a good time, moving her forward in the months following Mike's death. But while she enjoyed it, the play carried a major challenge – the memorization of long sections of dialogue, something she hadn't attempted in more than 25 years. "I didn't know if I would be able to do it, because I didn't know if I could memorize anymore," she says. "It's easy for kids to memorize stuff, but for adults, the older you get, the harder it gets, and the harder you have to work. I just canceled my life, more or less, for six weeks and worked day and night. I listened to tapes every time I got in the car and just really had to work hard to get it down." She did rise to the occasion, though. "I was scared to death, but only until the dress rehearsal. Then I was okay."

Singing a solo, a duet and portions of several other songs, she also winds up as the love interest of the thirsty title character in this goofy spoof.

The experience left her eager to perform but braced her with the reality of aging in the theatre. "The problem is, I'm a little bit old," she says. "I played this one okay because it was a spoof, and it came off well. It was close, though. It might not have. I was more the get-the-guy character because I'm vampy. But I'm not young enough to be the vamp or the ingenue, and I really don't look character enough to be the older lady."

But her bright eyes, dazzling smile and child-like exuberance were just right for the approaching Christmas season, during which Karolyn flew from coast to coast and several points in between, reimbursed only by modest fees and travel expenses. First came a post-Thanksgiving weekend autograph session at Decades, a collectibles shop in the Detroit suburb of Royal Oak. One week later, in the Seattle area, she headlined an "Angels in Our Midst" exhibit at the Rosalie Whyel

Museum of Doll Art and auctioned a Zuzu doll at the Holiday Gala for the Fred Hutchinson Cancer Research Center. The next week, at the behest of the chamber of commerce in the Boston suburb of Newburyport, Karolyn topped the bill for the community's Christmas celebration. She even squeezed in gigs closer to home, in the Kansas cities of Lawrence and Cottonwood Falls.

Karolyn greets fans purchasing her Zuzu doll at the Decades collectibles shop in Royal Oak, Michigan, in November 1994.

At each event, people were abuzz with the recent news that Republic Pictures had successfully regained control of the distribution of *It's a Wonderful Life* when the estate of Dimitri Tionkin, whose score for the film was separately copyrighted, reasserted the music rights. Republic then negotiated an exclusive three-year deal with NBC-TV, whereby the movie would be televised just once each Christmas season, starting that month.

The topic fell squarely in Karolyn's lap. The popularity of *It's a Wonderful Life* had risen because of its frequent screenings. Reporters covering her appearances asked her what she thought would happen to the film's following, given just one airing a year. They found a blunt defender of the movie's formerly free availability. "I feel like they stole the American movie from the American people," Karolyn told the Newburyport *Daily News*. "Before, it got the exposure that it needed, but now, I don't know if it will continue to live on." With icy insight, she told a reporter for the Toledo, Ohio, *Blade*, "Whoever had that idea [of airing the film once a year] was probably a good businessman, but he'll be like Potter in the end. He'll be lonely."

Karolyn hardly lacked for company on her gigs, however. Each event yielded big crowds and memorable moments of warmth, as people at every locale seemingly couldn't get enough of the *It's a Wonderful Life* aura.

"In Boston," says Karolyn, "when I was at the airline terminal to come back to Kansas City, I walked up to the gate, and a gal came up to me and said, 'You're Zuzu.' I said, 'Yes, I am.' And she said, 'I saw you on TV yesterday. My boyfriend's from Newburyport.' I said, 'Great!' Well, she walked off, but pretty soon she came back with a voucher and said, 'Here, I bumped you to first class. That's the pilot's favorite movie.' So after I got on the plane, the stewardesses and all the passengers in first class wanted autographs, and I sold three dolls, but that wasn't all. The captain got on the speaker, saying, 'Now, ladies and gentlemen, I want to remind you that the most wonderful movie ever made is going to be on TV tonight, the only time it's going to be shown this season, *It's a Wonderful Life*. It was just the biggest commercial. 'And by the way,' he said, 'we have aboard with us Karolyn Grimes . . .' Oh, it was just wonderful.

"Then the plane stopped in Detroit to change the crew, and a guy came in doing the janitorial work, and he said, 'I heard you's Zuzu.' I said, 'Yes, I am.' He said, 'You know, I watched that movie about eight years ago. I didn't have a job, I didn't have anything, I was going downhill. I watched that movie and it changed

'I feel like they stole the American movie from the American people. Before, it got the exposure that it needed, but now, I don't know if it will continue to live on.'

Karolyn in the Newburyport Daily News

my whole life. I knew I could do something. I made the right decisions just because of that movie.' It just makes you feel so good. Here he was, a janitor on a plane, but he was happy, he was joshing with the stewardesses, and he loved it, you could see that. You can't trade that kind of feeling that you get from people. And somehow or other they attribute this to me, because I was a part of it, so I get the credit, in a way. I'll tell you, it's just a great feeling."

The feeling intensified as she traveled to her final appearance of the season, a comparatively small gathering hosted by Jerry Baker on Dec. 19 in Aurora, Illinois. This time, Baker had invited Karolyn to his party for 30 friends and family and used his church as the meeting place. Ted Warner showed up, too, and he and Jerry managed to surprise Karolyn that night with their long-contemplated brainchild – the formation of a fan club called The Zuzu Society.

'Jerry and I kept saying that Karolyn gets so much fan mail that we have to do something, so we came up with the fan club.'

Ted Warner, co-founder, The Zuzu Society

"Jerry and I kept saying that Karolyn gets so much fan mail that we have to do something, so we came up with the fan club," says Ted. "When we announced it at the party, it was half serious and half tongue-in-cheek, so that if she didn't want it to happen, it would have been no problem. We had some business cards printed up, and she got a big kick out if it, and after the party was over, she said, 'Are you really going to do it?' and after I hemmed and hawed, she said, 'Go ahead and do it. But if you do, make the prices as low as possible and give the members as much as possible for it.' So we had certificates made up and got it started."

Soon, The Zuzu Society mushroomed into a mailing list of more than 700 people from nearly every state in the country (plus a few international locales) who receive a free newsletter that details Karolyn's films, provides updates on her gigs and offers opportunities to buy signed movie stills, Christmas ornaments, T-shirts and the like, all to cover expenses of the newsletter production.

Besides serving those interested in *It's a Wonderful Life* and Karolyn's other films, Ted and Jerry envision the

Jerry Baker introduces Karolyn at his 1994 IT'S A WONDERFUL LIFE party, at which he and Ted Warner launched The Zuzu Society.

fan club as a vehicle to promote Karolyn's availability for gigs. "The Zuzu Society," says Ted, "should be about her life and career and charities and her feel for things, because people want to know. The idea is to humanize her. In many people's minds, she's still the little girl from the movie, and that's great, but she's more than that. Her career is more than one movie."

Even so, Ted says, the Zuzu role is how people identify Karolyn, hence the use of the name in the fan club's title. "I think those who want to be part of this just want to be identified with *It's a Wonderful Life* in some way. It's not like Karolyn's going to become an Elizabeth Taylor-type star. There's a different spirit that moves these people. I think *It's a Wonderful Life* has moved them almost to a spiritual experience, and Karolyn is almost like an apostle. She was there. She was part of it. She's the living part of the movie, since Mr. Stewart is not accessible anymore. The other children are alive, but their roles in the film really don't have the draw that Karolyn's role has.

"And Karolyn herself is such a delight. People expect to see a diva when they think of a movie star, and instead, when they see Karolyn, they still see the little girl. She's really little Zuzu. She does have a sophisticated side, she can act and be what she needs to be, but she also is the little Zuzu who's still daddy's little girl on the inside. When people meet her, they instantly feel this. That's a rare quality to find now."

That "little girl" quality, plus the public's emotional connection to *It's a Wonderful Life*, make for a potent combination. Deena, Karolyn's second daughter, learned this firsthand when Karolyn took her to New York City in early 1995. "It was the first time she and I had ever been together on a trip alone," Karolyn says. "I was showing her 'my' New York, and the first night we were there, after dinner at Sardi's, we went to one of those trendy star bars, where you often see celebrities. As we sat there, I asked Deena, 'Okay, what do you think the bartender would think if he knew I was Zuzu?' She said, 'Oh, for heaven's sakes, this is New York. He sees real stars.' I said, 'Okay, kid, I'll bet you $5 it'll mean something to him.' So she told him who I was, and the man just absolutely went ape, he went crazy. It was that way everywhere we went, and by the end of the trip she was introducing me to people as Zuzu just to see their reaction. It was incredible."

Confirming this New York-based bedazzlement is Michael Lintecum, a Kansas City-based drama sponsor who had produced an Off-Broadway play, *The Cover of Life*, which Karolyn had backed. Lintecum says that a New York friend of his raved over having seen Karolyn at the opening night party the previous November. "My friend," he says, "was almost reverent, asking me, 'Do you know who I met?' He was into a demonic stage in describing her. It was so funny and unbelievable because at the party we had stars like Christian Slater and Mary Stuart Masterson, but people are fascinated that Karolyn is still around, and she

The first two editions of Karolyn's fan club newsletter, THE ZUZU NEWS, free for those on the club's mailing list. To get on the list, write P.O. Box 225, Stilwell, KS 66085.

plays the role so well. She's as sweet as the character in the movie." Michael's friend obviously agreed. Someone shot a photo of the friend with Karolyn, and the friend framed it and hung it on his living room wall, choosing to stuff a similar photo with Slater into his desk drawer.

Karolyn believes that kind of reaction is not a chance occurrence. Her faith is firm that everything happens for a reason. In fact, one of her favorite phrases is: "There are no coincidences." Certainly another event in Karolyn's life one day in January 1995 defied a conventional explanation – the loss of a 14-carat gold bracelet her husband Mike had given her shortly before his death the year before. Suspended from the bracelet were two gold charms in the shape of hearts, and inscribed was a message of love.

Karolyn with Paul "Fredrocks" Adams, 1995.

"That morning, I put the bracelet on, and that night I had dinner at a restaurant with some of my friends, and I was feeling out of place because they were all married and talking about their husbands and the things they did together," Karolyn says. "When I got home, the bracelet was gone. It was huge and had a guard on it, so there was no way it would fall off without my knowing. I looked everywhere and asked everybody about it but couldn't find it.

"The next morning at 7:30, I got a call from a local radio personality who had interviewed me over the phone before Christmas. At the time, he had told me he was impressed and said, 'You sound so young.' He'd wanted a copy of the Jimmy Stewart Christmas greeting tape from the Target tour, so I sent him that and popped in a picture of myself so he would know what I look like. He had gotten the photo, and he was calling me again to ask me out. And I decided to go. It was as if losing the bracelet was a release, saying it was okay. I follow those things."

'All of a sudden I'm walking down the street and people are seeing me holding hands with a man, and it felt good.'

The radio personality was 39-year-old Paul "Fredrocks" Adams, a longtime Kansas City morning radio host who had just weathered a divorce from high-profile former local TV news anchor Cynthia Smith. Paul and Karolyn started dating, "spent 24 hours a day together from the get-go," as Karolyn puts it, and landed at the top of the gossip column in the Jan. 31, 1995, *Kansas City Star*. "I'm robbing the cradle, but age is relative," 54-year-old Karolyn told columnist Christopher Hearne Jr. Countering that comment was one from Paul: "Here's a nice lady that I just happened to meet. She's a little older than me, but who cares as long as people get along together?"

This new relationship provided Karolyn with many welcome changes. First, Paul introduced her to Grand Avenue Temple, an older United Methodist Church in downtown Kansas City whose unpretentious services and meals cater to the city's homeless and hungry. Karolyn jumped in and attended regularly. "I feel like this place is serving a purpose," she says. "This is really God's work, working with the people who are less fortunate. It's a wonderful opportunity to help humanity."

Paul also dislodged Karolyn's aversion to being touched. "I'd been the frigid queen of America, but after I started studying the Shusta philosophy in the 1980s,

I made an effort to comfort people physically by holding them in my arms," Karolyn says. "After I met Paul, though, I started to enjoy it when people held me. He just woke that up in me. First time he laid eyes on me, he grabbed me and hugged me and kept saying over and over, 'I knew it. I knew you were the one I've been waiting for.' That whole night, all the way through a movie, he held my hand like I was a little schoolgirl. So all of a sudden I'm walking down the street and people are seeing me holding hands with a man, and it felt good. It was a really emotional experience to realize that I needed that. I'd read it, and I'd heard people say it, but I didn't understand it until that night."

With her dog Kobe, Karolyn shows off the IT'S A WONDERFUL LIFE room in her new home in Overland Park, Kansas, 1995.

Equally important, Paul brought his musical talent into Karolyn's life. An accomplished theater organist, Paul took quickly to the piano in Karolyn's home. He played, she sang, and the two quickly came up with the idea of expanding her Zuzu gigs to include Karolyn singing to Paul's accompaniment. Over the coming months, they honed an act of show tunes and clips from Karolyn's films. In September, the two provided a five-minute preview during a festival celebrating the 100th anniversary of the birth of Buster Keaton in the film comic's hometown in nearby Iola, Kansas. There, Karolyn sang "Without a Sound," a tribute to silent films that Gloria Swanson once had performed on television.

'Music makes me go round – makes me happy, sad, up, down, all around.

'It's just like honey to a bee. I need it.'

The opportunity connected with Karolyn's deepest yearnings. "Music makes me go round – makes me happy, sad, up, down, all around," she says. "It's just like honey to a bee. I need it." (Her sentiment brings to mind the bywords printed on the music holder for the piano she plays in *The Private Affairs of Bel Ami* from 1947: "If music be the food of life, play on.")

Requests for Karolyn's presence at local and regional events multiplied during 1995, and she accommodated them all, managing to fit in a whirlwind move from the huge Wilkerson family house in Stilwell to a smaller one in nearby Overland Park. (There, her *It's a Wonderful Life* "shrine" is intact, with an ever-growing assortment of posters, plates, videos, canisters, figurines and afghans.) Karolyn's 1995 appearances included a March hospital benefit in Paul's hometown of Aledo, Illinois, a May junior women's symphony fund-raiser in Kansas City and an October CD release party in Kansas City for 57-year-old jazz/blues singer

Queen Bey. As the Christmas season approached, she received a humanitarian award from the local Indian Missionary Society and headlined a Boy Scout fund-raiser. She also returned to suburban Detroit on Thanksgiving weekend, autographing photos and angel figurines for 400 people at December's Special Place in Southgate.

While in Detroit, Karolyn helped promote the city's America's Day Parade on Thanksgiving with Tim Allen, star of television's *Home Improvement*. Allen, a native of the Motor City, was starring in the just-released film comedy *The Santa Clause*, and Karolyn couldn't resist the opportunity to kid him. "Looks like my Christmas movie is getting some competition from your Christmas movie," she told him with a laugh. "Oh, I think your movie will have a bit more staying power," he graciously replied.

Karolyn meets with Detroit native Tim Allen, star of TV's HOME IMPROVEMENT *during the city's Thanksgiving Day parade, 1995.*

Twice in the fall of 1995, Karolyn experienced unusual renditions of *It's a Wonderful Life*. In Lamar, Colorado, where she spoke and sang to school classes and judged a town decorating contest, she also watched high-school students put on a two-act play adapted from the movie in 1993 by James W. Rodgers. The script opens with George Bailey contemplating suicide on the Bedford Falls bridge, then proceeds in a chronological flashback similar to the film. And in Leavenworth, Kansas, Karolyn attended a River City Community Players performance of a musical version of *It's a Wonderful Life* different from the one she had seen two years prior in Indiana, Pennsylvania. The songs, written by Thomas M. Sharkey, included "Save George," "A Frustrated Man," "You've Never Been Born" and "Daddy, Won't You Fix My Flower." Of the two 1995 productions, Karolyn favored the non-musical one, but she also maintained her firm suspicion that it's nearly impossible to improve upon the original film.

Karolyn speaks – and sings "White Christmas" – to more than 100 high-school students in Lamar, Colorado, 1995.

The year of 1996 – a landmark, given the 50th anniversary of *It's a Wonderful Life* – began with a bang, as she and Paul put on the first full-scale performance of her show-tune/film clip revue in March for a Kansas City audience of 400.

The next month brought an astounding eye-opener, however. Karolyn discovered that during the previous December Tabetha Dunn had ceased the printed version of her three-year-old *Zuzu's Petals Quarterly*, which at its height had just 160 subscribers. Instead, Tabetha assembled a computerized version as an ongoing World Wide Web site called "Zuzu's Petals Quarterly Online," a resource with 1,500 links for writers, editors, poets, performers and researchers. In its first four months on the Web, Dunn's site experienced a jaw-dropping 150,000 "hits," or inquiries, from interested Internet surfers. Dunn surmises that, because an explanatory link on the site's home page labeled "What's a Zuzu?" had only 1,000 hits, most of those visiting the site already recognized the cinematic Zuzu character.

The Web site gave birth to a new, separate site that links browsers to a variety of information on Karolyn and her movies, and those links are becoming

'Looks like my Christmas movie is getting some competition from your Christmas movie.'

Karolyn to Tim Allen

The icon for Karolyn's Web site. The address on the Internet: http://www.lehigh.net/wonderful

Karolyn signs autographs after her one-woman show in Kansas City, March 1996.

Karolyn dons the garb of Mrs. Whatsit, in the children's play A WRINKLE IN TIME,1996.

increasingly popular. For instance, in its first month on the Web in April and May 1996, an on-line Karolyn filmography page notched more than 1,000 hits.

Karolyn reignited her passion for live theater in the late spring of 1996 by winning a key part in Madeleine L'Engle's *A Wrinkle in Time*, a children's play put on by Kansas City's Coterie Theater from July 16 through Aug. 4. In the time-travel fantasy, Karolyn played Mrs. Whatsit, one of three supernatural beings who help a girl and her brother save their father. The production drew strong reviews and houses full of youthful smiles.

The Donna Reed Festival, held June 19-22 in the late actress' hometown of Denison, Iowa, was another destination for Karolyn in mid-1996. There, she rejoined other surviving *It's a Wonderful Life* cast members, including Argentina Brunetti (Mrs. Martini), Todd Karns (Harry Bailey) and Bobby Anderson (the young George Bailey), as well as her movie siblings Jimmy Hawkins and Carol Coombs Mueller. To the delight of the hundreds who attended, Karns unveiled a poster and series of greeting cards inspired by the settings of *It's a Wonderful Life*, and based upon canvases he had painted at his home in Ajijic, Mexico.

As full as 1996 was through late summer, the highlights of the year for Karolyn undoubtedly will come in the fall. It promises to be the biggest Zuzu season ever, as the golden anniversary of *It's a Wonderful Life* falls on Dec. 19. Early bookings included another cast reunion in early December in Jimmy Stewart's hometown of Indiana, Pennsylvania, as well as a November return to suburban Detroit and a pre-Christmas appearance at West Seattle's Admiral Theater for a double-bill of *It's a Wonderful Life* and *The Bishop's Wife*. The event will be a benefit for the Fred Hutchinson Cancer Research Center, the same institution whose Hutch Holiday Gala Karolyn headlined two years prior.

Enhancing these outings will be two book projects on which Karolyn collaborated that were slated for late 1996 release. Besides participating in the preparation of this biography, Karolyn co-authored *Zuzu's It's a Wonderful Life Cookbook* with publicist Franklin Dohanyos of Royal Oak, Michigan. Laced with stills from her signature movie, the collection of recipes from Karolyn and others connected with *It's a Wonderful Life* will be published by Carol Publishing.

The 1996 holiday season for *It's a Wonderful Life* is a milestone that Karolyn is embracing, not fully knowing the multitude of events and contacts that will greet her. Yet another wave of recognition for her is due simultaneously, with the scheduled Dec. 20 release by Disney of *The Preacher's Wife*, a black musical remake of *The Bishop's Wife*, directed by Penny Marshall and starring Denzel Washington as the angel, Courtney Vance as the cleric, Whitney Houston as his wife and Lionel Richie and Gregory Hines in other roles. The new movie is bound to refocus the media and the public on the charming, Academy Award-nominated 1947 original.

"I like to make friends with fans of these movies. I like to be one-on-one with people," Karolyn says. "Whatever happens this year, it'll be great. I could live out of a suitcase my whole life."

That statement is an exaggeration, though, as Karolyn still relishes her role as a mother. All her children are grown, with changing and growing families of their own that have so far provided Karolyn with six grandchildren (including one little girl with the first name of Bailey, in honor of Karolyn's Zuzu Bailey character). While she doesn't consider herself "the grandmother type," Karolyn does provide a rudder – and extra bedroom space, when needed – for her brood. "I'm not hard, but I have both feet on the ground," she says, "and I think my kids come to me to get that feeling. If one of them gets into trouble, they're old enough that I'm not going to run over and hold their hand anymore. But I can try to be rational and realistic and let them know I love them and care for them, and even put them up for awhile."

Karolyn also has taken in what she affectionately calls her "strays": two young men who have lived in her house off and on since Mike died. They perform odd jobs and provide a feeling of security, and their occupations and the women in their lives keep Karolyn on her toes. "We all kind of take care of each other," she says. "It's just nice to know there's somebody there who takes care of you, and the guys really are sweet."

Karolyn visits with Argentina Brunetti (Mrs. Martini in IT'S A WONDERFUL LIFE above) and actress Shelley Fabares (who played Donna Reed's daughter in television's THE DONNA REED SHOW) at the Donna Reed Festival in Denison, Iowa, June 1996.

Those close to Karolyn return the sentiment.

"She's remarkable," says her scrapbook friend Karen Treschl. "We're closer than most sisters, and I feel so fortunate. I don't know anyone who could have overcome the obstacles she has faced. Her personal life is not a fairy tale. Hers is like a tragedy that keeps happening, and you wonder what will come next. To have lost two parents, two husbands and a child, that's a lot of giving up, but she keeps trying to give. Even if her reward isn't on earth, it'll be in heaven."

"She's just a giving person," adds Beth Johnson, the friend who helped launch Karolyn's Zuzu dolls. "She would help anybody. She will not only buy things for people but give her own belongings away, including anything to do with *It's a Wonderful Life*. If she knows that you don't have the money for it, she'll make sure that you have it. And she's such a good listener. When she's being Zuzu,

'I like to make friends with fans of these movies. I like to be one-on-one with people.'

people sense that. I think they see Zuzu as daddy's little girl, maybe daddy's favorite, and people seem to like the favored child. I think people love that idea. She'll sign a sympathy card and say, 'I'm ringing a bell for you,' and honestly, it does mean quite a bit to think of Zuzu, in relationship to your higher spirit, actually ringing a bell for this person. It sounds strange, but it goes right to your heart, without a doubt."

For Karolyn to have survived and surmounted more than a lifetime's share of adversity and still be ringing that bell in her 56th year is an accomplishment approaching the angelic.

S ome movies – the best ones – have a way of bringing things full circle.

In *It's a Wonderful Life*, Zuzu helps deepen her father's appreciation of adult reality.

In her real-life childhood, Karolyn Grimes lost her mother and father and, with them, much of her childhood reality.

Decades later, the American people revived a tiny segment of her youth, changing forever Karolyn's adult reality.

She now carries a dual identity of Karolyn/Zuzu. It's intertwined with her charming films and her rugged personal history, with logic and religion, with angels and "real people," with material things and unexplainable forces, with her image of herself and the image others have of her.

The following conversation with Karolyn – a composite of interviews conducted at various times from 1994 through 1996 – covers all of those facets and sheds more light on this unusual woman. It also delves into the insight she draws from her most famous film, and reveals why another Christmas angel fable, *The Bishop's Wife*, is even more significant to her.

• • •

With *It's a Wonderful Life* and the Zuzu role, you're on a ride right now. Do you have any idea where it's going to end?

I don't know if it's going to keep going or if it'll start to peter out, but I want to stay on the ride. I love it. If it does end, I have a lot of wonderful memories. It's been wonderful. I wouldn't trade it for anything.

I feel like I'm one of the most fortunate people in the world because I was chosen to be a part of that movie. In a sense, I haven't really had a wonderful life, but on the other hand, what a special privilege I've been granted, to share in the love and the specialness of that movie. It's made up for everything. It's a balance, a healing balance. It heals all the other stuff that I've had to go through, and somehow it helps me have more compassion for the people I meet.

Who are the biggest fans of *It's a Wonderful Life*?

From what I can tell, if I were doing a study, the statistics would show that the blue-collar

"What a special privilege I've been granted, to share in the love and the specialness of that movie. It's made up for everything. It's a healing balance."

guys are the ones the movie means the most to. That's because they can identify with the situation George Bailey was in. Their dreams were never met, and things probably didn't go the way they wanted.

They're feeling stuck by their position.

Exactly – where the guys who are out there working all the time and making money don't have time to watch TV, and if they do, they're not going to watch an old black-and-white movie. Their dreams are met, and they have little reason to identify with that movie. That's what I've found, that when I go into areas like Detroit and Boston where you have the blue-collar worker, then the people really come out. When I go to Los Angeles, it's not quite the same.

There's a jadedness?

Yes. And when I go to some elite affairs, there isn't that outpouring and the same kind of – oh, it's not adoration, it's more empathy. There's not that emotional bonding. It's not that thread that everybody can cling to and identify with. It's not the same.

'It could have been anybody in the whole world, but somebody decided it was going to be me.

. . .

'Because of that movie, I feel that I need to do what I can today for this world, and for humanity.'

Do you have any insight about why you won the part of Zuzu?

There had to be a reason. It could have been anybody in the whole world, but, for some reason or other, somebody decided it was going to be me. There had to be a reason I was chosen to do that, because I feel a responsibility to that movie, and to what it stands for, and to what it has done for other people. Because of that movie, I feel that I need to do what I can today for this world, and for humanity.

Why not be content to sit back and say it was just the luck of the draw that you were in *It's a Wonderful Life*?

I'm a little weird about that. I'm very observant. I have to be logical about everything. There have to be reasons, and I have to think things through. I am the kind of person who will walk into a room of people and notice everything. I'll assess things, put things together. That's the way I've always been. I just walk in and analyze. I'm just really awful about that.

So I analyze the fact that I was chosen to be this little girl in this movie that has touched so many lives and means so much to so many people and families every year at Christmas. Well, I also was chosen to go through a hell of a life. I didn't make everything happen to me. Some things I did – bad choices, wrong choices or maybe just choices – I don't know if they were good or bad. But I didn't have control over everything that happened to me. So there had to be a reason for me to learn to feel compassion, to learn to feel the gamut of emotions a person can feel. Whether it be fear or happiness or dread, I've felt it with my life. I've had to. It's just happened to me over the years.

I can see my own character developing more and more, and in the end I'm still growing. Everyone is still becoming and moving. We're all a source of energy that is constantly changing. I feel that by experiencing all these things, I have more facets, perhaps, than someone who grows up in the all-American small-town home, loves their family, knows the same people all their life, went to school with them and still lives in this town. There's a difference between that and my life. I've lived 10 to 20 lives over my lifespan. In doing so, I've increased my knowledge and my emotional capabilities of expanding and controlling and everything that you can do to get through life. I'm surviving.

That's why I still think that, for some reason or another, that movie ties in to my life. There are hundreds of people who were in movies when they were kids, and no one ever knows it or even thinks about it or cares about it. But because of that one movie, it's become such a major part of my life. It's like I have two sides, and that's one of my sides. I really do have an alter ego. I'm that little girl. I am that person. I've grown up to be that person.

Who do you think that little girl is? Who is Zuzu?

Well, I think she has a mission. She's innocent and pure. She represents the all-American little girl who probably grew up to be a mother and had everything just like her mother. She had her babies and raised them, she did the right thing, she volunteered in the PTA, she was all of these things that everybody wants. Every man wants a woman like that to be his wife, and that was her goal in life, to be a mother and wife and all of that.

Essentially she became a Mary Bailey?

In a way, yes, because she has the support of her mother and father and family, and I get the impression that she would want to stay in that circle.

You can see all of that in such a small part?

I can, and I think that's what everybody sees as happening to this little girl. Her daddy loved her, perhaps a little more than the other kids, or seemed to. She wasn't even the baby. Tommy was the baby. But she got special attention in this movie, and it was pretty obvious there was a special bond between her and her dad, and that probably helped her get through life.

Well, I think that's a totally different person from who I am, and there has to be a reason for my turning out the way I did, so somewhere in there I have to keep these two people separated. They are two different people. I'm far from innocent, I'm far from that little girl. But yet I am.

More than a hint of the "innocent and pure" persona of Zuzu shines from this Christmastime photo of 4-year-old Karolyn in front of the Grimes family house on Norton Street in West Hollywood.

I'm naive about so many things, I'm so darn trusting of people, and I really am that little, innocent girl in a way. There's a lot of overlapping there. So it's an enigma.

You are one part of the movie, but the entire movie has captured people's hearts, more than any other Christmas movie. Why is that?

I think it's because of all the exposure it got. It's been a household word for many years. It was in all the cartoons, people made fun of it all the time, and it was on television all the time. That kept it in the public eye, and that made it what it is today. I'm not so sure it'll stay there if it continues to be shown only once a year, but I hope it will, because of the message.

'I'm far from innocent, I'm far from that little girl. But yet I . . . really am that little, innocent girl in a way.'

So it's the exposure as well as the content that created the phenomenon?

If people see it, they get the message, but they have to be able to see it.

What if a film like *Miracle on 34th Street* (starring Edmund Gwenn, Natalie Wood, Maureen O'Hara and John Payne) were to get the same exposure? It's a Christmas movie, it came out just a year after *It's a Wonderful Life* and it has a warm message.

'I'm not acting, I am love, I am reaching out and touching other people. It's this gift I've been given, that I can help others, and that's the most wonderful gift in the world.'

But it's not the same kind of movie, because it doesn't appeal as much to the little man. It doesn't have the same story. It's the story of *It's a Wonderful Life* that people can identify with. *Miracle on 34th Street* is about Santa Claus, but it doesn't apply as much to real life. *It's a Wonderful Life* is real life because it's the story of George Bailey. This man had a dream from day one, and constantly ran into roadblocks that stopped this dream from happening. Even his own emotions betrayed him when he fell in love with Mary. He made that choice, and as they're leaving to go on their honeymoon, with their money in their pocket, bingo-bang, there's another roadblock. It's the story of my life. That has been my life. That has been most everybody's life, because it happens. That's the way people have problems. Something like that always happens.

George Bailey couldn't control a lot of the things that happened to him, so in the end, when Uncle Billy lost the money, it was the straw that broke the camel's back. He had all these kids, this rickety old house, the building and loan was always on a thread, just barely making it, and then this happens and he still has to bow down to Mr. Potter. This is the end of his life. It really is. What is the point of going on? He's in pain, he's suffering, he's worked so hard, he's given up his dreams, his life, to keep this stupid business afloat, and then one silly mistake, one drunken old man happens to do this, and then boom, what's the point of his life? There was no point. I've felt like that many times, and I know other people have, too. You go back through your life and think, "If this had only happened, if that had only happened, I could be here, there or whatever."

Then, of course, when George Bailey reflects and sees what he really did accomplish and what it would have been like had he not been there, his life really is worth something, and he realizes the value of what he did have. He realizes he had the love of his wife that you can't buy, he had normal, wholesome children that you can't buy, he had the love of his community that you can't buy. You can't value these things that he had with a material value. These are emotional things, from the heart, from other people. There's just no way you can achieve that except from your work or from who you are. That's your character, that's your very being. You can go on a lot of trips, you can see the world, but have you really accomplished anything? Who knows?

He really realized that, and that's when he knew that he was a happy man, and it didn't matter that he didn't have any money, didn't matter if he lost the building and loan. What mattered was, he had that old house that was full of love, he had the best wife in the world and the most wonderful children. He was happy as a lark because you can't buy love.

That's why I think most people who watch the movie today identify with it. Maybe they sit back and look at their lives a little bit and think, "You know, I really am lucky to have these people who love me and care about me." It's all about love. The whole damn movie is about love and friendships and how you do things for people and you don't even remember or realize that you're doing it for them. Maybe it's just a smile. Maybe it's just a greeting: "Hi, how are you doing?" But maybe that meant more to that person than you can ever realize. You have to realize that you're "on" your whole life.

It's something I realize and try to do. I try to smile because I just think it's really important. I try to be as nice as I can, and hopefully it'll rub off on these people a little bit, and they'll turn around and give it to somebody else.

You obviously identify with the movie's themes, but how does that translate into taking the next step – to embracing it publicly?

Once I realized what this movie was about, I started trying to put it in perspective with my own life. It really gave me the feeling that it's okay to be on this mission, to impart to other people that I am a part of this story that you can get help from. I feel that if people feel so dearly about the movie, and it's in their hearts so much just to be able to touch a person who was a part of it and it makes them feel good, well, hey, I'll touch the world.

Karolyn visits with Manny Gravame of Madison Heights, Michigan, during a signing event at December's Special Place angel shop in nearby Southgate.

You don't know how gratifying it is. It's the most wonderful thing in the world. It's not like being a movie star and giving an autograph. That's a shallow, "Oh, she's famous," and blah blah blah. This is different. It's not like I'm famous, but I'm a part of the American way. I'm a part of love. I'm a part of something that is a tradition in everybody's home every year at Christmastime. I'm not acting, I am love, I am reaching out and touching other people. It's this gift I've been given, that I can help others, and that's the most wonderful gift in the world. It has nothing to do with money or anything else. It's trying to make the world a better place. I just think I'm so fortunate.

You began thinking about what the movie meant when you started getting the phone calls from reporters and so forth. But before then, you hadn't given the movie a second thought. What were you thinking about the obstacles you had faced up to that point?

For some reason or other I had a real positive outlook. I always knew down the road that things would be the way I wanted them to be, or things would be better. I always had that in my heart. Every single thing that happened to me, I always knew it was temporary and that it would get better, and I always looked for the positive in the worst situations.

My high school years in Osceola were probably the worst years of my life, yet the drama teacher Fern Lyons and the music teacher Blanche Remington gave me such self-confidence and love, and I just thought they were so neat. They gave me the inspiration that I was good and that I could perform. They kept my heart alive, so all of a sudden I looked forward to going to school, when I had hated school in California.

'I always knew down the road that things would be the way I wanted them to be, or things would be better.

'I always had that in my heart.'

I've never questioned anything that has ever happened to me. I don't say, "Why? Why? Why?" I say, "OK, it happened, let's analyze this, and let's see what we can pull out of this that's good."

When my son John killed himself, I looked at the situation, and he must have been a very unhappy little boy. Well, he's happy now. He's free of pain. He isn't hurting anymore. That's good, and that's the most important thing. I don't think he realized the consequences of what he'd done. I don't think he realized that it was permanent. I think he was really sick. I could dwell on the regrets that I have, but I never did anything consciously to hurt him, so I look at the fact that he's not in pain, and that's the most positive thing that can come from this – plus the outpouring of people who came and shared with me their problems of the same nature.

I just felt at the time a burden was lifted off my shoulders because I knew he was happy. A lot of people pray to dead people, but I will not allow myself to do that. I will never do that with John because I don't want to hold him here. I want him to go on to wherever he wanted to go to be happy. In my heart, I know I'll see him again. I can say I'm sorry or whatever I need to do, but a lot of friendships that I had grew closer because it's during times like this you know who your friends are. I think that there's always a positive that comes out of everything.

***It's a Wonderful Life* enhanced your feeling about that.**

Certainly. It taught me to look for the positive situations in all negative situations, and the negatives are constant.

Did your angel line in the movie ("Every time a bell rings, an angel gets his wings") ring true to you as well?

Yes, and I learned to accept the angel theme long before the movie became this thing it is today. I used to think reincarnation was a sin to even think about because I was raised so strictly. Well, in 1981 I started studying and reading about different theories on living, and I was taught Shusta, which is a metaphysical study of colors and a way of living life. In those teachings, there are beings who watch over you, and I consider those to be guardian angels.

I'm not really a Bible thumper, or a God-and-heaven-and-hell person, because I don't necessarily believe that. But I do believe that there is someone or something you can turn to. There's an entity that you can ask, "Please be with me, please guide me, please show me the way." I don't know that it's a heavenly, winged creature by any means, but that's the way we as humans see something beautiful, and I do consider it beautiful. I think whatever is there is beautiful. It's there to help us to grow mentally and physically, up the ladder with more goodness each time, to be more God-like or supreme-being-like.

Angels adorned Karolyn's Christmas tree in 1995.

Even the Bible – which people interpret a thousand different ways – says faith can move mountains, and I really do believe that. If you want something to happen, you can make it happen. I believe that with all my heart. It's just positive thinking.

So the angel stuff in the movie is pretty meaningful to you.

Absolutely.

It's not just a plot device, as in "It's nice, but it's not real."

No, no, no. It's not a gimmick. I think it is very real. I think that angels give you the opportunities, and you have to be aware enough to take advantage of them to make your life or somebody else's better. There are no coincidences, and whatever happens to you, there is a message, and you must look for that message and work with it. I think we're all made up of energy, and I think that we get energy from these beings. I think that we're like a conduit from the supreme source of energy, and that we have the opportunity to do good or evil. I think that the energy is like karma, and if you do bad, it'll come back to get you, if not in this lifetime, then another lifetime. You will pay. So I think angels do have a place in reality.

The notion of angels, or something that's there for everybody, is not just in *It's a Wonderful Life*. It's in another Christmas movie you made, *The Bishop's Wife*.

That's right. The Episcopal bishop [played by David Niven] asked for help, and he got an angel named Dudley [Cary Grant], and when the angel left, he took himself away from everybody's memory.

You often say that you like *The Bishop's Wife* more than *It's a Wonderful Life*. Why is that?

It's because, even though *It's a Wonderful Life* has had a profound effect on my life, *The Bishop's Wife* applies to me more directly as a person.

I have a very big problem of being obsessed by material things. I think my mother rather instilled that in me. I like possessions, I like fine art, I like beautiful things. When I was a child, I pretty much got everything I wanted. Then I went through a period of my life, in Osceola, when I was almost destitute. That makes you want even more, when that happens. I survived, I knew that I would survive, and I worked till I did okay. Then I married a man who ended up having plenty of money to throw away, and he was generous, so I could feed my obsession, or whatever you want to call it, with whatever I wanted. There was nothing material that I lacked for.

That can become a bottomless pit.

Yes, it can be, and it's hard, but there's so little satisfaction in that. I can acquire art pieces, and I love them, I love to look at them, and I'm proud to own them, and I feel that they're a part of history, but at the same time it's shallow. I don't think it's healthy to live like that, and that's why *The Bishop's Wife* hits me more, because it's about priorities. It's about human beings giving of themselves, and really intermingling with the people who need you, rather than having a huge cathedral, a cold and empty edifice of religion.

It's also about an older woman who had married a man she didn't love, and she felt extremely guilty and bitter her whole life because she had deceived him and lived in a life where she was totally unhappy. She knew that she had lost her love because she couldn't deal with the priorities. She didn't want to live poor. So she

'I think that angels give you the opportunities, and you have to be aware enough to take advantage of them to make your life or somebody else's better.

'There are no coincidences, and whatever happens to you, there is a message, and you must look for that message and work with it.'

gave up love for financial stability. She wanted to build a huge cathedral in her husband's memory to ease her conscience. So she had the same problem that the bishop had.

I think that's a common thing today. A lot of people have that problem. So priorities, to me, are very important. Where are your priorities, you know? I think about fathers who are divorced from their kids, and it's pretty easy to go out and buy a $400 little Jeep that they can pedal rather than taking them out for a camping trip and things like that. That's priorities, giving of yourself instead of being in love with material things. So that's why *The Bishop's Wife* hits me a little more, because I have a problem with that.

***It's a Wonderful Life* is about priorities, too.**

Yes, but in *The Bishop's Wife*, that theme is more pronounced. It shows the parish in the poor part of town where the boys are singing, and the parish is kind of falling apart. There's no continuity, the boys aren't coming to choir practice, and they really need someone to give them direction, and the bishop's not there. It's the same thing of giving of yourself, and you can't buy that, you can't pay for it, and you need to help humanity rather than put money into an empty thing that looks good, maybe, but is cold and serves no purpose.

The movie is also a great love story. The wife of the bishop [Loretta Young] is naive and beautiful and loves life and gives to people from herself. In the end, though, when the angel is talking about loving her and not wanting to leave her, all of a sudden she realizes, "Oh, no, I belong here." But you also know that she really does love Dudley, too. Yet, she knows her priorities, and she can't necessarily follow her heart. She knows the right thing to do, and what she has to do.

There is an edge, when you watch *The Bishop's Wife*. You feel almost uncomfortable that the angel, who is supposed to be a force for good, is going to wreck this home and take the wife away, and that edge keeps you going. You're not totally sure what Cary Grant is going to do.

And the bishop is realizing he's losing her, he's been made to look like a fool, he feels he's lost his parish, and everything, really. So he goes to the professor, who tells him, "Oh, but you have the edge, because he's an angel, and you're a human." That's all it took. Then he has his confidence back and realizes that he can do the right thing. Again, it's priorities.

Sometimes when you're out in public and not on a Zuzu gig, you like to tell people – even teen-agers and college students, people whose parents may not have even been born when the movie came out – that you played Zuzu. It's almost like you're testing them.

A lot of young people like old stuff, including that movie. They really do, particularly the ones who are intellectually strong, the smart ones. I just follow my intuition, and I listen to my inner voice. I think it's fun, and it's the right thing to do.

'Where are your priorities, you know? I think about fathers who are divorced from their kids, and it's pretty easy to go out and buy a $400 little Jeep that they can pedal rather than taking them out for a camping trip and things like that.

'That's priorities, giving of yourself instead of being in love with material things.'

There's no hint of embarrassment about it.

Sometimes I act like I'm embarrassed, but I'm actually thrilled to death because I get to be "on." The only time I'm embarrassed is if somebody doesn't know the movie. Then I feel like a fool. But for the most part, strange as it might seem, the older people often don't know the movie, but it's a cult for young people. Teachers show their kids this movie in school. It just happens.

It's astonishing how one movie can have that kind of magic with so many people. Is the message of *The Bishop's Wife* as universal?

Those movies are two different avenues, and they reach two different groups of people. Priorities, I don't think, are necessarily going to reach the middle class as much as George Bailey's story does, because priorities are more of an elitist message. The middle-class guy doesn't really ever have those choices to make, in a way. Yet, everyone really does, every day of their lives. It just isn't noticeable or obvious.

But *It's a Wonderful Life* is the film that has had a huge effect on you.

Oh God, tons. It is my alter ego. It really is the case. It is my life. That is me. It has become me, I should say.

You have allowed it to become you.

Absolutely.

You could just say, "Forget it, I'm not going to do that."

Oh, but I love it. I love the people. When you look at their faces, they're so excited to meet you, and it's not you, but it's the *It's a Wonderful Life* thing, too. It's the movie. It's history.

Karolyn signs autographs at the Decades memorabilia shop in Royal Oak, Michigan, 1994.

When you talk with people and autograph things for them, do they see Karolyn or do they see Zuzu?

I don't think they bother to think about distinguishing. I just think they think that I'm her. They associate the movie so much with me that they really feel like that's who I really am, and I would never want to besmirch that image.

It's a nice image to have.

It is, and I feel a responsibility to uphold it.

Where do you feel that responsibility from, though?

The people.

But nobody's told you to take on this persona.

You can just tell the way people act. They cry and they just get so wrapped up in it, and it's like I really am Zuzu.

What attributes of Zuzu do you have?

I think I'm a very giving person. Even during that long time when I wasn't a touchy-feely person, people still clung to me with their problems. I've always been like that, I think, because I've been through so much. People draw to me because they've seen me survive all the things that I've gone through, and maybe they need to draw some strength from it.

It seems that you've built up a serenity over time.

Well, there's a crisis in my life every day, usually, sometimes more than one, but I just go with the flow. I've learned that the best way to handle a bad situation is to look for something good in it, because there always is. You just have to look for it, and that's what you focus in on. You just always look for those things. They're there.

There are many of those gems that I live by, like "There are no coincidences," and there is a message for you when those "coincidences" happen. There's something there for you to find. That's why they happen.

You're not talking about these things in overly religious tones.

Oh, my divine source is there. I know there is someone who has a hand in things. I pray, I meditate. I feel like God is within me because that's where I look for God. I pray for him to come into me, and then that's the way I live my life. I have his help – be it God, be it a karmic lord, be it whatever's there. I'm not one who quotes Bible scripture that says there's going to be a new world and all that sort of thing. I don't believe in that.

But think about how many galaxies there are in this life that we have today. There are billions. Do you actually think that this is the only planet that has life on it? We are, I think, a very young civilization, and the whole spectrum is unlimited. I don't think we are developed enough to ever figure out what's going on. There's got to be more than what we know. I do believe there is life after death. I'm very strong on that. I believe that energy is something that exists, and that we function on. I believe that we have the power to let people die or keep them here when they're ill. There's this energy that we all exist on, and there can be negative energy or positive energy.

I've met people who dwell in hate and bitterness and negative thoughts. Nothing ever goes right and it never will, and those people are so pitiful. I don't believe in that. I think there is good in everything, and you can look for it and it's all energy. It fills you with such goodness sometimes that you just want to burst. It's wonderful. Energy is what makes the world go round. It's what life is about.

Do you have regrets?

I wish I hadn't quit college. That's the main regret of my life, because my life would have had a different path altogether. Everything would have been different.

What would your life have been like if you had stayed in Los Angeles, the city of angels?

Well, it's not exactly that. I can only guess what might have happened to me if I'd stayed, but I think I would have been a mess. Life was so fast there. Everybody else my age was drinking, and even though it was the 1950s, kids were already into drugs there. I probably would have fallen into that and gone down the wrong path. I think there were some guardian angels who plucked me up and placed me back in the Midwest and saved my life.

'To make it into the movies, a child has to have an extremely pushy mother or father, a stage parent all the way – obnoxious, pushy, everything you don't want to be.

'If you've got that strong, burning desire for your child, I guess you have to do it, but your children pay the price. They work all day, they live in a whole different world than other children do, and they don't get a childhood.'

When God took me out of that life in California, it was the best thing that ever happened to me because it showed me a different world. Maybe it wasn't good for me to live with the people I did in Osceola, but I guess it had to help develop my character. There had to be a reason for it, and it was a great gift, because I met real people, and people are what make the world what it is. Without other people there would be nothing.

You cringe a bit when someone calls you a child star.

I don't even consider myself a starlet. I was a bit player, just a character kid with buns and braids. There's no two other ways about it. I happened to be in the right movie.

What is your advice to parents who want to put their children in the movies?

I would say, "Don't." To make it into the movies, a child has to have an extremely pushy mother or father, a stage parent all the way – obnoxious, pushy, everything you don't want to be. If you've got that strong, burning desire for your child, I guess you have to do it, but your children pay the price. They work all day, they live in a whole different world than other children do, and they don't get a childhood.

To compete in today's world, it's got to be worse than what I went through when I was a child. But I took violin lessons, piano lessons, acting lessons, dialect lessons, vocal coaching, dancing, singing. It was a constant onslaught of lessons of some sort. Your whole life is that, rather than being a child growing up. I could never play sports because I might damage my hands or hurt my voice by screaming, so I missed out on a lot of things other children benefited from. I became sort of a loner.

In this undated photo, 4- or 5-year-old Karolyn acts as a model in what appears to be a newspaper or magazine advertisement for grocery products. No accompanying papers to document this job survive, and Karolyn can recall nothing of it, but it is perhaps for a Safeway ad because she was told long ago that the checker is her father LaVan.

Do you think your own childhood in the movies hurt you as an adult?

It didn't bother me that badly. Maybe it'll catch up with me later, but I doubt it. I'm able to take whatever life hands me and deal with it. I've always been like that.

What is it about being "on" that you like so much?

I like to make people wake up their emotions and have compassion and feeling. I like to be able to stir that up. I think that's a real talent.

'To compete in today's world, it's got to be worse than what I went through.'

What do you do with comments from people who say that you're beautiful?

Right now, I'd kiss them on the feet. It feels so good.

But there's also the notion that real beauty lies within.

I am thankful every day of my life that I had something to work with, because that has been important to me. I don't know if my mother instilled that, but physical appearance is important to me. However, it's not so important that I'm willing to do narcissistic workouts to my body like a 20-year-old. I'm not that disciplined, and I don't care about it that much. But I really appreciate keeping my nails and my hair done and looking nice.

Have you always felt that way about your appearance?

I knew I could turn a head when I was younger, but I've never thought of myself as gorgeous or anything like that. I was just taught that to look pretty is good, if you can.

But is it really good?

I've been taught that, and I feel good if I'm looking nice. As the years are passing, though, I have a hard time dealing with the aging factor. I don't look pretty, to me, anymore. That is something I'm having to deal with, so we'll see down the road how much that really was important to me. It may have been more important than I thought.

Where do you see *It's a Wonderful Life* and your role in it five years from now?

I don't know. I just can't conceive of it. But I do make permanent relationships wherever I go, and they're true friendships. It's like during the Target tour when the Bailey kids were reunited. We have a bond. Now we're like real brothers and sisters. It's so cool. It's just the neatest thing.

"I'm having a heyday. Anyone who thinks life is over after 50 is wrong!"

Do you see doing Zuzu gigs in your 60s and 70s and beyond?

Yes, I do, but it probably depends a lot on whether the movie is shown on television just once a year. Whatever happens, though, I'm looking forward to it.

What aspects of *It's a Wonderful Life* will endure long after we're all gone?

Opposite page: Karolyn poses for one of the many promotional photos arranged by her mother Martha.

It's a movie that will help anyone survive any kind of adversity that comes their way. I know I have used it as a source of energy to turn my thinking around and make me a survivor, and I feel that's what I am. I'll keep fighting to the end because that movie gives me the courage to do that. The movie is bound to have that appeal for people long into the future. There's something in that movie for everyone. It's like a flower that's continually unfolding. It's timeless, really.

The movie is like a fragile thread that's trying to hold onto a special time of truth and honesty. Today, we keep pursuing that thread to try to regain part of a lost era that we miss and we need. We're trying to heal a society that's really hurting. In the movie, George Bailey never reached his goals, but he actually maintained much more and contributed so much, and he inspires us all to continue

to go after what we want, but at the same time to look at what we've done.

Each year, I go more places as Zuzu, and I keep meeting young people who are trying to make a difference. This movie gives them the tools to work with.

Would you call your own life inspirational?

If anything, *It's a Wonderful Life* has inspired my life. I mean, I live that movie. If I didn't, I think I would have collapsed by now.

I think I've been more of a survivor than an inspiration. I'm a survivor of life, and life isn't always easy. It would be awfully boring if it was. You have to go through some bad times to know what the good times are.

And these are good times. In fact, I'm having a heyday. Anyone who thinks life is over after 50 is wrong! When people share their joys and their grief and their dreams with me, I feel like I'm Mother Earth. I, who never had a family, so to speak, have the biggest family in the world, and it gets bigger all the time. I just have an affinity with people in pain or hurt, and it ends up being a really good thing.

Zuzu seems to be your persona for life.

It's so much a part of me that I think it's with me forever, and it's the most wonderful, fulfilling thing. I'm a very gregarious person. I love to do presentations, and I love to talk to people. And people really do treat me with a certain reverence because *It's a Wonderful Life* is so much a part of their lives.

'If I can touch someone's life and make it better for even just a few minutes, my God, how many people can do that?

'What a thrill, what a joy, what an opportunity to make the world a little different.'

If I can touch someone's life and make it better for even just a few minutes, my God, how many people can do that? What a thrill, what a joy, what an opportunity to make the world a little different. It's so special, and it's just a wonderful, wonderful feeling when I do that. I just feel so privileged. It's like a conduit. The holy spirit of somebody is coming through me.

I don't really know why I get to do this. But maybe it's because God's been kind of rough in some other ways and he's giving me a balance to make me a better person, because every little thing you go through that's painful and horrible makes you grow. You have more compassion for others, and I think that's the key in life – compassion, touching others' lives.

I have the opportunity that most people never have, to touch others' lives with compassion and caring. I have so many friends that I probably am the luckiest person in the world.

Without fans, no movie can succeed. As *It's a Wonderful Life* approached its golden anniversary on Dec. 19, 1996, no other American film could claim more dedicated fans than this Christmas classic.

Unquestionably the most active and appealing present-day ambassador for *It's a Wonderful Life*, Karolyn Grimes has traveled to every corner of the country this decade, drawing thousands of enthusiastic fans of all ages and walks of life. It's only fitting that a biography of Karolyn gives her fans the last word.

This chapter has two sections. A "best of" collection from Karolyn's hundreds of fan letters starts the chapter, followed by the comments of those who crowded into one of her most recent Zuzu gigs.

Peruse these sentiments with anticipation, for it's a safe bet you will find your own thoughts and feelings. Such is the magic of *It's a Wonderful Life* – and of Karolyn.

• • •

As Karolyn gained national visibility from the Target tour of 1993, her mailbox swelled with letters from well-wishers. Their postmarks hailed from every state in the union, plus several international addresses. Their occupations ran the gamut, from an English teacher and a police lieutenant to Georgia's secretary of state (the inspiring paraplegic Max Cleland). Most sought Karolyn's autograph, and a few offered unusual news, such as Nancy Holmes, of Alexandria, Virginia, who wanted Karolyn to know that her family had named its Delaware beach house "Zuzu's Petals."

Several of the letters prompted smiles, tears or both. Excerpts from the best of those appear below. (And if you wish to write Karolyn and get on the mailing list for the newsletter of The Zuzu Society, the address is P.O. Box 225, Stilwell, KS 66085.)

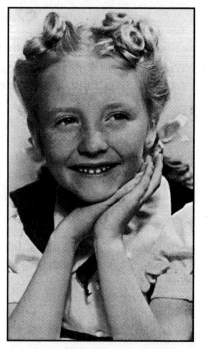

A portrait of Karolyn at 6 years old, the age at which she played Zuzu in IT'S A WONDERFUL LIFE.

From Ron Mariwell, of Chicago, Illinois:

It truly is a wonderful life. I even proclaim my fondness by a sign across my garage door at Christmas time that says, "That-a-boy, Clarence!" Sorry it wasn't one of your lines. My wife thinks it's silly for a 41-year-old man to break into tears every time when Harry says, "To my big brother George, the richest man in town."

My wife's girlfriend hates the movie because she says it would never happen. She has no faith in people. I have enclosed an envelope with her address on it. You could do me a big favor and just write her a few lines. With me working on her here and you sending a message, maybe we could convince her, it truly is a wonderful life!

'Remember, no man is a failure who has friends.'

(The best of Karolyn's fan mail, and in-person interviews with her fans, 1993-1995)

From Greg and Lisa Wilson, of Clarksburg, West Virginia:

We named our daughter Taylor Zuzu. We can only hope that she has an idyllic home life as shown in the movie.

From Robert J. Robertson, of Edmonton, Alberta:

It's a Wonderful Life is my personal favorite film. It is certainly a lovely sentiment to base one's existence around. When things become bleak, I always, always find inspiration and meaning in that movie to continue on, no matter what is in front of me. And the simplicity inherent in the innocent message of a child is heavenly in itself.

From Sharon Espiau, of Pomona, California:

Thank you for the wonderful photographs you sent me. I certainly didn't expect to receive such a nice response. I want you to know that my husband and I will treasure these pictures forever. I have framed them and display them proudly in my living room. In front of the three movie photos, I've placed the recent picture of you. You've turned out as beautiful as any Hollywood leading lady.

Last night, I sat transfixed looking at the pictures, imagining you playing your scenes with all those great actors and actresses. We've all heard those stories about child actresses being selfish brats, but your kindness and generosity dispel any such notion about you. Thank you for making my life a little more wonderful.

From Robert Perts, inmate, of Huntington, Pennsylvania:

We're allowed to have a TV in our cells. I have an older (in his mid-50s) cellmate who had (remarkably) never watched *It's a Wonderful Life*. It was only the hundredth time or so that I've seen it. I never miss it while it's on! My "cellie" is doing 10 to 20 years for murder and doesn't display much in the way of emotions. When you said, "Look daddy, teacher says, every time a bell rings, an angel gets his wings," I saw a tear streak down his face. I made like I didn't notice. Thank you, "Zuzu."

'Your performance was one of the best that anyone has ever done – ever!

'To get to my "cellie" was more than a performance. It was a miracle!'

Robert Perts

Your performance was one of the best that anyone has ever done – ever! To get to my "cellie" was more than a performance. It was a miracle! May God forever bless you, and may you always have the heart of Zuzu! The world sorely needs more Zuzus. (A couple more Jimmy Stewarts wouldn't hurt, either!) Thank you so very much just for being you.

From Richard Alan Lebow, M.D., of Baltimore, Maryland:

Prescription: Autographed photo.

Name: Zuzu.

Age: Forever young.

It would be a great thrill if you could honor my prescription! I can't begin to tell you how much "the movie" means to me. As a physician, I often urge my depressed patients to experience the motivational power of *It's a Wonderful Life*.

From John R. Mencl, of Independence, Missouri:

(Mencl, an attorney, sent Karolyn a lengthy letter, explaining the part *It's a Wonderful Life* played in a September 1990 civil trial, in which he presented the widow of Robert Stratton, a farmer accidentally killed in a truck accident. How to value the premature loss of Stratton's life was a major issue in the case. He had left no children behind and was going bankrupt at the time of his death, so the trucking company argued for a low financial value. Mencl, however, focused on his client's life, calling witnesses from Stratton's farm community whom Stratton had helped, sometimes to Stratton's monetary detriment. One man described on the stand how Stratton had saved his son's life because Stratton knew cardiopulmonary resuscitation.

(Mencl had no economic damages to put into evidence and could not ask the jury to consider the widow's grief. But Missouri law allowed the jury to evaluate the loss the widow would have for the rest of her life. The following is an excerpt from Mencl's closing argument.)

Karolyn talks with Independence, Missouri, attorney John Mencl and his wife Ruth (above) at the Donna Reed Festival, held in June 1996 in Denison, Iowa. Later in the summer, she visited the Mencls' home, including the family "shrine" to IT'S A WONDERFUL LIFE (below).

"Robert and Elaine worked at their marriage. They had an investment in their marriage, and they had a right to cash in on that investment. They had a right to some golden years together. Maybe things and times wouldn't be so tough. Maybe there would be better days. As long as Robert was around, Elaine always had hope. . . .

"You know, this case kind of reminds me, maybe in a roundabout way, of that movie they show around Christmas time – Jimmy Stewart in *It's a Wonderful Life*. Remember that? He plays George Bailey, and the angel takes him back and shows him what life would've been like if he had never been born, and there were some changes. Well, there would have been some changes if Robert Stratton had never been born. His life had value. There's one little boy down in Windsor who probably wouldn't even be alive now without him. That is something to be proud of.

"At the end of that movie, I remember they looked in a book, and this was after all of the friends had come to Jimmy Stewart's aid. Remember that? They're all bringing in cash to help him out. And the book said, 'No man is a failure who has friends.'

"Robert Stratton had a lot of friends. His best friend is sitting right here. . . . Just do your honest best to put a value on what she's lost – what she had and what she's lost, and what she'll continue losing for the next 30-some-odd years. I ask you to do that and return a verdict that you'll be proud of in your heart, and then you can say that you rendered full and complete justice."

(The jury returned its verdict in less than two hours. The verdict was 14 times more than the highest settlement offer the defendant had been willing to make before the trial.)

From Jane Andrews, of Eastman, Georgia:

It's a Wonderful Life has been part of our family's Christmas since 1976. One of the first questions my unmarried 31-year-old son asks a date is, "Do you like *It's a Wonderful Life*"?

From Doug LeTendre, of Milwaukee, Wisconsin:

1. Will you marry me? (OK, never mind.)

2. I think you are so damn cute in that movie – are you still cute?

3. Do you cry when you see the movie?

You were an angel. I hope you still are. I bet you are.

● ● ●

On Thanksgiving weekend 1995, Karolyn visited Detroit, Michigan, to help promote the annual America's Day Parade with that city's famous native son, Tim Allen of TV's *Home Improvement*. However, the culmination of her trip came on Saturday afternoon, Nov. 25, when – for five hours nonstop – she autographed photos, ornaments and figurines for 400 people who crowded into an angel shop called December's Special Place in suburban Southgate. Some of the fans had Karolyn personalize Christmas gifts for family and friends, while others just wanted to meet her and share a smile and a moment of conversation. Here are excerpts from the reflections of 33 of those fans, interviewed at random:

Mary Kruso, of Wyandotte:

I use *It's a Wonderful Life* as my philosophy of life. I, too, lost my parents at a very young age. I was 14 when my mom died of emphysema, and my father died of a massive heart attack when I was 21. I have four brothers and sisters, though, and I was blessed to have them. I'm the youngest, so they always took care of me and watched out for me.

This was always my favorite movie, because it's true that life is bittersweet, and you take the good with the bad and you go on. I was always brought up that there was always something bigger and better, that the angels always watched out for you. I've always used that as my motto. I've felt in my life that angels watched out for me, and some of them had to have earned their wings by now.

My husband and I have two children, 2-year-old John and 4-year-old Michael, and they call it the George movie. They watch it just as much as Barney. It's very much a part of our life. When we decorate our tree, I have a special bell that we put on, the bell that rings.

To me, meeting Zuzu was the ultimate fantasy. It's important to me to see that the characters in the movie aren't just characters, that they are real people, especially her, because I had read that she, too, had lost her parents at a young age. As she says, it's not that great, but you can make the best out of it.

To me, she's a person who was created with a very special gift that God gave her. She is not concealing it. She is rejoicing in the message that she has, and she's delivering it to people, to whoever will listen.

'To me, meeting Zuzu was the ultimate fantasy.

'It's important to me to see that the characters in the movie aren't just characters, that they are real people, especially her, because I had read that she, too, had lost her parents at a young age.'

Mary Kruso

When George came back from his episode with Clarence the angel, the first thing he checked for, besides his bloody lip and that it was snowing, was Zuzu's petals in his pocket. That's what brought him back to reality, because that was his reality. And now I have two children, and they are my reality.

I'm so glad for the popularity of the movie because we need it. We need to know that there is more than what's here. If more people believed in angels and listened to children and heeded what they had to say, I think that it would be a much better place. I find it a much better world because of listening to children and believing in angels – and knowing that, yeah, sometimes you do owe $8,000, and, yeah, there is death in this world. But there's also life, and people who are very giving.

Sandra Evans, of Dearborn Heights:

It's a Wonderful Life just shows that no matter how bad things get, you can always get through, and everyone has a significance, everyone's special.

I came to see Karolyn because I thought it would be fun to meet someone who played in a movie that is so old that still means so much today in society. There's so much going on today that's so wrong, and this just puts everything back in perspective – the simple things you realize are most important, your family and friends. It doesn't matter if you have $1 million or two cents. It just puts it all into perspective.

Alice Sperry, of LaGrange, Indiana:

I drove three hours to come here because I collect angels, and Karolyn was in the movie that started the "whenever a bell rings." I lost my son in January, and I've taken an interest.

I hadn't ever met anybody who was in the public eye, and it all ties together with the Christmas season and angels. She seems like a nice person – and, you know, the angels are all around us. We're just now starting to really realize it.

Pat Longton, of Southgate:

I like to think that there is someone taking care of us, and I like to watch *It's a Wonderful Life*. It's always been a favorite movie, and to meet someone who played in one of my favorites is exciting. She's still Zuzu, the same warm, caring, generous person.

Jane Cady and daughter Stephanie, 9, both of Riverview:

Stephanie: I'm here because my mom told me about it.

Jane: It's our special movie.

Stephanie: I think it's maybe just for us.

Jane: I'm really sick that they put it on only once a year, though. She and I used to cuddle up on the couch and watch it, every time.

Stephanie: It's one of these classics for people to watch.

Jane: I will not buy the video, because I will only watch it at Christmastime. It's not fun to watch in July. I'm surprised Karolyn would come so far to be here.

'You know, the angels are all around us. We're just now starting to really realize it.'

Alice Sperry

I had figured that the people from the movie just kind of went their own way. I brought my daughter because it's a very special movie to me, and it's going to be a lot more memorable now that she's met her. And of course, angels just put a meaning on Christmas, a meaning of life.

Susan Walker, of Trenton, and Kathy Oberdorf, of Flat Rock:

Susan: My husband Steven is obsessed with *It's a Wonderful Life*. If it's on 20 times, he watches it 20 times.

Kathy: It's a lot about family values. If you have family and you have friends, you can get through just about anything in life. Everybody likes money, but that's not the important thing.

Susan: I've been obsessed with angels for two years now. I think everybody has a guardian angel, and I think that when you need it the most, you don't realize that there's somebody there to help you get through it. I think we need that hope.

Kathy: Right, I think we need to go back to the old values that taking time for our families is important instead of this fast pace.

Susan: Anybody from the movie, we would have come to see today.

Kathy: We don't get to meet famous people, and just to think that Karolyn worked with Jimmy Stewart. I just think he's just great – and so is she!

Pura Martinez, of Lincoln Park:

My brother and his wife met watching *It's a Wonderful Life* on a blind date 10 years ago, and they make it a big occasion every year. After they got married, they used to scan the schedule to see when it was on. They'd each set the alarm clock and get up at 2 in the morning, watch the movie, go back to bed and then get up and go to work in the morning.

My little nephew is in love with Zuzu, but he doesn't know that she's older now. He thinks that she's still a young girl.

We come from a large family, and we all have the video. It takes you back into a different time, a better time. You know, when all of the friends come together and give George Bailey the money to rescue him, that's great. People don't do that anymore. And when the angel gets his wings, that's it. I cry every time when I hear the bell ring.

Maureen Budny, of Southgate:

You know how sometimes you run into that whole feeling of depression at Christmastime and how it can overtake a lot of people? Well, the more materialistic it gets, the more you have to stop and think about what the meaning of Christmas is.

I think the end of *It's a Wonderful Life*, when all the people help George Bailey out, is such a pick-me-up. It puts a little more zip back into you. You start to think there are still people out there who care, who think like that.

Sandra Hudzinski, of Wyandotte:

We watch *It's a Wonderful Life* every year, over and over again. It's like *The Bishop's Wife*. I love that one, too – anything that has to do with angels. They're

'My little nephew is in love with Zuzu, but he doesn't know that she's older now. He thinks that she's still a young girl.'

Pura Martinez

there. They're watching you. Some people see them. I feel them.

Just to meet Karolyn, she's somebody who's different. In *The Bishop's Wife*, she was the little girl who got to talk to Cary Grant, who was supposed to be an angel. For all we all know, there might have been one there.

Bill Brang, of Southgate:

It's a Wonderful Life is ageless. You can watch it over and over again. It's a Christmas tradition. The entire family watches it, from my father onward.

It says that you should never give up and feel sorry for yourself. Sometimes you don't think you're very important, but you are actually helping people in your own way, even though you may not realize it. George Bailey found that out. He thought he was failing in life, then Clarence showed him that he'd done all these wonderful things.

I feel that way almost every day. Sometimes I get an inspiration to be something greater than I am in life, but in my own way I'm helping others – like one of the pictures I had Karolyn sign is to help raise money for Leader Dogs for the Blind. I'm in a science-fiction club called Alien Empire, and we have a convention coming up. I'm going to give the photo to our auction, and I'm sure it'll bring in quite a bit of money.

Karolyn autographs a book for an IT'S A WONDERFUL LIFE fan at December's Special Place in Southgate, Michigan, Thanksgiving weekend 1995.

I guess angels play a very important part in our lives. Somebody must help me once in a while when I'm feeling a bit blue and depressed.

Karen Reitz, of Flat Rock:

It's a Wonderful Life is our family's favorite. Every year we watch it, usually Christmas Eve. It has the message that good can come out of anything, and we all like that.

I got Karolyn's autograph for my brother because he's a huge fan. He has everything there is that's *It's a Wonderful Life*, and his birthday is Christmas Eve.

It's exciting. To see anybody from the movies in person makes the movie that much more special. When I see the movie again, I'm going to be thinking about her all the time. I like her character because she's little, and the innocence of it all. She doesn't see the evil and all that's going on, only the good.

Emmanuel "Manny" Gravame, of Madison Heights:

I've watched *It's a Wonderful Life* every year since 1947 or 1948 when I was still in high school. It's a beautiful movie, and I love it.

My dad died when I was 3, my mother was sick with tuberculosis, and I lived with my grandfather until I was 10. There were a lot of hard times, but there were good times, and Christmas was always the special time.

The movie means so much to me because things would go wrong, or sometimes I got into arguments with my stepfather, and there were a couple of times that I

'I guess angels play a very important part in our lives. Somebody must help me once in a while when I'm feeling a bit blue and depressed.'

Bill Brang

wished I was dead. By looking at him [George Bailey] – and I know this is all fiction, but still – what he did, asking God to bring it all back to what it was, and then all the people who were behind him, it becomes a personal thing. It seems to all happen to me. I always think of how it would have been if my dad would have lived.

Karolyn is a doll. She's friendly, a down-to-earth person, somebody who could be your next-door neighbor. I came to see her when she was in Royal Oak last year. I broke down crying then, and I'm doing it now.

*'Everybody can relate to **It's a Wonderful Life** because it gives you hope, and it's something about mankind.*

'Bedford Falls and all of that might be a fantasy in some writer's imagination, but I think it depicts some part of us, what we like to keep, and it's up to us to live it out, if we can.'

Sharon Mandell

Debbie Boren and Shari Dobrovich, both of New Boston:

Debbie: We're always reading anything we can about *It's a Wonderful Life*. It's our favorite Christmas movie.

Shari: It's a good movie for family values and morals. A lot of people are depressed over the holidays, and it lifts your spirits.

Debbie: It happens to me every year until I watch that. Then I realize how blessed I am.

Shari: We believe in angels. I lost a family member last year, and I believe I've got a guardian angel. It's her. I do believe in them.

Debbie: Karolyn's fantastic, and at the end of the movie, her line about ringing the bell always sticks in my mind.

Shari: That's the highlight of the movie. My kids even talk about it after we see the movie. When we're in the stores they always remember, "Mom, there's a bell ringing. You know what that means." It's great to see her because the way she smiles, that's what she did in the movie. You can just connect her.

Sharon and Paul Mandell, of Grosse Ille:

Sharon: I surprised my husband with this. He's the biggest fan, he has two copies of the video, and he didn't know we were coming until I got him up this morning and said, "We've got to be someplace right now."

Paul: Zuzu is like the spirit of Christmas, because she's sick and she helps her father realize there's more to life than himself and what a person wants of himself.

Sharon: Everybody can relate to *It's a Wonderful Life* because it gives you hope, and it's something about mankind. Bedford Falls and all of that might be a fantasy in some writer's imagination, but I think it depicts some part of us, what we like to keep, and it's up to us to live it out, if we can.

Lisa Withrow-Tringali, of Riverview:

I watch *It's a Wonderful Life* about five times a year, and I started about 10 years ago when I was in high school. It's such a heartwarming story, and at the end, when they sing, I always cry. It's just nice to see that everybody pulled together for them, that everybody was there and cared. You watch the news beforehand and you get depressed, and then you watch that and you realize, well, hey, there's still some good out there.

Becky Mulrooney, of Farmington Hills:

I'm a fan of *It's a Wonderful Life*, and my mother instilled it in me. She's an even bigger fan. I think what makes it most special is seeing George Bailey go through the whole period of having to be confused, and then all of a sudden having everything come together in the end. I think all of us have times when we have to go through that sort of thing, and to just see it all work out, it's nice.

Pat Colucci, of Gibraltar:

When I watch *It's a Wonderful Life*, I always look for the kids. They're a special part of the movie to me. It was exciting to meet Karolyn. She was really sweet, and she mentioned that she was named after Karo syrup, and I told her that's why she's so sweet.

It's nice that she does something like this, and people appreciate this kind of thing. She just has the look of a really special lady.

Sandy Richards, of Taylor:

My daughter, who's 27, is a big fan of *It's a Wonderful Life*. She always says my husband and I always like the "la-la" movies, which are the older movies, so for somebody her age to enjoy a movie of that vintage says a lot for it.

I think the movie emphasizes family first, and it points out that you don't realize how much you mean to people. Sometimes you get down on yourself and you think you're not living up to expectations, and you don't realize how important you are in somebody's life. Everybody has their faults, but you stay together and you love each other and you support each other through the good times and the bad times, and that's what George Bailey's family did. They supported him, and he them.

Zuzu was a big part of the movie because she was daddy's little girl, and she was innocence. She wasn't aware of all the big problems that were going on. She just knew that she loved her dad and she loved her family and Christmas was exciting to her. It wasn't a time when the mortgage was going to be due or whatever, so she could see the world through the innocence of a child.

And it was very nice to meet the one who played Zuzu. Karolyn is very sweet, and I admire her for taking the time to sign all of the autographs. She seems to be someone who doesn't tire out. I said that her hand must be cramped, and she said, "Oh no, I love doing it."

It's great to have her here because the movie does promote family values, and we need to do more of that to emphasize how important the family is. I don't see it as her going out to make money. I see it as her going out to promote the movie and what it stands for.

John and Sue Ural, of Southgate:

John: I've liked *It's a Wonderful Life* since I was in grade school back in about 1964. I always thought it really captured a spirit or emotion of Christmas, of good will, of somebody giving back what he's done for the community.

Sue: Meeting someone from the movie makes the character real to you, and then you have a connection because you've met the person who played the role.

'Zuzu was a big part of the movie because she was daddy's little girl, and she was innocence.

'She wasn't aware of all the big problems that were going on. She just knew that she loved her dad and she loved her family and Christmas was exciting to her.'

Sandy Richards

And Karolyn is stunning. She was a really cute little girl, but cute little girls don't usually grow up to be that stunning. She also seems like a lovely person. Her personality reflects what she was in the movie.

Larry Rockensuess, of Trenton:

It's a Wonderful Life is my all-time favorite. We have a copy of it, and I watch it probably three or four times a year, even in the summertime. It stands for great American family values. When the chips are down, people will pitch in and help. It's something that I look forward to myself trying to be part of in somebody else's life, because I'm a minister now.

Anytime you can meet someone from the movie, even if it was a small part, it's great to see that she exhibits today what the movie portrayed. I don't think anybody could say that great smile of hers still isn't as charming today as it was in the movie.

Janice Basley, of Allen Park:

She was in two of my favorite movies, *It's a Wonderful Life* and *The Bishop's Wife*, and they have two of my favorite actors, Jimmy Stewart and Cary Grant. My parents are from that era, and I was brought up on black-and-white movies.

I'm staying home to raise my daughter to have the feeling that I had, to give her what my mother and father gave to me when I was growing up. I love old movies, and I think when you watch them, that's what it reminds you of.

Karolyn is an important part of *It's a Wonderful Life* because of the closeness of the family at the end. When she says, "Every time a bell rings," I just bawl my eyes out, every time.

Jennifer Maxwell, of Lincoln Park:

I first saw *It's a Wonderful Life* in 1984, the year I met my husband, and he died two years ago. The first holiday party we hosted together, we were changing the channel constantly to see how many times we could get it. It's just not Christmas unless you watch it once all the way through.

It got to be a family joke where we call each other up and say "hee-haw" and try to outdo each other to see how many parts of the movie we knew. I always write "hee-haw" in my Christmas cards, because a lot of people know what that is.

The movie is a reaffirmation of the preciousness of life and the grace of God and all that good stuff. The rose petals and Zuzu made for a poignant, epiphanal moment for her father. He's thinking, "My God, this is my baby, and she's putting her trust and hope in me." I think everybody who's a parent goes through that. Being a widow, I still go through that with my own kids.

My brother's going through a divorce, and I just want to say, "Stick it out like George Bailey." He'll know in two seconds what I'm talking about. I came here to get him a little book for Karolyn to sign, and she was really nice. She signed it, "Keep the faith. It really is a wonderful life." I think he'll listen to that. He's a fan, big-time.

'The rose petals and Zuzu made for a poignant, epiphanal moment for her father.

'He's thinking, "My God, this is my baby, and she's putting her trust and hope in me."

'I think everybody who's a parent goes through that. Being a widow, I still go through that with my own kids.'

Jennifer Maxwell

Judy Danish, of Lincoln Park:

We always have to watch *It's a Wonderful Life*. It's just a happy movie – sad but happy. It makes you feel good watching it and puts you in the Christmas spirit.

I think everybody can relate to it. You always feel that you're not perfect, and with Christmas you have the pressure on to do so much.

All the kids' parts are important in the movie. They're all the innocent ones, and back then they were more innocent than kids are nowadays.

Karolyn seems to take her time with everybody, not pushing or rushing people, but I'm sure she must be tired after doing this for so long. She seems like she could be your neighbor next door, a really nice person. She just seems like the Zuzu character grown up.

Wendy Rushlow, of Southgate

In the movie, Zuzu's just like the typical little girl: "Well, Da-ad, look what you've done to my flowers." I could see any one of us doing that, and he's trying to fix it and he's getting frustrated and he's upset. That's what's so real about it. He reacted the same way most people would, and she was just a little girl and didn't understand what she was doing.

Karolyn was such a fantastic little actress, also in *The Bishop's Wife*, another one of my favorites. She didn't look like she was acting. She looked like that was her personality, that little girl. And to see her today, she's an extremely nice person. She doesn't seem like an oh-wow movie star.

Angela Lang and Diane Buzymowski, sisters, of Allen Park:

Angela: Our family always watched *It's a Wonderful Life* when we were kids. I think it was a bonding time for our whole family to sit down and watch it, both physically and spiritually – the angels and the message that friends are more important than money.

Diane: I always liked Zuzu's innocence, being pure in thought and believing in the angels and listening to what the teacher had told her, that there really are angels.

Angela: I could identify with the character when I was growing up. There was a special connection between the daughter and the father.

Diane: It was terrific to actually meet her today. She seems so young, and she laughed at my corny jokes. When she said she couldn't write and talk to us at the same time, I said, "Oh, you must be a true blonde," and she liked that.

Angela: And only because you're a blonde, you can say it. We also have another connection. When I was a toddler and Diane wasn't born yet, we had a 2-year-old sister who died in a fire of smoke inhalation, and our father had always said that she was our special angel. So from the time we were little and watching the movie, we believed. There was no questioning.

Diane: We believe in them, and this movie points that out to people who may never have thought of it. It can help people believe that there are angels, and angels don't have to be strangers. You can actually know people who become angels.

'I could identify with the character when I was growing up. There was a special connection between the daughter and the father.'

Angela Lang

Charise Copeland, of Plymouth:

I had to come today. I was so excited, my boss let me take the afternoon off. *It's a Wonderful Life* is so inspirational for family unity, and I've watched it a lot – particularly one Christmas when my daughter had a four-foot python snake, and it had gotten out that night, and I was so scared to go to sleep. The movie was on again and again all night long, and I stayed up and watched it over and over, just curled up in my covers.

Carole Newberry, of Wyandotte:

'People need to start realizing that . . . they have to make the best of what they have and that what God gave them was one of the best things, and that is life itself.'

Carole Newberry

In May of last year, I was rear-ended by a drunk-driver who was going 85 mph, and I was catapulted 300 feet out of my car into a brick garage. I was code blue, and the police and fire department said I wasn't going to make it. I wore a back brace for a year. Then in March of this year they detected breast cancer. Since then, I've gone through three surgeries and eight weeks of radiation, and as of the last check, everything is fine. The last surgery was done three days after our house burned down, but thankfully my husband, my 8-year-old grandson and our pets all made it out of the fire okay.

I learned from my parents that there's always a positive out of the negative, and I think *It's a Wonderful Life* bred that into me as well. I've watched that movie every year for the last 20 years or so, and I think that's probably what got me through the last two years, to realize that it's not time to give up. I'm here for a reason, and obviously I've got somebody watching over me. The way I look at it, when God gives you a second lease on life, you don't sneer at him.

Zuzu is important in the movie because she's a child. Children are so important, and it's hard for them to understand when things are happening around them. With my grandson, it was the same thing. He kept saying, "Why is all this happening to us?" I kept showing him that other things are happening to other people, and that it was just happening to us right now. So now he starts to look for the good with the bad. With Zuzu in the movie, it's the same thing. She had to deal with what was happening between her parents and the shortcomings that they had.

I told my grandson, "We'll cast away the old memories, and we'll have to make new ones now." It is a wonderful life. People need to start realizing that – regardless of what they have, regardless of what life has given them. They have to make the best of what they have and realize that what God gave them was one of the best things, and that is life itself.

For a childhood film career that lasted only seven years, Karolyn Grimes appeared in a string of movies remarkable for both their variety and quality. Her 16 movies cover a wide range of genres. None of the films is a dud. In fact, several can rank proudly at or near the top of any cinema fan's list of favorites.

Karolyn's screen time in these movies totals about 87 minutes (it is difficult to calculate precisely without being able to see *Sweet and Low*), which, fittingly enough, approximates the average length of a feature film from the mid-1940s to the early 1950s.

This filmography gathers pertinent details and rates the films according to a four-bell system (four is excellent, three is good, two is fair and one is poor). It also indicates whether each listing has been released on video. Of the 16, seven remain unreleased. Perhaps this list, and this book, will encourage studios who own rights to these films to make them available to the public. Each of the unreleased films is a treat, not only for those interested in Karolyn's career but also for fans of their respective genres.

That Night with You

🔔🔔🔔🔔

84 minutes, black and white, Universal

Release date: Fall 1945

Director: William A. Seiter

Stars: Franchot Tone, Susanna Foster, David Bruce, Buster Keaton

Karolyn's role: Filmed June 30 and July 2-3, 1945. Unbilled, she plays one of six orphans and has 5 minutes of screen time in two consecutive segments near the end of the film. She has only two spoken lines, but they are more than throwaways.

Sure, that's Karolyn Grimes, second from the left in the row of six orphans from THAT NIGHT WITH YOU, but who's the maid escorting them into the room? See text below.

Comment: Hopelessly dated and mired in overacting, *That Night with You* is fascinating nonetheless. Tone is suave, Foster appealing and Bruce just right as the romantic diner owner whose vision of getting married and having six kids flies in the face of Foster's dreams of stardom. The "father-daughter" relationship between Tone and Foster is curiously risqué for its time. More curious, however, is why Buster Keaton is wasted in a nothing role. Ironically, the film's final sequence, a special-effects laugher that ties the plot up in a neat bow, is quite Keatonesque.

For trivia buffs: Playing the ever-frustrated maid in Tone's apartment who escorts Karolyn and the other orphans into the presence of Tone's would-be wife Susanna Foster is the young Irene Ryan, best known 20 years later as Granny in TV's *Beverly Hillbillies*.

Karolyn along with Rita Johnson and Fred MacMurray, as they appeared on a lobby card for PARDON MY PAST.

Pardon My Past

88 minutes, black and white, Columbia

Release date: Feb. 8, 1946

Director: Leslie Fenton

Stars: Fred MacMurray, Marguerite Chapman, Akim Tamiroff, Rita Johnson, Harry Davenport, William Demarest

Karolyn's role: Filmed May 1945. Eighth in the credits, she plays Stephani, the daughter of one of the MacMurray characters, and has 7 minutes of screen time.

Comment: It's centuries old, but the plot device of mistaken identity works well here, largely because of a clever script and MacMurray's ability to carve two characters who are different from each other, but not so different to be unbelievable as identical twins. It's also easy to see why Karolyn drew favorable press attention. Hers is a performance quite credible for a child not yet 5 years old.

For trivia buffs: It's fun to see MacMurray's easy rapport with sidekick Demarest, as the two teamed up similarly in the 1960s on TV's *My Three Sons*.

Karolyn's five-minute segment with Bing Crosby is a high point of BLUE SKIES.

Blue Skies

104 minutes, color, Paramount

Release date: July 25, 1946

Director: Stuart Heisler

Stars: Bing Crosby, Fred Astaire, Joan Caulfield, Billy De Wolfe

Karolyn's role: Filmed Sept. 6-8, 1945. Eighth in the credits, she plays Mary Elizabeth, the daughter of the Crosby character and has one 5-minute segment of screen time.

Comment: Few musicals can rise beyond the limitations of formula. In this one, the producers apparently decided not to worry about such aspirations. They were content to pack in as many Irving Berlin songs as possible, stringing them together with the barest of plot. With that understanding, *Blue Skies* is a lot of fun to watch. The songs and Astaire's dancing are engaging, and Karolyn's segment with Crosby for "Getting Nowhere" is a genuine high spot. The only real problem is a dated, interminably long would-be comedy routine by De Wolfe.

For trivia buffs: Look for a stage hand played by Frank Faylen, who one year later became Ernie the cab driver in *It's a Wonderful Life* and went on to play Dobie' father in the TV situation comedy *The Many Loves of Dobie Gillis*.

Available on video.

Sister Kenny

118 minutes, black and white, RKO Radio Pictures

Release date: Sept. 28, 1946

Director: Dudley Nichols

Stars: Rosalind Russell, Alexander Knox, Dean Jagger, Philip Merivale

Karolyn's role: Filmed between November 1945 and January 1946. Unbilled, she plays a polio victim named Carolyn (no name spelling is indicated, however) and has 1 minute of screen time.

Playing the title role, Rosalind Russell carries Karolyn to an outdoor examination table in SISTER KENNY.

Comment: As film biographies go, this one's not bad, and it follows the story of an underdog/outcast in the medical profession with grace. The sincerity and skill of the Australian nurse played by Russell are credible, but to its credit, the movie stops short of fully endorsing her unconventional approach to treating childhood polio. The ambiguity of the story nicely prompts a desire to read the autobiography upon which the film was based.

For trivia buffs: Another *It's a Wonderful Life* actress, Beulah Bondi, (George Bailey's mother) appears in *Sister Kenny* in a brief supporting role.

Available on video.

It's a Wonderful Life

129 minutes, black and white, Liberty Films/RKO Radio Pictures

Release date: Dec. 19, 1946

Director: Frank Capra

Stars: James Stewart, Donna Reed, Lionel Barrymore, Thomas Mitchell, Henry Travers, Beulah Bondi, Gloria Grahame

Karolyn's role: Filmed She is 33rd in the credits, plays Zuzu Bailey and has 6 minutes of screen time.

Comment: One of the best movies – if not the best – of all time, untouchable in its grasp of the desires and principles that fuel the American spirit. Despite its glum premise (a contemplated suicide), this is a film guaranteed to prompt tears of joy. Considering the movie's power, its 30-year dormancy is remarkable, and its revival an enduring gift.

For trivia buffs: Though they never shared screen time in this film, Karolyn and Bobby Anderson (the young George Bailey) acted together in a key segment from another Christmas/angel film released on year later, *The Bishop's Wife*.

Available on video.

As Zuzu, Karolyn holds the high-school principal's watch in the final scene of IT'S A WONDERFUL LIFE.

The Private Affairs of Bel Ami

🔔🔔🔔

112 minutes, black and white, United Artists

Release date: Feb. 25, 1947

Director: Albert Lewin

Stars: George Sanders, Angela Lansbury, Ann Dvorak, John Carradine

Karolyn's role: Filmed in the fall of 1946. She is 17th in the credits, plays Laurine and has four segments totaling 2 minutes of screen time.

Comment: Literate, talky and pretentious, this film professes to examine the wickedness of selfishness, personified by the Sanders character. He is anything but the bel ami (best friend) of the title. By today's standards, *Bel Ami* moves too slowly and offers no intriguing plot twists, but the acting of Sanders and Lansbury commands interest, as does the Parisian setting. Karolyn does her best to warm the heart of Sanders, but it's questionable whether his character even has one. For a somber, perhaps cynical mood only.

For trivia buffs: The precursors to Sanders' tour de force as Addison deWitt in 1950's *All About Eve* are on full display here.

Available on video.

Sweet and Low

🔔🔔🔔 (?)

Karolyn beckons to composter Harlan Kane (Griff Barnett) in SWEET AND LOW.

19 minutes (short subject), color, Paramount

Release date: March 28, 1947

Director: Jerry Hopper

Stars: Richard Webb, Catherine Craig, Willie Mastin Trio featuring Sammy Davis, Jr.

Karolyn's role: Filmed July 31-Aug. 3, 1946. She is third in the credits, plays Tammie and, as detailed in an early script under the working title "The Masque Ball," has perhaps as many as 9 minutes of screen time.

Comment: This short subject may be a gem. As the film is apparently unavailable for viewing, it's hard to say. The innocence and honesty of Karolyn's character help her parents achieve what they, with their adult sensibilities, cannot achieve by themselves. It's a well-worn theme, but always worth revisiting if played out well.

For trivia buffs: *Sweet and Low* could be the earliest appearance on film of the legendary Davis, who was 20 at the time. (His earliest feature film, *The Benny Goodman Story*, came nine years later, in 1955.) Could there be a better reason to make it available to the public?

Philo Vance's Gamble

Pam Roberts (Karolyn) brandishes a gun before a couple of police detectives, but the cunning Philo Vance (Alan Curtis) knows the weapon is plastic.

62 minutes, black and white, Producers Releasing Corporation

Release date: April 1947

Director: Basil Wrangell

Stars: Alan Curtis, Terry Austin, Frank Jenks, Tala Birell

Karolyn's role: Filmed sometime in December 1946 and January 1947. Unbilled, she plays Pam Roberts and has 6 minutes of screen time.

Comment: Weapons emerging ominously from behind curtains, secrets galore, all on a dark, murderous night – this is the B-movie detective formula played to a T. What brightens and shakes up the proceedings, though, is the important plot presence of a little girl who likes to surprise strangers by brandishing a toy gun. Made of plastic, the gun is really a shell to hold rock candy, and in this case, a stolen emerald. Fun all around.

For trivia buffs: Less-known than other fictional private eyes, the Philo Vance character nevertheless headlined 14 films from 1929 to 1947.

Mother Wore Tights

107 minutes, color, 20th Century Fox

Release date: Aug. 19, 1947

Director: Walter Lang

Stars: Betty Grable, Dan Dailey, Mona Freeman

Karolyn's role: Filmed sometime from October 1946 through January 1947. She is unbilled, plays young Iris and has 30 seconds of screen time.

Comment: Producers of this musical let too much plot get in the way of the songs, but this movie is still colorful, energetic and fun.

For trivia buffs: Remember Señor Wences' charming ventriloquism act, a mainstay of TV's *Ed Sullivan Show*? A early version appears here.

Unconquered

146 minutes, color, Paramount

Release date: Oct. 3, 1947

Director: Cecil B. DeMille

Stars: Gary Cooper, Paulette Goddard, Howard Da Silva, Boris Karloff, Cecil Kellaway

Karolyn's role: Filmed in the fall of 1946. She is 133rd in the cast list, plays a "little girl" lying dead in her mother's arms and has 15 seconds of screen time.

Comment: Overacted to the point of melodrama, and overlong even by today's standards, *Unconquered* is a curiosity, though an intriguing one. Fans of Cooper and Goddard (once Charles Chaplin's paramour and co-star) will enjoy these stars trying to bring some credibility to this depiction of pre-Revolutionary War America. Ultimately, it's as lifeless as the tiny role played by Karolyn. DeMille never did learn that less is more.

For trivia buffs: Bert and Ernie from *It's a Wonderful Life* each show up in one of Karolyn's films. This time it's Ward Bond (Bert the cop), who has a meaty supporting role in this colonial tale.

Available on video.

The Bishop's Wife

108 minutes, black and white, Samuel Goldwyn Productions / RKO Pictures

Release date: Dec. 25, 1947

Director: Henry Koster

Stars: Cary Grant, Loretta Young, David Niven, Monty Woolley, James Gleason

Karolyn's role: Filmed in the summer of 1947. She is ninth in the credits, plays Debby Brougham and has 7 minutes of screen time.

Comment: Not as viscerally emotional, and a little distant from mainstream audiences because of its upper-crust setting, *The Bishop's Wife* nevertheless ranks with *It's a Wonderful Life* as a classic. The actors' chemistry enhances this angel fable, and the outcome is never quite certain until the end. Delightful sequences fill the film, from the hilarious symbolism of Niven (the bishop) stuck to a donor's chair, to a warming harp interlude and a stunning hymn from the Mitchell Boychoir. And Karolyn is in the thick of it all.

For trivia buffs: For the magical skating sequence, professional skaters were used, their faces covered with masks in the images of Grant and Young.

Available on video.

Albuquerque

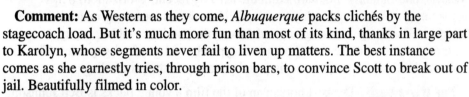

89 minutes, color, Paramount-Clarion

Release date: Feb. 20, 1948

Director: Ray Enright

Stars: Randolph Scott, Barbara Britton, Gabby Hayes, Lon Chaney Jr., Catherine Craig

Karolyn's role: Filmed sometime from March through June of 1947. She is 10th in the credits, plays Myrtle Walton and has 12 minutes of screen time.

Karolyn, Catherine Craig and Gabby Hayes' double ride a stagecoach into town while filming the 1948 Western, ALBUQUERQUE.

Comment: As Western as they come, *Albuquerque* packs clichés by the stagecoach load. But it's much more fun than most of its kind, thanks in large part to Karolyn, whose segments never fail to liven up matters. The best instance comes as she earnestly tries, through prison bars, to convince Scott to break out of jail. Beautifully filmed in color.

For trivia buffs: Lest anyone think Lon Chaney Jr. was only a staple of horror movies, *Albuquerque* shows him off as an ominous henchman. Here, he and Scott engage in one of the longest and most vicious fistfights in film history.

Lust for Gold

90 minutes, black and white, Columbia

Release date: May 31, 1949

Director: Sylvan Simon

Stars: Ida Lupino, Glenn Ford, Gig Young, Paul Ford

Karolyn's role: Filmed in late 1949. She is unbilled, plays young Martha Bannister and has 40 seconds of screen time.

Comment: The narration in this self-titled "documentary Western" strains to emphasize the film's real-life story, and at times the legendary hype seems a bit melodramatic. But as Saturday matinee fare for impressionable kids, this fills the bill. In the tussle between greed and the secrets of Superstition Mountain, the outcome is never in question. Ford, Lupino and half a dozen bit players, plus the film's flashback structure, make *Lust for Gold* interesting nonetheless.

For trivia buffs: Paul Ford plays a present-day sheriff, and portraying one of his deputies is Jay Silverheels, the man who played Tonto for many years on TV's *The Lone Ranger.*

Available on video.

Rio Grande

105 minutes, black and white, **Republic Pictures**

Release date: Nov. 2, 1950

Director: John Ford

Stars: John Wayne, Maureen O'Hara, Ben Johnson, Harry Carey Jr., Victor McLaglen, Claude Jarman Jr.

Karolyn's role: Filmed in June and July 1950. She is 13th in the credits, plays Margaret Mary and has 6 minutes of screen time.

Comment: On the surface, this is a lesser **John Ford Western**, but viewed more than once, a delicate interplay of family, duty and destiny emerge. The gorgeous location photography (not harmed in the least by recent colorization) helps enormously. Wayne, underplaying, and O'Hara are an intriguing match, and the intertwined activity of young, untried calvarymen and their older, crusty counterparts is far more complex than in typical good-guy/bad-guy tales. The Sons of the Pioneers add symbolism and gallantry to the proceedings.

For trivia buffs: The best horseman of the film's young bucks is Ben Johnson, better known to latter-day audiences for his weathered, Academy Award-winning supporting role in 1971's *The Last Picture Show*.

Available on video.

Honeychile

90 minutes, color, **Republic Pictures**

Release date: Nov. 12, 1951

Director: R.G. Springsteen

Stars: Judy Canova, Eddie Foy Jr., Alan Hale Jr., Walter Catlett

Karolyn's role: Filmed in November 1950. She is sixth in the credits, plays Effie and has 20 minutes of screen time.

Comment: Laced with cleverly written gags, this is pure corn all the way. There's a big crisis as a music publishing company has mistakenly pressed 200,000 records of a love song that the country-livin' Canova had submitted on a lark. The city folks connive to buy her song, "Honeychile," for a pittance, but it's not that easy in this rural romp. Karolyn has more screen time in this than any other film, and she exhibits a naturalness as the niece who takes care of Canova's household. Still, this slick effort is Canova's film all the way, her brash, brassy singing voice on full display.

For trivia buffs: The man in Canova's life is none other than Alan Hale Jr., who played the Skipper in TV's *Gilligan's Island*.

Hans Christian Andersen

120 minutes, color, RKO Radio Pictures

Release date: Nov. 25, 1952

Director: Charles Vidor

Stars: Danny Kaye, Farley Granger, Jeanmaire

Karolyn's role: Filmed in May 1952. She is unbilled, plays a match girl and has 10 seconds of screen time.

Comment: The ebullient Danny Kaye is a delight as Hans, particularly in his singing scenes with youngsters. The music and colorful sets are worth slogging through a leaden plot that feels contrived from the outset. A more true-to-life biography may have provided the substance needed to elevate this oversentimental tale from simplistic children's fare.

For trivia buffs: Karolyn's last film role is also her shortest. Unlike most of her other films in which she played the only child, or one of a few, in this movie there are dozens of younger, would-be Karolyns.

Available on video.

*Photo/
graphic
credits*

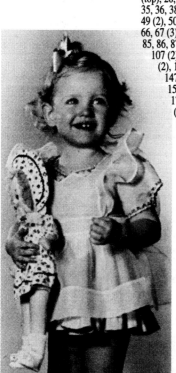

Karolyn at age 2.

Front cover photo by Larry Levenson (Copyright © 1996 Larry F. Levenson/Kansas City)

Illustrations by Sandy Johnson, LaConner, Washington (Copyright © 1996, All Rights Reserved): title page, 2, 3, 7, 9, 10, 227-235

Reprinted by permission and courtesy of the collection of Karolyn Grimes: title page (4), 4, 13, 17 (top), 18, 19, 20 (top), 21 (top), 22, 23 (3), 24 (bottom), 25 (2), 26 (2), 27 (top), 28, 29 (2), 30 (top), 31 (top), 32 (top), 33 (2), 34 (2), 35, 36, 38 (4), 40 (3), 41 (2), 42, 43, 44, 45 (2), 46, 47, 48, 49 (2), 50 (2), 52, 53, 54 (2), 55 (2), 56, 59, 60, 63, 64, 65, 66, 67 (3), 69, 70, 71, 72, 75, 76, 77, 78, 79, 80, 81, 82, 83, 85, 86, 87, 88, 89, 91, 94 (2), 97, 98, 100, 103, 104 (2), 107 (2), 109, 111, 113, 115, 117 (bottom), 118 (4), 119 (2), 120 (2), 121, 124, 126, 128, 132, 133 (2), 145, 147 (top), 149, 150, 153, 154, 155 (2), 156, 157, 158, 159, 160 (2), 161 (3), 163, 165, 166, 168, 170, 171 (2), 172, 175, 178, 179, 180 (2), 181 (2), 182 (bottom), 183, 184, 185, 186 (2), 187 (3, top, middle), 188 (2), 189 (2), 191, 192, 193, 194, 195, 196, 197 (top), 198 (middle, bottom), 199 (2), 203, 206, 211, 213, 215, 227, 228 (2), 230, 231, 233, 236, 237, 239, 240, 241, 243, 245, back cover (3 insets)

Reprinted by permission and courtesy of Bill Campsey: 5

Reprinted by permission and courtesy of the Fred Hutchinson Cancer Research Center (photos by Gary Kissel): 11, 12, 14

Reprinted by permission and courtesy of Columbia Pictures ("PARDON MY PAST" Copyright © 1945, renewed 1972 Columbia Pictures Industries, Inc., All Rights Reserved): 43, 44, 45 (2), 46, 47, 228 (top), back cover (inset, bottom left).

Reprinted by permission and courtesy of MCA Publishing Rights, a Division of MCA Inc. (Copyright 1945 by Universal City Studios, Inc., All Rights Reserved): 48, 227

Reprinted by permission and courtesy of MCA Publishing Rights, a Division of MCA Inc. (Copyright 1946 by Universal City Studios, Inc., All Rights Reserved): 49 (2), 50 (2), 52, 53, 228 (bottom), back cover (inset, top right).

Lyric excerpts of "Getting Nowhere (Running Around in Circles)" by Irving Berlin reprinted by permission and courtesy of Williamson Music, New York (Copyright © 1945, Irving Berlin, Copyright Renewed, International Copyright Secured, All Rights Reserved): 50

Reprinted by permission and courtesy of Turner Entertainment Co. (Copyright © 1946 RKO Pictures, Inc., All Rights Reserved): 51 (bottom), 229 (top)

Reprinted by permission of Academy of Motion Picture Arts and Sciences, Center for Motion Picture Study, Margaret Herrick Library: 52, 69, 70, 72, 75, 230, 231, 240

From the State Historical Society of Missouri at Columbia: 51 (top), 71, 84, 144

Reprinted by permission and courtesy of *Newsweek* (Copyright © 1946, Newsweek, Inc., All Rights Reserved): 55 (top)

Reprinted by permission and courtesy of Nabisco Brands Co, (Copyright © 1904, All Rights Reserved): 56

Logo reprinted by permission and courtesy of the *Los Angeles Times* (Copyright © 1946, All Rights Reserved): 65

Copyright © 1947 Paramount Pictures, All Rights Reserved: 69, 70, 230, 240

Reprinted by permission and courtesy of MCA Publishing Rights, a Division of MCA Inc. (Copyright 1947 by Universal City Studios, Inc., All Rights Reserved): 72

Reprinted by permission and courtesy of Republic Pictures (Copyright © 1947, Republic Entertainment Inc., All Rights Reserved): 73

Copyright © 1947 Producers Releasing Corporation, Renewed 1975 Pathe Industries, Inc. All Rights Reserved: 75, 231

Reprinted by permission and courtesy of MCA Publishing Rights, a Division of MCA Inc. (Copyright © 1948 by Universal City Studios, Inc. All Rights Reserved): 77, 78, 79, 80, 81, 233

Reprinted by permission and courtesy of Goldwyn Entertainment Company (Copyright © 1947, Samuel Goldwyn, All Rights Reserved): 85, 86, back cover (inset, bottom right)

Reprinted by permission and courtesy of Republic Pictures (Copyright © 1950, Republic Entertainment Inc., All Rights Reserved): 92

Reprinted by permission and courtesy of Republic Pictures (Copyright © 1951, Republic Entertainment Inc., All Rights Reserved): 96

From the St. Clair County, Missouri, Library: 117 (top)

Reprinted by permission and courtesy of Gail Taylor Adams: 123, 127, 129, 130, 131, 134, 135

Reprinted by permission and courtesy of *The Sun Newspapers* (Copyright © 1990, All Rights Reserved): 176

Reprinted by permission and courtesy of Rick Detorie and Creators Syndicate (Copyright © 1991, All Rights Reserved): 180

Reprinted by permission and courtesy of Scott Willis of the *San Jose Mercury News* (Copyright © 1992, All Rights Reserved): 181 (top)

Reprinted by permission and courtesy of *Chile Pepper* magazine (Copyright © 1992, All Rights Reserved, toll-free phone: 1-888-SPICY HOT): 181 (bottom)

Reprinted by permission and courtesy of Universal Press Syndicate (THE FAR SIDE © 1992 FARWORKS, INC./ Distributed by UNIVERSAL PRESS SYNDICATE. All Rights Reserved): 182 (bottom)

Reprinted by permission and courtesy of the *Star Tribune* (Copyright © 1993, All Rights Reserved): 184

Reprinted by permission and courtesy of Ward Sutton, *Twin Cities Reader* (Copyright © 1993, All Rights Reserved): 185

Reprinted by permission and courtesy of Target Stores, Inc. (Copyright © 1993, All Rights Reserved): 186 (top)

Reprinted by permission and courtesy of TwinTone Records (Copyright © 1992, All Rights Reserved, photo by Brian Garrity): 190

Courtesy of Emmanuel "Manny" Gravame: 192, 209

Courtesy of Tara Morris, Lamar, Colorado: 197 (bottom)

Reprinted by permission and courtesy of John Mencl: 217 (2)

Reprinted by permission and courtesy of Zuzu's Petals Quarterly Online (Copyright © 1996, All Rights Reserved): 198 (top)

From the collection of the author: 21 (bottom), 39

By the author: 20 (bottom), 24 (top), 27 (bottom), 30 (bottom), 31 (bottom), 32 (bottom), 37, 119 (top), 122, 136, 139, 141, 142, 143 (bottom, 2), 146, 182 (top), 187 (bottom), 201, 205, 212, 221, back cover (upper left)

A s I put the final touches on this book, the cheery ditty "Hooray for Hollywood" is playing in the background. It's an inimitable carol to the magic of the movies, and it comes straight from the elusive "good old days" that so many people seem to long for.

This book is about the movies, in a sense, for movies are a mixture of illusion and reality – and so is life. We all go through our waking hours in the real world with an ever-changing wellspring of anticipation dancing in our thoughts.

The challenge of capturing a person's life in a biography has danced through my own mind for many years. Something wonderful – could it have been a guardian angel? – brought Karolyn Grimes to me for that dance to become reality.

One underlying theme of this book is that Karolyn, like all of us, has always been searching, not always knowing for what. As bubble-headed as it may sound, I believe that when she and I met at my employer's Hutch Holiday Gala in December 1994, she was searching for me, or someone like me, to write her life's story. I do know that I was searching for something to do that offered personal meaning, and I feel fortunate to have been able to seize the opportunity.

The overall tone of this book is journalistic, as befits my training, but the book does shift back and forth in its focus. It's an account of Karolyn's life as a survivor, and how she and others view it. But it's also an analysis of her childhood films and her parts in them, particularly her Zuzu role from *It's a Wonderful Life*.

To me, this dichotomy of purpose makes sense, particularly because Karolyn feels deeply that Zuzu is her alter ego. At times, in public, she even lapses back and forth between the two identities. An exploration of the Zuzu character – and the other similar roles she played – seems to be an essential element to examine in depth in any attempt to write Karolyn's life story.

In that vein, I made a point to see as much of Karolyn's screen work as possible, and I was able to track down copies of all her films except the short subject *Sweet and Low*. Unfortunately, I struck out trying to view any of her scattered TV appearances. Perhaps the missing shows will surface someday for all to enjoy.

Any serious biographer seeks to represent his or her subject accurately, and while accuracy is a highly subjective matter, it is aided by a tenacious search for ever more information. I trust that in my seemingly endless digging and interviewing I have captured enough of Karolyn's past, and of her present personality, to help readers understand something of the affection and admiration I hold for this unusually warm, generous, strong, courageous, funny and unpretentious woman.

In the process, I also hope to have brought to life the wondrous innocence and idealistic devotion that Hollywood filmmakers of the 1940s thought could be expressed best by children – and which I'm convinced that we need more of today in our everyday, non-movie lives.

"Hooray for Hollywood," indeed.

Clay Eals

Afterword

'I'm going to build things.'

The author and Karolyn Grimes at December's Special Place, Southgate, Michigan, Thanksgiving weekend, 1995

Further reading

The books below provided information and inspiration, both many years prior and up through the last-minute stages of proofreading.

If you enjoyed the biography you hold in your hand, you are bound to find some or all of these works useful and interesting.

Comprehensive reference works:
• *A Wonderful Life: The Films and Career of James Stewart*, Tony Thomas, Citadel Press, 1988, 250 pages.
• *Academy Awards: An Ungar Reference Index*, compiled by Richard Shale, Ungar Publications, 1982, 691 pages.
• *Leonard Maltin's 1996 Movie & Video Guide*, edited by Leonard Maltin, Signet/Penguin, 1996, 582 pages.
• *Leonard Maltin's Movie Encyclopedia*, edited by Leonard Maltin, Dutton/Penguin, 1994, 976 pages.

A fascinating pair, separately and together:
• *Frank Capra: The Catastrophe of Success*, Joseph McBride, Simon & Schuster, 1992, 768 pages.
• *The Name Above the Title: An Autobiography*, Frank Capra, Belvedere Publishers, 1982, 562 pages.

Inside perspectives on child stardom:
• *Twinkle, Twinkle, Little Star (but don't have sex or take the car)*, Dick Moore, Harper & Row, 1984, 303 pages.
• *Hollywood's Children: An Inside Account of the Child Star Era*, Diana Serra Cary, Houghton Mifflin Co., 1978, 290 pages.

An illuminating look at the complexities of *Rio Grande*:
• *The Western Films of John Ford*, Janey Ann Place, Citadel Press, 1974, 246 pages.

Invaluable for the *It's a Wonderful Life* fan:
• *The 'It's a Wonderful Life' Book*, Jeanine Basinger, Alfred A. Knopf, 1986, 366 pages.
• *The 'It's a Wonderful Life' Trivia Book*, Jimmy Hawkins and Paul Petersen, Crown Publishers, 1992, 128 pages.

The nuts and bolts of writing and publishing:
• *How to Write a Book Proposal*, Michael Larsen, Writer's Digest Books, 1990, 113 pages.
• *The Self-Publishing Manual*, Dan Poynter, 1996, Para Publishing, 458 pages.

Colophon

This book was prepared on an Apple Power Macintosh 7100/66 computer. The main software applications used were Microsoft Word, version 6.0 for the Power Macintosh; ofoto, version 2.0.1; and Adobe PageMaker, version 6.0 Power PC.

Fonts used on the cover are Amasis MT Italic, Biffo MT, Ellington MT Extra Bold and Times. Fonts used on the inside pages are Pepita MT and Times. Cover stock is 10 point Cornwall C1S Cover. The colors are PMS 186 and 341. Inside paper stock is 50 pound Opaque Offset.

Consolidated Press of Seattle, Washington, printed, bound and trimmed the book and separated the color photo on the cover. Special thanks to Phil Melberg, Sandi Johns, Kurt Baserman and Ann Marie Sewell at Consolidated for their advice and assistance. Data Index of Redmond, Washington, prepared the ISBN barcode on the back cover.

*N*o book, particularly a non-fiction work with a variety of sources, is a solitary pursuit. The success of this one depended upon the assistance and moral support of countless people who hold many roles in my life – all of whom I am fortunate to call my friends.

Thanks go first to Karolyn Grimes herself, who took seriously my six-page, handwritten February 1995 proposal to write her life story. Her adventurous embrace of the idea made this book possible, and our genuine collaboration has become one of the high points of my life. As she aptly puts it, with no untoward ambiguity intended, this has been an affair of the heart.

A critical source of information was the wealth of clippings, letters, photos, pay stubs and other scraps of paper that Karolyn's mother Martha meticulously saved. That they survived half a century to be sifted for the benefit of posterity borders on the miraculous. This book would be immeasurably poorer without them.

A book person from way back . . .

To the people other than Karolyn who served as sources, a hearty thanks, as well. Those I interviewed, and whose observations and sentiments are reflected in the text, included Gail Taylor Adams and Gene Adams, Marie and Marion Barnes, Charlene Broughton, Wanda Lyke Firestone, Beverly Vannice Fridley and Don Fridley, Don and Nancy Gates, Bill Grimes, Marsha Grimes, Louise Grovenburg, Helen and Ralph Hart, Jimmy Hawkins, Marsha Ann Heidler, Beth Johnson, Barbara Karnes, Beryl Keifer, Michael Lintecum, Mary Jo Miller, Lewis Lee Motley, Lilly "Cookie" Motley, St. Clair County Circuit Court Clerk Jim Naylor, Glendena Perkins, Catherine Craig Preston, Butch Rigley, Otto M. Spurny M.D., Karen Treschl, Perry Vannice, Ted Warner, Jack Wolf M.D. and Pam Yarbrough.

Sources who steered me to invaluable information, provided keen advice and/or lent incalculable help and encouragement were Faye Thompson, Sam Gill and Robert Cushman at the Margaret Herrick Library of the Academy of Motion Picture Arts and Sciences in Los Angeles; Alan Gevinson of the American Film Institute in Los Angeles; Ned Comstock of the University of Southern California Cinema and TV Library; Lou Ellen Kramer of the University of California at Los Angeles Film and TV Archive; Leith Johnson of the Frank Capra Archives at Wesleyan University, Middletown, Connecticut; Ara Kaye of the State Historical Society of Missouri at Columbia; Eleanor Ratliffe of the St. Clair County, Missouri, Library; Mary Beth Cauthon of the St. Clair County Recorder's Office; Eddie Brant's Saturday Matinee video store in North Hollywood; Jim Kline, author of *The Complete Films of Buster Keaton*; Paul Bergman, co-author of *Reel Justice: The Courtroom Goes to the Movies*; Val Bennett and Audrey Murray of Osceola High School; John Strauss of Sherman Oaks, Calif.; Therese December and her staff at December's Special Place, Southgate, Mich.; Franklin Dohanyos of Royal Oak, Mich.; Stephanie Ogle of Cinema Books, Seattle, Washington; Kevin Whitaker, Wally Bramblage and Paul "Fredrocks" Adams, all of Kansas City; Roger Senders of Playa del Rey, California; film historian Leonard Maltin of Los Angeles; Rosalie Heacock and Bill Miller-Jones of Santa Monica, California; Carlos, Cenia, Karla, Vanessa and Nicole Bonilla of West Hollywood, California; William Arnold of the *Seattle Post-Intelligencer*; Cynthia Stevens of Bothell, Washington; Eduardo Jorge de Mendonça of Bellevue, Washington; Sallie Tisdale of Portland, Oregon; Jay Rubin of Indiana, Pennsylvania; Tara Morris of Lamar, Colorado; and members of Karolyn's family, including her daughters Haleen, Deena, Carey and Kylan and son Chris.

I also wish to single out several people for special mention:

■ Wade Williams of Kansas City searched and screened key reels from his film library, making it possible for Karolyn and me to see films featuring Karolyn that she had never seen before and that I would not have experienced otherwise.

'Thanks for the wings!'

A critical source of information was the wealth of clippings, letters, photos, pay stubs and other scraps of paper that Karolyn's mother Martha meticulously saved.

This book would be immeasurably poorer without them.

■ Tabetha Dunn of Allentown, Penn., established Karolyn's Web site on the Internet. Her devotion to the Zuzu mystique translated into untold hours of volunteer work that helped – and will continue to help – spread the word about Karolyn and this book via the latest communications technology.

In SWEET AND LOW, playwright Harlan Kane (Griff Barnett) reads a bedtime story to Tammie, played by Karolyn.

■ Attorney John Mencl of Independence, Mo., lent a much-needed last-minute boost by writing an emotionally powerful endorsement letter for Karolyn's fan club newsletter, *The Zuzu News*.

■ Venice Buhain, a University of Washington student and friend of my daughter's, became my volunteer editor. Her zeal, insights and understanding crucially bolstered this project.

■ Co-workers in the Development and Community Relations Division of the Fred Hutchinson Cancer Research Center, particularly my supervisor Jerry VanderWood (and his supervisor Karen Lane), sensitively handled my requests for work schedule adjustments. Without Jerry's moral support in particular, I would not have pulled off the researching, writing and self-publishing of this book during the past year and a half. Division staff, especially Marilee McCorriston, Nancy Greenwood, Polly Diaz and Amy Hampson, along with guild volunteer Mary Beth Barbour, contributed vision, enthusiasm and commitment in the effort to connect the book with its Seattle audiences.

Those who plowed through the manuscript as it progressed deserve helpings of appreciation. These readers and advisers included Rita Burns, Abigail Coble, Susan Coles, Leslie Cottle, Marcia Gaul, Stephanie Hill, Kathleen Kealey, Diana Lynn, Gregory and Carolyn Malcolm, Karen Mathieson, Tab Melton, Renee Renshaw-Myrwang and Eve Ruff.

Most important to me in this litany of gratitude are the members of my family. Relatives – including Maxine Kobylk; Dorothy, Wilbur and Beverly Johnson; Donna Tiffan; Margaret and Ed Whaley; and Mary Drane Owen – demonstrated unflagging interest, and a cousin, Elizabeth Cramer, and her family even put me up for several days during a research trip to Los Angeles.

My parents, Henry and Virginia Eals, long accustomed to my idealism, antsy career shifts and unconventional ideas of success, consistently and generously perceived the project as a worthwhile labor of love.

My 20-year-old daughter Karey Eals, no doubt a future author herself in some form, supplied a welcome reality check as her view of the project evolved from skepticism and wariness to intrigue and pride. Her sense of humor, intelligence, facility with words and good heart inspire me. Karey's contribution to the book will, in my estimation at least, be more fully reflected as she continues to rack up achievements of her own.

Finally, I can only try to thank my wife, Meg Bakken. She intimately understands how this book fulfills several of my passions – for trying new and challenging kinds of work, for researching, writing and promoting a book, for the movies in general and Karolyn's signature movie in particular, and for believing that, indeed, *It's a Wonderful Life*. She reminds and comforts me that we are better together for allowing each other to fulfill our individual dreams, and that our entire family's enjoyment of the work, of the movie and of the relationship with Karolyn will endure long after the project's challenges and hurdles are past. Ever will I endeavor to reciprocate in kind. It may be cliché to say that Meg is the Mary Hatch to my George Bailey, a notion that Meg herself has advanced, but the truth to be found in that statement is profound.

Clay Eals

Index

Karolyn at 5, in one of the many photos from her portfolio.

Newspaper movie writers found much in Karolyn's early performances to promote – even outside the United States. This Portuguese article from the Brazilian publication CARIOCA is probably from early 1946. Its headline labels her a "baby star" with "30 kilos of personality," who will follow in the footsteps of Margaret O'Brien and Shirley Temple. Five-year-old Karolyn's movie idols at the time, according to the article, were Bing Crosby and Bob Hope. "She is crazy for them at the cinema or on the radio."

Index of fans

Did you enjoy this book?

Would you like to share it with others?

Here's how to order more copies for your family members and friends!

Every Time a Bell Rings

The ultimate book about the woman who played **Zuzu Bailey** and roles in 15 other Hollywood movies.

Jam-packed with anecdotes, fan comments and 250 photos, plus a personal look at the beloved family film **It's a Wonderful Life** as it reaches its golden anniversary!

The Wonderful Life of Karolyn Grimes

By Clay Eals

ORDER FORM

❑ Please send me _____ copies of *Every Time a Bell Rings: The Wonderful Life of Karolyn Grimes*. I understand that I may return any books for a full refund – for any reason, no questions asked.

❑ Please put my name and address on the mailing list for receiving *The Zuzu News*, the free newsletter of Karolyn Grimes' fan club.

Name: _____

Address: _____

City: _____ State: _____ Zip: _____ – _____

Telephone: (_____) _____

For each book, please send $24.95, plus $5 postage/handling. Please make out checks to **Pastime Press**.

Please mail this order form, with your check, to **Pastime Press**, 4310-¹/₂ S.W. Raymond St., Seattle, WA 98136-1444.

If you would like your copy(ies) of *Every Time a Bell Rings: The Wonderful Life of Karolyn Grimes* personalized with a signature and message from Karolyn Grimes, please indicate here, or on a separate sheet of paper:

Book #1 message _____

Book #2 message _____

Book #3 message _____